Venice &
the Veneto

"All you've got to do is decide to go
and the hardest part is over.

So go!"

TONY WHEELER, COFOUNDER – LONELY PLANET

Contents

(left) **Ca' Rezzonico p76** A mansion full of masterpieces.

(above) **Vogalonga p154** Take part in this festive rowing race.

(right) **Torre Dell'Orologio p57** A 15th-century timepiece.

Murano, Burano & the Northern Islands p147

Cannaregio p105

San Polo & Santa Croce p84

San Marco p48

Castello p117

Dorsoduro p71

Giudecca, Lido & the Southern Islands p136

Welcome to Venice & the Veneto

Imagine the audacity of building a city of marble palaces on a lagoon – and that was only the start.

Epic Grandeur

Never was a thoroughfare so aptly named as the Grand Canal, reflecting the glories of Venetian architecture lining its banks. At the end of Venice's signature waterway, Palazzo Ducale and Basilica di San Marco add double exclamation points. But wait until you see what's hiding in narrow backstreets: neighbourhood churches lined with Veroneses and priceless marbles, Tiepolo's glimpses of heaven on homeless-shelter ceilings, and a tiny Titian that mysteriously lights up an entire cathedral.

Venetian Feasts

Garden islands and lagoon aquaculture yield speciality produce and seafood you won't find elsewhere – all highlighted in inventive Venetian cuisine, with tantalising traces of ancient spice routes. The city knows how to put on a royal spread, as France's King Henry III once found out when faced with 1200 dishes and 200 bonbons. Today such feasts are available in miniature at happy hour, when bars mount lavish spreads of *cicheti* (Venetian tapas). Save room and time for a proper sit-down Venetian meal, with lagoon seafood to match views at canalside bistros and toasts with Veneto's signature bubbly, *prosecco*.

Historic Firsts

The city built on water was never afraid to attempt the impossible. When plague struck, Venice consulted its brain trust of Mediterranean doctors, who recommended a precaution that has saved untold lives since: quarantine. Under attack by Genovese rivals, Venice's Arsenale shipyards innovated the assembly line, producing a new warship every day to defeat Genoa. After Genoa backed Christopher Columbus' venture to the New World, Venice's shipping fortunes began to fade – but Venice wasn't about to relinquish the world stage, going on to become the launching pad for baroque music and modern opera.

Defying Convention

Eyeglasses, platform shoes and uncorseted dresses are outlandish Venetian fashions that continental critics sniffed would never be worn by respectable Europeans. When prolific Ghetto publishing houses circulated Renaissance ideas, Rome banned Venice from publishing books. The city was excommunicated for ignoring such bans – but when savvy Venice withheld tithes, Rome recanted. Venice's artistic triumphs over censorship now grace the magnificent Gallerie dell'Accademia.

Why I Love Venice

By Cristian Bonetto, Author

Venice is the consummate magician. It makes marble palaces vanish into silent fogs, labyrinthine *calli* (streets) disappear at the whim of moody tides, and can even turn the most pedestrian of people into fantastical, masked creatures. Just like its world-famous Carnevale, Venice thrives on mystery and awe, from the secret passageways that riddle Gothic Palazzo Ducale, to the esoteric powers of the Basilica di Santa Maria della Salute, to the inexplicable radiance of Titian's *Assunta* altarpiece. After countless sojourns, I am yet to tire of the place. Some spells are simply too hard to break.

For more about our authors, see p288.

Venice's
Top 10

Palazzo Ducale *(p53)*

1 Other cities have government buildings; Venice has the Palazzo Ducale, a monumental propaganda campaign. To reach the halls of power, you must pass the Scala dei Censori (Stairs of the Censors) and Sansovino's staircase lined with 24-carat gold, then wait in a Palladio-designed hall facing Tiepolo's *Venice Receiving Gifts of the Sea from Neptune*. Veronese's *Juno Bestowing her Gifts on Venice* graces the trial chambers of the Consiglio dei Dieci (Council of Ten), Venice's CIA. Upstairs is the Piombi attic-prison, where Casanova was confined in 1756 until his escape.

⊙ *San Marco*

Basilica di San Marco *(p50)*

2 Early risers urge you to arrive when morning sunlight bathes millions of *tesserae* with an otherworldly glow, and jaws drop to semiprecious-stone floors. Sunset romantics lobby you to linger in Piazza San Marco until fading sunlight shatters portal mosaics into golden shards, and the Caffè Florian house band strikes up the tango. Yet no matter how you look at it, the basilica is a marvel. Two eyes may seem insufficient to absorb 800 years of architecture and 8500 sq metres of mosaics – Basilica di San Marco will stretch your sense of wonder.

⊙ *San Marco*

Tintoretto's Masterpieces *(p109)*

3 During Venice's darkest days of the Black Death, flashes of genius appeared. Tintoretto's loaded paintbrush streaks across stormy scenes inside the Scuola Grande di San Rocco (p86) like a lightning bolt, revealing glimmers of hope in the long shadow of the plague that reduced Venice's population by a third. Angelic rescue squads save lost souls until the very last minute of the master's *Last Judgement* in Madonna dell'Orto (p109) – as long as they hold back that teal tidal wave, even a lowly mortal might catch a glimpse of heaven on earth. BELOW: SCUOLA GRANDE DI SAN ROCCO

◉ *San Polo & Santa Croce, Cannaregio*

Cruising Canals *(p25)*

4 Traffic never seemed so romantic as at sunset in Venice, when smooching echoes under the Ponte dei Sospiri (Bridge of Sighs) from passing gondolas. Venice's morning rush hour may lull you back to sleep with the gentle sounds of footsteps heading to the *vaporetto* (water bus) and oars slapping canal waters. Road rage is not an issue in a town with no actual roads but over 400 licensed *gondolieri*, who call 'Ooooooeeee!' around blind corners to avoid collisions. Hop on board, or try your hand at the oar with Row Venice (p154).

🕺 *Tours*

Gallerie dell'Accademia *(p73)*

5 They've been censored and stolen, raised eyebrows and inspired generosity: all the fuss over Venetian paintings becomes clear at the Accademia. The Inquisition did not appreciate Venetian versions of biblical stories – especially Veronese's *Last Supper,* a wild dinner party of drunkards, dwarves, dogs, Turks and Germans alongside apostles. But Napoleon quite enjoyed Venetian paintings, warehousing them here as booty. Wars and floods took their toll, but international donations have restored Sala dell'Albergo's crowning glory: Titian's *Presentation of the Virgin,* where a young Madonna inspires Venetian merchants to help the needy.

◉ *Dorsoduro*

Padua's Scrovegni Chapel
(p164)

6 Squint a little at Giotto's 1303–05 Cappella degli Scrovegni frescoes, and you can see the Renaissance coming. Instead of bug-eyed Byzantine saints, Giotto's biblical characters evoke people you'd recognise today: a middle-aged mother (Anne) with a miracle baby (Mary), a new father (Joseph) nodding off while watching his baby boy (Jesus), a slippery schemer (Judas) breezily air-kissing a trusting friend (Jesus). Giotto captures human nature in all its flawed and complex beauty, making a detour to elegant, erudite Padua well worth the effort.

⊙ *Day Trips from Venice*

Opera at Teatro La Fenice
(p58)

7 Before the curtain rises, the drama has already begun at La Fenice. Wraps shed in lower-tier boxes reveal jewels, while in top loggie (balconies), *loggione* (opera critics) predict which singers will be in good voice, and which understudies may merit promotions. Meanwhile, architecture aficionados debate whether the theatre's faithful reconstruction after its 1998 arson was worth €90 million. But when the overture begins, all voices hush. No one wants to miss a note of performances that could match premieres here by Stravinsky, Rossini, Prokofiev and Britten.

☆ *San Marco*

Venice Biennale (p39)

8 When Venice dared the world to show off its modern masterpieces, delegations from Australia to Venezuela accepted the challenge – who turns down an invitation to Venice? Today the Venice Biennale is the world's most prestigious creative showcase, featuring art (in odd-numbered years) and architecture (in even-numbered years), and hosting the Venice Film Festival and performing-arts extravaganzas annually. Friendly competition among nationals is obvious in the Giardini's pavilions, which showcase architectural sensibilities ranging from magical thinking (Austro-Hungary) to repurposed industrial cool (Korea). LEFT: *THE PORTRAIT OF SAKIP SABANCI* BY KUTLUĞ ATAMAN

🎭 *Entertainment*

Venetian Artisans *(p41)*

9 In Venice, you're not just in g
you're in highly skilled ones.
done for centuries, artisans here
trades, those that don't involve a
mouse, such as glass-blowing, pa
marbling and oarlock-carving. Ye
craft traditions have fossilised int
bygone eras, Venetian artisans ha
their creations current. A modern
glass chandelier morphs into an i
octopus, marbled paper turns int
handbags, and oarlocks custom-
rock-and-roll legends are mantelp
tures that upstage any marble bu

🔒 *Shopping*

Veneto Wines *(p33)*

10 Toast your arrival in Venice
Veneto is overflowing with
Conegliano to explore the very ho
in Bassano del Grappa for a mout
tured whites in Soave, and fall in l
northwest of Verona. For someth
ViniVeri, Italy's natural-process w

🍷 *Drinking & Nightlife*

What's New

A New Exhibition Program

With Gabriella Belli (ex-director of the Museo di Arte Moderna e Contemporanea di Trento e Rovereto) now at the helm of Venice's civic museums (www.visitmuve.it), you can expect great things. She's signed a four-year deal with exhibition organisers 24 Ore Cultura (www.24orecultura.com), giving them the run of the 11 museum spaces for shows that have already included Henri Rousseau at the Palazzo Ducale, Cy Twombly at Ca' Pesaro and Leslie Hirst at the Burano Lace Museum.

Museo del Vetro

Murano's restored Glass Museum has been transformed from a hopeless clutter of artefacts into a beautifully curated collection spread over double the space. (p150)

VèneziaUnica

Venice's new, online, one-ticket solution for public transport and tourist cards covers all major museums, sights, churches, special events and even parking and wi-fi. (p246)

Arsenale Aperto

As part of the continuing regeneration of the Arsenale, this open weekend in April allows the public to explore Venice's vast industrial shipyards, even giving access to usually restricted military areas. (p119)

Yoga

Given the urban rigours of the Rialto how does one keep fit in Venice? Yoga, of course. Now available in Giudecca gardens, the Giardini's 19th-century greenhouse and the Palestra di San Giorgio. (p146)

Burano's Albergo Diffuso

The forward-thinking Bisol family behind Venissa have renovated a few fishermen's cottages on Burano to create Venice's first *albergo diffuso*. Guests can make themselves at home in their cottage, but still have access to Venissa's gourmet goodies if they want. (p157)

Palazzo Mocenigo

Long famed for its collection of historical fashion, Palazzo Mocenigo now allows visitors to explore the history, science and art of fragrance with the opening of a new perfume exhibit. (p91)

Improved Disabled Access

With 11% of travellers to Venice having a disability, wheelchair-accessible boat travel from Gondolas 4 All and L'Altra Venezia couldn't come soon enough. (p251)

Chiesa di San Sebastiano

Blockbuster painting cycles by Veronese, Titian and Tintoretto will soon have a dazzling new lustre thanks to a major restoration effort at Chiesa di San Sebastiano. (p77)

Surfing & Paddling

Watersports enthusiasts, children and lagoon lovers will cheer the advent of stand-up paddleboard (SUP) tours (p135) and the new kid-friendly Surf Club Venezia on the Lido (p145).

For more recommendations and reviews, see **lonelyplanet.com/italy/venice**

Need to Know

For more information, see Survival Guide (p239)

Currency
Euro (€)

Language
Italian and Veneto (Venetian dialect)

Visas
Not required for EU citizens. Nationals of Australia, Brazil, Canada, Japan, New Zealand and the USA do not need visas for visits of up to 90 days.

Money
ATMs widely available; credit cards accepted at most hotels, B&Bs and shops.

Mobile Phones
GSM and tri-band phones can be used in Italy with a local SIM card.

Time
GMT/UTC plus one hour during winter, GMT/UTC plus two hours during summer daylight saving.

Tourist Information
Azienda di Promozione Turistica (☑041 529 87 11; www.turismovenezia.it; Piazza San Marco 71f; ☺8.30am-7pm) is Venice's tourism office, providing information on events, attractions, day trips, transport and shows.

Daily Costs

Budget:
Less than €120
➡ Dorm bed: €22–€30
➡ Basilica di San Marco: free
➡ *Cicheti* at All'Arco: €5–€15
➡ Chorus Pass: €12
➡ Organ vespers at Chiesa di Santa Maria della Salute: free
➡ *Spritz:* €2.50–€4

Midrange:
€120–€250
➡ B&B: €70–€180
➡ Civic Museum Pass: €24
➡ Happy hour in Piazza San Marco: €9–€15
➡ Interpreti Veneziani ticket: €27
➡ Dinner at Antiche Carampane: €30–€45

Top End:
More than €250
➡ Boutique hotel: €180-plus
➡ Gondola ride: €80
➡ Palazzo Grassi & Punta della Dogana ticket: €20
➡ Dinner at Da Rioba: €45–€60
➡ La Fenice ticket: from €45

Advance Planning

Two months before Book accommodation for high season and snap up tickets to La Fenice operas, Venice Film Festival premieres and Biennale openings.

Three weeks before Check special-event calendars at www.unospitedivenezia.it and www.veneziadavivere.com, and reserve boat trips.

One week before Make restaurant reservations for a big night out; skip the queues by booking tickets to major attractions and events online at www.venetoinside.com or www.veneziaunica.it.

Useful Websites

Lonely Planet (www.lonelyplanet.com) Expert travel advice.

Venice Comune (www.comune.venezia.it) City of Venice official site with essential info, including high-water alerts.

VeneziaUnica (www.veneziaunica.it) A one-ticket solution for public transport and tourist cards covering museums, churches and special events.

Venezia da Vivere (www.veneziadavivere.com) Music performances, art openings, nightlife and child-friendly events.

2Venice (www.2venice.it) Updated events listings and info on restaurants, bars and shopping.

WHEN TO GO

Autumn offers warm days, sparse crowds and low rates. Winter has chilly days and sociable nights. Spring is damp but lovely as ever indoors.

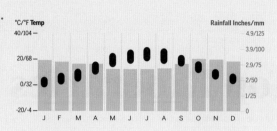

°C/°F Temp

Rainfall Inches/mm

Arriving in Venice

Marco Polo Airport (VCE) Located on the mainland 12km from Venice, east of Mestre. Alilaguna operates a ferry service (€15) to Venice from the airport ferry dock (an eight-minute walk from the terminal); expect it to take 45 to 90 minutes to reach most destinations. Water taxis to Venice from airport docks cost from €110, or from €25 for shared taxis with up to 10 passengers. ATVO buses (€6) depart from the airport every 30 minutes from 7.50am to 12.20am, and reach Venice's Piazzale Roma within 20 to 30 minutes, traffic permitting.

Piazzale Roma This car park is the only point within central Venice accessible by car or bus. *Vaporetto* (water-bus) lines to destinations throughout the city depart from Piazzale Roma docks.

Stazione Santa Lucia Venice's train station. *Vaporetto* lines depart from Ferrovia (Station) docks.

Stazione Venezia Mestre Mestre's mainland train station; transfer here to Stazione Santa Lucia.

For much more on **arriving** see p240

Getting Around

➡ **Vaporetto** Venice's main public transport. Single rides cost €7; for frequent use, get a timed pass for unlimited travel within a set period (one-/two-/three-/seven-day passes cost €20/30/40/60). Tickets and passes are available dockside from ACTV ticket booths and ticket vending machines, or from tobacconists.

➡ **Gondola** Daytime rates run to €80 for 30 minutes (six passengers maximum) or €100 for 35 minutes from 7pm to 8am, not including songs (negotiated separately) or tips.

➡ **Traghetto** Locals use this daytime public gondola service (€2) to cross the Grand Canal between bridges.

➡ **Water taxi** Sleek teak boats offer taxi services for €15 plus €2 per minute, plus €5 for pre-booked services and extra for night-time, luggage and large groups. Ensure the meter is working when boarding.

For much more on **getting around** see p243

Sleeping

With many Venetians opening their homes to visitors, you can become a local overnight here. Venice was once known for charmingly decrepit hotels where English poets quietly expired, but new design-literate boutique hotels are spiffing up historic palaces and attracting a rock-star following. Expect to pay €110 to €200 midrange, plus tourist tax (hostels are exempt). Some upscale hotels offer vouchers for parking in Tronchetto; otherwise it's at least €21 per day.

Useful Websites

➡ **BB Planet** (www.bbplanet. com) Search Venice B&Bs by neighbourhood, price range and facilities.

➡ **Lonely Planet** (www. lonelyplanet.com/italy/ venice/hotels) Expert author reviews, user feedback, booking engine.

➡ **Airbnb** (www.airbnb.com) Rooms and apartments rented straight from the owners.

➡ **Luxrest Venice** (www. luxrest-venice.com) Carefully curated apartments from €950 per week.

For much more on **sleeping** see p186

Top Itineraries

Day One

San Marco (p48)

 Begin your day in prison on the Secret Passages tour of the **Palazzo Ducale**, then break for espresso at the counter of **Caffè Lavena** before the Byzantine blitz of golden mosaics inside **Basilica di San Marco**. Browse boutique-lined backstreets to **Museo Fortuny**, the palace fashion house whose goddess-style gowns freed women from corsets.

> ✕ **Lunch** Perfect prosciutto above a cinema at DOK Dall'Ava LP26 (p64).

Dorsoduro (p71)

Pause atop wooden **Ponte dell'Accademia** for **Grand Canal** photo ops, then surrender to timeless drama that no camera can convey inside **Gallerie dell'Accademia**. Wander past **Squero di San Trovaso** to glimpse gondolas under construction, then bask in the reflected glory of Palladio's **Il Redentore** along waterfront **Zattere**. Stop at tiny **Chiesa di San Sebastian**, packed with Veroneses, then hop between artisan boutiques along Calle Lunga San Barnaba before '*spritz* o'clock' (cocktail hour) in **Campo Santa Margherita**.

> ✕ **Dinner** Swoon over seasonal, succulent flavours at Ristorante La Bitta (p79).

Dorsoduro (p71)

 Leap back into the 1700s at nearby Scuola Grande dei Carmini, the evocative setting for costumed classical concerts by **Musica in Maschera**. Alternatively, end the night on a saxy note at modern veteran **Venice Jazz Club**.

Day Two

San Polo & Santa Croce (p84)

 Kick off day two with a crash course in local surf and turf at produce-packed **Rialto market**, side-stepping it to **Drogheria Mascari** for gourmet pantry fillers and regional wines, and to **All'Arco** for a cheeky morning *prosecco*. Boutiques and artisan studios punctuate your way to Campo San Rocco, home to Gothic showoff **I Frari** and its sunny Titian altarpiece. Once admired, slip into **Scuola Grande di San Rocco** for prime-time-drama Tintorettos.

> ✕ **Lunch** Market-fresh bites and impeccable wines at vibrant Estro (p81).

Dorsoduro (p71)

Explore the modern art that caused uproars and defined the 20th century at the **Peggy Guggenheim Collection**, and contrast it with works that push contemporary buttons at **Punta della Dogana**. Duck into Baldassare Longhena's domed **Chiesa di Santa Maria della Salute** for blushing Titians and legendary curative powers, then cross the **Grand Canal** on Venice's only wooden bridge, Ponte dell'Accademia.

> ✕ **Dinner** Superlative Venetian cuisine at Trattoria e Bacaro da Fiore (p65).

San Marco (p48)

 The hottest ticket in town during opera season is at **La Fenice**, but classical-music fans shouldn't miss Vivaldi played with contemporary verve by **Interpreti Veneziani**.

Day Three

Castello (p117)

 Stroll **Riva degli Schiavoni** for views across the lagoon to Palladio's **San Giorgio Maggiore**. See how Carpaccio's sprightly saints light up a room at **Scuola di San Giorgio degli Schiavoni**, then seek out Castello's hidden wonder: **Chiesa di San Francesco della Vigna**. Get stared down by statues atop **Ospedaletto** on your way to Gothic **Zanipolo**, home to 25 marble doges. The Renaissance awaits two bridges away at **Chiesa di Santa Maria dei Miracoli**, a polychrome marble miracle made from Basilica di San Marco's leftovers.

> **Lunch** Housemade pasta lures *gondolieri* at Osteria Ruga di Jaffa (p130).

Cannaregio (p105)

Wander serene *fondamente* (canal banks) past statue sentries ringing **Campo dei Mori** to reach **Chiesa della Madonna dell'Orto**, the neighbourhood Gothic church Tintoretto pimped with masterpieces. Tour the Ghetto's newly renovated **synagogues** and the restored historic pawnshop, **Banco Rosso**, until Venice's happiest hours beckon across the bridge at **Al Timon**.

> **Dinner** Inventive Venetian cuisine beside the canal at Da Rioba (p112).

Cannaregio (p105)

Take a romantic **gondola** ride through Cannaregio's long canals, seemingly purpose-built to maximise moonlight.

Day Four

Murano, Burano & the Northern Islands (p147)

 Make your lagoon getaway on a *vaporetto* bound for Technicolor **Burano** and green-and-gold **Torcello**. Follow the sheep trail to Torcello's Byzantine **Cattedrale di Santa Maria Assunta**, where the apse's golden Madonna calmly stares down the blue devils opposite. Catch the boat back to Burano to admire extreme home-design colour schemes and handmade lace at **Museo del Merletto**.

> **Lunch** Sunny Mazzorbo vineyards and inspired cuisine at Venissa (p157).

Murano, Burano & the Northern Islands (p147); Giudecca, Lido & the Southern Islands (p136)

Take in the fiery passions of glass artisans at Murano's legendary *fornaci* (furnaces), and see their finest moments showcased at the fabulously renovated **Museo del Vetro** (Glass Museum). After Murano showrooms close, hop the *vaporetto* to **Giudecca** for some spa-loving at the **Bauer Palladio** and unbeatable views of San Marco glittering across glassy waters.

> **Dinner** Wine and dine with artists and celebrities at Trattoria Altanella (p142).

San Marco (p48)

 Celebrate your triumphant tour of the lagoon with a *prosecco* toast and tango across Piazza San Marco at time-warped **Caffè Florian**; repeat these steps as necessary.

If You Like...

Hidden Gems

Chiesa di San Francesco della Vigna All-star Venetian art showcase and Palladio's first commission. (p128)

Chiesa di Santa Maria dei Miracoli The little neighbourhood church with big Renaissance ideas and priceless marble. (p109)

Basilica di Santa Maria Assunta Lambs bleat encouragement as you traverse the overgrown island of Torcello towards golden glory in apse mosaics. (p149)

Ghetto synagogues Climb to rooftop synagogues on tours run by Museo Ebraico. (p107)

Palazzo Contarini del Bovolo A secret spiral staircase in an ancient courtyard sets the scene for a clandestine smooch. (p59)

Boats

Arsenale Venice's legendary shipyards built a warship in a day on the world's first assembly line. (p119)

Squero di San Trovaso Watch gondolas being shaped by hand and custom-sized to match the weight and height of the gondolier. (p81)

Museo Storico Navale Four floors of nautical wonders, from the *bucintoro* (ducal barge) to WWII battleships. (p128)

Gilberto Penzo Scale-model gondolas for your bathtub and build-your-own-boat kits from a master artisan. (p100)

Gelati

Row Venice Learn to row across lagoon waters standing like a gondolier. (p154)

Fashion

Museo Fortuny Glimpse inside the palatial, radical fashion house that freed women from corsets and innovated bohemian chic. (p59)

Palazzo Mocenigo Find fashion inspiration in a palace packed with Venetian glamour, from bustles and knee breeches to dashing waistcoats. (p91)

Fiorella Gallery Rock subversive Venetian looks, including lilac silk-velvet jackets hand-printed with red rats. (p68)

Antica Modisteria Giuliana Longo Dive into this historic milliner for handcrafted pieces, from Louise Brooks cloches to authentic gondolier hats. (p68)

Declare Bold, contemporary leather bags and accessories from a young-gun duo. (p100)

Backstreet Bars

All'Arco Lip-smacking *cicheti* (Venetian tapas) invented daily with Rialto Market's freshest finds, plus perfect wine pairings – all for the price of a pizza. (p95)

Vino Vero Venice's only *bacaro* (hole-in-the-wall bar) dedicated to biodynamic wines paired with gourmet bar bites. (p112)

Bacaro Risorto A pocket-sized bar packed with *cicheti* and good spirits, whenever they feel like opening. (p133)

Cantina Aziende Agricole A tried-and-tested *bacaro* serving well-priced *ombre* (half-glasses of wine) and generously heaped *cicheti*. (p110)

Trattoria e Bacaro Da Fiore Affordable wines and authentic Venetian snacks in the heart of pricey San Marco. (p65)

Curiosities

Museo della Follia 'Museum of Madness' is as creepy as it sounds, featuring 'cures' happily no longer in use on the island of San Servolo. (p140)

Museo di Storia Naturale di Venezia Dinosaurs, two-headed calves, monstrous Japanese spider crabs and other bizarre scientific specimens brought home by intrepid Venetian explorers – all inside a Turkish fortress. (p91)

Museo d'Arte Orientale The attic of Ca' Pesaro is lined with Japanese samurai gear, thanks to an Italian prince's 1887–89 Asian shopping binge. (p90)

Fondazione Vedova Robots designed by Renzo Piano display Emilio Vedova's abstract canvases, then whisk them back into storage. (p77)

Sweet Treats

Alaska Gelateria Made-from-scratch organic gelato in refreshing flavours like cardamom, white peach and artichoke. (p97)

VizioVirtù From edible plague-doctor masks to *vino*-infused pralines, this artisan chocolate maker is terrific-calorific. (p101)

Pasticceria Da Bonifacio Almond *curasan* (croissants), *zaletti* (cornmeal biscuits) and other Venetian treats rich enough to satisfy a doge. (p131)

Panificio Volpe Giovanni A kosher bakery peddling heavenly pastries with the rabbi's blessing. (p111)

For more top Venice spots, see the following:

➡ Eating (p27)
➡ Drinking & Nightlife (p33)
➡ Entertainment (p37)
➡ Sports & Activties (p39)
➡ Shopping (p41)

Pasticceria Tonolo Flakey apple strudel and mini-profiteroles bursting with hazelnut-chocolate mousse provide energy to take on Titian at I Frari. (p79)

Local Hang-outs

Lido Beaches When temperatures nudge upwards of 29°C, Venice races to the Lido-bound *vaporetto* (ferry) to claim sandy beachfront. (p142)

Campo San Giacomo dell'Orio bars Kids tear through the *campo*, while parents watch through the bottom of glasses of natural-process *prosecco*. (p98)

Rialto Market Whet your appetite as grandmothers and Michelin chefs drive hard bargains with witty grocers. (p89)

Via Garibaldi Venetian workers heading home always make time for one last *spritz* in Via Garibaldi bars. (p132)

Murano Linger after the day-trippers disperse for soothing glasses of Lugana and Venice's best pizza. (p156)

Month by Month

February

Snow occasionally falls in Venice, blanketing gondolas. Velvet costumes and wine fountains warm February nights, when revellers party like it's 1699 at masked balls – in its baroque heyday, Carnevale lasted three months.

Carnevale

Masqueraders party in the streets for two weeks preceding Lent. Tickets to the extraordinary St Valentine's Masquerade Ball run up to about €800, but there's no shortage of less expensive diversions at Carnevale (www.carnevale.venezia.it), from public costume parties in the *campi* (squares) to Grand Canal flotillas.

April

The winning springtime combination of optimal walking weather and reasonable room rates lasts until Easter, when art-history classes on holiday briefly flood the city.

Vinitaly

Good spirits abound at Italy's premier expo of wine and spirits (www.vinitaly.com), drawing over 155,000 visitors to Verona's VeronaFiere pavilions. The four-day expo starts in sober earnest, with expert-guided tastings of rare vintages and Slow Food and wine pairings – but by the final afternoon it's a proper bacchanal.

Su e Zo Per I Ponti

'Up and Down the Bridges' is a 12km non-competitive race through Venice (www.suezo.it), with 10,000 to 15,000 participants crossing 43 bridges to raise funds for charity and enjoying free music gigs to get them in the mood.

Festa di San Marco

Join the celebration of Venice's patron saint on 25 April, when Venetian men carry a *bocolo* (rosebud) in

processions through Piazza San Marco, then give them to the women they love.

May

As summer edges closer, it's time for headline-grabbing contemporary art and mystical seafaring celebrations.

Biennale di Venezia (Venice Biennale)

In odd years the Art Biennale usually runs May to November, and in even years the Architecture Biennale kicks off in September – but every summer, the Biennale (www.labiennale.org) also features avant-garde dance, theatre, cinema and music.

Vogalonga

This 32km 'long row' (www.vogalonga.com) starts with 1800 boats in front of the Palazzo Ducale, loops past Burano and Murano, and ends with cheers and *prosecco* at Punta della Dogana.

Festa della Sensa

If Venice loves the sea, why don't they get married? Consider it done. Vows have been professed annually since AD 1000 in the Sposalito del Mar (Wedding to the Sea), with celebrations including outdoor markets and Mass on the Lido. The event takes place on the Feast of the Ascension.

June

As the weather warms further, a former cathedral turns into a party backdrop.

✈️ Festa di San Pietro di Castello

The Festival of St Peter of Castello (www.sanpiero decasteo.org) takes place in the last week of June at the steps of the church that was once the city's cathedral, with Mass, games, puppetry, rustic fare and live music.

July

Fireworks over Giudecca illuminate balmy summer nights, and performances by jazz greats end sunny days on a sultry note.

✈️ Festa del Redentore

Walk on water across the Giudecca Canal to Il Redentore via a pontoon bridge on the third Saturday and Sunday in July. Join the massive floating picnic along the Zattere, and don't miss the fireworks (www. turismovenezia.it).

☆ Venice Jazz Festival

International legends from Wynton Marsalis to Burt Bacharach bring down the house at La Fenice, while crowd-favourite acts play venues as diverse as the Peggy Guggenheim Collection and Isola di San Clemente. Check the calendar for

shows in Vicenza, Verona, Treviso and Bassano del Grappa year-round (www. venetojazz.com).

September

Movie stars bask in flattering autumnal light along Venice Film Festival's red carpets, and regattas make the most of optimal weather.

☆ Venice International Film Festival

The only thing hotter than Lido beaches this time of year is the red carpet at this star-studded event (www.labiennale.org/en/ cinema), running for 11 days from late August or early September.

🏃 Regata Storica

Never mind who's winning, check out the gear: 16th-century costumes and eight-oared gondolas re-enact the Venice arrival of the Queen of Cyprus (www. regatastoricavenezia.it). A floating parade is followed by four races, where kids and adult rowers compete for boating bragging rights.

✈️ Burano Regata

Fishing island Burano angles for attention the third Sunday in September with Venice's only mixed men's and women's rowing regatta (www.comune. venezia.it). The last regatta of the rowing season, its victors are celebrated at the island after-party over fish, polenta and *prosecco*.

✈️ Riviera Fiorita

Relive the glory days of 1627 along the Brenta river with a flotilla of antique boats, baroque costume balls at Villa

Widmann Rezzonico Foscari and Villa Pisani Nazionale, historically correct country fairs, period music and gelato in baroque-era flavours. It's usually held the second Sunday in September.

October

High tourism season ends, festival crowds disperse and hotel rates lower.

✈️ Festa del Mosto

A country fair on 'garden isle' Sant'Erasmo, held on the first Sunday in October (www.comune.venezia.it). The wine-grape harvest is celebrated with a parade, farmers market, gourmet food stalls, live music and free-flowing *vino*.

🏃 Venice Marathon

On the fourth Sunday in October, 8000 runners work up a sweat over 42km of spectacular scenery, dashing along the Brenta river before heading into Venice and crossing the Grand Canal on a floating bridge (www.venicemarathon.it).

November

Venice gives thanks for its miraculous survival before kicking off another year of revelry on 1 January.

✈️ Festa della Madonna della Salute

If you'd survived plague and Austrian invasion, you'd throw a party too. Every 21 November since the 17th century, Venetians have crossed a pontoon bridge across the Grand Canal to light a candle in thanks at Santa Maria della Salute and splurge on sweets.

For Free

Despite its centuries-old reputation as a playground for Europe's elite, some of Venice's finest moments are freebies, from glittering glimpses of heaven in Basilica di San Marco to soothing vespers at the healing Basilica di Santa Maria della Salute.

Historical Sites

Some of the most pivotal sites in Venetian history have free entry: Rialto Market (p89), where an empire sprang up around fishmongers; Basilica di Santa Maria della Salute (p76), the domed church built as thanks for Venice's salvation from plague; and the Basilica di San Marco (p50), the apotheosis of Venice's millennium of brilliant self-invention. While the Basilica di Santa Maria della Salute offers free afternoon organ vespers concerts, the Basilica di San Marco runs free guided tours of its astounding mosaics.

Arts & Architecture

While entry to the main art and architecture Biennale shows and Venice Film Festival premieres isn't free, many citywide dance, music, cinema and ancillary arts programs are. Art lovers will appreciate the superb (and often free) shows at Palazzo Franchetti (p63). Commercial art galleries and Murano glass showrooms are yours to enjoy at no cost, and state-run museums such as Palazzo Grimani (p124) are *gratis* on the first Sunday of the month. Then there is Venice's spectacular architecture. Take in Grand Canal *palazzi* (palaces) for the price of a *vaporetto* (ferry) ticket, or discover hidden gems like Palazzo Contarini del Bovolo on a San Marco walking tour (p62).

Island Getaways

A timed *vaporetto* ticket lets you do laps of the lagoon without paying extra. The Lido offers three free-access beaches, a miniature version of Venice at Malamocco, a superb Tuesday produce market (p143), and free summer concerts. Giudecca comes with mesmerising views, galleries, a 14th-century church and the Fortuny showroom. Visit the haunting cemetery isle of San Michele on your way to Murano, where you can glimpse glass-makers at work, and spot dragon's bones among the Byzantine mosaics of San Donato. Take a photography expedition to Technicolor Burano and while you're there, spot masterpieces inside Chiesa di San Martino (p154). For welcome stretches of green, hop off at Torcello, Mazzorbo, Sant'Erasmo and Le Vignole.

Top Bargains

Access some of Venice's finest masterpieces in 16 churches with a Chorus Pass. It costs €12 (for a total saving of €35), and includes such spectacular sights as I Frari, Chiesa di Santa Maria dei Miracoli, Chiesa di San Sebastiano and Chiesa della Madonna dell'Orto.

The San Marco Museums Pack (€17) covers the Palazzo Ducale, Museo Correr, Museo Archeologico Nazionale and Biblioteca Nazionale Marciana. Or get even more history for your money: for €7 extra, buy the Civic Museum Pass, which grants access to an extra seven museums.

Ditch those €80 gondola rides for the cheap thrill of standing on the *traghetto* (public gondola) as you cross the Grand Canal (€2 per ride). If you *must* hop on a gondola, **Tu.Ri.Ve** (www.turive.it) offers rides at €31 a pop.

With Kids

Adults think Venice is for them; kids know better. This is where fairy tales come to life, where prisoners escape through the roof of a palace, Murano glass-blowers breathe life into pocket-sized sea dragons, and spellbound Pescaria fish balance on their tails. Top that, JK Rowling.

Attractions

Make an early morning run down the Grand Canal for hot chocolates at Florian (p65); the cafe's fairy-tale interiors are plucked straight out of a giant storybook. Slip into Palazzo Mocenigo (p91) to explore the Cinderella fashions of the past, then roam the secret attic-prisons of the Doge's Palace (p53). Check out giant samurai swords at the Museo d'Arte Orientale in Ca' Pesaro (p90), or the massive sea monsters and dinosaurs at the Museo di Storia Naturale (p91). Grab your sailor hat and shout out 'Ship Ahoy!' at the Museo Storico Navale (p128), jam-packed with golden princely barges, model warships and enough cannons to make any pirate nervous.

Most attractions in Venice offer reduced admission for children. City-run museums (visitmuve.it) generally give a 60% to 70% discount to visitors aged six to 14, and free entry to those aged five and under. State-owned museums (www.polomuseale. venezia.beniculturali.it) are free for those aged under 18.

Tours for Kids

Friend in Venice

History and culture dished up by your **Friend in Venice** (☑338 9196695; http:// friendinvenice.com; tours €120-300), Nadia, with engaging anecdotes and quotidian details perfect for kids aged seven and up.

Monica Caserato

Ghost tours (www.monicacesarato.com; tours €35) packed with tales of grizzly murders, plague, drownings and beheadings are delivered with Monica's mesmerising Marco Polo storytelling skills, and will hook kids aged seven to 14.

Context Travel

Scholarly tours for the curious minded, **Context** (☑06 9672 7371; www.contexttravel. com; group tours €315-345) will have you lion hunting round town, investigating Venetian life and exploring the secrets and science of the lagoon with a marine biologist. For kids aged five to 12, plus separate tours for teens.

Outdoor Activities

Beaches & Picnics

Lido beaches and lagoon picnics on Torcello, Mazzorbo and Le Vignole give the whole family some reinvigorating downtime.

Boating, Kayaking & Surfing

Glide across teal-blue waters to desert islands with Terra e Acqua (p150); kayak down canals and across the open lagoon with Venice Kayak (p159); or hit the Lido beaches at Surf Club Venezia (p145).

Photography Walks

Teens will love Venice Photo Walk (p68) with Marco Secchi, especially when his professional tips make their Instagram shots the envy of all their social media peers.

Island Biking

Team up on tandem bikes for leisurely Lido itineraries, or strike out on two-wheeled nature excursions on the garden island of Le Vignole.

Hands-On Learning

Rowing & Sailing

Kids tall and strong enough to hold an oar can learn to row like *gondolieri* do with Row Venice (p154). Alternatively, sign up for a week of lagoon sailing with Vento di Venezia (p25), with courses for budding sailors aged seven to 13 as well as for older teens.

Arts & Crafts

Kids inspired by watching Venetian artists and artisans at work can make their own Carnevale masks at Ca' Macana (p83), and even build their own gondolas with scale-model kits from Gilberto Penzo (p100). Ideal for kids aged seven and up.

Pasta Making

Spend the morning eyeing up sci-fi-like lagoon creatures at Rialto Market (p89), then head to the Acquolina Cooking School (p30) to learn the art of making pasta and tiramisu. Suitable for teens.

Learning the Lingo

Ordering gelato is an essential skill, so give your kids a head start with a fun, engaging morning language session at the Venice Italian School (p246). For kids aged five and up.

Food

When feet and spirits begin to drag, there's pizza and pasta galore to pick them back up. For an impromptu tea party, settle in with freshly baked brownies and other sweet treats at Tea Room Beatrice (p81), Rosa Salva (p133) and La Serra dei Giardini (p132). Unless your kids are super adventurous, navigating *cicheti* (Venetian tapas) may be hard. The best compromise is to opt for restaurants that serve full menus as well as *cicheti*. The Lido is the land of pizza lovers and ice-cream shops. Other popular take-away options good for a cheap, quick feed include Antico Forno (p97), Bar alla Toletta (p79), Rosticceria Gislon (p64), Cip Ciap (p131) and Osteria al Duomo (p156). The last of these has a lovely outdoor dining area, as does Agriturismo da Zangrando (p155). That done, challenge your budding

gastronomes to try asparagus ice-cream at Alaska Gelateria (p97).

Given the expense of eating out, many families find that opting for a self-catering apartment is a life saver. Not only does it offer the flexibility of having your own kitchen, but the experience of shopping at the Rialto or the city's floating produce barges is a memorable cultural experience.

Kid Hang-outs

Campo San Giacomo dell'Orio

Marathon games of tag in this *campo* probably started around the time its namesake medieval church was built. These days the square is dotted with bar tables where parents can keep an eye on kids, *prosecco* in hand.

Giardini & Parco delle Rimembranze

Parents are wowed by the sweeping lagoon views and backdrop of Biennale pavilions, but kids know they've found paradise when they spot the swings, slides and sandlots of Venice's best park playgrounds.

The Lido

The Lido's breezy summer vibe and bike-loving culture is a winner with kids wanting to retreat from the stony Rialto to play ball on the beach and pedal madly down the *lungomare* (seafront promenade).

Tours

To get to know Venice from the inside out, first you have to see the lagoon city as Venetians have for a millennium – by water – then dive into the calli (lanes) and ascend secret staircases for glimpses of Venetian life behind the scenes and above the fray.

nalside buildings

Tours on Water

The following outings offer maritime adventures down canals and out on the lagoon. Reserve ahead, bring sunscreen and check weather forecasts, as trips are subject to climatic conditions.

Rowing

Find your footing on the lagoon as Olympic-trained rowing coach Jane Caporal and her team of rowers at Row Venice (p154) show you how to propel a handcrafted Venetian *batellina coda di gambero* (shrimp-tailed boat) standing up. The outfit also offers night lessons and a combined rowing and *cicheti* (Venetian tapas) bar hop.

Kayaking & Paddling

Venice Kayak (p159) offers a highly unique way to experience La Serenissima's waterways and quieter islands. Both group and private tours are offered, including half- and full-day explorations. Swimming skills and some prior paddling experience is required. Beginners are able to join a more experienced paddler in a two-person kayak.

Also open to confident paddlers over the age of 14 are stand-up paddleboard tours with art historian and paddler Eliana Argine of SUP in Venice (p135). The two-hour tour weaves through the quieter canals of Castello and Cannaregio and out on the lagoon.

Sailing

Eolo Cruises (www.cruisingvenice.com) covers the lagoon on a double-masted 1946 fishing *bragozzo* (flat-bottomed fishing boat) for one- to eight-day trips (per person from €2000 for six to 10 people), including on-board cooking tours. Guests sleep in select villas and *palazzi*, spend the day sailing and eat seafood lunches on board.

Vento di Venezia (☎041 520 85 88; www. ventodivenezia.it; Isola della Certosa; 🚤; 🚢Certosa) 🚲 offers sailing classes for the day or longer, plus stays at the marina hotel, Il Certosina.

Boating

Eco-friendly Terra e Acqua (p150) offers wild rides to the outer edges of the lagoon.

KIMBERLEY COOLE / GETTY IMAGES ©

Itineraries can cover abandoned plague-quarantine islands, fishing and birdwatching hot spots, Burano and Torcello. Lunch is served on board or at a local trattoria, and trips accommodate up to 12 people on a sturdy motorised *bragozzo*.

River Cruising

Luxury day cruises are possible between Venice and Padua on **Il Burchiello** (☑049 876 02 33; www.ilburchiello.it; adult/reduced half-day cruise from €55/45, full day €99/55), a modern barge that plies the villa-lined Brenta canal between March and October. The tranquil trip passes through nine swivel bridges and five locks, stops for guided tours of some of the villas and lunch at a canalside restaurant.

Tours on Land

Guided Tours of Major Sights

Many major sights offer guided tours, especially Venice civic museums. Basilica di San Marco (p50) offers free tours run by the diocese; the Itinerari Segreti (Secret Passages) tour (p26) of the Palazzo Ducale leads through hidden doorways to the attic prison; Palazzo Mocenigo (p91) offers monthly guided visits to see fragile antique fashions inside the palace's walk-in closet attic; and Museo del Vetro (p150) offers tours, including glass-blowing demonstrations. The only way to visit the Torre dell'Orologio (Clocktower, p57) and see the ancient clockworks in action is by pre-arranged tour.

For additional tours offered by Venetian churches and sights, consult the website of the **Venice Comune** (www.comune.venezia. it), or the free publication *Un Ospite di Venezia* (A Guest in Venice), distributed in most hotels. Tourist offices (p250) can also set you up with authorised tour guides and can book well-priced tours through accredited providers.

Walking Tours

Venice Urban Adventures (p99) offers year-round *cicheti* tours, covering five back-street *bacari* (hole-in-the-wall bars) on a local-guided Venetian bar crawl.

Venicescapes (☑041 520 63 61; www. venicescapes.org; 4-6hr tour incl book 2 adults US$250-290, additional adult US$60, under 18yr US$30), a nonprofit historical society, runs intriguing walking tours with themes such as 'A City of Nations – Foreigners and Immigrants', exploring multiethnic Venice through the ages. Proceeds support ongoing Venetian historical research.

Off-the-beaten-track tours with **Passeggiate Italiane** (☑331 267 18 59; www. secretvenice.it; tours €250-370) focus on the secret and esoteric side of Venice, and include private night tours of the basilica and a ghost tour with Venetian historian and writer Alberto Toso Fei. Veneto tours cover Padua, Vicenza and Cittadella.

Walks Inside Venice (☑041 524 17 06; www.walksinsidevenice.com; 2½hr group tours per person €60; ☑) has a spirited team that helps you explore the city's major monuments and hidden backstreets. Group tours include explorations of San Marco and San Polo, while private tour options include contemporary art and photography, and Venice's lagoon islands.

Whether you're a lens-literate pro or a smartphone-clutching Instagram addict, photojournalist Marco Secchi of Venice Photo Walk (p68) will have you capturing Venice from impressive new angles. His snap-happy walking tours are packed with information on both the city and the finer points of photography.

Caffè Florian (p65), Piazza San Marco

Eating

The visual blitz that is Venice tends to leave visitors bleary-eyed, weak-kneed and grasping for the nearest panino (sandwich). But there's more to La Serenissima than simple carb-loading. For centuries Venice has gone far beyond the call of dietary duty, and lavished visitors with wildly inventive feasts. Now it's your turn to devour addictive cicheti (Venetian tapas), lustful pastries and a lagoon's worth of fresh, succulent seafood.

Venetian Cuisine

'Local food!' is the latest foodie credo, but it's nothing new in Venice. Surrounded by garden islands and a seafood-rich lagoon, Venice dishes up local specialities that never make it to the mainland, because they're served fresh the same day in Venetian *bacari* (hole-in-the-wall bars) and *osterie* (casual eateries). A strong sea breeze wafts over the kitchens of the lagoon city, with the occasional meaty dish from the Veneto mainland and traditional, local options of rice and polenta in addition to classic Italian pastas and gnocchi. But side dishes of Veneto vegetables often steal the show, and early risers will notice Venetians risking faceplants in canals to grab *violetti di Sant'Erasmo* (tender purple baby artichokes), *radicchio trevisano* (ruffled red bitter chicory) and prized Bassano del Grappa white asparagus from produce-laden barges.

Cross-cultural fusion fare is old news here, dating back to Marco Polo's heyday. Thirteenth-century Venetian cookbooks include recipes for fish with galangal, saffron

NEED TO KNOW

Prices

With some notable exceptions in Venice (eg *cicheti*, sandwiches, pizza and gelato), a meal typically consists of two courses, a glass of house wine, and *pane e coperto* (bread and cover charge). Meal prices are defined as follows:

€ less than €25
€€ €25 to €45
€€€ more than €45

Opening Hours

Cafe-bars generally open from 7am to 8pm, although some stay open later and morph into drinking hang-outs. Restaurant kitchens generally close at 2.30pm or 3pm at lunch and around 10pm or 10.30pm at dinner.

Reservations

Call ahead to book a table at restaurants and *osterie* (taverns) whenever possible, especially for lunch in high season. You may get a table when you walk in off the street, but some restaurants buy ingredients according to how many bookings they've got – and when the food runs low, they stop seating. *Cicheti* are a handy alternative.

Pane e Coperto

'Bread and cover' charges range from €1.50 to €6 for sit-down meals at most restaurants.

Service Charges

Service may be included in *pane e coperto* (especially at basic *osterie*) or added onto the bill (at upscale bistros and for large parties). Read the fine print before you leave an additional tip.

and ginger; a tradition that still inspires dishes at nosh spots like Osteria Trefanti (p97). Don't be surprised if some Venetian dishes taste vaguely Turkish or Greek rather than strictly Italian, reflecting Venice's preferred trading partners for over a millennium. Spice-route flavours from the Mediterranean and beyond can be savoured in signature Venetian recipes such as *sarde in saor,* traditionally made with sardines in a tangy onion marinade with pine nuts and sultanas.

Exceptional ingredients from other parts of Italy sneak into Venetian cuisine, such as Tuscan steaks, white truffles from Alba, aromatic Amalfi lemons and Sicilian pistachios and blood oranges. Just don't ask for pesto: the garlicky basil spread hails from Genoa, Venice's chief trade-route rival for 300 years, and some Venetians still hold culinary grudges.

Cicheti

Even in unpretentious Venetian *osterie* and *bacari,* most dishes cost a couple of euros more than they might elsewhere in Italy – not a bad mark-up, considering all that fresh seafood and produce brought in by boat. But *cicheti* are some of the best culinary finds in Italy, served at lunch and from around 6pm to 8pm with sensational Veneto wines by the glass. *Cicheti* range from basic bar snacks (spicy meatballs, fresh tomato and basil bruschetta) to highly inventive small plates: think white Bassano asparagus and plump lagoon shrimp wrapped in pancetta at All'Arco (p95); pungent gorgonzola paired with sweet, spicy *peperoncino* (chilli) jam at Dai Zemei (p95); or fragrant, bite-sized bread rolls crammed with tuna, chicory and horseradish at Al Mercà (p98).

Prices start at €1 for tasty meatballs and range from €3 to €6 for gourmet fantasias with fancy ingredients, typically devoured standing up or perched atop stools at the bar. Filling *cicheti* such as *crostini, panini* and *tramezzini* (sandwiches on soft bread, often with mayo-based condiments) cost €1.50 to €6. Nightly *cicheti* spreads could easily pass as dinner.

Peckish? Venice's *cicheti* hot spots include:

Cannaregio Along Fondamenta degli Ormesini and off Strada Nova.

San Polo & Santa Croce Around the Rialto Market and Ruga Ravano.

Castello Via Garibaldi and Calle Lunga Santa Maria Formosa.

San Marco Around Campo San Bartolomeo, Campo Santo Stefano and Campo della Guerra.

The Menu

Cicheti are fresh alternatives to fast food worth planning your day around, but you'll also want to treat yourself to a leisurely sit-down meal while you're in town, whether it's in a back-alley *osteria* or canalside restaurant. If you stick to tourist menus you're bound to be disappointed, but adventurous diners who order seasonal specialities are richly rewarded, and often spend less, too.

PIATTI (COURSES)

No one expects you to soldier through multiple courses plus antipasti and dessert, but we wouldn't blame you for trying either, given the many tempting *piatti* on the local menu. Consider your à la carte options:

Antipasti (appetisers) vary from lightly fried *moeche* (tiny soft-shell crabs) and lagoon-fresh *crudi* (Venetian sushi) such as sweet mantis prawns, to old-school *baccala mantecato* (whipped salted cod with olive oil) and traditional platters of cheeses and rustic cured meats.

Primi (first courses) usually include the classic Italian pasta or risotto; one Venetian speciality pasta you might try is *bigoli*, a thick wholewheat pasta, often served *in salsa* (with salted anchovies, Chioggia onions and black pepper). Equally loved are *pasta e fagioli*, a soupy concoction of pasta and borlotti beans, and *risi e bisi*, a risotto-like classic made with peas, pancetta and parmesan. Many Venetian restaurants have adopted a hearty Verona speciality: gnocchi. Another regional option is polenta, white or yellow cornmeal formed into a cake and grilled, or served semisoft and steaming hot. As the Venetian saying goes, '*Xe non xe pan, xe poenta*' (If there's no bread, there's still polenta).

Secondi (second or main courses) are usually seafood or meat dishes. Adventurous eaters will appreciate a traditional Venetian *secondo* of *trippa* (tripe) or *fegato alla veneziana* (calf's liver lightly pan-roasted in strips with browned onion and a splash of red wine). If you're not an offal fan, you can find standard cuts of *manzo* (beef), *agnello* (lamb) and *vitello* (veal) on most menus. Committed carnivores might also try carpaccio (a dish of finely sliced raw beef served with a sauce of crushed tomato, cream, mustard and Worcestershire sauce dreamed up by Harry's Bar (p66) and named for the Venetian painter Vittore Carpaccio, famous for his liberal use of blood-red paint). Popular surf options include *fritto misto*, a golden mix of fried fish and seafood, sometimes accompanied by tempura-style seasonal vegetables.

Contorni (vegetable dishes) are more substantial offerings of *verdure* (vegetables). For vegetarians, this may be the first place to look on a menu – and meat-eaters may want to check them out, too,

since *secondi* don't always come with a vegetable side dish. Go with whatever's fresh and seasonal.

Dolci (desserts) are often *fatti in casa* (housemade) in Venice, especially Veneto-invented tiramisu, Vienna-influenced *bigne* (cream puffs) and strudel, and safffron-scented Burano *esse* (S-shaped cookies). Otherwise, gelaterie (ice-cream shops) offer tempting options for €1.50 to €5.

DAILY SPECIALS

Here's one foolproof way to distinguish a serious Venetian *osteria* from an imposter: lasagne, spaghetti Bolognese and pizza are not Venetian specialities, and when all three appear on a menu, avoid what is essentially a tourist trap. Look instead for places where there's no menu at all, or one hastily scrawled on a chalkboard or laser-printed in Italian only, preferably with typos. This is a sign that your chef reinvents the menu daily, according to what looked best that morning at the market.

Although fish and seafood are increasingly imported, many Venetian restaurant owners pride themselves on using only fresh, local ingredients, even if that means getting up at the crack of dawn to get to the Pescaria (fish market). Lagoon tides and changing seasons on the nearby garden island of Sant'Erasmo bring a year-round bounty to Venetian tables at the Rialto Market.

Beware any menu dotted with asterisks, indicating that several items are *surgelati* (frozen) – seafood flown in from afar is likely to be unsustainable, and indigestible besides.

DRINKS

No Venetian feast would be complete without at least one *ombra* (glass of wine) – and that includes lunch. Fishmongers at the Pescaria get a head start on landlubbers, celebrating the day's haul at 9am by popping a cork on some *prosecco* (sparkling white wine), the Veneto's beloved bubbly. By noon, you already have some catching up to do: start working your way methodically through the extensive seafood menu of tender octopus salad, black squid-ink risotto, and *granseola* (spider crab), paired with appropriate *ombre*.

Many Venetian dishes are designed with local wines specifically in mind to round out the flavours – especially delicate lagoon seafood, whose texture may be changed by the powerful acidity of lemon juice. Some *enoteche* (wine bars) and *osterie* have wine selections that run into the hundreds of labels, so don't be shy about soliciting suggestions from your server or bartender.

Of course, no meal is complete without a glass of the Veneto's own fire water – grappa. Far from the rocket fuel you may be accustomed to, respected distilleries such as Bassano del Grappa's Poli produce sophisticated versions that are equally smooth and nuanced.

Vegetarians & Vegans

Even in a city known for seafood, vegetarians need not despair: with a little advance savvy, vegetarian visitors in Venice can enjoy an even wider range of food choices than they might at home. Island-grown produce is a point of pride for many Venetian restaurants, and *primi* such as polenta, pasta and risotto *contorni* make the most of such local specialities as asparagus, artichokes, radicchio and *bruscandoli* (wild hops). Venetian *contorni* include grilled local vegetables and salads, and *cicheti* showcase marinated vegetables and Veneto cheeses.

There are eateries that serve a good range of meat-free dishes at all price points. Meat-free and cheese-free pizza is widely available, and *gelaterie* offer milk-free *sorbetto* (sorbet) and gelato with *latte di soia* (soy milk). Self-catering is always an option for vegans and others with restricted diets, but if you call ahead, specific dietary restrictions can usually be accommodated at restaurants and *osterie*.

Self-Catering

Picnicking isn't allowed in most *campi* (squares) – Venice tries to keep a lid on its clean-up duties, since all refuse needs to be taken out by barge – but you can assemble quite a feast to enjoy at your B&B, rental apartment or hotel. For lunch with sweeping lagoon views, pack a picnic and head to the Lido beaches, the Biennale gardens or the northern lagoon islands of Mazzorbo, Torcello, Le Vignole and Sant'Erasmo.

FARMERS MARKETS

The Rialto Market (p89) offers superb local produce and lagoon seafood at the centuries-old Pescaria. Second only to it is the Lido's Tuesday food market, Mercato Settimanale de Lido (p143). For produce fresh from prison, head to Giudecca on Wednesday morning for its organic farmers market (p143), where sales of fruit, vegetables and herbs

grown by a cooperative in Giudecca's prison fund job-retraining programs. For produce that floats, make a beeline for the produce barge on the Rio di Sant'Anna at the end of Via Garibaldi in Castello, or the one pulled up alongside Campo San Barnaba in Dorsoduro, near Ponte dei Pugni.

GROCERIES

The area around Rialto Market has gourmet delis and speciality shops. Close to the airport bus and train station is **Coop** (☏041 296 06 21; Piazzale Roma, Santa Croce; ⊙8.30am-8pm; ◉Piazzale Roma), an agricultural cooperative grocery with a good deli section. You'll find other branches throughout the city, including at Campo San Giacomo dell'Orio. The small supermarket chain **Rizzo** (☏041 71 83 22; www.rizzovenezia.it; Campo San Leonardo 1355; ◉Guglie) stocks sandwiches at its deli counters.

Cooking Courses

If all that produce and tradition inspires the chef within, consider signing up for a Venetian cooking course. **Acquolina Cooking School** (www.acquolina.com) runs four- and eight-hour courses, the latter option including a morning trip to the Rialto Market. It also offers multiday courses, including accommodation. Local market trawls are also on the menu at Cook in Venice (p113), whose one- and three-day cooking courses include gluten- and lactose-free nosh on request.

Mealtimes

Restaurants and bars are generally closed one day each week, usually Sunday or Monday. If your stomach growls between official mealtimes, cafes and bars generally open from 7am to 8pm and serve snacks all day.

Prima colazione (breakfast) is eaten between 7am and 10am. Venetians rarely eat a sit-down breakfast, but instead bolt down a cappuccino with a *brioche* (sweet bread) or other type of pastry (generically known as *pastine*) at a coffee bar before heading to work.

Pranzo (lunch) is served from noon to 2.30pm. Few restaurants take orders for lunch after 2pm. Traditionally, lunch is the main meal of the day, and some shops and businesses close for two or three hours to accommodate it. Relax and enjoy a proper sit-down lunch, and you may be satisfied with *cicheti* for dinner.

Cena (dinner) is served between 7pm and 10.30pm. Opening hours vary, but many places begin filling up by 7.30pm and few take orders after 10.30pm.

Dining Etiquette

With thousands of visitors trooping through Venice daily demanding to be fed, service can be slow, harried or indifferent. By showing an interest in what Venice brings to the table, you'll get more attentive service, better advice and a more memorable meal. You'll win over your server and the chef with these four gestures that prove your mettle as *una buona forchetta* ('a good fork', or good eater):

Ignore the menu. Solicit your server's advice about seasonal treats and house specials, pick two options that sound interesting, and ask your server to recommend one over the other. When that's done, snap the menu shut and say, *'Allora, facciamo cosi, per favore!'* (Well then, let's do that, please!) You have just won over your server, and flattered the chef – promising omens for a memorable meal to come.

Drink well. Bottled water is entirely optional; *acqua del rubinetto* (tap water) is perfectly potable and highly recommended as an environment-saving measure. But fine meals call for wine, often available by the glass or half-bottle. Never mind that you don't recognise the label: the best small-production local wineries don't advertise or export (even to other parts of Italy), because their yield is snapped up by Venetian *osterie* and *enoteche*.

Try primi without condiments. Your server's relief and delight will be obvious. Venetian seafood risotto and pasta are rich and flavourful enough without being smothered in Parmesan or hot sauce.

Enjoy lagoon seafood. No one expects you to order an appetiser or *secondo*, but if you do, the tests of any Venetian chef are seasonal seafood antipasti and *frittura* (seafood fry). Try yours *senza limone* (without lemon) first: Venetians believe the subtle flavours of lagoon seafood are best complemented by salt, pepper and subtle trade-route spices like star anise. Instead, try washing down seafood with citrusy Veneto white wines that highlight instead of overwhelm briny flavours.

Gourmet Hot Spots

Bad advice has circulated for decades about how it's impossible to eat well and economically in Venice, which has mis-informed day trippers clinging defensively to congealed, reheated pizza slices in San Marco. Little do they realise that for the same price a bridge away, they could be dining on *crostini* topped with scampi and grilled baby artichoke, or tuna tartare with wild strawberries and balsamic reduction. Luckily for you, there's still room at the bar to score the best *cicheti*, and reservations are almost always available at phenomenal eateries – especially at dinner, after the day trippers depart.

To find the best Venetian food, dodge restaurants immediately around San Marco, near the train station and along main thoroughfares. Instead, aim for these gourmet trails and outstanding island eateries:

Cannaregio Along Fondamenta Savorgnan, Fondamenta della Sensa and Calle Larga Doge Priulli.

San Polo & Santa Croce Around the Rialto Market.

Castello Around Campo Bandiera e Moro and Zanipolo.

San Marco Along Calle delle Botteghe, Calle Spezier and Frezzeria.

Dorsoduro Along Calle Lunga San Barnaba, Calle della Toletta and Calle Crosera.

Giudecca Along Fondamenta delle Zitelle.

Northern Islands Locanda Cipriani (p157) on Torcello, Gatto Nero (p157) and Da Romano on Burano, and Venissa (p157) on Mazzorbo.

Eating by Neighbourhood

➡ **San Marco** *Panini*, *cicheti* and high-end, traditional restaurants. (p63)

➡ **Dorsoduro** Snug bistros, *campo*-side bar bites and pizza by the slice. (p79)

➡ **San Polo & Santa Croce** Market-inspired cuisine, creative *cicheti*, pizza and vegetarian fare. (p95)

➡ **Cannaregio** Traditional *cicheti*, authentic *osterie* and canalside dining. (p110)

➡ **Castello** Daring creative cuisine, pizza and bargain *cicheti*. (p130)

➡ **Giudecca, Lido & the Southern Islands** Traditional seafood and waterfront dining. (p142)

➡ **Murano, Burano & the Northern Islands** Just-caught lagoon seafood and garden dining. (p156)

Lonely Planet's Top Choices

All'Arco (p95) *Panini* are decoys for day trippers; stick around and let Venice's *cicheti maestri* ply you with market-fresh *fantasie*.

da Rioba (p112) Romantic noshing with fresh, family-picked Sant'Erasmo produce.

Trattoria Corte Sconta (p132) Superlative surf antipasti, inspired pasta dishes, and subtle modern subversion.

Osteria Trefanti (p97) Venetian traditions meet contemporary innovation at this new gastronomic darling.

Locanda Cipriani (p157) The Cipriani family's rustic retreat, where soulful flavours are yours by a crackling fire or beneath a scented pergola.

Best by Budget

€

All'Arco (p95) Stand-up gourmet bites made with prime Rialto produce.

Dai Zemei (p95) Inspired *cicheti* combos and hand-picked regional wines.

Osteria Ruga di Jaffa (p130) An artsy *osteria* serving refined, time-tested classics.

€€

Acquastanca (p156) Contemporary regional flavours in a reformed Murano bakery.

Ai Mercanti (p64) Globally influenced Italian and a sharply curated wine list.

Osteria Trefanti (p97) Intimate, pared-back elegance meets blue-ribbon produce, textures and arresting wines.

€€€

Trattoria e Bacaro Da Fiore (p65) Maurizio Martin's seafood concoctions shine bright on culinary radars.

Trattoria Corte Sconta (p132) Unexpected ingredients revamp tired classics.

Al Covo (p132) Just-caught, just-sourced local ingredients keep Al Covo on the foodie radar.

Best for Cicheti

All'Arco (p95) Market-fresh morsels, zingy *prosecco* and corner conviviality close to the gut-rumbling Rialto Market.

Osteria alla Vedova (p112) Flavour-packed, good-value bites in a veteran *osteria*.

Dai Zemei (p95) Unexpected, creative concoctions from food- and *vino*-obsessed twins.

Osteria Al Squero (p81) Classic and lesser-seen *cicheti* opposite a gondola workshop.

Best for Waterfront Dining

Trattoria Altanella (p142) Wine, dine and sigh on a balcony that hovers right over the water.

La Palanca (p142) Panoramic waterfront dining at mere-mortal prices.

Trattoria al Gatto Nero (p157) Canalside seafood with crayon-coloured Burano backdrop.

Best for Vegetarians

Le Spighe (p131) Vegetarian and vegan edibles made with seasonal, organic ingredients.

Osteria La Zucca (p97) Market-driven menus in a snug, canalside bolthole.

Frary's (p98) Pan-Mediterranean and Middle Eastern flavours in the shadow of a Gothic giant.

Best for Sustainable Food

Le Garzette (p143) Organic ingredients and gorgeous rustic fare at a tranquil *agriturismo* (farmstay).

Venissa (p157) Most ingredients are grown on-site at this vine-laced island getaway.

Alaska Gelateria (p97) Seasonal ingredients get creative at this cult-status ice-cream maker.

Best for Classic Venetian

Antiche Carampane (p97) Respectable *crudo* (raw seafood) and moreish *fritto misto* in Venice's former red-light corner.

Al Ponte di Borgo (p143) Fresh, succulent seafood and spot-hitting *cicheti* on the sinuous Lido.

Ristorante Ribot (p97) Beautifully cooked classics meet an enviable cellar and summertime courtyard dining.

Best for Inventive Venetian

Venissa (p157) Graze on the island landscape in lagoon-inspired dishes by rising culinary talents.

Trattoria Corte Sconta (p132) Clever antipasti and pasta dishes in a sneaky Castello courtyard.

Osteria Trefanti (p97) Refreshing tweaks give Venetian classics elegant new verve.

CoVino (p131) A pocket-sized showcase for Slow Food produce cooked with modern soul.

WALTER BIBIKOW / GETTY IMAGES ©

Musicians performing at Piazza San Marco

🍷 Drinking & Nightlife

When the siren sounds for acqua alta (high tide), Venetians dutifully close up shop and head home to put up their flood barriers – then pull on their boots and head right back out again. Why let floods disrupt a toast or two? It's not just a turn of phrase: come hell or high water, Venetians will find a way to have a good time.

Happy Hour(s)

The happiest hour (or two) in Venice begins around 6pm at *bacari* (hole-in-the-wall bars) serving booze and *cicheti* (Venetian tapas). If you're prompt, you might beat the crowds to the bar for *un'ombra* (a 'shade'; a small glass of wine), which can go for as little as €0.60 at cupboard-sized Bacareto Da Lele (p99). Heading in early also means grabbing *cicheti* while they're fresh. *Osterie* (taverns) and *enoteche* (wine bars) are also renowned for their *vino*-friendly bites.

Giro d'Ombra

An authentic Venetian *giro d'ombra* (pub crawl) begins around the Pescaria by 9am, drinking *prosecco* with fishermen toasting a hard day's work that began at 3am. For layabouts, Venice offers a second-chance *giro d'ombra* with *cicheti* at *bacari* ringing the Rialto Market around noon. Afterwards, it's a long four-hour dry spell until the next *giro d'ombra* begins in buzzing spots around Campo Santa Margherita in Dorsoduro, Fondamenta degli Ormesini in Cannaregio,

NEED TO KNOW

Opening Hours

Cafe-bars generally open from 7am to 8pm, although some stay open later and morph into drinking hang-outs. Pubs and wine bars are mostly shut by 1am to 2am.

Events Calendars

Check listings and special events at **Venezia da Vivere** (www.veneziadavivere.com), **2Venice** (www.2venice.it) and **VeNews** (www.venezianews.it). For events in Lido di Jesolo and around the lagoon, see www.turismovenezia.it

Noise Regulations

Keep it down to a dull roar after 10pm: sound travels in Venice, and worse than a police bust for noise infractions is a scolding from a Venetian *nonna* (grandmother).

Campo Maria Formosa in Castello, and the warren of *calli* (streets) around Campo San Bartolomeo and Campo Manin in San Marco.

What to Order

No rules seem to apply to drinking in Venice. No mixing spirits and wine? Venice's classic cocktails suggest otherwise; try a *spritz,* made with *prosecco,* soda water and bittersweet Aperol, bitter Campari or herbaceous Cynar. Price is not an indicator of quality – you can pay €2.50 for a respectable *spritz,* or live to regret that €16 bellini tomorrow (ouch). If you're not pleased with your drink, leave it and move on to the next *bacaro.* Don't be shy about asking fellow drinkers what they recommend; happy hour is a highly sociable affair.

LOCAL FAVOURITES

Prosecco The crisp, sparkling white that's the life of any Venetian party, from nonvintage to DOCG Conegliano Prosecco Superiore. Persistent bubbles and straw-yellow hues.

Spritz A stiff drink at an easy price, this *prosecco* cocktail is a cross-generational hit with students and pensioners at bars across Venice – except at *enoteche.*

Soave A well-balanced white wine made with Veneto Garganega grapes, ideal with seafood in refreshing young versions or as a conversation piece in complex Classico versions.

Amarone The Titian of wines: a profound, voluptuous red blended from Valpolicella Corvina grapes. Complex and costly (€6 to €18 per glass), but utterly captivating while it lasts.

Ribolla Gialla A weighty white with all the right curves from Friuli-Venezia Giulia, this wine gets more voluptuous with age; irresistible with buttery fish, gnocchi and cheese.

Valpolicella A versatile grape that's come into its own with a bright young DOC namesake red wine more food-friendly than Amarone, a structured, aged version called DOG Valpolicella Ripasso, and DOCG sweet late-harvest Recioto della Valpolicella.

Lugana A mineral-rich, well-structured white from Trebbiano grapes grown at the border of Veneto and Lombardy; a favourite with gastronomes.

Refosco dal Peduncolo Rosso Intense and brooding, a Goth rocker that hits the right notes. This order is guaranteed to raise your sommelier's eyebrow, and probably your bill.

Raboso One of Italy's top reds at full maturity, rich in tannins, packed with flavour and with a bouquet of spicy cherries. Perfect with aged cheeses, game and grilled red meats.

Morgana beer A worthy Venetian craft beer from the owners of La Cantina: unpasteurised, unfiltered and undeniably appealing on hot summer days.

Cafes

To line your stomach with coffee and pastry before your next *giro d'ombra,* check out Venice's legendary cafe-bars, and skip milky cappuccino for a stronger *macchiatone* (espresso with a 'big stain' of hot milk). For local flavour, try the Torrefazione Marchi (p112) *noxea:* coffee beans roasted with hazelnuts. House-roasted speciality blends are also the order of the day at Caffè del Doge (p99).

Historic baroque cafes around Piazza San Marco like Caffè Florian (p65) and Caffè Quadri (p65) serve coffee and hot chocolate with live orchestras – though your heart might beat a different rhythm once you get the bill. Hint: Caffè Lavena (p66) offers a €1 espresso at the counter.

Enoteche

Request *qualcosa di particolare* (something interesting), and your sommelier will accept the challenge to reach behind the bar for one of Veneto's obscure varietals or

VENETO: WHERE DRINKING COMES NATURALLY

Detour through the Veneto's glorious wine country for a day, and you'll see why the region is setting Italy's trend for natural-process wines – an umbrella term describing wines made with organic, biodynamic, natural-fermentation and other unconventional methods. With speciality grapes thriving on the Veneto's unspoilt volcanic hills, who needs pesticides, additives and industrial processing? Instead, growing numbers of Veneto vintners are doing what comes naturally, and experimenting with low-intervention, natural-process approaches.

Taste their results for yourself at **ViniVeri** (www.viniveri.net), the natural-process wine showcase held in Verona every April, or sample outstanding natural-process wines year-round at **Vino Vero** (p112), **Cantina Aziende Agricole** (p110) and **Al Prosecco** (p98). *Salute* – here's to your health, and the Veneto's, too.

PLAN YOUR TRIP DRINKING & NIGHTLIFE

innovative wines. Even ordinary varietals take on extraordinary characteristics in growing areas that range from marshy to mountainous.

Speciality *enoteche* like Vino Vero (p112), Estro (p81), Al Prosecco (p98) and La Cantina (p111) uphold Venice's time-honoured tradition of selling good stuff by the glass, so you can discover new favourites without committing to a bottle.

To dive deeper into Veneto wines, sign up for a tasting session with Venetian Vine (p113), join a *cicheti* crawl led by Monica Cesarato from Cook in Venice (p113), or request a *vino*-versed guide on a *cicheti* rowing tour with Row Venice (p154).

DOC Versus IGT

In Italy, the official DOC *(denominazione d'origine controllata)* and elite DOCG (DOC *garantita* – guaranteed) designations are usually assurances of top-notch *vino*. Taste the DOCG wines that put the Veneto on the world wine-tasting map at select wineries in Valdobbiadene and Conegliano *(prosecco)*, Soave (Soave Superiore and Recioto di Soave) and Valpolicella (Amarone and Valpolicella).

Yet, successful as its wines are, the Veneto also bucks the DOC/DOCG system. Many of the region's small-production wineries can't be bothered with such external

validation as they may already sell out to Venetian *osterie* and *enoteche*. As a result, some top producers prefer the IGT *(indicazione geografica tipica)* designation, which guarantees grapes typical of the region but leaves winemakers room to experiment with non-traditional blends and methods, such as natural-yeast fermentation.

Drinking & Nightlife by Neighbourhood

➡ **San Marco** High-end cocktails and DOC wines with DJs. (p65)

➡ **Dorsoduro** Bargain booze, buzzing *osterie*, and rivers of *spritz*. (p80)

➡ **San Polo & Santa Croce** Inspired *ombre* (wine by the glass) and *cicheti* at historic *bacari*. (p98)

➡ **Cannaregio** Happy hour sun spots on southern facing canal banks. (p112)

➡ **Castello** Drink like a sailor at local *bacari*, or join *artistes* for pre-Biennale cocktails. (p132)

➡ **Giudecca, Lido & the Southern Islands** Fall film festivals, summer beach clubs and year-round happy hours. (p144)

➡ **Murano, Burano & the Northern Islands** A quiet drink with a local crowd. (p156)

Lonely Planet's Top Choices

Vino Vero (p112) Superlative wines from small and biodynamic producers, top-notch *cicheti*, and an effortlessly cool vibe.

Al Prosecco (p98) Organic grapes, wild-yeast fermentation, biodynamic methods: with Italy's finest natural-process wines, toasts come naturally.

Al Mercà (p98) Intriguing DOC regional wines, cheeses and small bites enjoyed by the Grand Canal docks.

Cantinone Già Schiavi (p80) Tiny bottles of beer and outsized neighbourhood personalities keep this historic canalside joint hopping.

Al Timon (p113) Canalside tables, *crostini* (open-face sandwiches), carafes of good house wine and occasional live music: idyllic.

Best Happy-Hour Hang-outs

Al Mercà (p98) Delectable DOC *vino*, bargain bar bites and alfresco conviviality beside Venice's best-loved market.

Al Timon (p113) Swill and swoon on a moored vessel with savvy local dreamers.

Il Caffè Rosso (p81) Cheap drinks and eclectic regulars define this Campo San Margherita veteran.

Cantinone Già Schiavi (p80) Appetite-piquing *cicheti* and a mixed local crowd by a Dorsoduro canal.

Bacareto Da Lele (p99) Filthy-cheap *ombre*, petite *panini* and crowds of loyal locals.

MQ10 (p113) Waterside mojitos at a trendy Cannaregio favourite.

Best for Wine

Vino Vero (p112) Natural, biodynamic and boutique drops in a standout Cannaregio wine bar.

Estro (p81) Has 500 personally chosen wines, plus handpicked cheeses, *salumi* (cured meats) and produce-driven menus.

Ai Pugni (p81) Nightly canalside crowds and a long, interesting, ever-changing choice of *vino* by the glass.

Cantina Aziende Agricole (p110) Get indecisive over 150 wines from renowned local producers.

Enoteca Mascareta (p133) Inspired wines by the glass, including the owner's very own organic *prosecco*.

Best for Beer

Agli Ormesini (p113) Venice's top beer bar keeps punters purring with over 100 brews.

La Cantina (p111) House-brand beer Gaston is a winner with sud-loving locals.

Il Santo Bevitore (p113) Trappist ales, seasonal stouts and chat-igniting football matches on the TV.

Birraria La Corte (p98) Sud sessions overlooking San Polo's sweeping namesake *campo*.

Best Signature Cocktails

Bar Terazza Danieli (p133) Apricot and orange mix with gin and grenadine in the Danieli.

Harry's Bar (p66) The driest classic in town is Harry's gin-heavy martini (no olive).

Locanda Cipriani (p157) Harry's famous white-peach bellini tastes even better at Cipriani's island retreat.

La Serra dei Giardini (p132) Venice's effervescent icon gets a vibrant twist with the pear bellini.

Best for Coffee & Tea

Caffè Florian (p65) An 18th-century time-warp in show-off Piazza San Marco.

Caffè Lavena (p66) Sip to the sound of violins at this former Richard Wagner hang-out.

Torrefazione Marchi (p112) A veteran coffee roaster famed for its hazelnut-laced espresso.

Tea Room Beatrice (p81) Soothing teas and a tranquil vibe.

Best Wine-Tasting Destinations

Vinitaly (p20) Italy's premier wine expo turns Verona into a mecca for professional oenophiles.

ViniVeri (p35) Verona's alternative wine show, dedicated to natural-process drops.

La Strada del Prosecco (p177) The Veneto's revered epicentre of *prosecco* production.

Soave (p184) Medieval walls and crisp, vibrant whites await east of Verona.

Valpolicella (p184) Northwest of Verona, the celebrated home of coveted red Amarone.

Best for Drinks with a View

Bar Terazza Danieli (p133) Late-afternoon cocktail sessions with canal and Palladio views.

Bar Longhi (p65) Exquisite cocktails and a view of La Salute.

L'Ombra del Leoni (p66) The Biennale's bargain bar on the Grand Canal.

Teatro La Fenice (p58)

⭐ Entertainment

After the fall of Venice's shipping empire, the curtain rose on the city's music scene. A magnet for classical-music fans for four centuries, Venice continues to fill its palaces with the sounds of arias, cantatas and freestyle sax. Outside, the city's waterways lure with the promise of aquatic thrills, from stand-up rowing to historic regattas.

Opera

Venice is the home of modern opera and the legendary, incendiary Teatro La Fenice (p58). One of the world's top opera houses since its founding in 1792, it was here that Giuseppe Verdi premiered *Rigoletto* and *La Traviata*. But the music doesn't stop when La Fenice takes its summer break: opera divas from around the world perform under the stars from June to early September at Verona's Roman Arena (p179), Italy's top summer opera festival.

Today you can see opera as Venetians did centuries ago, inside a whimsical pleasure-palace music room at Palazzetto Bru Zane (p100), in Grand Canal palace salons with Musica a Palazzo (p67), among heavenly frescoes at Scuola Grande di San Giovanni Evangelista (p100), and in period costume at Scuola Grande dei Carmini (p78).

Classical Music

Venice is the place to hear baroque music in its original and intended venues, with notes

NEED TO KNOW

Advance Tickets

Shows regularly sell out in summer, so purchase tickets online at the venue website, www.veneziaunica.it or www. musicinvenice.com. Tickets may also be available at the venue box office or from HelloVenezia ticket outlets, located near key *vaporetto* (ferry) stops and ACTV public-transport ticket points.

Opening Hours

Event start times vary, with doors at evening concerts typically opening from 7pm to 8.30pm. Due to noise regulations in this small city with big echoes, live music venues are limited, and shows typically end by 11pm.

Music Calendar

For schedules of upcoming performances, Venetian discographies and online ticket sales, see www.musicinvenice.com. For upcoming openings, concerts, performances and other cultural events, check listings at www.veneziadavivere.com (mostly in Italian) and www.turismo venezia.it.

Cover

Entry is often free at bars, but the cover runs from €10 to €25 for shows in established venues; pay in advance or at the door.

Free Shows

In summer, don't miss Venice Jazz Festival outdoor events, plus free beach concerts on the Lido and on Lido di Jesolo. Year-round in good weather, you might luck into outdoor happy-hour shows around Campo San Giacomo dell'Orio and Fondamenta degli Ormesini.

soaring to Sebastiano Ricci–frescoed ceilings at Palazzetto Bru Zane (p100), sweeping through the salons at Palazzo Querini Stampalia (p126) and reverberating through La Pietà (p128), the original Vivaldi venue. Between opera seasons, summer symphonies are performed by **La Fenice's Philharmonic Orchestra** (www.filarmonica-fenice. it) at the opera house or affiliated Teatro Malibran (p114).

Interpreti Veneziani plays Vivaldi and other baroque classics on original instruments with radical verve, in a style known in Italy as 'baroque-n-roll' or 'ba-rock'. Tickets can be purchased on site or at Museo della Musica (p59), an informative museum of baroque music and instruments with free admission provided by Interpreti Veneziani.

Music becomes a religious experience surrounded by Venetian art masterpieces during organ vespers at Basilica di Santa Maria della Salute (p74) and occasional sacred music concerts at other Venetian churches.

Jazz, Rock & Pop

July's Venice Jazz Festival showcases international stars like Keith Jarrett, Cassandra Wilson and Jack Savoretti in iconic venues throughout the city, including La Fenice (p58) and Peggy Guggenheim Collection (p75). Its organising body, VenetoJazz (www.venetojazz.com), delivers year-round concerts in numerous towns across the Veneto, including Padua and Bassano del Grappa. Year-round tributes to Miles Davis, Chet Baker and Charles Mingus await at Venice's only dedicated jazz venue, Venice Jazz Club (p81).

A handful of bars sporadically host live music acts, usually rock, reggae, folk and *leggera* (pop). For all-ages alt-rock and punk, check events at Laboratorio Occupato Morion (p133). Bars with regular musical interludes include Paradiso Perduto (p114), Al Timon, Bagolo, Bacarando (p66) and Il Santo Bevitore (p113). But don't expect to roll in late and still catch the show: according to local noise regulations, bars are expected to end concerts at 11pm.

Summer concerts – including DJ sets from world-renowned names – are held on beaches on the Lido and on Lido di Jesolo – check the local press in July and August.

Cinema

International star power and Italian fashion storm Lido red carpets during the Venice International Film Festival, where films are shown in their original language. Year-round, catch award-winning films (sometimes subtitled) and blockbusters (usually dubbed) at Multisala Rossini (p67), a three-screen venue with digital sound in the heart of San Marco. Check Venice Co-

VENICE BIENNALE

Europe's premier arts showcase since 1907 is something of a misnomer: the **Venice Biennale** (www.labiennale.org) is actually held every year, but the spotlight alternates between art (odd-numbered years, eg 2015, 2017, 2019) and architecture (even-numbered years, eg 2016, 2018, 2020). The summer art biennial is the biggest draw, with some 300,000 visitors viewing contemporary-art showcases in 30 national pavilions in the Giardini, with additional exhibitions in venues across town. The architecture biennial is usually held in autumn (fall), with architects filling the vast boat sheds of the Arsenale with avant-garde conceptual structures.

But the Biennale doesn't stop there. The city-backed organisation also organises an International Festival of Contemporary Dance, not to mention the iconic Venice International Film Festival. Running parallel to the Venice Biennale is a growing number of fringe arts events, offering opportunities to see hidden corners of the city usually off-access to the public. Check the Biennale website for upcoming event listings, venues and tickets.

mune (www.comune.venezia.it) for upcoming movie-screening schedules.

Theatre & Dance

Although dance performances are staged year-round in Venice, they are especially prolific during the Venice Biennale's International Festival of Contemporary Dance, usually held the first two weeks in June. For more modern movement, check the schedule at Teatro Fondamenta Nuove. Ballet performances are usually staged at Teatro Goldoni (p67), which also delivers contemporary theatre and Shakespeare, usually in Italian.

Sports & Activities

CYCLING

Though cycling is banned in central Venice, the Lido is a prime stretch of waterfront cycling turf, with tandem bicycle rentals available. Another good option is Sant'Erasmo, where Il Lato Azzurro (p198) rents bikes and offers suggestions for a soothing, tranquil exploration of Venice's famed food-bowl isle.

JOGGING

Jogging is increasingly popular in Venice, with favourite running spots including the Giardini, the Zattere, and along Castello's *fondamente* (canal banks) from Sant'Elena to the Riva degli Schiavoni. In October, sure-footed runners attempt the mad dash from the Brenta riverbanks to San Marco in the Venice Marathon (p21).

WATER SPORTS

Sailing is a year-round passion, with classes available at the Isola di Certosa. The island is also home to Venice Kayak (p159), which runs kayaking tours of the Venetian lagoon. Paddleboard standing up with SUP in Venice (p135), or learn to row standing up (*voga alla veneta*) at Row Venice (p154), run by regatta champ Jane Caporal. The city's world-renowned regattas run from spring's ambitious 32km Vogalonga (p154) through autumn's costumed Regata Storica (p21). For a summertime swim, hit the beaches on the Lido or Lido di Jesolo.

Entertainment by Neighbourhood

➡ **San Marco** Opera, classical music, dance, theatre, cinema, DJs. (p67)

➡ **Dorsoduro** Jazz. (p81)

➡ **San Polo & Santa Croce** Cinema, outdoor theatre, live music nights. (p100)

➡ **Cannaregio** Dance, live music nights, cinema, casino. (p114)

➡ **Castello** Classical music, dance, live music nights. (p133)

➡ **Giudecca, Lido & the Southern Islands** Cinema and DJ-fuelled beach parties on the Lido. (p144)

➡ **Murano, Burano & the Northern Islands** DJs and clubs on Lido di Jesolo. (p158)

Lonely Planet's Top Choices

Venice Biennale (p39) Europe's signature art and architecture biennials draw international crowds, while musicians and dancers perform in summer showcases.

Teatro La Fenice (p58) Divas hit new highs in this sumptuous, legendary theatre for under 1000 lucky ticket-holders.

Venice International Film Festival (p21) A paparazzi-packed spectacle of silver-screen royalty and international premieres.

Verona's Roman Arena (p179) Larger-than-life tenors rock the Roman amphitheatre June to early September, rousing choruses of *Bravo!* from 30,000 fans.

Interpreti Veneziani (p67) Venice's breakthrough classical talents play baroque with such bravado you'll fear for their antique instruments.

Best Modern Music Events

Venice Jazz Festival (p21) A-list names play theatres, palaces and galleries.

Venice Biennale (p39) A jam-packed program of new works, including numerous world premieres.

Teatro Fondamenta Nuove (p114) Unexpected and cutting-edge sounds from Italy and beyond.

Laboratori Occupato Morion (p133) A radical backdrop for rocking regional bands.

Fondazione Giorgio Cini (p139) Occasionally serves up top-notch, modern world music at the Teatro Verde.

Best for Opera

Teatro La Fenice (p58) Top-tier productions in one of Italy's grandest theatres.

Verona's Roman Arena (p179) Summertime arias in an ancient Roman stadium.

Musica a Palazzo (p67) Historic compositions sung in sumptuous palace surrounds.

Scuola Grande di San Giovanni Evangelista (p100) Sopranos belt out baroque where flagellants once flogged.

Scuola Grande dei Carmini (p78) Costumed opera in a jewel-box former hostel.

Best for Classical Music

Interpreti Veneziani (p67) Vivaldi played with cliché-smashing verve.

Palazzetto Bru Zane (p100) Renowned musicians and lesser-played compositions in the presence of cheeky cherubs.

Teatro La Fenice (p58) A robust program of grand symphonies and choral concerts.

Teatro Malibran (p114) Intimate chamber music concerts in a 17th-century theatre.

Best for Theatre & Dance

Venice Biennale (p39) Envelope-pushing moves at an international dance fest.

Teatro Goldoni (p67) Mighty classics in the city's starring theatre.

Teatro Junghans (p144) Thought-provoking work from Venice's acting academy.

Teatro Fondamenta Nuove (p114) Edgy performance art and theatre in a vibrant local hub.

Best for Cinema

Venice International Film Festival (p21) Red carpet pre-mieres and Hollywood royalty on the Lido.

Multisala Rossini (p67) Venice's newest and largest cinema screens the odd original-language film.

Cinema Giorgione Movie d'essai (p114) Two screens play-ing film-fest favourites, classics and kid-friendly animations.

Best Live Music Nights

Laboratorio Occupato Morion (p133) World music, hip hop and folk-rock orchestras to shake up Venice.

Paradiso Perduto (p114) Jazz, salsa and the odd legend in an arty, old-school tavern.

Venice Jazz Club (p81) Jazz great tributes and sultry Latin rhythms.

Il Santo Bevitore (p113) Oc-casional pop, blues and funk in a beer-lover's paradise.

Best Outdoor Activities

Row Venice (p154) Hone your Venetian rowing skills on a tradi-tional shrimp-tailed boat.

Su e Zo Per I Ponti (p20) Cross 43 Venetian bridges for a good cause.

Lido Tandem-biking to Malam-occo, summer beach time, or holes-in-one on a historic golf course.

🛍 Shopping

Beyond the world-famous museums and architecture is Venice's best-kept secret: the shopping. No illustrious shopping career is complete without trolling Venice for one-of-a-kind, artisan-made finds. All those souvenir tees and kitschy masks are nothing more than the decoys for the amateurs. Dig deeper and you'll stumble across the prized stuff – genuine, local and nothing short of inspiring.

Artisan Specialities

Your Venice souvenirs may be hard to describe back home without sounding like you're bragging. 'It's an original', you'll say, 'and I met the artisan'. Venice has kept its artisan traditions alive and vital for centuries, especially glass, paper, textiles and woodworking.

STUDIO VISITS

For your travelling companions who aren't sold on shopping, here's a convincing argument: in Venice, it really is an educational experience. In backstreet artisans' studios, you can watch ancient techniques used to make strikingly modern *carta memorizzata* (marbled-paper) travel journals (from €12) and Murano glass waterfalls worn as necklaces (from €35). Studios cluster together, so to find unique pieces, just wander key artisan areas: San Polo around Calle Seconda dei Saoneri; Santa Croce around Campo Santa Maria Mater Domini; San Marco along Frezzeria and Calle de la Botteghe; Dorsoduro around the Peggy Guggenheim Collection; and Murano.

Glass showrooms and shelves of fragile handicrafts may be labelled '*non toccare*' (don't touch) – instead of chancing breakage, just ask to see any piece. The person who shows it to you may be the artisan who made it, so don't be shy about saying '*Complimenti!*' (My compliments!) on impressive pieces.

Venetian Shopping Highlights

Italian style earns its international reputation for impeccable proportions, eye-catching details, luxe textures and vibrant colours – but Venice goes one step further, with eclectic fashion statements, highly creative artisanal accessories, limited-edition sunglasses and no shortage of prized and intriguing antiques.

CLOTHING

Venice has the standard Italian designer brands you can find back home, from Armani to Zegna, along Larga XXII Marzo and Marzaria in San Marco – but for original fashion and better value, venture into Venice's backstreets. The chances of a colleague back home showing up to the office party in the same hot orange and teal-blue Virginia Preo jacket (p116), Venetia Studium goddess dress (p69), hand-printed Fiorella Gallery smoking jacket (p68) or Arnoldo & Battois sculpted silk frock (p69) are infinitesimal. Then there are the Japanese-inspired tube scarves at Anatema (p102), driven by the same whimsical flair that sees vintage fabrics reborn as contemporary threads at Cannaregio's L'Armadio di Coco (p115), and Tibetan cashmere transformed into wearable artwork at Giudecca's Laura Mirè Design (p145).

ACCESSORIES

Don't call Venetian artisans designers: their highly skilled handicrafts can't be mass produced, and stand out in a globalised fashion crowd. Paris' latest 'it' bags seem uninspired compared to purses made of marbled paper

NEED TO KNOW

Opening Hours

Shops generally open around 10am to 1pm and 3.30pm to 7pm Monday to Saturday. A growing number of shops in tourist areas stay open 10am to 7pm daily, while shops off the main thoroughfares may remain closed on Monday morning. Most Murano glass showrooms close by 6pm. Many shops close for major Italian holidays, and for all or part of August.

Shipping

Never mind arbitrary airline luggage limits: most home decor and Murano glass showrooms offer shipping services at reasonable costs, especially within Europe. On new merchandise, customs duties may apply in your home country – check before you buy.

Taxes

Visitors from outside the EU may be entitled to VAT sales tax refunds on major purchases (p249).

at San Polo's Cárte (p100), while Tiffany appears somewhat clichéd once you've glimpsed the glass-ring selection in Murano.

Indeed, the choice of Venetian-made objects are as eclectic as they are irresistible: organic statement jewellery at Michela Pavan Gallery (p101), handcrafted Venetian slippers at Pied à Terre (p101), even world-renowned *forcole* (gondola oarlocks) at Franco Furlanetto (p102). Add Le Burle Veneziane (p68) vintage-bead-fringed cocktail purses and custom-fit shoes with leather heels sculpted like gondola prows from Giovanna Zanella (p135) and there really is no point of comparison.

EYEWEAR

Centuries before geek chic, the first eyeglasses known to Europe were worn in the Veneto c 1348, and Venetian opticians have been hand-grinding lenses and stylish frames ever since. Bring your prescription to San Marco's Ottica Carraro (p69) or San Polo's Ottica Vascellari (p104), or snap up a replica of Peggy Guggenheim's outrageous frames at the Peggy Guggenheim Collection gift shop (p75) in Dorsoduro.

ANTIQUES

Venice's penchant for conjuring up the past goes beyond Byzantine domes and baroque salons. The city is a giant attic of rare, well-worn trinkets and treasures, from 19th-century postcards and lithographs to centuries-old leather-bound books. Dorsoduro is a good place to start your antiques hunt, whether you're looking for vintage lighting at L'Angolo del Passato (p82), turn-of-the-century Venetian prints, erotic literature or baroque card games at Segni nel Tempo (p83), or *fin de siècle* miniatures and repurposed earrings at Antiquariato Claudia Canestrelli (p83). Italian design fiends lust after 20th-century glassware at San Polo's Campiello Ca' Zen (p103), whose inventory includes cult-status Venini items. San Polo is also home to Scriba (p103), where contemporary art is sold alongside old maps. More vintage cartography awaits at Cannaregio's Antichità al Ghetto (p116), whose beautifully curated collection includes Jewish liturgical objects, damask and 18th-century cameos. Across in Castello lies Ballarin (p135), its own eclectic, well-priced booty spanning everything from long-forgotten toys to hand-painted glassware. Last but not least is San Marco's **Mercatino dell'Antiquariato** (www.mercatinocamposan maurizio.it), a much-loved antiques flea market held several weekends a year in Campo San Maurizio. Head in early for the best finds, among them vintage Campari posters, Venetian postcards, Murano glassware and delicate Burano lace.

Shopping by Neighbourhood

➡ **San Marco** Art galleries, international designers and high-end artisan showcases. (p67)

➡ **Dorsoduro** Antique shops and fashion-forward boutiques. (p82)

➡ **San Polo & Santa Croce** Artisan studios: glass, paper, fashion, gondolas. (p100)

➡ **Cannaregio** High-street retail and artisan bargains. (p114)

➡ **Castello** Cutting-edge artisans and quirky curios. (p133)

➡ **Giudecca, Lido & the Southern Islands** Heritage textiles, paper-made design and sculptural knits. (p145)

➡ **Murano, Burano & the Northern Islands** Handmade lace and the world's finest art glass. (p158)

Lonely Planet's Top Choices

ElleElle (p158) Murano art glass balancing modernity and tradition, with essential shapes and dramatic colours.

Cárte (p100) Marble endpaper breaks free of books and turns into handbags, cocktail rings and jewellery boxes.

Marina e Susanna Sent Studio (p158) Minimalist Murano glass jewellery with vivid colours and architectural impact.

Sigfrido Cipolato (p67) Venetian pirate-king skull rings and enamelled baroque diadems in gold and gems, exquisitely hand-crafted.

Chiarastella Cattana (p67) Locally loomed linens as plush as velvet, in history-inspired modern designs and Venetian colours.

Best Original Venice Souvenirs

Gilberto Penzo (p100) Scale-model *gondole*.

I Vetri a Lume di Amadi (p100) Glass mosquitoes.

Pied à Terre (p101) *Furlane* (gondolier shoes).

Gianni Basso (p114) Calling cards with the lion of San Marco.

Paolo Brandolisio (p134) Miniature *forcole* (carved gondola oarlocks).

Best Venetian Home Decor

Fortuny Tessuti Artistici (p145) Luxury, handmade textiles from an Italian style icon.

Chiarastella Cattana (p67) Sophisticated linens to restyle every corner of your *palazzo*.

Caigo Da Mar (p69) Dramatic homewares for seasoned individualists.

Madera (p82) Forward-thinking objects, from chopping blocks to floor lamps.

Danghyra (p82) One-of-a-kind ceramics merging elegance and whimsy.

Best Venetian Fashion

Fiorella Gallery (p68) Head-turning couture for style rebels.

Godi Fiorenza (p69) Beautifully tailored couture at approachable prices.

Virginia Preo Cashmere (p116) Contemporary cashmere frocks, tops and more for work and play.

Malefatte (p69) Poptastic, good-cause wearables and accessories with playful Venetian themes.

Gualti (p83) Sculptural wraps guaranteed to make you the star at any premiere.

Best Jewellery

Sigfrido Cipolato (p67) Arresting, detailed pieces bursting with imagination and intrigue.

Marina e Susanna Sent (p82) Striking, contemporary wearables good enough for MoMA.

Oh My Blue (p101) Cutting-edge creations from local and foreign designers.

Michela Pavan Gallery (p101) Sculptural statements from emerging artistic talent.

Atelier Leonardo (p115) Exclusive glass jewellery from revered Murano artisans.

Best for Antiques

Ballarin (p135) A treasure chest packed with period furniture, lamps, glass and more.

Antichità al Ghetto (p116) A nostalgic mix of Venetian maps, art and jewellery.

Campiello Ca' Zen (p103) Paintings, furniture and glassware from cult names like Venini.

Segni nel Tempo (p83) A burst of rare books, prints and historic oddities.

Best Gifts for Gourmands

Drogheria Mascari (p101) Must-have pantry fillers and coveted wines.

VizioVirtù (p101) Artisan chocolates in unexpected flavours.

Atelier Alessandro Merlin (p134) Talking-point ceramics for a provocative cup of coffee.

Madera (p82) Contemporary kitchenware and tableware from edgy designers.

ElleElle (p158) Fetching sets of affordable hand-blown glasses.

Best Leather Goods

Daniela Ghezzo (p69) Custom-made shoes created with rare leather and seasoned style.

Arnoldo & Battois (p69) Hand-crafted bags with historically inspired details.

Balducci Borse (p115) Shoes and bags from a master leather craftsman.

Declare (p100) Hip bags and accessories in striking tones.

Kalimala Cuoieria (p135) Natural tanning and top-shelf leather underlines goods for men and women.

Explore Venice & the Veneto

VENICE'S
TOP SIGHTS

Basilica di San Marco (p50)

Neighbourhoods at a Glance

① San Marco p48

So many world-class attractions are packed into San Marco, some visitors never leave – and others are loath to visit, fearing crowds. But why deny yourself the pleasures of Teatro La Fenice, Basilica di San Marco, Palazzo Ducale and Museo Correr? Judge for yourself whether they earn their reputations – but don't stop there. The backstreets are packed with galleries, boutiques and *enoteche* (wine bars).

② Dorsoduro p71

Dorsoduro covers prime Grand Canal waterfront with Ca' Rezzonico's gilded splendour, the Peggy Guggenheim Collection's modern edge, Gallerie dell'Accademia's Renaissance beauties and Punta della Dogana's ambitious installation art. The neighbourhood lazes days away on the sun-drenched Zattere, and convenes in Campo Santa Margherita for *spritz* and flirtation.

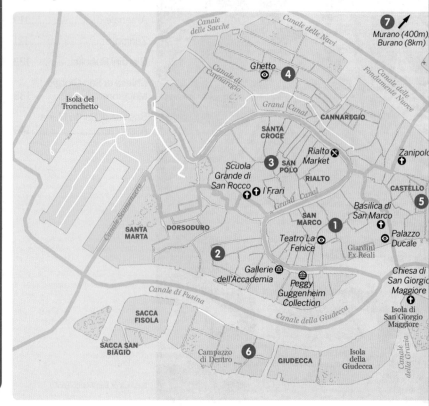

❸ San Polo & Santa Croce p84

Heavenly devotion and earthly delights co-exist in San Polo and Santa Croce, where divine art rubs up against the ancient red-light district, now home to artisan workshops and *osterie* (taverns). Don't miss fraternal-twin masterpieces: Titian's glowing Madonna at I Frari and turbulent Tintorettos at Scuola Grande di San Rocco. Quirky museums fill Grand Canal *palazzi* (mansions) with fashion and oddities, while island-grown produce crams the stalls of the Rialto Market.

❹ Cannaregio p105

Anyone could adore Venice on looks alone, but in Cannaregio you'll fall for its personality. A few streets over from bustling Strada Nova, footsteps echo along moody Fondamenta della Misericordia, and there's not a T-shirt kiosk in sight. Between the Gothic wonder of Madonna dell'Orto and the Renaissance miracle of Santa Maria dei Miracoli are Venice's top *osterie* and the tiny island Ghetto, a living monument to the outsized contributions of Venice's Jewish community.

❺ Castello p117

Sailors, saints and artists made Castello what it is today: home to seafood restaurants, ethereal icons and the Biennale. Some 5000 shipbuilders once worked at the Arsenale; their output is documented at Museo Storico Navale. Byzantine churches are gilt to the hilt, luxury hotels sprawl along the waterfront, and Vivaldi echoes from the orphanage where he worked. When it's time to unwind, hit the Giardini, *campo* (square) cafes and chatty *bacari* (bars).

❻ Giudecca, Lido & the Southern Islands p136

Architecture fans have headed here for centuries: have you seen the Palladios on Isola di San Giorgio Maggiore? Giudecca was an elite garden getaway before it became an industrial outpost; there's still a women's prison here alongside luxe spas, art galleries and romantic restaurants. Lido is Venice's 12km island escape, with sandy beaches, an A-list film festival and Liberty villas. Island resorts ring the Lido, alongside monasteries, abandoned quarantine islands and San Servolo's Museo della Follia.

❼ Murano, Burano & the Northern Islands p147

Other cities have suburban sprawl; Venice has a teal-blue northern lagoon dotted with blown-glass sculptures and rare wildlife. Serious shoppers head to Murano for one-of-a-kind glass art. Escapists prefer lazy days boating on the lagoon, mooring for seafood feasts and wine tasting on the islands of Burano and Mazzorbo, and glimpses of heaven in Torcello's golden mosaics.

NEIGHBOURHOODS AT A GLANCE

jewel-

secrets
bitions
le of
).

opher
Titian
per-
Libreria

Nazionale Marciana in **Museo Correr** (p57).

5 Tangoing across Piazza San Marco at sunset to the tune of the **Caffè Florian** (p65) orchestra.

Explore San Marco

The neighbourhood of San Marco is Venice's oldest and most famous. Everything started here when Doge Partecipazio built his rosy palace overlooking the lagoon and commissioned Venice's fairytale golden basilica to house the bones of St Mark the Evangelist.

With the palace, prisons, government offices, mint and library crowding around the basilica, Piazza San Marco was the fulcrum of Venetian power and it still attracts throngs of visitors today. You could spend days here, so start early and choose one big sight a day before striking out east towards the Accademia bridge. Just as in the past, your path from Campo San Moisè to Campo Santo Stefano is lined with purveyors of dazzling luxury goods and fevered shoppers. The throngs only thin out when narrow *calli* (lanes) disgorge them, blinking, into sunny *campi* (squares) faced by the lavishly decorated churches of Santa Maria del Giglio, San Maurizio and Santo Stefano. The latter is ringed with cafes and is a perfect pitstop.

In the evening, the red carpets and gilt boxes of La Fenice and Teatro Goldoni beckon music and theatre enthusiasts for high-brow operas, intimate classical music concerts, ballet and low-brow *opera buffa*. Alternatively, take a pew on the Gritti terrace for sunset views over Salute or dive down canyon-like *calli* near the Rialto for cheap eats, welcoming *trattorias* and endless glasses of *vino*.

Local Life

➡ **Drinks with character** Some things are worth a splurge and Venetians prefer to splash their cash at Harry's Bar (p66), Bar Longhi (p65) and Caffè Florian (p65).

➡ **Music and theatre** Start on a high note at La Fenice (p58), go for baroque at Interpreti Veneziani (p67) and laugh along to *opera buffa* at Teatro Goldoni (p67).

➡ **Artisan finds** Global marques can't compete with the workmanship of Venice's finest artisans: Sigfrido Cipolato (p67), Carlo Moretti at L'Isola (p68), Venetia Studium (p69), Le Burle Veneziane (p68) and Chiarastella Cattana (p67).

Getting There & Away

➡ **Vaporetto** *Vaporetti* 1 and N stop along the Grand Canal at several points in San Marco, including Rialto, Sant'Angelo, San Samuele, Santa Maria del Giglio and San Marco.

➡ **Walking** Follow yellow-signed shortcuts from the Rialto through shop-lined Marzaria del Capitello, Marzaria San Zulian and Marzaria Orologio to Piazza San Marco.

Lonely Planet's Top Tip

In San Marco, the price of a sit-down cappuccino seems more like rent. Take your coffee standing at a bar for just €1.50 to €2.50, spend a couple more euros for sunshine and people-watching at a *campo* table, or luxuriate in the baroque cafes of Piazza San Marco. There's usually a €6 music surcharge for outdoor seating in Piazza San Marco, so you may as well get your money's worth and tango.

✖ Best Places to Eat

➡ Trattoria e Bacaro Da Fiore (p65)

➡ Trattoria Vini da Arturo (p65)

➡ Ai Mercanti (p64)

➡ Bistrot de Venise (p65)

➡ Gelateria Suso (p63)

For reviews, see p63. ➡

🍷 Best Places to Drink

➡ Caffè Florian (p65)

➡ Bar Longhi (p65)

➡ Harry's Bar (p66)

➡ DOK Dall'Ava LP26 (p64)

➡ Osteria all'Alba (p67)

For reviews, see p65. ➡

◉ Best Interior Decor

➡ Museo Correr (p57)

➡ Palazzo Ducale (p53)

➡ Museo Fortuny (p59)

➡ Negozio Olivetti (p58)

➡ Palazzo Grassi (p63)

For reviews, see p50. ➡

DON'T MISS...

➡ Facade lunette mosaics dating from 1270

➡ Dome of Genesis

➡ Dome of the Prophets

➡ Pala d'Oro

➡ Loggia dei Cavalli

PRACTICALITIES

➡ St Mark's Basilica

➡ Map p268, H4

➡ 🕿 041 270 83 11

➡ www.basilicasan marco.it

➡ Piazza San Marco

➡ admission free

➡ ⏱9.45am-5pm Mon-Sat, 2-5pm Sun summer, to 4pm Sun winter

➡ 🚢San Marco

ery: over Greek columns and a Moorish arch is a lacy screen that might have been a Turkish sultan's balcony. Grand entrances are made through the central portal, under an ornate triple arch with Egyptian purple porphyry columns and 13th- to 14th-century reliefs of vines, virtues and astrological signs.

Dome Mosaics

Blinking is natural upon your first glimpse of the basilica's 8500 sq metres of glittering mosaics, many made with 24-carat gold leaf fused onto the back of the glass to represent divine light. Just inside the narthex (vestibule) glitter the basilica's oldest mosaics: *Apostles with the Madonna*, standing sentry by the main door for more than 950 years. The atrium's medieval **Dome of Genesis** depicts the separation of sky and water with surprisingly abstract motifs, anticipating modern art by 650 years. *Last Judgment* mosaics cover the atrium vault and the Apocalypse looms large in vault mosaics over the gallery.

Mystical transfusions occur in the **Dome of the Holy Spiri**t, where a dove's blood streams onto the heads of saints. In the central 13th-century **Cupola of the Ascension**, angels swirl overhead while dreamy-eyed St Mark rests on the pendentive (dome peak). Scenes from St Mark's life unfold over the main altar, in vaults flanking the **Dome of the Prophets** (best seen from the Pala d'Oro).

The roped-off circuit of the church interior is free and takes about 15 minutes. Silence is requested, but gasping understandable. For entry, dress modestly (ie knees and shoulders covered) and leave large bags around the corner at Ateneo di San Basso's free one-hour **baggage storage** (10am-4.30pm).

Pala d'Oro

Tucked behind the main altar containing **St Mark's sarcophagus** is the **Pala d'Oro** (Map p268; admission €2; ⊙9.45am-5pm Mon-Sat, 2-5pm Sun summer, to 4pm winter; ⊠San Marco), studded with 2000 emeralds, amethysts, sapphires, rubies, pearls and other gemstones. But the most priceless treasures here are biblical figures in vibrant cloisonné, begun in Constantinople in AD 976 and elaborated by Venetian goldsmiths in 1209. The enamelled saints have wild, unkempt beards and wide eyes fixed on Jesus, who glances sideways at a studious St Mark as Mary throws up her hands in wonder – an understandable reaction to such a captivating scene. Look closely to spot touches of Venetian whimsy: falcon-hunting scenes in medallions along the bottom, and the by-now-familiar scene of St Mark's body smuggled out of Egypt on the right.

PLANNING YOUR VISIT

The grandest entrances to the basilica are with a crowd. Luckily, the queue moves quickly – waits are rarely more than 15 minutes. Book 'Skip the Line' access online April to October (www.venetoinside.com; €2 booking fee) and head directly into the central portal. Arrive at odd times to avoid tour groups, which tend to arrive on the hour or half-hour. Free **guided tours** (☑041 241 38 17; www.basilicasanmarco.it; ⊙11am Mon-Sat summer) from the diocese explaining the theological messages in the mosaics also enter through the central portal. Reservations required.

Attending evening vespers allows you to enter the basilica after hours, minus tour groups. Worshippers come in through a side door and are expected to sit quietly for the duration of services; visits beyond the side chapel are not allowed.

BASILICA DI SAN MARCO

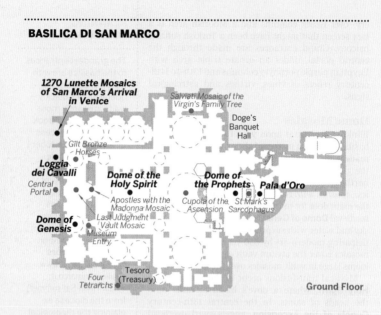

1270 Lunette Mosaics of San Marco's Arrival in Venice

Salviati Mosaic of the Virgin's Family Tree

Doge's Banquet Hall

Gilt Bronze Horses

Loggia dei Cavalli

Central Portal

Dome of the Holy Spirit

Dome of the Prophets

Pala d'Oro

Apostles with the Madonna Mosaic

Cupola of the Ascension

St Mark's Sarcophagus

Dome of Genesis

Last Judgment Vault Mosaic

Museum Entry

Four Tetrarchs

Tesoro (Treasury)

Ground Floor

Museum

San Marco remained the doge's chapel until 1807, and the ducal treasures upstairs in the **Museo** (Basilica di San Marco Museum; Map p268; admission €5; ⏰9.45am-4.45pm summer, to 3.45pm winter; ⛴San Marco) put a king's ransom to shame. Gilt bronze horses taken by Venice from Constantinople were stolen in turn by Napoleon, but eventually returned to the basilica and installed in the 1st-floor gallery. Portals lead from the gallery on to the giddiness-inducing **Loggia dei Cavalli**, where reproductions of the horses gallop off the balcony over Piazza San Marco.

In the Museo's displays of restored 13th- to 16th-century mosaic fragments, the Prophet Abraham is all ears and raised eyebrows, as though scandalised by Venetian gossip. On an interior balcony, Salviati's restored 1542–52 **mosaic of the Virgin's family tree** shows Mary's ancestors perched on branches, alternately chatting and ignoring one another, as families do. Hidden over the altar is the **doge's banquet hall**, where dignitaries wined and dined among lithe stucco figures of Music, Poetry and Peace.

Treasury

Holy bones and booty from the Crusades fill the **Tesoro** (Treasury; Map p268; admission €3; ⏰9.45am-5pm Mon-Sat, 2-5pm Sun summer, to 4pm winter; ⛴San Marco), including a 10th-century rock-crystal ewer with winged feet made for Fatimid Caliph al-'Aziz-bi-llah. Don't miss the bejewelled 12th-century Archangel Michael icon, featuring tiny, feisty enameled saints that look ready to break free of their golden setting and mount a miniature attack on evil. Velvet-padded boxes preserve doges' remains alongside alleged saints' relics, including St Roch's femur, St Mark's thumb, the arm St George used to slay the dragon and even a lock of the Madonna's hair.

TOP SIGHT
PALAZZO DUCALE

Don't be fooled by its genteel Gothic elegance: behind that lacy, pink-chequered facade, the doge's palace shows serious muscle and a steely will to survive. The seat of Venice's government for nearly seven centuries, this powerhouse stood the test of storms, crashes and conspiracies – only to be outwitted by Casanova, the notorious seducer who escaped from the attic prison.

Exterior
After fire gutted the original palace in 1577, Venice considered Palladio's offer to build one of his signature neoclassical temples in its place. Instead, Antonio da Ponte won the commission to restore the palace's Gothic facade with white Istrian stone and Veronese pink marble. Da Ponte's Palazzo effortlessly mixes past with present and business with pleasure, capping a graceful colonnade with medieval capitals depicting key Venetian guilds. The **loggia** along the *piazzetta* (little square) may seem like a fanciful flourish, but it served a solemn purpose: death sentences were read between the ninth and 10th columns from the left. Facing the piazza, Zane and Bartolomeo Bon's 1443 **Porta della Carta** (Paper Door) was an elegant point of entry for dignitaries, and served as a public bulletin board for government decrees.

Courtyard
Entering through the colonnaded courtyard you'll spot Sansovino's brawny statues of Apollo and Neptune flanking Antonio Rizzo's **Scala dei Giganti** (Giants' Staircase). Recent restorations have preserved charming cherubim propping up the pillars, though slippery incised-marble steps remain off-limits. On the east

DON'T MISS
➡ Sala dello Scudo
➡ Scala d'Oro
➡ Anticollegio
➡ Sala Consiglio dei Dieci
➡ Collegio

PRACTICALITIES
➡ Ducal Palace
➡ Map p268, H5
➡ 🎧 041 271 59 11
➡ www.palazzoducale.
visitmuve.it
➡ Piazzetta San Marco 52
➡ incl Museo Correr adult/reduced €18/11
➡ ⏰8.30am-7pm summer, to 5.30pm winter
➡ 🚤San Zaccaria

PALAZZO DUCALE'S TOP FIVE PROPAGANDA PAINTINGS

The following are not be missed:

➡ Veronese's *Juno Bestowing Her Gifts on Venice*
➡ Tiepolo's *Venice Receiving Gifts of the Sea from Neptune*
➡ Titian's *Doge Antonio Grimani Kneeling before Faith*
➡ Tintoretto's *Minerva Dismissing Mars*
➡ Veronese's *Virtues of the Republic*

....

At the top of the Scala d'Oro to your left you'll notice the face of a grimacing man with his mouth agape. This *bocca di leoni*, lion's mouth, was a postbox for secret accusations. These slanders reported any number of unholy acts, from cursing and tax avoidance (forgiveable) to Freemasonry (punishable by death). The notes, which had to be signed by two accusers, were then investigated by Venice's dreaded security service, led by the Council of Ten.

PALAZZO DUCALE

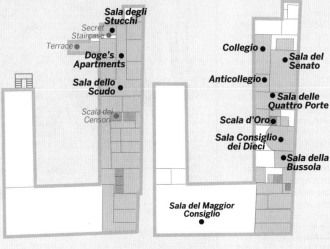

First Floor   **Second Floor**

wand over Justice and Peace. Father–son team Jacopo and Domenico Tintoretto attempt similar flattery, showing Venice keeping company with Apollo, Mars and Mercury in their *Triumph of Venice* ceiling for the **Sala del Senato** (Senate Hall), but frolicking lagoon sea-monsters steal the scene.

Government cover-ups were never so appealing as in the **Sala Consiglio dei Dieci** (Trial Chambers of the Council of Ten; Room 20), where Venice's star chamber plotted under Veronese's *Juno Bestowing her Gifts on Venice*, a glowing goddess strewing gold ducats. Over the slot where anonymous treason accusations were slipped into the **Sala della Bussola** (Compass Room; Room 21) is his *St Mark in Glory* ceiling.

The cavernous 1419 **Sala del Maggior Consiglio** (Grand Council Hall) features the doge's throne with a 22m-by-7m *Paradise* backdrop (by Tintoretto's son, Domenico) that's more politically correct than pretty: heaven is crammed with 500 prominent Venetians, including several Tintoretto patrons. Veronese's political posturing is more elegant in his oval *Apotheosis of Venice* ceiling, where gods marvel at Venice's coronation by angels, with foreign dignitaries and Venetian blondes rubbernecking on the balcony below.

Prisons

Only visitors on the Itinerari Segreti (secret passages tour, p110) can access the secret Council of Ten headquarters and **Piombi** attic prison. Pass through the **Sala del Magistrato alle Leggi** (Hall of the Legal Magistrate) featuring ominous scenes by the master of apocalyptic visions, Hieronymus Bosch. Follow the path of condemned prisoners across the **Ponte dei Sospiri** (Bridge of Sighs) to Venice's 16th-century **Priggione Nove** (New Prisons). Dank cells are covered with

DEAD DOGES

On the death of the doge, the Council announced: 'With much displeasure we have heard of the death of the most serene prince, a man of such goodness and piety; however, we shall make another.' The signet ring, symbol of his power, was then slipped from his finger and broken in half. The doge's family had three days to vacate the palace and remove all their furniture. Three Inquisitors were also appointed to scrutinise the doge's past office and, if necessary, punish his heirs for any fraud or wrongdoing.

In the Sala del Maggior Consiglio, the wall frieze depicts the first 76 doges of Venice, but note the black space: Doge Marin Falier would have appeared there had he not lost his head for treason in 1355.

Arcade,

graffitie
with ma
sacking

Secret

Discover
attic on
erari Se
adult/red
10.45am
10.20am
and thro
unadorn
yond thi
is lined
reports
cusation
and judg
accused
tion Ro
sometim
a rope.
prison co
years' co
the more
As descr
genious
guard he
night. Ho
spy for th

◉ SIGHTS

BASILICA DI SAN MARCO BASILICA
See p50.

PALAZZO DUCALE MUSEUM
See p53.

CAMPANILE TOWER
Map p268 (Bell Tower; www.basilicasanmarco.
it; Piazza San Marco; admission €8; ⊘9am-9pm
summer, to 7pm spring & autumn, 9.30am-3.45pm
winter; 🚤San Marco) The basilica's 99m-tall
bell tower has been rebuilt twice since its
initial construction in AD 888. Galileo Gali-
lei tested his telescope here in 1609, but today visitors head to the top for 360-degree
lagoon views and close encounters with the
Marangona, the booming bronze bell that
originally signalled the start and end of the
working day for the craftsmen *(marangoni)*
at the Arsenale shipyards. Today it rings
twice a day, at noon and midnight.

The tower's distinctive profile was the
brainchild of Bartolomeo Bon, whose 16th-
century design was initially criticised for
being ungainly. However, when the tower
suddenly collapsed in 1902, the Venetians
painstakingly rebuilt it exactly as it was,
brick by brick.

Sansovino's classical marble loggia at the
base of the Campanile is decidedly mythi-
cal, showcasing bronzes of pagan deities
Minerva, Apollo and Mercury, plus Peace.

TORRE DELL'OROLOGIO LANDMARK
Map p268 (Clock Tower; ☎041 4273 0892; www.
museicivicivicieneziani.it; Piazza San Marco; adult/
reduced with Museum Pass €12.50/7.50; ⊘tours
in English 10am & 11am Mon-Wed, 2pm & 3pm Thu-
Sun, in Italian noon & 4pm daily, in French 2pm
& 3pm Mon-Wed, 10am & 11am Thu-Sun; 🚤San
Marco) The two hardest-working men in
Venice stand duty on a rooftop around the
clock, and wear no pants. No need to file
workers' complaints: the 'Do Mori' (Two
Moors) exposed to the elements atop the
Torre dell'Orologio are made of bronze, and
their bell-hammering mechanism runs like,
well, clockwork. Below the Moors, Venice's
gold-leafed 15th-century timepiece tracks
lunar phases.

The clock, designed by Zuan Paolo Rain-
ieri and his son Zuan Carlo in 1493–99, had
one hitch: the clockworks required constant upkeep by a live-in clockwatcher and
his family until 1998. After a nine-year renovation, the clock's works are now in independent working order – 132-stroke chimes

SAN MARCO SIGHTS

◉ TOP SIGHT
MUSEO CORRER

Napoleon filled his Piazza San Marco palace with the
doges' riches, and took Venice's finest heirlooms back to
France. But the greatest treasure here couldn't be lifted:
the **Libreria Nazionale Marciana**, arguably Europe's
first public library, lavishly painted with larger-than-life
philosophers by Veronese, Titian and Tintoretto.

Napoleon lost Venice to Austrian emperor Franz Joseph before completing the construction of this palace.
The Habsburgs loved luxury and **Empress Sissi's suite**
showcases her 19th-century penchant for brocade-
swagged curtains, silk-swathed walls and frescoed
ceilings – shocking, considering the abject poverty of
Venice's citizenry at the time.

Over the years, Venice has successfully reclaimed
many of Napoleon's pilfered maps, statues, cameos and
weapons. In addition, four centuries of artistic masterpieces are held in the **Pinacoteca**. Not to be missed are
Paolo Veneziano's 14th-century sad-eyed saints (room
25); Jacopo di Barbari's minutely detailed woodblock
perspective view of Venice; an entire room of bright-
eyed, peach-cheeked Bellini saints (room 36); and a
wonderful anonymous 1784 portrait of champion rower
Maria Boscola, five-time regatta winner (room 47).

DON'T MISS...
➡ Libreria Nazionale
Marciana
➡ Empress Sissi's
suite
➡ Drinks in frescoed
Caffè dell'Art

PRACTICALITIES
➡ Map p268, F5
➡ ☎041 4273 0892
➡ http://correr.visit
muve.it/
➡ Piazza San Marco 52
➡ incl Palazzo Ducale
adult/reduced €18/11
➡ ⊘10am-7pm sum-
mer, to 5pm winter
➡ 🚤San Marco

keep time in tune, moving barrels indicate minutes and hour on the world's first digital clock face (c 1753), and wooden statues of the three kings and angel emerge from side panels annually on Epiphany and the Feast of the Ascension. Tours climb steep four-storey spiral staircases past the clockworks to the roof terrace, for giddy, close-up views of the Moors in action.

Children must be over 6 years old to climb the tower and the steep climb is not recommended for pregnant women and those suffering from vertigo or claustrophobia.

NEGOZIO OLIVETTI   LANDMARK

Map p268 (Olivetti Store; ☑041 522 83 87; www. negoziolivetti.it; Piazza San Marco 101, Procuratie Vecchie; adult/reduced incl audio tour €5/2.50; ☺11am-6.30pm Tue-Sun summer, to 4.30pm winter; ☻San Marco) Like a revolver pulled from a petticoat, ultra-modern Negozio Olivetti was an outright provocation when it first appeared under the frilly arcades of Piazza San Marco in 1958. High-tech pioneer Olivetti comissioned Venetian architect Carlo Scarpa to transform a narrow, dim souvenir shop into a showcase for its sleek typewriters and 'computing machines' (several 1948–54 models are displayed).

Instead of fighting the elements, Scarpa invited them indoors. He sliced away walls to let light flood in, included a huge planter for tall grasses and added a black slab-marble fountain as a wink at *acque alte* (high tide). Semicircular porthole windows resemble eyes open wide to the historic piazza, and the Architecture Biennale's modernist horizons.

CHIESA DI SAN ZULIAN   CHURCH

Map p268 (☑041 523 53 83; Campo San Zulian; ☺9am-6.30pm Mon-Sat, 9am-7.30pm Sun; ☻San Marco) **FREE** Founded in 829, San Zulian got a Sansovino makeover funded by physician Tomasso Rangone, who made his fortune by selling syphilis cures and secrets to living past 100 (he died at 84). The doctor is immortalised in bronze over the portal, holding sarsaparilla – his VD 'miracle cure'. Inside are works by Palma il Giovane and Veronese's *Dead Christ and Saints*.

CHIESA DI SAN MOISÈ   CHURCH

Map p268 (☑041 528 58 40; Campo di San Moisè; ☺9.30am-12.30pm & 3.30-6.30pm Mon-Sat, 9.30-11am & 2.30-6.30pm Sun; ☻San Marco) **FREE** Icing flourishes of carved stone across the 1660s facade make this church appear

---

⦿ TOP SIGHT
TEATRO LA FENICE

Once its dominion over the high seas ended, Venice discovered the power of high Cs, hiring San Marco choir-master Claudio Monteverdi, the father of modern opera, and opening La Fenice ('The Phoenix') in 1792. Rossini and Bellini staged operas here, making La Fenice the envy of Europe – until it went up in flames in 1836.

Venice without opera was unthinkable, and within a year the opera house was rebuilt. Verdi premiered *Rigoletto* and *La Traviata* at La Fenice, and international greats Stravinsky, Prokofiev and Britten composed for the house. But La Fenice was again reduced to ashes in 1996; two electricians found guilty of arson were apparently behind on repairs. A €90-million replica of the 19th-century opera house reopened in late 2003 (though some critics had lobbied for Gae Aulenti's avant-garde design), and the reprise performance of *La Traviata* was a sensation.

From January to July and September to October, opera season is in full swing. Tours of the gilt encrusted venue are also possible with advance booking. Check also for chamber music concerts staged at La Fenice's sister venue, **Teatro Malibran** (p114).

DON'T MISS...

➡ Opera season

➡ *Intermezzo* (intermission) at the baroque bar

➡ Summer symphonies

➡ Carnevale balls

PRACTICALITIES

➡ Map p268, D5

➡ ☑041 78 66 75

➡ www.teatrolafenice.it

➡ Campo San Fantin 1965

➡ theatre visits adult/reduced €9/6.50, opera tickets from €66

➡ ☺tours 9.30am-6pm

➡ ☻Santa Maria del Giglio

positively lickable, although 19th-century architecture critic John Ruskin found its wedding-cake appearance indigestible. From an engineering perspective, Ruskin had a point: several statues had to be removed in the 19th century to prevent the facade from collapsing under their combined weight.

The remaining statuary by Flemish sculptor Heinrich Meyring (aka Merengo in Italian) includes scant devotional works but a sycophantic number of tributes to church patrons. Among the scene-stealing works inside are Tintoretto's *Washing of the Feet*, in the chapel to the left of the altar, and Palma il Giovane's *The Supper*, on the right side of the chapel.

PALAZZO CONTARINI DEL BOVOLO MANSION
Map p268 (Calle Contarini del Bovolo 4299; ⬚Sant'Angelo) **FREE** No need to wait for San Marco sunsets to inspire a snog: this romantic Renaissance 15th-century *palazzo* with an external spiral *bovolo* (snail-shell) stairwell is closed for restoration, but its shady courtyard offers stirring views and privacy.

MUSEO FORTUNY MUSEUM
Map p268 (☏041 098 81 07; http://fortuny. visitmuve.it/; Campo San Beneto 3758; adult/ reduced with Museum Pass €13/11; ⊘10am-6pm Wed-Mon; ⬚Sant'Angelo) Find design inspiration at the palatial home-studio of Art Nouveau designer Mariano Fortuny y Madrazo, whose shockingly uncorseted Delphi-goddess frocks set the standard for bohemian chic. First-floor salon walls are eclectic mood boards: Fortuny fashions and Isfahan tapestries, family portraits and the odd dress made of peacock feathers. Art shows in Fortuny's attic warehouse are often overshadowed by the striking architecture and rooftop views.

If these salons inspire design schemes, visit Fortuny Tessuti Artistici (p145) in Giudecca, where textiles are still hand-printed according to Fortuny's top-secret methods.

CHIESA DI SANTA MARIA DEL GIGLIO CHURCH
Map p268 (Santa Maria Zobenigo; www.chorus venezia.org; Campo di Santa Maria del Giglio; admission €3, or with Chorus Pass free; ⊘10am-5pm Mon-Sat; ⬚Santa Maria del Giglio) Experience awe through the ages in this compact church with a 10th-century Byzantine layout, charmingly flawed maps of Venice territories c 1678 on the facade, and three

WAGNER SAYS 'SHHHH!'

By the 19th century, Venice's great families were largely ruined and could not afford to heat their enormous *palazzi* (mansions). La Fenice served as a members-only club where Venetian society would spend much of the day gambling, gossiping and providing running commentary during performances. When he first performed at La Fenice, German composer Richard Wagner miffed the notoriously chatty Venetian opera crowd by insisting on total silence during performances.

intriguing masterpieces. Veronese's *Madonna with Child* hides behind the altar, Tintoretto's four evangelists flank the organ, and Peter Paul Rubens' *Mary with St John* in the **Molin Chapel** features a characteristically chubby baby Jesus.

Admiral Antonio Barbaro commissioned this reconstruction of the original 9th-century church by Giuseppe Sardi for the glory of the Virgin, Venice, and of course himself – his statue gets prime facade placement. This self-glorifying architectural audacity enraged 19th-century architectural critic John Ruskin, who called it a 'manifestation of insolent atheism'.

MUSEO DELLA MUSICA MUSEUM
Map p268 (☏041 241 18 40; http://www.inter pretiveneziani.com/en/museo-della-musica.php; Campo San Maurizio 2761; ⊘10am-7pm; ⬚Santa Maria del Giglio) **FREE** Housed in the restored neoclassical **Chiesa di San Maurizio**, this collection of rare 17th- to 19th-century instruments is accompanied by informative panels on the life and times of Venice's Antonio Vivaldi. To hear these instruments in action, check out the kiosk with CDs and concert tickets for Interpreti Veneziani (p67), which funds this museum.

CHIESA DI SANTO STEFANO CHURCH
Map p268 (www.chorusvenezia.org; Campo Santo Stefano; admission €3, or free with Chorus Pass; ⊘10am-5pm Mon-Sat; ⬚Accademia) The freestanding **bell tower** behind it leans disconcertingly, but this brick Gothic church has stood tall since 1325. Credit for ship-shape splendour goes to Bartolomeo Bon for the marble entry portal and to Venetian shipbuilders, who constructed the vast wooden

Palazzo Grassi
French magnate François Pinault scandalised Paris when he relocated his contemporary art collection here, to be displayed in galleries designed by Gae Aulenti and Tadao Ando.

①

Ca' Rezzonico
See how Venice lived in baroque splendour at this 18th-century art museum with Tiepolo ceilings, silk-swagged boudoirs and even an in-house pharmacy.

⑫

⑪

⑬ Ponte dell'Accademia

⑭ Peggy Guggenheim Collection

Chiesa di Santa Maria delle Salute

⑮

Punta della Dogana
Minimalist architect Tadao Ando creatively repurposed abandoned warehouses as galleries, which now host contemporary art installations from François Pinault's collection.

Fondaco dei Turchi

Recognisable by its double colonnade, watchtowers, and dugout canoe parked at the Museo di Storia Naturale's ground-floor loggia.

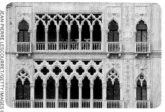

Ca' d'Oro

Behind the triple Gothic arcades are priceless masterpieces: Titians looted by Napoleon, a rare Mantegna and semiprecious stone mosaic floors.

te di Calatrava

ts starkly streamlined fish-fin shape, the bridge was the first to be built over the d Canal in 75 years.

- ② Palazzo Vendramin
- ③
- ④
- ⑤
- ⑥ Pescaria
- ⑦ Rialto Market
- Palazzo Grimani ⑨
- ⑩ Palazzo Corner-Spinelli
- ⑧ Ponte di Rialto

Ponte dei Sospiri ⑱

Palazzo Ducale ⑰

Ponte di Rialto

Antonio da Ponte beat out Palladio for the commission of this bridge, but construction costs spiralled to 250,000 Venetian ducats – about €19 million today.

'esaro

ally designed by Baldassare Longhena, this o was bequeathed to the city in 1898 to house lleria d'Arte Moderna and Museo d'Arte ale.

SAN MARCO SIGHTS

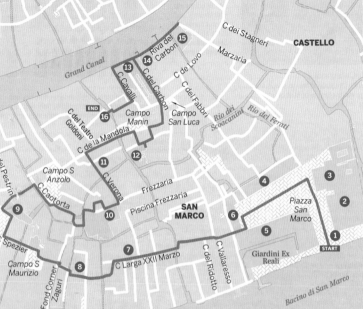

Neighbourhood Walk
San Marco Circuit

START PIAZZETTA SAN MARCO
END DOK DALL'AVA LP26
LENGTH 3KM; 1½ HOURS

Venetians still hurry past the granite ①**Columns of San Marco**, site of public executions for centuries. Past ②**Palazzo Ducale** (p53) is the ③**Basilica di San Marco** (p50) flanked by Mauro Codussi's 16th-century ④**Procuratie Vecchie** and Scamozzi-designed and Longhena-completed ⑤**Procuratie Nuove**. Today the Museo Correr occupies the Procuratie Nuove and ⑥**Ala Napoleonica**, the palace Napoleon brazenly razed San Geminiano church to build.

Follow ⑦**Calle Larga XXII Marzo** towards baroque ⑧**Chiesa di Santa Maria del Giglio** (p59), covered in peculiar maps charting Venetian vassal states c 1678–81. Further west, Bartolomeo Bon's marble Gothic portals grace the red brick ⑨**Chiesa di Santo Stefano** (p59), while next door its leaning bell tower looks as though it's had one *spritz* too many.

From here, head north through Campo San Anzolo turning right down Calle Caotorta to reach ⑩**Teatro La Fenice** (p58). Take canyon-like Calle Verona into the shadows past ⑪**Calle dei Assassini**. Corpses were so frequently found here that in 1128, Venice banned the full beards assassins wore as disguises. Snogging in *campi* is another established Venetian pastime – just off Campo Manin you can duck into the romantic courtyard of ⑫**Palazzo Contarini del Bovolo** (p59).

Along Calle del Carbon is city hall ⑬**Palazzo Loredan**. Outside, a plaque honours philosopher Eleonora Lucrezia Corner Piscopia, the first woman to earn a Padua University PhD, in 1678. Along the quay is 14th-century Gothic ⑭**Palazzo Dandolo**, home of blind doge and erstwhile Crusader Enrico Dandolo, who sacked Constantinople in 1203. Next door is Sansovino-designed ⑮**Palazzo Dolfin-Manin** (1547), where the last doge, Ludovico Manin, died in seclusion in 1802. End your grand tour with an *aperitivo* at ⑯**DOK dall'Ava LP26** (p64).

carena di nave (ship's keel) ceiling that resembles an upturned Noah's Ark.

Enter the cloister museum to see Canova's 1808 funerary stelae featuring gorgeous women dabbing their eyes with their cloaks. Also worth looking at are Tullio Lombardo's wide-eyed 1505 saint, and three brooding 1575–80 Tintorettos – *Last Supper*, with a ghostly dog begging for bread; the gathering gloom of *Agony in the Garden*; and the abstract, mostly black *Washing of the Feet*.

CHIESA DI SAN VIDAL   CHURCH
Map p268 (www.chorusvenezia.com; Campo di San Vidal 2862; admission €3, or with Chorus Pass free; ⊙9am-6.30pm Mon-Sat, 10am-6pm Sun; ⛴Accademia) Built by Doge Vitale Falier in the 11th century, Chiesa di San Vidal got a 1706–14 Palladian facelift to comemmorate Doge Francesco Morosoni's victory over Turkish foes. Inside is *St Vitale on Horseback and Eight Saints* by Vittore Carpaccio, featuring his signature traffic-light red and miniaturist's attention to detail. The deconsecrated church now serves as a concert venue (p67).

PONTE DELL'ACCADEMIA   BRIDGE
Map p268 (btwn Campo di San Vidal & Campo della Carità; ⛴Accademia) The wooden Ponte dell'Accademia was built in 1933 as a temporary replacement for an 1854 iron bridge, but this span, arched like a cat's back, remains a beloved landmark. Engineer Eugenio Miozzi's notable works include the Lido Casino, but none has lasted like this elegant little footbridge – and recent structural improvements have preserved it for decades to come.

PALAZZO FRANCHETTI   PALACE
Map p268 (Istituto Veneto di Scienze Lettere ed Arti; ☑041 240 77 11; www.istitutoveneto.it; Campo Santo Stefano 2842; ⊙10am-6pm Mon-Fri; ⛴Accademia) Three Venetian families originally lived at this Gothic 16th-century Grand Canal palace, and they didn't agree on decor. When Archduke Frederick of Austria snapped it up in the 19th century, he unified competing styles with a modern makeover. The Franchetti family lived here after independence and restored its Gothic fairy-tale look, including an **art nouveau staircase** dripping with dragons.

The palace was home to a private bank from 1922–99, when the Veneto Institute of Sciences, Letters and Arts moved in and began hosting arts expositions and academic conferences (see website). The **Palazzo Franchetti Caffè** (Map p268; ☑041 240 77 11; www.istitutoveneto.it; Campo Santo Stefano 2945; exhibits adult/student €9/6, cafe admission free; ⊙10am-6pm Mon-Fri; ⛴Accademia) in the garden cloisters has baroque-patterned window screens for a secluded espresso away from San Marco crowds.

★PALAZZO GRASSI   MUSEUM
Map p268 (☑box office 199 13 91 39, 041 523 16 80; www.palazzograssi.it; Campo San Samuele 3231; adult/reduced €15/10, 72hr ticket incl Punta della Dogana €20/15; ⊙10am-7pm Wed-Mon mid-Apr-Nov; ⛴San Samuele) Grand Canal gondola riders gasp at first glimpse of massive sculptures by contemporary artists like Thomas Houseago docked in front of Giorgio Masari's 1749 neoclassical palace. French billionaire François Pinault's provocative art collection overflows Palazzo Grassi, while clever curation and shameless art-star namedropping are the hallmarks of rotating temporary exhibits. Still, despite the artistic glamour, Tadao Ando's creatively repurposed interior architecture steals the show.

Postmodern architect Gae Aulenti peeled back twee rococo decor to highlight Masari's muscular classicism in 1985–86, and minimalist master Ando added stage-set drama in 2003–05 with ethereal backlit scrims and strategic spotlighting. Ando's design directs attention to contemporary art, without detracting from baroque ceiling frescoes. Don't miss the cafe overlooking the Grand Canal, with interiors redesigned by contemporary artists with each new show.

Next door, the **Teatrino** occupies a space that once served as the palace's garden before it was converted into a theatre. Here, once again, Ando has worked his magic, transforming the interior into a curvaceous, 220-seat, concrete auditorium which now hosts concerts, conferences and film projections.

 EATING

★GELATERIA SUSO   GELATERIA €
Map p268 (☑348 564 65 45; www.gelatovenezia.it; Calle della Bissa 5453, Cannaregio; gelati €2-5; ⊙10am-8pm; ⛴; ⛴Rialto) 🍃 Indulge in gelato as rich as a doge, in original seasonal flavors like marscapone cream with fig sauce and walnuts. All Suso's gelati are

locally made and free of artificial colours, and even the gluten-free flavours are extra creamy. A waffle cone with hazelnut and extra-dark chocolate passes for dinner.

ROSA SALVA
BAKERY €

Map p268 (☎041 522 79 34; www.rosasalva.it; Mercerie 5020; pastries €1.20-3; ☉7.30am-8pm Thu-Tue; ☎ �; 🚇Rialto) With just-baked strudel and reliably frothy cappuccino, Rosa Salva has provided Venetians with fresh reasons to roll out of bed for over a century. Cheerfully efficient women working the spotless granite counter ensure that no *curasan* (croissant) order waits for more than a minute, and supply gale-force espresso and turbo-loaded chocolate profiteroles to power you across 30 more bridges.

MARCHINI TIME
BAKERY €

Map p268 (☎041 241 30 87; www.marchinitime.it; Campo San Luca 4598; pastries €1.20-2, sandwiches €1.50-3; ☉7.30am-8.30pm Mon-Sat, 8am-8.30pm Sun; 🚇Rialto) Elbow your way through the morning crush to bag a warm croissant filled with runny apricot jam or melting Nutella. Everything here is freshly baked, which is why the crowd hangs around as croissants give way to foccacia, *pizette* (mini pizza) and generously stuffed *panini*.

CAFFÈ MANDOLA
PANINI €

Map p268 (☎041 523 76 24; Calle della Mandola 3630; panini €3-7; ☉9am-7pm Mon-Sat; 🚇Sant'Angelo) Carbo-load before the opera or between museums with fresh focaccia stuffed with tangy tuna and capers or lean *bresaola* (air-cured beef), rocket and seasoned Grana Padano cheese. On cold days, get your *porchetta* (pork) and gorgonzola cheese panini toasted to gooey perfection. Plan your breaks before 1pm or after 3pm to snag a stool indoors (no extra charge).

ROSTICCERIA GISLON
VENETIAN, DELI €

Map p268 (☎0415 22 35 69; Calle de la Bissa 5424; meals €15-25; ☉9am-9.30pm Tue-Sun, 9am-3.30pm Mon; 🚇Rialto) Serving San Marco workers since the 1930s, this no-frills *rosticceria* has an ultramarine canteen counter downstairs and a small eat-in restaurant upstairs. Hot to trot you'll find *arancini* (rice balls), deep fried mozzarella balls, croquettes and fish fry ups. No one said it was going to be healthy! Those with more time might indulge in surprisingly good seafood risottos, grilled cuttlefish and, of course, the perennially popular roast chicken.

★AI MERCANTI
OSTERIA €€

Map p268 (☎041 523 82 69; www.aimercanti.com; Corte Coppo 4346/A; meals €40-45; ☉noon-3pm & 7-11pm Tue-Sat, 7-11pm Mon; 🚇Rialto) With its pumpkin-coloured walls, gleaming golden fixtures and jet-black tables and chairs, Ai Mercanti effortlessly conjures up a romantic mood. No wonder dates whisper over glasses of DOC Veneto wines from the 300+ bottles in the wine cellar before ordering contemporary dishes of risotto with mullet and nori seaweed. If you fancy something simpler, opt for the superb 'smokey' burger and a glass of Barolo.

★DOK DALL'AVA LP26
ITALIAN €€

Map p268 (☎041 296 07 64; www.dallava.com; Campo San Luca 3989; meals €18-30; ☉10am-3.30pm & 5.30pm-1am; 🚇Sant'Angelo) The new kid on the block is a trendy *prosciutteria* with the muscle (and the 24-month aged prosciutto) of one of San Daniele's biggest prosciutto houses behind it. It's been an instant hit, not least because it combines a coffee bar, an open-plan restaurant overlooking a canal and an enviable roof terrace bar, with live music on summer evenings. Aside from the hard-to-turn-down prosciutto, you can order stone-ground pizzas with Gragnano tomatoes or succulent Chianina burgers.

The entrance to the restaurant is at the back of the Rossini cinema.

HOSTARIA DA ZORZI
OSTERIA €€

Map p268 (☎041 520 45 89; Calle dei Fuseri 4359; meals €20-30; ☉noon-2.30pm & 7-10pm Mon-Sat; 🚇Rialto) With over a hundred years of history, Zorzi has served many a weary traveller tramping through San Marco. A set lunchtime menu (€20) guarantees a hearty Venetian meal of *bigoli* (pasta) with onions and anchovies, followed by pan-fried pork or grilled Adriatic fish. The fixed price menu even includes wine and water – no wonder thrifty, off-duty *gondolieri* come here for lunch.

OSTERIA DA CARLA
OSTERIA, CICHETI €€

Map p268 (☎041 523 78 55; Frezzaria 1535; meals €20-30; ☉10am-9pm Mon-Sat; 🚇Vallaresso) For the price of hot chocolate in Piazza San Marco, diners in the know duck into this hidden courtyard to feast on handmade ravioli with poppyseed, pear and sheep's cheese. Expect a wait at lunch and happy hour, when *gondolieri* abandon ship for DOC Soave and *sopressa crostini* (soft salami on toast).

ANONIMO VENEZIANO ITALIAN €€

Map p268 (☑041 528 97 30; Calle del Fruttariol 1847; meals €25-35; ☺noon-3pm & 5.30-9.30pm Mon-Wed, Fri & Sat, 5.30-9.30pm Sun; ▣Santa Maria del Giglio) A casual charmer with classic fare at eminently reasonable prices – under €10 for pasta and €4 for a small carafe of house Friulano white – and impeccable social graces. Dapper bow-tied servers may not allow you to leave until you've enjoyed a grappa-filled chocolate, and they graciously help ladies don their coats only after return visits are promised.

★ TRATTORIA E
BACARO DA FIORE VENETIAN, CICHETI €€€

Map p268 (☑041 523 53 10; www.dafiore.it; Calle delle Botteghe 3461; meals €45-80, cicheti €10-15; ☺12.30-2.30pm & 7.30-10.30pm Tue-Sat; ▣San Samuele) Possibly the best bang for your buck in San Marco, this elegant trattoria with its rustic-chic decor serves superlative Venetian dishes composed of carefully selected seasonal ingredients from small Veneto producers. Maurizio Martin is justly famous for his seafood dishes such as seabass with balsamic vinegar, although during the Feast of the Redeemer you shouldn't pass up the *castradino* (a sort of Irish stew).

Next door, the *cicheti* (bar snacks) counter serves excellent *cicheti* at more democratic prices. Hurrah! Here, you can fill a plate with *baccala mantecato* (creamed cod), octopus-fennel salad, *arancini* (risotto balls), and Venetian *trippa* (tripe) to enjoy on a stool at the bar or in the *calle*.

★ TRATTORIA
VINI DA ARTURO ITALIAN €€€

Map p268 (☑041 528 69 74; Calle dei Assassini 3656; meals €50-70; ☺noon-2.30pm & 7.30-11pm Mon-Sat; ▣Sant'Angelo) Everyone in this corridor-sized restaurant comes for the same reason: the steak, studded with green peppercorn, soused in brandy and mustard or rare on the bone. Your host will happily trot out irrefutable proof that Nicole Kidman actually eats and that producer Joel Silver managed to escape *The Matrix* for steak here.

★ BISTROT DE VENISE VENETIAN €€€

Map p268 (☑041 523 66 51; www.bistrotde venise.com; Calle dei Fabbri 4685; tasting menu €95, meals €50-80; ☺noon-3pm & 7pm-midnight; ▣Rialto) Indulge in some culinary time travel at this fine dining bistro where owner Sergio Frangiacomo has revived the recipes of

Renaissance chef Bartolomeo Scappi. Dine like a doge in the red-and-gilt dining room on braised duck with wild apple and onion pudding, or enjoy the reprised Jewish recipe of goose, raisin and pinenut pasta. Even the desserts are beguilingly exotic, such as the Bianca Reale, a soft ricotta pudding spiced with ginger and rosewater.

🍷 DRINKING & NIGHTLIFE

★ CAFFÈ FLORIAN CAFE

Map p268 (☑041 520 56 41; www.caffeflo rian.com; Piazza San Marco 56/59; drinks €10-25; ☺9am-midnight; ▣San Marco) One of Venice's most famous cafes, Florian maintains rituals (if not prices) established c 1720: white-jacketed waiters serve cappuccino on silver trays, lovers canoodle in plush banquettes and the orchestra strikes up a tango as the sunset illuminates San Marco's mosaics.

Piazza seating during concerts costs €6 extra, but dreamy-eyed romantics hardly notice.

Among Italy's first bars to welcome women and revolutionaries, Florian maintains its radical-chic reputation with contemporary art installations.

CAFFÈ QUADRI CAFE, BAR

Map p268 (☑041 522 21 05; www.alajmo.it; Piazza San Marco 120; drinks €6-25; ☺9am-11.30pm; ▣San Marco) Powdered wigs seem appropriate in this baroque cafe, serving royal happy hours since 1638. The upstairs restaurant charges a king's ransom for three-Michelin starred fare and views over Piazza San Marco, while the gilded downstairs cafe serves a princely €12 hot chocolate with *panna* (whipped cream). Reserve ahead during Carnevale, when costumed Quadri revellers party like it's 1699.

★ BAR LONGHI COCKTAIL BAR

Map p268 (☑041 79 46 11; www.hotelgrittipal acevenice.com; Campo di Santa Maria del Giglio 2467; drinks €16-22; ☺11am-1am; 🛜; ▣Santa Maria del Giglio) The Gritti's beautiful Bar Longhi may be hellishly expensive, but if you consider the room – with its Fortuny fabrics, intarsia marble bar, 18th-century mirrors and million-dollar Piero Longhi paintings – its signature balsamic Martini (the work of art that it is) starts to seem reasonable. Between May and October you'll have to choose between the twinkling interior and a spectacular Grand Canal terrace fringed with baby-pink carnations.

★ HARRY'S BAR
BAR

Map p268 (☏041 528 57 77; Calle Vallaresso 1323; cocktails €12-22; ☺10.30am-11pm; ⛴San Marco) Aspiring auteurs hold court at bistro tables well scuffed by Ernest Hemingway, Charlie Chaplin, Truman Capote and Orson Welles, enjoying the signature €16.50 bellini (Giuseppe Cipriani's original 1948 recipe: white-peach juice and *prosecco*) with a side of reflected glory. Upstairs is one of Italy's most unaccountably expensive restaurants – stick to the bar to save the financing for your breakthrough film.

OSTERIA SAN MARCO
WINE BAR

Map p268 (☏041 528 52 42; www.osteriasan marco.it; Frezzaria 1610; drinks €3-7; ☺12.30-11pm Mon-Sat; ⛴Vallaresso) Romance is in the air in Venice – but the top-notch wines lining these exposed-brick walls surely help. From 6:30pm till 8pm, locals crowd the bar for prime selections from the chalkboard list of wines available by the glass. Starters and mains here are variable, costly and occasionally microwaved, but cheese plates and a book-size wine list make this a post-concert destination.

A DRINK WITH A VIEW

Eating options in San Marco boil down to a simple choice: good food or a view. Getting both is impossible, especially at reasonable prices – still you can enjoy a coffee or *aperitivi* with superlative views at these great bars:

➡ **Bar Longhi** (p65) The Gritti's jewel-box bar is hung with priceless artworks and has a Grand Canal terrace fringed with flowers.

➡ **Caffé dell'Art** The cafe of the **Museo Correr** (p57) offers frescoed rooms and first-floor views of Basilica di San Marco.

➡ **L'Ombra del Leoni** (p66) The Biennale's Grand Canal terrace offers a triple-whammy view of the Salute, Dogana and San Giorgio Maggiore.

➡ **DOK Dall'Ava LP26** (p64) Floor-to-ceiling windows offer views over the Rio di San Luca and the church of the same name.

CAFFÈ CENTRALE
LOUNGE

Map p268 (☏041 296 06 64; www.caffecentralev enezia.com; Piscina Frezzaria 1659b; drinks €3.50-15; ☺7pm-1am; ⛴San Marco) Under moody Murano-chandelier lighting, you might spot Salma Hayek, Spike Lee and sundry America's Cup sailors within these exposed-brick walls. Meals are pricey and canalside VIP tables chilly, but Centrale draws La Fenice post-opera crowds with signature foamy *spritz* cocktails, midnight snacks, chill-out DJ sets and occasional live jazz.

L'OMBRA DEL LEONI
CAFE, BAR

Map p268 (☏041 521 87 11; www.labiennale.org; Calle Ridotto 1364a; drinks €3-6; ☺9am-midnight summer, 9am-9pm winter; ⛴San Marco) Lucky Biennale folk have Grand Canal views from their upstairs offices in Ca' Giustinian, but you too can enjoy the *palazzo's* peerless waterside position in the downstairs cafe-restaurant, which is open to the public. In keeping with the democratic spirit of the institution, drink prices are a bargain, especially if you manage to nab a seat on the outdoor terrace. At lunch there are simple sandwiches and salads.

BACARANDO
BAR

Map p268 (☏041 523 82 80; Corte dell'Orso 5495; ☺9.30am-midnight; ⛴) If you've managed to find this warm, wood-panelled bar in the warren of streets off San Bartolomeo, toast yourself with a radical rum cocktail (this place has over 150 different labels) and order a huge burger or a plate of heaped *cicheti*. Thanks to its clubby vibe and a lively programme of cultural events and live music, its popular with a hip young crowd.

TEAMO
CAFE, BAR

Map p268 (☏041 528 37 87; www.teamowinebar. com; Rio Terà della Mandola 3795; ☺8am-9pm; ⛴Sant'Angelo) Sunny tearoom by day, sleek backlit alabaster bar by night, and fabulous full time. Arrive by 6.30pm for first choice of fresh *cicheti* at the bar and lookers in the leather banquettes – this bar swings both ways, so there's something for everyone.

CAFFÈ LAVENA
CAFE

Map p268 (☏041 522 40 70; www.lavena.it; Piazza San Marco 133/4; drinks €1-12; ☺9.30am-11pm; ⛴San Marco) Opera composer Richard Wagner had the right idea: when Venice leaves you weak in the knees, get a pick-me-up at Lavena. The €1 espresso at Lavena's mirrored bar is a baroque bargain – never mind the politically incorrect antique 'Moor's head' chandeliers. Spring for piazza seating to savor *caffè corretto* (coffee 'corrected' with liquor) accompanied by Lavena's nimble violinists.

⭐**OSTERIA ALL'ALBA**   WINE BAR
Map p268 (☑340 124 56 34; Ramo del Fontego dei Tedeschi 5370; drinks €4-6; ⊙10am-1am; ⛴Rialto) That roar behind the Rialto means the DJ's funk set is kicking in at All'Alba. Squeeze inside to order salami sandwiches (€1 to €2.50) and DOC Veneto wines, and check out walls festooned with vintage LPs and effusive thanks scrawled in a dozen languages.

ENOTECA AL VOLTO   BAR
Map p268 (☑041 522 89 45; Calle Cavalli 4081; cicheti €2-4, meals under €25; ⊙10am-3pm & 5.30-10pm Mon-Sat; ⛴Rialto) Join the bar crowd working its way through the vast selection of *cicheti* in this historic wood-panelled bar that feels like the inside of a ship's hold. Lining the ceiling above the golden glow of the brass bar lanterns are hundreds of wine labels, from just some of the bottles of regional wines that are cracked open every night. Cash only.

☆ **ENTERTAINMENT**

INTERPRETI VENEZIANI   CLASSICAL MUSIC
Map p268 (☑041 277 05 61; www.interpre tiveneziani.com; Chiesa San Vidal, Campo di San Vidal 2862; adult/reduced €27/22; ⊙doors open 8.30pm; ⛴Accademia) Everything you've heard of Vivaldi from weddings and mobile ring tones is proved fantastically wrong by Interpreti Veneziani, which plays Vivaldi on 18th-century instruments as a soundtrack for living in this city of intrigue – you'll never listen to *The Four Seasons* again without hearing summer storms erupting over the lagoon, or snow-muffled footsteps hurrying over footbridges in winter's-night intrigues.

MUSICA A PALAZZO   OPERA
Map p268 (☑340 971 72 72; www.musicapalaz zo.com; Palazzo Barbarigo-Minotto, Fondamenta Barbarigo o Duodo 2504; tickets incl beverage €75; ⊙doors open 8pm; ⛴Santa Maria del Giglio) Hang onto your *prosecco* and brace for impact: in palace salons, the soprano's high notes imperil glassware, and thundering baritones reverberate through inlaid floors.

During 1½ hours of selected arias from Verdi or Rossini, the drama progresses from receiving-room overtures to parlour duets overlooking the Grand Canal, followed by second acts in the Tiepolo-ceilinged dining room and bedroom grand finales.

TEATRO GOLDONI   THEATRE
Map p268 (☑041 240 20 14; www.teatrostabi leveneto.it; Calle Teatro Goldoni 4650b; tickets €8-29; ⊙box office 10am-1pm & 3-6.30pm Mon-Wed, Fri & Sat, 10am-1pm Thu; ⛴Rialto) Named after the city's great playwright, Venice's main theatre has an impressive dramatic range that runs from Goldoni's comedy to Shakespearean tragedy (mostly in Italian), plus ballets and concerts. Don't be fooled by the huge modern Brutalist bronze doors: this venerable theatre dates from 1622, and the jewel-box interior seats just 800.

MULTISALA ROSSINI   CINEMA
Map p268 (☑041 241 72 74; Calle San Benedetto 3997a; adult/reduced €7.50/6, 3D films €10/9; ⊙shows Tue-Sun; ♿; ⛴Rialto) Film buffs who miss the proverbial boat to the annual Venice Film Festival on the Lido, rejoice: award-winning films and blockbusters screen year-round at the city's newest and largest cinema. Sala 1 is the largest of three screening rooms, with seating for 300 and excellent sound. Some films are screened in the original language, but most are dubbed in Italian.

🛍 **SHOPPING**

⭐**CHIARASTELLA CATTANA**   HOMEWARES
Map p268 (☑041 522 43 69; www.chiarastellacat tana.it; Salizada San Samuele 3357; ⊙10.30am-1pm & 3-7pm Mon-Sat; ⛴San Samuele) Transform any home into a thoroughly modern *palazzo* with these locally woven, strikingly original Venetian linens. Whimsical cushions feature a chubby purple rhinoceros and grumpy scarlet elephants straight out of Pietro Longhi paintings, and hand-tasseled Venetian jacquard hand towels will dry your royal guests in style. Decorators and design aficionados, save an afternoon to consider dizzying woven-to-order napkin and curtain options here.

⭐**SIGFRIDO CIPOLATO**   JEWELLERY
Map p268 (☑041 522 84 37; www.sigfridocipola to.com; Calle della Mandola 3717/a; ⊙11am-8pm

SEEING VENICE WITH AN ARTIST'S EYE

Wandering through sun drenched *campi* and over glassy canals, it's easy to see why Venice has inspired an endless stream of artists. From Veronese and Tiepolo to Canaletto, Turner and Monet, each tried to capture the elusive quality of the city's light-filled beauty and psychedelic colour palette, and many of their efforts are crammed in the museums, *palazzi* (mansions) and galleries of San Marco. Why not join them and try your hand at painting or photographing the city light with the experts?

Painting In Venice (☑340 544 52 27; www.paintinginvenice.com; 3-hour private lesson €90, 2-/4-day workshop €250/580) Sign up for a session with professionally trained and practising artists Caroline, Sebastian and Katrin and you'll strike out into tranquil *campi* in the tradition of classic Venetian *vedutisti* (outdoor artists). Beginners learn the basic concepts of painting 'en plein air', while those with more advanced skills receive tailormade tuition. It's a great way to slow down and really appreciate the colour and composition of each view. Materials can be provided at an extra cost and are yours to keep after the course. Lessons are offered in English, Italian, French and German.

Venice Photo Walk (☑041 963 73 74; www.msecchi.com; 2-/3-/6-hr walking tour for up to 4 people €210/300/600) Throughout San Marco you'll be tripping over iPhone touting tourists waving selfie sticks. Everyone, it seems, wants to capture the perfect Venetian scene. Getty photojournalist, Marco Secchi, will show you how. When he's not on a global assignment, he's happy to walk you around the secret corners of the city in a friendly, in-depth tutorial, showing you how to really capture the nuances of light and helping you to frame that masterpiece for the mantle. He can work with all types of cameras, tailors tours to personal interests and can arrange boat tours.

Mon-Sat; ☀Rialto) Booty worthy of pirates is displayed in this fishbowl-size window display: a constellation of diamonds in star settings on a ring, a tiny enamelled green snake sinking its fangs into a pearl, and diamond drop earrings that end in enamelled gold skulls. Though they look like heirlooms, these small wonders were worked on the premises by master jeweller Sigfrido.

FIORELLA GALLERY FASHION

Map p268 (☑041 520 92 28; www.fiorellagallery.com; Campo Santo Stefano 2806; ☺9.30am-1.30pm & 3.30-7pm Tue-Sat, 3-7pm Mon; ☀Accademia) Groupies are the only accessory needed to go with Fiorella's silk-velvet smoking jackets in louche lavender and oxblood, printed by hand with skulls, peacocks or a Fiorella signature: wide-eyed rats. Shock frock coats starting in the mid-three figures make Alexander McQueen seem retro – Fiorella's been pioneering rebel couture since 1968. Hours are approximate; as the sign says, 'we open sometime'.

ANTICA MODISTERIA
GIULIANA LONGO HATS

Map p268 (☑041 522 64 54; www.giulianalongo.com; Calle del Lovo 4813; ☀Rialto) Giuliana's shop is the dream hat-cupboard of any true sartorialist. Styles range from hand-woven

Montecristi panama hats – as modelled by client Sean Connery – to a fuchsia felt number that looks like a doge's cap for Peggy Guggenheim. Giuliana is here most days, polishing leather aviator hats or affixing a broad band to a *baretero,* the wide-brimmed gondolier's hat best worn with a rakish tilt (from €45).

L'ISOLA GLASS

Map p268 (☑041 523 19 73; www.lisola.com; Calle de la Botteghe 2970; ☺10.30am-2pm & 3-7.30pm Mon-Sat; ☀Vallaresso, San Marco) Backlit chalices and spotlit vases emit an otherworldly glow at this shrine to Murano modernist glass master, Carlo Moretti. Strict shapes contain freeform swirls of orange and red, and glasses etched with fish-scale patterns add a wink to high-minded modernism. Prices for signature water glasses start at €98.

LE BURLE VENEZIANE JEWELLERY

Map p268 (☑041 522 21 50; www.leburleveneziane.com; Piscina San Samuele 3436; ☺10.30am-7.30pm; ☀San Samuele) The window of Monica Burcovich's shop-cum-studio is filled with feminine treasures: silk bags trimmed with vintage seed beads, feathered fascinators and necklaces fashioned from the tiniest strands of microbeads, crystals and pearls. Some chokers are so finely wrought they look like sparkling pieces of lace. Monica works in the studio so you can see just how painstaking the creative process is.

MALEFATTE — ACCESSORIES

Map p268 (www.rioteradeipensieri.org; Campo Santo Stefano kiosk; ⊙2-7pm Mon-Sat Feb-Dec; 🚤Accademia) 🢩 'Misdeeds' is the name of this nonprofit initiative by and for incarcerated workers, but its pop-art man-bags made from recycled-vinyl museum banners are clever indeed. T-shirts showing *acqua alta* measurements and aprons silk screened with the *spritz* recipe are souvenirs with a difference. All proceeds support training and transitions from jail on Giudecca to new lives and productive careers in Venice.

OTTICA CARRARO — ACCESSORIES

Map p268 (☎041 520 42 58; www.otticacarraro.it; Calle della Mandola 3706; ⊙9.30am-1pm & 3-7.30pm Mon-Sat; 🚤Sant'Angelo) Lost your sunglasses on the Lido? Never fear: Ottica Carraro can make you a custom pair within 24 hours, including the eye exam. The store has its own limited-edition 'Venice' line, ranging from cat-eye shades perfect for facing paparazzi to chunky wood-grain frames that could get you mistaken for an art critic at the Biennale.

GODI FIORENZA — FASHION

Map p268 (☎041 241 08 66; Rio Tera San Paternian 4261; ⊙9.30am-6.30pm Mon-Sat; 🚤Rialto) Impeccably tailored midnight-blue silk-satin dresses with exuberant woolly shoulders showcase the Savile Row skills of sisters Patrizia and Samanta Fiorenza, but also their vivid imaginations. Evening dresses come embellished with tiny Murano glass beads, pearls or antique lace and they also do a line of jewellery in gold, brass and copper. They specialise in couture at off-the-rack prices. For under €100, hand-beaded antique-lace collars add turn-of-the-century elegance to modern minimalism.

ARCOBALENO — ART SUPPLIES

Map p268 (☎041 523 68 18; Calle delle Botteghe 3457; ⊙9.30am-1.30pm & 3-7pm Mon-Sat; 🚤Accademia) After seeing umpteen Venetian art masterpieces, anyone's fingers will start twitching for a paint brush. Arcobaleno provides all the raw materials needed to start your own Venetian art movement, with shelves fully stocked with jars of all the essential pigments: Titian red, Tiepolo sky-blue, Veronese rose, Bellini peach and Tintoretto teal.

DANIELA GHEZZO — SHOES

Map p268 (☎041 522 21 15; www.danielaghezzo.it; Calle dei Fuseri 4365; ⊙10am-1pm & 3-7pm Mon-Fri, 10am-1pm Sat; 🚤Vallaresso) A gold chain pulled across this historic atelier doorway means Daniela is already consulting with a client, discussing rare leathers while taking foot measurements. Maestra Ghezzo custom makes every pair, so you'll never see your emerald ostrich-leather boots on another diva, or your dimpled manta-ray brogues on a rival mogul. Each pair costs €700 to €1100 and takes about six weeks for delivery.

ARNOLDO & BATTOIS — FASHION, ACCESSORIES

Map p268 (☎041 528 59 44; www.arnoldoebattois.com; Calle dei Fuseri 4271; ⊙10am-1pm & 3.30-7pm Mon-Thu & Sat; 🚤Rialto) Handbags become heirlooms in the hands of Venetian designers Massimiliano Battois and Silvano Arnoldo, whose handcrafted clutches come in bold, buttery turquoise and magenta leather with baroque closures in laser-cut wood. Artfully draped emerald and graphite silk dresses complete the look for Biennale openings.

VENETIA STUDIUM — ACCESSORIES, FASHION

Map p268 (☎041 523 69 53; www.venetiastudium.com; Palazzo Zuccato 2425; ⊙10am-7.40pm Mon-Sat, 10.30am-6.30pm Sun; 🚤Santa Maria del Giglio) Get that 'just got in from Monaco for my art opening' look beloved of bohemians who marry well. The high-drama Delphos tunic dresses make anyone look like a high-maintenance modern dancer or heiress (Isadora Duncan and Peggy Guggenheim were both fans), and the hand-stamped silk-velvet bags are more arty than ostentatious (prices from €60).

CAIGO DA MAR — HOMEWARES

Map p268 (☎041 243 32 38; www.caigodamar.com; Calle delle Botteghe 3131; ⊙11am-1pm & 4-7pm Mon-Fri, 11am-7pm Sat; 🚤San Samuele) Venetian pirates once headed to Constantinople for all their interior-decoration needs, but today they'd need look no further than Caigo da Mar. This tiny treasure trove brims with dramatic black Murano glass candelabras and a designer booty of Fornasetti cushions, plus enough octopus-shaped lamps and nautilus-shell dishes to make any living room look like the lost city of Atlantis.

VENETIAN DREAMS — ACCESSORIES

Map p268 (☎041 523 02 92; http://venetiandreams.altervista.org; Calle della Mandola

3805a; ⊙11am-6.30pm Wed-Mon; ⊠Sant'Angelo) High fashion meets *acqua alta* in Marisa Convento's aquatic accessories. La Fenice divas demand her freshwater pearl–encrusted velvet handbags, while Biennale artistes snap up octopus-tentacle glass-bead necklaces. Between customers, Marisa can be glimpsed at her desk, painstakingly weaving coral-branch collars from antique Murano *conterie* (seed beads). To wow Carnevale crowds, ask about custom costume orders.

GALLERIA LA SALIZADA GALLERY

Map p268 (⊠041 241 07 23; www.lasalizada.it; Calle de la Botteghe 3448; ⊙10am-1pm & 3.30-7.30pm Tue-Sat, 3.30-7.30pm Mon; ⊠Santa Maria del Giglio) Showcases rare vintage prints of Venice from the Fratelli Alinari photographic archives alongside the work of practising photographic greats such as Elio Ciol and Luisa Menazzi Moretti. Smaller prints are affordable and make wonderful keepsakes.

ESPERIENZE GLASS, JEWELLERY

Map p268 (⊠041 521 29 45; www.esperienze venezia.com; Calle degli Specchieri 473b; ⊙10am-noon & 3-7pm; ⊠San Marco) When an Italian minimalist falls in love with a Murano glassblower, the result is spare, spirited glass jewellery. Esperienze is a collaborative effort for husband–wife team Graziano and Sara: he breathes life into her designs, including matte-glass teardrop pendants and cracked-ice earrings. Their mutual admiration for Guggenheim Collection modernists shows in colourful necklaces that resemble Calder mobiles and Kandinsky paintings.

LE BOTTEGHE
DELLA SOLIDARIETÀ GIFTS, HOMEWARES

Map p268 (⊠041 522 75 45; www.coopfilo.it; Salizada Pio X 5164; ⊙10am-7pm Mon-Sat; ⊠Rialto) Italian design sensibilities meet Venetian trading smarts at this fair-trade boutique on the steps of the Rialto. Gondola rides call for straw hats woven by a Bangladeshi collective and refreshing Libera Terra wine from vineyards reclaimed from the Mafia, while kids are placated by organic chocolate and recycled cans fashioned into toy Vespas.

LIBRERIA STUDIUM BOOKS

Map p268 (⊠041 522 23 82; Calle di Canonica 337; ⊙9am-7.30pm Mon-Sat, 9.30am-1.30pm & 2-6pm Sun; ⊠San Zaccaria) Consult bibliophile staff for worthy vacation reads, page-turning Venetian history or top picks from shelves groaning under the weight of Italian cookbooks. Many titles are available in English and French, and there's a respectably vast Lonely Planet section (not that we're biased). Don't miss conversation-starting 'Eye on Venice' pamphlets addressing current Venetian issues, from lagoon aquaculture to palace preservation.

MATERIALMENTE JEWELLERY, HOMEWARES

Map p268 (⊠041 528 68 81; www.material mente.it; Mercerie San Salvador 4850; ⊙10am-7pm Mon-Sat; ⊠Rialto) Prolific sibling artisans Maddelena Venier and Alessandro Salvadori pack their tiny boutique with modern Venetian luxuries, casting skull signet rings, hand-silkcreening mirrors with baroque ballgown patterns, and weaving fish-skeleton chandeliers from wire. It also stocks whimsical, affordable works by young Italian designers, including free-form porcelain earrings and anime-inspired mobiles.

CHARTA BOOKS

Map p268 (⊠041 522 98 01; www.chartaonline. com; 831 Calle del Fabbri; ⊙10am-12:30pm & 4-7.30pm; ⊠Vallaresso) Even pulp fiction becomes high art at Charta, where favourite books are custom bound. *Twilight* has vampire bitemarks, Dostoyevsky's *Brothers Karamozov* is emblazoned with three brothers joined at the beard, and a manual of Freemason's rites is enshrined in a gilt temple. Limited editions start around €30, while customised antique books run €150 to €850.

CAMUFFO GLASS

Map p268 (Calle delle Acque 4992; ⊙10am-12:30pm & 1-5pm Mon-Sat; ⊠Rialto) Kids, entomologists and glass collectors seek out Signor Camuffo in this cabinet of miniature natural wonders. Expect to find him wielding a blowtorch as he fuses metallic foils and molten glass into shimmering wings for the city's finest lampworked glass beetles and dragonflies. Between bugs, he'll chat about his work and sell you strands of Murano glass beads at excellent prices.

PAGINE E CUOIO ACCESSORIES

Map p268 (⊠041 528 65 55; Calle del Fruttariol 1845; ⊙9.30am-7pm Mon-Sat; ⊠Santa Maria del Giglio) The lion of San Marco looks fashionably fierce embossed upon a turquoise billfold by leather artisan Davide Desanzuane. Unexpected colours update Venetian heraldry for the 21st century on Davide's tablet cases, smartphone carriers and business-card holders – and since they're all one of a kind, they make singular fashion statements.

Dorsoduro

Neighbourhood Top Five

1 Getting a crash course in Venetian painting at **Gallerie dell'Accademia** (p73), a former convent now positively blushing with masterpieces of glowing colours, censored subjects, prime-time drama and breathless elegance.

2 Schmoozing with Picasso, Pollock, Giacometti and Kapoor at the former Grand Canal pad of an American heiress at **Peggy Guggenheim Collection** (p75).

3 Waltzing through baroque palace boudoirs filled with social graces and sharp wits at **Ca' Rezzonico** (p76).

4 Comparing, contrasting and debating fearless contemporary art and boldly repurposed architecture at **Punta della Dogana** (p78).

5 Testing the curative powers of Longhena's mystical marbles and finding hidden Titian wonders inside **Basilica di Santa Maria della Salute** (p76).

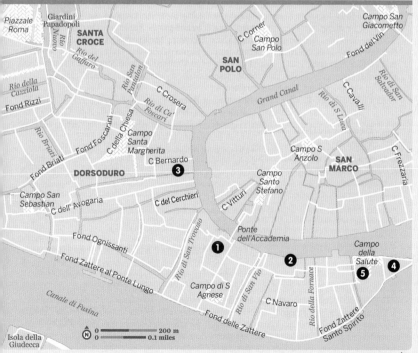

For more detail of this area see Map p272 and p273 ➡

Lonely Planet's Top Tip

New in town? Save a couple of euro on admission to the Peggy Guggenheim Collection by bringing your Trenitalia Freccia train or Alitalia airline ticket to the museum. Don't dawdle: the offer is good for new arrivals with train tickets no more than three days old, and Alitalia airline passengers with tickets up to seven days old.

Best Places to Eat

→ Ristorante La Bitta (p79)
→ Enoteca Ai Artisti (p80)
→ Al Vecio Marangon (p79)
→ Grom (p79)

For reviews, see p79. ➡

Best Places to Drink

→ Cantinone Giá Schiavi (p80)
→ Estro (p81)
→ Il Caffè Rosso (p81)
→ Ai Pugni (p81)

For reviews, see p80. ➡

Best Venetian Views

→ *Feast in the House of Levi*, Gallerie dell'Accademia (p73)
→ Grand Canal alongside *Angel of the City*, Peggy Guggenheim Collection (p75)
→ Ando's water-gate windows, Punta della Dogana (p78)
→ Vedutisti Gallery, Ca' Rezzonico (p76)

For reviews, see p73. ➡

TOP SIGHT
GALLERIE DELL'ACCADEMIA

Hardly academic, these galleries contain more murderous intrigue, forbidden romance and shameless politicking than the most outrageous Venetian parties. The former Santa Maria della Carità convent complex maintained its serene composure for centuries, but ever since Napoleon installed his haul of Venetian art trophies in 1807, there's been nonstop visual drama inside these walls.

Rooms 1–5

The grand gallery you enter upstairs features vivid early works that show Venice's precocious flair for colour and drama. Case in point: Jacobello Alberegno's late-14th-century *Apocalypse* (Room 1) shows the whore of Babylon riding a hydra, babbling rivers of blood from her mouth. In the same room but at the opposite end of the emotional spectrum is Paolo Veneziano's 1553–59 *Coronation of Mary*, where Jesus bestows the crown on his mother with a gentle pat on the head to the tune of an angelic orchestra.

UFO arrivals seem imminent in the eerie, glowing skies of Carpaccio's lively *Crucifixion and Glorification of the Ten Thousand Martyrs of Mount Ararat* (Room 2). But Giovanni Bellini's *Pala di San Giobbe* shows hope on the horizon, in the form of a sweet-faced Madonna and Child emerging from a dark niche as angels play their instruments. The martyrs surrounding them include St Roch and St Sebastian, suggesting that this luminous, uplifting work dates from the dark days of Venice's second plague in 1478.

Lock eyes with fascinating strangers across portrait-filled Room 4. Hans Memling captures youthful stubble and angst with the exacting detail of a Freudian miniaturist in *Portrait of a Young Man*, while Giorgione's sad-eyed *La Vecchia* (Old Woman) points to herself as the words 'with time' unfurl ominously by her arm. Trumping them both, however, is Giovanni Bellini's sublimely elegant *Madonna and Child between St Catherine and Mary Magdalene*.

Rooms 6–11

Venice's Renaissance awaits in Room 6, where you'll find Titian and Tintoretto. The latter's *Creation of the Animals* is a fantastical bestiary suggesting God put forth his best efforts inventing Venetian seafood (no argument here).

In Room 10, Tintoretto's 1562 *St Mark Rescues a Saracen* is an action-packed blockbuster, with fearless Venetian merchants and an improbably muscular, long-armed saint rescuing a turbaned sailor. In the same room, Titian's 1576 *Pietà* was possibly finished posthumously by Palma il Giovane, but notice the smears of paint Titian applied with his bare hands and the column-base self-portrait, foreshadowing Titian's own funeral monument.

Artistic triumph over censorship underlines Paolo Veronese's monumental *Feast in the House of Levi*, originally called *Last Supper* until Inquisition leaders condemned him for showing dogs, drunkards, dwarves, Muslims and Reformation-minded Germans cavorting with Apostles. He refused to change a thing, besides the title, and Venice stood by this act of defiance against Rome. Follow the exchanges, gestures and eye contact among the characters, and you'll concede that not one Turkish trader, clumsy server, gambler or bright-eyed lapdog could have been painted over without losing an essential piece of the Venetian puzzle.

DON'T MISS...

➡ Veronese's *Feast in the House of Levi*

➡ Titian's *Presentation of the Virgin*

➡ Tintoretto's *Creation of the Animals*

➡ Bellini's *Miracle of the True Cross*

➡ Sala dell'Albergo

PRACTICALITIES

➡ Map p272, E3

➡ ☎041 520 03 45

➡ www.gallerie accademia.org

➡ Campo della Carità 1050

➡ adult/reduced €11/8 plus supplement during special exhibitions, first Sun of the month free

➡ ⏱8.15am-2pm Mon, to 7.15pm Tue-Sun

➡ 🚤Accademia

SKIP THE QUEUES & SAVE

....

To skip ahead of the Accademia queue in high season, book tickets in advance by calling ☎041 520 03 45 (booking fee €1). Otherwise, queues tend to be shorter in the afternoon. The last entry is 45 minutes before closing, and proper visits take at least 90 minutes. The gallery audio guide (€6) is mostly descriptive and largely unnecessary – better to avoid the wait and just follow the explanatory wall tags. Bags larger than 20x30x15cm need to be stored in the lockers, which require a refundable €1 coin.

....

The Accademia represents Venice's single most important art collection – and the work of several of its finest architects. Bartolomeo Bon completed the spare, Gothic-edged Santa Maria della Carità facade in 1448. A century later in 1561, Palladio took a classical approach to the Convento dei Canonici Lateranensi, which was absorbed into the Accademia. From 1949 to 1954, modernist Carlo Scarpa chose a minimalist approach to restorations, taking care not to upset the delicate symmetries achieved between architects over the centuries.

TOP SIGHT
PEGGY GUGGENHEIM COLLECTION

After tragically losing her father on the *Titanic*, heiress **Peggy Guggenheim** befriended Dadaists, dodged Nazis and changed art history at her palatial home on the Grand Canal. Peggy's Palazzo Venier dei Leoni is a showcase for surrealism, futurism and abstract expressionism by some 200 breakthrough modern artists, including Peggy's ex-husband Max Ernst and Jackson Pollock (among her many rumoured lovers).

Collection

Peggy collected according to her own convictions rather than for prestige or style, so her collection includes inspired folk art and lesser-known artists alongside Kandinsky, Picasso, Magritte, Man Ray, Rothko, Mondrian, Joseph Cornell and Dalí. Major modernists also contributed custom interior decor, including the Calder silver bedstead hanging in the former bedroom. In the corners of the main galleries, you'll find photos of the rooms as they appeared when Peggy lived here, in fabulously eccentric style.

For this champion of modern art who'd witnessed the dangers of censorship and party-line dictates, serious artwork deserved to be seen and judged on its merits. The Jewish American collector narrowly escaped Paris two days before the Nazis marched into the city, and arrived in Venice in 1948 to find the city's historically buoyant spirits broken by war. More than a mere tastemaker, Peggy became a spirited advocate for contemporary Italian art, which had largely gone out of favour with the rise of Mussolini and the partisan politics of WWII.

Peggy sparked renewed interest in postwar Italian art and resurrected the reputation of key Italian Futurists, whose dynamic style had been co-opted to make Fascism more visually palatable. Her support led to reappraisals of Umberto Boccioni, Giorgio Morandi, Giacomo Balla, Giuseppe Capogrossi and Giorgio de Chirico, and aided Venice's own Emilio Vedova and Giuseppe Santomaso. Never afraid to make a splash, Peggy gave passing gondoliers an eyeful on her Grand Canal quay: Marino Marini's 1948 *Angel of the City*, a bronze male nude on horseback, is visibly excited by the possibilities on the horizon.

Garden & Pavilion

The Palazzo Venier dei Leoni was never finished, but that didn't stop Peggy Guggenheim from filling every available space indoors and out with art. Wander past bronzes by Moore, Giacometti and Brancusci, Yoko Ono's *Wish Tree*, as well as intriguing granite creations by Anish Kapoor and Isamu Noguchi in the **sculpture garden**. The city of Venice granted Peggy an honorary dispensation to be buried beneath the Giacometti sculptures and alongside her dearly departed lapdogs in 1979. Through the gardens is a **pavilion** housing a sunny cafe, a bookshop, bathrooms, and temporary exhibits highlighting underappreciated modernist rebels. Around the corner from the museum, on Fondamenta Venier dei Leoni, is a larger **museum shop**, selling art books in several languages and replicas of Peggy's signature glasses – winged, like the lion of San Marco.

DON'T MISS...

→ Rotating permanent collection
→ Calder silver bedstead
→ *Angel of the City*
→ Sculpture garden
→ Temporary pavilion shows

PRACTICALITIES

→ Map p272, F3
→ ☎041 240 54 11
→ www.guggenheim-venice.it
→ Palazzo Venier dei Leoni 704
→ adult/reduced €15/9
→ ⏰10am-6pm Wed-Mon
→ 🚤Accademia

⊙ SIGHTS

GALLERIE DELL'ACCADEMIA GALLERY
See p73.

PEGGY GUGGENHEIM COLLECTION MUSEUM
See p75.

CA' DARIO PALACE
Map p272 (Ramo Ca' Dario 352; ⚐Salute) Grand Canal palaces rank among the world's most desirable real estate, and multi-coloured marble Gothic marvel Ca' Dario casts a mesmerising reflection painted by no less than Claude Monet – but there's a catch. Starting with the daughter of its original owner, Giovanni Dario, an unusual number of Ca' Dario occupants have met untimely deaths. According to local legend, the palace is associated with at least seven deaths; gossips claim this effectively dissuaded Woody Allen from buying it in the 1990s.

The former manager of The Who, Kit Lambert, moved out after complaining of being hounded by the palace's ghosts, and was found dead shortly after. One week after renting the place for a holiday in 2002, The Who's bass player, John Entwhistle, died of a heart attack.

★BASILICA DI SANTA MARIA DELLA SALUTE BASILICA
Map p272 (La Salute; ☎041 241 10 18; www.seminariovenezia.it; Campo della Salute 1b; admission free, sacristy adult/reduced €3/1.50; ☺9am-noon & 3-5.30pm; ⚐Salute) Guarding the entrance to the Grand Canal, this 17th-century domed church was commissioned by Venice's plague survivors as thanks for their salvation. Baldassare Longhena's uplifting design is an engineering feat that defies simple logic; in fact the church is said to have mystical curative properties. Titian eluded the plague until age 94, leaving 12 key paintings in the basilica's art-slung sacristy.

Longhena's marvel makes good on an official appeal by the Venetian Senate directly to the Madonna in 1630, after 80,000 Venetians had been killed by plague brought in by a carpenter working on Venice's quarantine island, the Lazzaretto Vecchio. The Senate promised the Madonna a church in exchange for her intervention on behalf of Venice – no expense or effort spared. Before 'La Salute' could even be started, at least 100,000 pylons had to be driven deep into the *barene* (mud banks) to shore up the tip of Dorsoduro.

⊙ TOP SIGHT
CA' REZZONICO

Baroque dreams come true at Baldassare Longhena's Grand Canal palace, also known as the Museum of the 18th Century. Giambattista Tiepolo's **Throne Room ceiling** is a masterpiece of elegant social climbing, showing gorgeous Merit ascending to the Temple of Glory clutching the Golden Book of Venetian nobles' names – including Tiepolo's patrons, the Rezzonico family.

In the **Pietro Longhi Salon**, sweeping Grand Canal views are upstaged by the artist's winsome satires of society antics observed by disapproving lapdogs. **Sala Rosalba Carriera** features Carriera's wry, unvarnished pastel portraits of socialites who aren't conventionally pretty but look like they'd be the life of any party. Giandomenico Tiepolo's swinging court jesters and preening parrots add cheeky humour to the reassembled **Zianigo Villa frescoes.**

On the top floor, don't miss Emma Ciardi's moody Venice canal views in the Vedutisti Gallery (Gallery Nine), and an **antique pharmacy** with 183 majolica ceramic jars of 18th-century remedies.

DON'T MISS...
➡ *Trompe l'œil* ceilings
➡ Pietro Longhi Salon
➡ Sala Rosalba Carriera
➡ Emma Ciardi's Venice paintings
➡ Antique pharmacy

PRACTICALITIES
➡ Map p272, E2
➡ ☎041 241 01 00
➡ www.visitmuve.it
➡ Fondamenta Rezzonico 3136
➡ adult/reduced €10.50/8
➡ ☺10am-6pm Wed-Mon summer, to 5pm winter
➡ ⚐Ca' Rezzonico

The Madonna provided essential inspiration, but La Salute draws its structural strength from a range of architectural and spiritual traditions. Architectural scholars note striking similarities between Longhena's unusual domed octagon structure and both Greco-Roman goddess temples and Jewish Kabbalah diagrams. The lines of the building ingeniously converge beneath the dome to form a vortex on the inlaid marble floors, and the black dot at the centre is said to radiate healing energy.

The sacristy is a wonder within a wonder, its glorious collection of Titian masterpieces including a vivid self-portrait in the guise of St Matthew and his earliest known work from 1510, *Saint Mark on the Throne.* Salute's most charming allegory for Venice's miraculous survival from plague is Palma Il Giovane's painting of Jonah emerging from the mouth of the whale, where the survivor stomps down the sea creature's tongue like an action hero walking the red carpet. Life in a time of plague is a miracle worth celebrating in Tintoretto's upbeat 1561 *Wedding Feast of Cana,* featuring a Venetian throng of multi-culti musicians, busy wine pourers, and Tintoretto himself in the pink, gently schooling a young, thin-bearded Paolo Veronese.

MAGAZZINI DEL SALE   ART GALLERY

Map p272 (⌨041 522 66 26; www.fondazionevedova.org; Fondamenta delle Zattere 266; adult/reduced €8/6; ⊙during shows 10.30am-6pm Wed-Mon; ⚓Zattere) A retrofit designed by Pritzker Prize–winning architect Renzo Piano transformed Venice's historic **salt warehouses** into **Fondazione Vedova** art galleries, commemorating pioneering Venetian abstract painter Emilio Vedova. Fondazione Vedova shows are often literally moving and rotating: powered by renewable energy sources, 10 robotic arms designed by Vedova and Piano move major modern artworks in and out of storage slots.

Although the facade is a neoclassical job from the 1830s, these nine salt warehouses were established in the 14th century, when the all-important salt monopoly made Venice's fortune. Before fridges and electricity, the only way to preserve foodstuffs was to cure or pack them in salt – and since preserved foods were essential for ocean voyages, salt was crucial to maritime commerce. By controlling the salt trade, Venice effectively controlled the seas for centuries.

SACRED MUSIC AT SALUTE

If you think the Longhena-designed dome of the **Basilica di Santa Maria della Salute** looks magnificent, wait until you hear how it sounds. Weekdays at 3.30pm, vespers are played on the basilica's original 1782–83 organ. These musical interludes are free, and the acoustics are nothing short of celestial.

Today's creatively repurposed salt warehouses are only fitting, now that Venice's most precious commodity is art, not salt. Neighbouring **Spazio Vedova** (at Zattere 50) includes a public art and performance space.

CHIESA DEI GESUATI   CHURCH

Map p272 (Church of Santa Maria del Rosario; www.chorusvenezia.org; Fondamenta delle Zattere 918; admission €3, or with Chorus Pass free; ⊙10am-5pm Mon-Sat; ⚓Zattere) That Tiepolo's 1737–39 ceiling frescoes star St Dominic is hardly surprising given that this baroque church – designed by Giorgio Massari and completed in 1735 – was built for the Dominicans. Overwhelming grief grips Mary in Tintoretto's sombre 1565 *Crucifixion,* a painting subsequently restored by Giambattista Piazzetta. Altogether lighter is Sebastiano Ricci's 1730–33 *Saints Peter and Thomas with Pope Pius V,* complete with comical cherubs performing celestial tumbling routines.

CHIESA DI SAN SEBASTIANO   CHURCH

Map p272 (www.chorusvenezia.org; Campo San Sebastiano 1687; admission €3, or with Chorus Pass free; ⊙10am-5pm Mon-Sat; ⚓San Basilio) Antonio Scarpignano's relatively austere 1508–48 facade creates a sense of false modesty at this neighbourhood church in Dorsoduro. Currently undergoing restoration, the interior is adorned with floor-to-ceiling masterpieces by Paolo Veronese, executed over three decades. According to popular local legend, Veronese found sanctuary at San Sebastiano in 1555 after fleeing murder charges in Verona, and his works in this church deliver lavish thanks to the parish and an especially brilliant poke in the eye of his accusers.

Veronese's virtuosity is everywhere here, from the horses rearing on the coffered ceiling to organ doors covered with his *Presentation of the Virgin.* In Veronese's *Martyrdom of Saint Sebastian* near the altar, the bound saint defiantly stares down his tormentors amid a Venetian crowd of socialites, turbaned traders and Veronese's signature frisky spaniel. St Sebastian was the fearless patron saint of Venice's plague victims, and Veronese suggests that, though sticks and stones may break his bones, Venetian gossip couldn't kill him.

Pay respects to Veronese, who chose to be buried here beneath his masterpieces – his memorial plaque is to the right of the organ – but don't miss Titian's 1563 *San Nicolò* to the right of the entry. Peek into the **sacristy** to glimpse Veronese's glowing 1555 *Coronation of the Virgin* on the ceiling.

**SCUOLA GRANDE
DEI CARMINI**   HISTORIC BUILDING
Map p272 (☑041 528 94 20; www.scuolagrande
carmini.it; Campo Santa Margherita 2617; adult/
reduced €5/4; ☉11am-4pm; ☒Ca' Rezzonico)

Eighteenth-century backpackers must have thought they'd died and gone to heaven at Scuola Grande dei Carmini, with its lavish interiors by Giambattista Tiepolo and Baldassare Longhena. The gold-leafed, Longhena-designed stucco **stairway to heaven**, glimpsed upstairs in Tiepolo's **nine-panel ceiling** of a rosy *Virgin in Glory.* The adjoining hostel room is bedecked in *boiserie* (wood carving).

This *scuola* (confraternity) was the first formed by women in the 13th century. It was also Venice's first known order of Battuti (Flagellants), who practiced self-mortification with a wooden rod – a practice that has since been discredited. The Carmini continued to extend hospitality to destitute and wayward travellers from the 13th century right through to the time of Napoleon's occupation of Venice. Sadly, cots are no longer available in this jewel-box building, but evening concerts are held here, and members of the Carmini continue to organise charitable works to this day.

TOP SIGHT
PUNTA DELLA DOGANA

Fortuna, the weathervane atop Punta della Dogana, swung Venice's way in 2005, when bureaucratic hassles in Paris convinced art collector François Pinault to showcase his works in Venice's long-abandoned customs warehouses.

Built by Giuseppe Benoni in 1677 to ensure that no ship entered the Grand Canal without paying duties, the warehouses re-opened in 2009 after a striking reinvention by Tadao Ando. Inside, the Japanese architect stripped back centuries of alterations, returning the interior to its pure form of red brick and wooden beams. Within this pared-back space, Ando added his own contemporary vision, cutting windows in Benoni's ancient water gates to reveal views of passing ships, adding floating concrete staircases in honour of innovative Venetian modernist Carlo Scarpa, and erecting his own trademark polished concrete panels.

The end result is a conscious and dramatic juxtaposition of the old and the new, one that simultaneously pays due to the city's seafaring history and its changing architecture, and one which provides a suitable scale and mood for Pinault's rotating exhibitions of ambitious, large-scale contemporary artworks from some of the world's most prolific and provocative creative minds.

DON'T MISS...

➡ Fortuna
➡ Tadao Ando interiors
➡ Rotating art installations
➡ Quayside sculpture displays

PRACTICALITIES

➡ Map p272, H3
➡ ☑041 271 90 39
➡ www.palazzograssi.it
➡ adult/reduced €15/10, incl Palazzo Grassi €20/15
➡ ☉10am-7pm Wed-Mon
➡ ☒Salute

EATING

BAR ALLA TOLETTA
SANDWICHES €

Map p272 (☑041 520 01 96; Calle la Toletta 1192; sandwiches €1.60-5; ☺7am-8pm; ☑☻; ☻Ca' Rezzonico) Midway through museum crawls from Accademia to Ca' Rezzonico, Bar Toletta satisfies starving artists with lip-smacking, grilled-to-order *panini*, including *prosciutto crudo* (cured ham), rocket and mozzarella, and daily vegetarian options. *Tramezzini* (triangular stacked sandwiches) are tasty, too. Get yours to go, or grab a seat for around a €1 more.

PIZZA AL VOLO
PIZZA €

Map p272 (☑041 522 54 30; Campo Santa Margherita 2944; pizza slices €2, small pizzas €4-7; ☺11am-2am; ☻; ☻Ca' Rezzonico) Peckish night owls run out of options fast in Venice once restaurants close their kitchens around 10.30pm – but slices here are cheap and tasty, with a thin yet sturdy crust that won't collapse on your bar-hopping outfit.

PASTICCERIA TONOLO
PASTRIES €

Map p272 (☑041 532 72 09; Calle dei Preti 3764; pastries €1-4; ☺7.45am-8pm Tue-Sat, 8am-1pm Sun, closed Sun Jul; ☻Ca' Rezzonico) Long, skinny Tonolo is the stuff of local legend, a fact confirmed by the never-ending queue of customers. Ditch packaged B&B croissants for flaky *apfelstrudel* (apple pastry), velvety *bignè al zabaione* (marsala cream pastry) and oozing *pain au chocolat* (chocolate croissants). Devour one at the bar with a bracing espresso, then bag another for the road.

GROM
GELATERIA €

Map p272 (☑041 099 17 51; www.grom.it; Campo San Barnaba 2461; gelati €2.50-5.50; ☺10.30am-11pm Sun-Thu, 10am-12.30am Fri & Sat, shorter hours winter; ☻Ca' Rezzonico) At Grom, gorgeous, fresh gelato is made using top-notch ingredients like Amalfi Coast lemons and Piedmontese hazelnuts. Seasonal flavours range from chestnut cream to apricot sorbet, with liquid treats including luscious hot chocolate. You'll find other branches in San Polo (Campo dei Frari 3006), Cannaregio (Strada Nova 3844) and at Stazione di Santa Lucia (train station).

★RISTORANTE LA BITTA
RISTORANTE €€

Map p272 (☑041 523 05 31; Calle Lunga San Barnaba 2753a; meals €35-40; ☺6.45-10.45pm Mon-Sat; ☻Ca' Rezzonico) Recalling a cosy, woody bistro, La Bitta keeps punters purring with

hearty rustic fare made using the freshest ingredients – the fact that the kitchen has no freezer ensures this. Scan the daily menu for mouthwatering, seasonal options like tagliatelle with artichoke thistle and gorgonzola or juicy pork *salsiccette* (small sausages) served with *verze* (local cabbage) and warming polenta. Reservations essential. Cash only.

RISTOTECA ONIGA
VENETIAN €€

Map p272 (☑041 522 44 10; www.oniga.it; Campo San Barnaba 2852; meals €19-35; ☺noon-2.30pm & 7-10.30pm Wed-Mon; ☻; ☻Ca' Rezzonico) ✐ Its menu peppered with organic ingredients, Oniga serves exemplary *sarde in saor* (sardines in tangy onion marinade), seasonal pastas, and the odd Hungarian classic like goulash (a nod to former chef Annika Major). Oenophiles will appreciate the selection of 100+ wines, handy for toasting to the €19 set lunch menu. Grab a sunny spot in the *campo*, or get cosy in a wood-panelled corner.

★AL VECIO MARANGON
VENETIAN €€

Map p272 (☑041 523 57 68; Calle Toletta; meals €30; ☺noon-10.30pm; ☻Ca' Rezzonico) It may sit on a backstreet, but snug Al Vecio Marangon is one of Dorsoduro's worst-kept secrets. Head in early or book ahead for one of the handful of tables, then tackle the *piatto di cicheti misti*, a generous tasting plate of succulent morsels like *baccala mantecato* (whipped codfish and olive oil), warming *polpette* (meatballs) and grilled vegetables.

AI QUATTRO FERI
VENETIAN €€

Map p272 (☑041 520 69 78; Calle Lunga San Barnaba 2754a; meals €35; ☺12.30-2.30pm & 7-10.30pm Mon-Sat; ☻Ca' Rezzonico) Adorned with artworks by some well-known creative fans, this honest, good-humoured *osteria* (casual tavern) is well known for its simple, classic seafood dishes like al dente *spaghetti con seppie* (with cuttlefish), grilled *orata* (sea bream) and tender calamari. Post-meal coffees are made using a traditional Italian percolator. No credit cards.

IMPRONTA CAFÉ ITALIAN €€
Map p272 (☑041 275 03 86; www.impronta cafevenice.com; Calle Crosera 3815; meals €34; ☺7am-1am Mon-Fri, 8am-1pm Sat; ☻; ☒San Tomá) When other restaurants close, slinky Impronta stays open to accommodate late lunches, tea sessions, and midnight snacks of club sandwiches. The menu is a mix of the contemporary and the classic, from the *mista di pesce alla fantasia dello chef*, a generous tasting plate of seafood concoctions, to comforting suckling pig confit with green apple and seasonal puree. Give the mediocre cheese platter a miss.

RISTORANTE SAN TROVASO VENETIAN €€
Map p272 (☑041 523 08 35; Rio Terà Carità 967; meals €30; ☺noon-3pm & 7-10pm; ☎; ☒Accademia) After the Accademia leaves you delirious with visual overload, come to your senses with fried calamari, polenta, *sarde in saor* and a carafe of the house Soave. Hidden behind the museum, this rustic restaurant hastens recovery with brisk service, a sunny garden seating and an airy, woodbeamed dining room.

ENOTECA AI ARTISTI ITALIAN €€€
Map p272 (☑041 523 89 44; www.enoteca artisti.com; Fondamenta della Toletta 1169a; meals €45; ☺noon-3pm & 7-10pm Mon-Sat; ☒Ca' Rezzonico) Indulgent cheeses, exceptional *nero di seppia* (cuttlefish ink) pasta, and tender *tagliata* (sliced steak) drizzled with aged balsamic vinegar atop arugula are paired with exceptional wines by your gracious oenophile hosts. Sidewalk tables for two make great people-watching, but book ahead for indoor tables for groups; space is limited. Note: only turf (no surf) dishes on Mondays.

🍷 DRINKING & NIGHTLIFE

★**CANTINONE GIÀ SCHIAVI** BAR
Map p272 (☑041 523 95 77; Fondamenta Nani 992; ☺8.15am-8.30pm Mon-Sat; ☒Zattere) Chaos cheerfully prevails at this legendary canalside spot, where Accademia art historians rub shoulders with San Trovaso gondola builders without spilling a drop. Regulars gamely pass along orders to timid newcomers, who might otherwise miss out on smoked swordfish *cicheti* (bar snacks) with top-notch house Soave, or *pallottoline* (mini-bottles of beer) with generous *sopressa* (soft salami) *panini*.

WORTH A DETOUR

CHIESA DI SAN NICOLÒ DEI MENDICOLI

Other churches in town might be grander, but none is more quintessentially Venetian. This striking brick Veneto-Gothic **church** (Map p272; ☑041 528 45 65; Campo San Nicolò 1907; ☺10am-noon & 3-5.30pm Mon-Sat, 10am-noon Sun; ☒San Basilio) dedicated to serving the poor hasn't changed much since the 12th century, when its cloisters functioned as a women's refuge and its **portico** sheltered *mendicoli* (beggars). The tiny, picturesque *campo* out front is Venice in miniature, surrounded on three sides by canals and featuring a pylon bearing the winged lion of St Mark – one of the few in Venice to escape target practice by Napoleon's troops.

Dim interiors are illuminated by an **18th-century golden arcade** and a profusion of clerestory paintings, including a Palma Il Giovane masterpiece. His *Resurrection* shows onlookers cowering in terror and awe, as Jesus leaps from his tomb in a blaze of golden light. The right-hand **chapel** is a typically Venetian response to persistent orders from Rome to limit music in Venetian churches: Madonna in glory, thoroughly enjoying a concert by angels on flutes, lutes and violins. The parish's seafaring livelihood is honoured in Leonardo Corona's **16th-century ceiling panel** *San Nicolò Guiding Sailors Through a Storm*, which shows the saint as a beacon guiding sailors rowing furiously through a storm.

Film buffs might recognise church interiors from the 1973 Julie Christie thriller *Don't Look Now* as the church Donald Sutherland was assigned to restore. Though the movie cast Venice in a spooky light, the publicity apparently helped San Nicolò; the British Venice in Peril Fund underwrote extensive church renovations, completed in 1977.

★ **ESTRO** WINE BAR

Map p272 (www.estrovenezia.com; Dorsoduro 3778; ☺11am-midnight Wed-Mon, kitchen closes 10pm) New-entry Estro is anything you want it to be: wine and charcuterie bar, *aperitivo* pitstop, or sit-down degustation restaurant. The 500 *vini* (wines) – many of them natural-process wines – are chosen by young-gun sibling owners Alberto and Dario, whose passion for quality extends to the grub, from *cicheti* topped with house-made *porchetta* (roast pork), to a succulent burger made with Asiago cheese and house-made ketchup and mayonnaise.

★ **AI PUGNI** BAR

Map p272 (☎041 523 98 31; Ponte dei Pugni 2859; ☺7am-10.30pm; ☐Ca' Rezzonico) Centuries ago, brawls on the bridge out the front once inevitably ended in the canal, but now Venetians settle differences with one of over 50 wines by the glass at this ever-packed bar, pimped with recycled Magnum-bottle lamps and wine-crate tables. The latest drops are listed on the blackboard, with *aperitivo*-friendly nibbles including *polpette* (meatballs) and cured local meats on bread. Cash only for bills under €25.

★ **IL CAFFÈ ROSSO** CAFE

Map p272 (☎041 528 79 98; Campo Santa Margherita 2963; ☺7am-1am Mon-Sat; ☎; ☐Ca' Rezzonico) Affectionately known as 'il rosso', this red-fronted cafe has been at the centre of the bar scene on Campo Santa Margherita since the late 1800s. It's at its best in the early evening, when locals snap up the sunny piazza seating to sip on inexpensive *spritzes*.

OSTERIA AL SQUERO BAR

Map p272 (Dorsoduro 943-944; ☺9am-9pm Tue-Sun; ☎; ☐Zattere) After a stroll along the Zattere, retreat to this snug local drinking hole, right opposite the city's oldest functioning gondola workshop. Wines are well priced and the crostini delicious and imaginative, with combos like artichoke with blue cheese, ricotta and mascarpone. On your own? Lose yourself in one of the well-worn books on Venice.

IMAGINA CAFÉ BAR

Map p272 (☎041 241 06 25; www.imaginacafe.it; Rio Terà Canal 3126; ☺7am-9pm Sun-Thu, to 1am Fri & Sat; ☎☐; ☐Ca' Rezzonico) Running the show at modern, upbeat Imagina are affable Stefano and Domenico, busy brew-

---

LOCAL KNOWLEDGE

SQUERO DI SAN TROVASO

The **wood-brick cabin** (Map p272; Campo San Trovaso 1097; ☐Zattere) along Rio di San Trovaso may look like a stray ski chalet, but it's one of Venice's handful of working *squeri* (shipyards), complete with refinished gondolas drying in the yard. When the door's open, you can peek inside in exchange for a donation left in the basket by the door. To avoid startling gondola-builders working with sharp tools, no flash photography is allowed.

---

ing top-notch espresso, pouring quaffable wines, and serving fresh, tasty salads, focaccias and cakes. Monthly exhibitions showcase local artists, while the free wi-fi makes it a handy, comfy spot to kick back and check on all those Instagram likes.

TEA ROOM BEATRICE TEA ROOM

Map p272 (☎041 724 10 42; Calle Lunga San Barnaba 2727a; ☺3-10pm; ☐Ca' Rezzonico) After long museum days, Beatrice offers a relaxing alternative to espresso bolted at a bar. Rainy days call for pots of organic genmaicha tea and comforting brownies, while sunshine brings iced drinks and salty pistachios to the garden patio.

AI DO DRAGHI BAR

Map p272 (☎041 528 97 31; Calle della Chiesa 3665; ☺10am-1am; ☐Ca' Rezzonico) '*Permesso!*' (Pardon!) is the chorus inside this hip, pocket-sized *bacaro* (bar), where the crowd spills onto the sidewalk and tries not to spill drinks in the process. Below a tangle of filament bulbs is the tiny wooden bar, peddling respectable *cicheti* and around 45 wines by the glass, most of which are organic or from smaller producers.

☆ ENTERTAINMENT

VENICE JAZZ CLUB LIVE MUSIC

Map p272 (☎041 523 20 56; www.venicejazzclub.com; Ponte dei Pugni 3102; admission incl 1st drink €20; ☺doors 7pm, set begins 9pm, closed Thu, Sun & Aug; ☐Ca' Rezzonico) Jazz is alive and swinging in Dorsoduro, where the resident Venice Jazz Club Quartet pays regular respects to Miles Davis and John Coltrane, as well as heating up with Latin and bossa nova beats on Tuesdays and Fridays. Drinks are steep, so starving artists should booze beforehand and arrive by 8pm to pounce on complimentary cold-cut platters. The venue closes for all of August and much of January.

🛍 SHOPPING

★ MARINA E SUSANNA SENT · · · GLASS
Map p272 (☎041 520 81 36; www.marinaesusan nasent.com; Campo San Vio 669; ☉10am-1pm & 1.30-6.30pm; 🚤Accademia) Wearable waterfalls and unpoppable soap-bubble necklaces are Venice style signatures, thanks to the Murano-born Sent sisters. Defying centuries-old beliefs that women can't handle molten glass, their minimalist art-glass statement jewellery is featured in museum stores worldwide, from Palazzo Grassi to MoMA. See new collections at this flagship store, their Murano studio, or the San Marco branch (at Ponte San Moisè 2090).

DANGHYRA · · · CERAMICS
Map p272 (☎041 522 41 95; www.danghyra.com; Calle de le Botteghe 3220; ☉10am-1pm & 3-7pm Tue-Sun; 🚤Ca' Rezzonico) Spare white bisque cups seem perfect for a Zen tea ceremony, but look inside: that iridescent lilac glaze is pure Carnevale. Danghyra's striking ceramics are hand-thrown in Venice with a magic touch – her platinum-glazed bowls make the simplest pasta dish appear fit for a modern doge.

PERLAMADREDESIGN · · · GLASS
Map p272 (☎340 8449112; www.perlamadre design.com; Calle de le Boteghe 3182; ☉10.30am-1pm & 3.30-6.30pm Mon-Sat; 🚤Ca' Rezzonico) Chances are you'll find glassmaker Patrizia Iacovazzi (known as Simona to her friends) at her work table, turning glass into striking, elegant wearables, from necklaces and bracelets, to earrings and cufflinks. Patrizia was born in Puglia, and the vibrant hues of her creations echo the rich, sun-drenched hues of southern Italy. With its frost-like finish and intriguing dual tones, the Sommerso range is especially irresistible.

MADERA · · · ACCESSORIES, HOMEWARES
Map p272 (☎041 522 41 81; www.shopmaderaven ezia.it; Campo San Barnaba 2762; ☉10am-1pm & 3.30-7.30pm Mon-Sat; 🚤Ca' Rezzonico) Restyle your life at this modern design showcase, which stocks a sharply curated selection of

Italian and international jewellery, accessories, homewares and gifts. The emphasis is on handmade and harder-to-find objects, whether it's sculptural chopping blocks and necklaces, or geometric serving trays and bags.

Further down the street, Madera's second **showroom** (Map p272; ☎041 241 83 10; Calle Lunga San Barnaba 2729; ☉10am-1pm & 3.30-7.30pm Mon-Sat) focuses on furniture and furnishings.

LAURETTA VISTOSI · · · ACCESSORIES
Map p272 (☎041 528 65 30; www.laurettavistosi. org; Calle Lunga San Barnaba 2866b; ☉10am-7pm; 🚤Ca' Rezzonico) Murano-born Renaissance artisan Lauretta Vistosi hand-crafted shoes, stationery and dresses before inventing her own signature craft: handmade handbags, iPad covers, journals, even wine bottle sleeves, emblazoned with Murano-glass bullseyes. Pieces are simultaneously playful and architectural, with hand-finished flourishes like contrasting orange outstitching and grid patterns in green ribbon. Prices are surprisingly reasonable for one-of-a-kind finds, starting at around €15. In winter, the shop closes at 6pm and is not open on Sundays.

LE FORCOLE DI SAVERIO PASTOR · · · HANDICRAFTS
Map p272 (☎041 522 56 99; www.forcole. com; Fondamenta Soranzo detta Fornace 341; ☉8.30am-12.30pm & 2.30-6pm Mon-Sat; 🚤Salute) Only one thing in the world actually moves like Jagger: Mick Jagger's bespoke *forcola*, hand-carved by Saverio Pastor. Each forked wooden gondola oarlock is individually designed to match a gondolier's height, weight and movement, so the gondola doesn't rock too hard when the gondolier hits a groove. Pastor's *forcole* twist elegantly, striking an easy balance on gondolas and mantelpieces alike.

L'ANGOLO DEL PASSATO · · · GLASS
Map p272 (☎347 1586638; Campiello dei Squelini 3276; ☉3.30-7pm Mon, 9am-12.30pm & 3.30-7pm Tue-Sat; 🚤Ca' Rezzonico) The 19th century bumps into the 21st in this hidden corner showcase of rare Murano glass, ranging from spun-gold chandeliers beloved of royal decorators to sultry smoked-glass sconces that serve Hollywood stars better than Botox. Contemporary creations line the shelves, from geometric-patterned vases to bold, Dali-esque drinking glasses.

PAOLO OLBI
HANDICRAFTS

Map p272 (☑041 523 76 55; http://olbi.atspace. com; Dorsoduro 3253a; ◷10.30am-12.40pm & 3.30-7.30pm Mon-Sat, 11.30am-12.40pm & 4-7.30pm Sun; ⓔCa' Rezzonico) Thoughts worth committing to paper deserve Paolo Olbi's keepsake books, albums and stationery, whose fans include Hollywood actors and NYC mayors (ask to see the guestbook). Ordinary journals can't compare to Olbi originals, handmade with heavyweight paper and bound with beautiful leather bindings. The €1 watercolour postcards of Venice make for beautiful, bargain souvenirs.

ARRAS
ACCESSORIES, CLOTHING

Map p272 (☑041 522 64 60; http://arrastessuti. wordpress.com; Campiello dei Squelini 3235; ◷9am-1.30pm Mon & Sat, 9am-1.30pm & 2-6.30pm Tue-Fri; ⓔCa' Rezzonico) ∅ The plush, handwoven silk-and-wool wraps piled high on Arras' shelves represent the combined efforts of this weaving cooperative, which offers vocational workshops for people with disabilities. Shimmering scarlet shawls deserve at least one summer sunset gondola ride, and cleverly draped wool jackets reduce Venice's winter chill factor even better than *prosecco*.

PAPUNI ART
JEWELLERY

Map p272 (☑041 241 04 34; www.papuniart.it; Ponte dei Pugni 2834a; ◷noon-7pm Mon-Sat; ⓔCa' Rezzonico) Handmade industrial chic isn't what you'd expect to find across the footbridge from baroque Ca' Rezzonico, but Ninfa Salerno's clients delight in the unexpected. The Venetian artisan gives staid pearl strands a sense of humour with bouncy black rubber, weaves fuschia rubber discs into glowing UFO necklaces, and embeds Murano glass beads in rubber daisy cocktail rings.

ANTIQUARIATO
CLAUDIA CANESTRELLI
ANTIQUES

Map p272 (☑340 577 60 89; Campiello Barbaro 364a; ◷10.30am-1pm & 3-5.30pm Mon & Wed-Sat, 10.30am-1pm Tue; ⓔSalute) Hand-coloured lithographs of fanciful lagoon fish, 19th-century miniatures of cats dressed as generals, and vintage cufflinks make for charming souvenirs of Venice's past in this walk-in curio cabinet. Collector-artisan Claudia Canestrelli brings back bygone elegance with her repurposed antique earrings, including free-form baroque pearls dangling from gilded bronze cats.

SEGNI NEL TEMPO
BOOKS

Map p272 (☑041 72 29 09; Calle Lunga San Barnaba 2856; ◷10.30am-1.30pm & 2.30-7.30pm; ⓔCa' Rezzonico) Not so much a bookshop as a tiny time machine, where cramped shelves might reveal a 16th-century edition of Giovanni Pontano's *De Prudentia* or a *History of Oxford* dating from 1676. Most titles are in Italian, with a good selection of Venetian history books. Bound beauties aside, you'll also find vintage prints of the city and the odd curiosity... perhaps an 18th-century card game of seduction.

GUALTI
JEWELLERY, ACCESSORIES

Map p272 (☑041 520 17 31; www.gualti.it; Rio Terà Canal 3111; ◷10am-1pm & 3-7.30pm Mon-Sat; ⓔCa' Rezzonico) Either a shooting star just landed on your shoulder, or you've been to Gualti, where iridescent orange glass bursts from clear resin stems on a supernova brooch. Pleated-silk evening wraps unfurl like jellyfish tendrils, while glowing rings evoke wild sea anemones. Smaller one-off designs start at around €45.

CA' MACANA
HANDICRAFTS

Map p272 (☑041 277 61 42; www.camacana.com; Calle de le Botteghe 3172; ◷10am-7.30pm Sun-Fri, 10am-8pm Sat; 🖼; ⓔCa' Rezzonico) Glimpse the talents behind the Venetian Carnevale masks that so impressed Stanley Kubrick, he ordered several for his final film *Eyes Wide Shut*. Choose your papier-mâché persona from the selection of coquettish courtesan's eye-shades, chequered Casanova disguises and long-nosed plague doctors' masks – or invent your own alter ego at Ca' Macana's one- to two-hour **mask-making workshops** (one-hour per person €47, two-hour per person from €68) for individuals and families. One-hour workshops are held 10am to noon and 2pm to 6pm Monday to Saturday, two-hour workshops negotiable.

SIGNOR BLUM
TOYS

Map p272 (☑041 522 63 67; Campo San Barnaba 2840; ◷9.30am-2pm & 2.30-7.30pm Mon-Sat; ⓔCa' Rezzonico) Kids may have to drag adults away from the 2D wooden puzzles of the Rialto bridge and grinning wooden duckies before these clever handmade toys induce acute cases of nostalgia. Calderesque mobiles made of colourful carved gondola prows would seem equally at home in an arty foyer and a nursery. And did we mention the Venice-themed clocks?

up a serious
er lagoon surf
gut-rumbling,
rsting **Rialto**
9).

ng the trail of
netian explorers
world of natural
d oddities at the
Storia Naturale
(p91).

5 Posing like a Venetian at
très-chic **Palazzo Mocenigo**
(p91), an aristocratic pad
turned ode to centuries of
fashion, furnishings and
exotic fragrances.

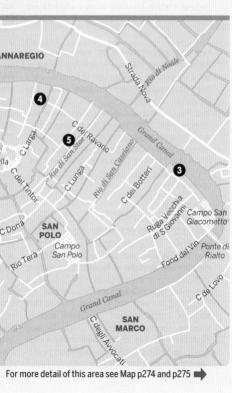

For more detail of this area see Map p274 and p275 ➡

Explore San Polo & Santa Croce

Start the morning among masterpieces at Scuola Grande di San Rocco, then bask in the glow of Titian's Madonna at I Frari. Shop backstreet galleries and artisan studios all the way to the Rialto Market, where glistening purple octopus and feathery red *radicchio treviso* (chicory) present Technicolor photo-ops.

Stop at All'Arco for *cicheti* (bar snacks) before breezing through elegant salons of fashion, art and scents at vainglorious Palazzo Mocenigo. Alternatively, zip through millennia of natural history at the epic Museo di Storia Naturale di Venezia.

Next, swing by Alaska for some of the city's best gelato, or head straight to medieval San Giacomo dell'Orio for happy hour at Al Prosecco. Appetite-piqued and buzzing, wander the maze of Venice's former red-light district to celebrated Antiche Carampane for dinner.

Local Life

➡ **Market mornings** Gently elbow fastidious chefs and *nonne* (grandmothers) on your quest for the morning's finest produce at Rialto Market (p89). Bag vegetables freshly pulled from Sant'Erasmo soil and shrimp caught in local waters, or detour to Casa del Parmigiano (p104) for picnic-friendly cheese and olives.

➡ **Bacaro-hopping** Ringing the Rialto are authentic, pocket-sized *bacari* (bars) offering inventive Venetian bites, best devoured standing with top-notch *ombre* (half-glasses of wine) at All'Arco (p95), Dai Zemei (p95), Al Mercà (p98) and Do Mori (p98).

➡ **Artisan studios** Despite skyrocketing rents and the inundation of foreign-made 'Venetian' souvenirs, local artisans continue to design, carve, sew and print in their studios and workshops, among them Gilberto Penzo (p100), Veneziastampa (p102), Laberintho (p103) and Gmeiner (p102).

➡ **Musical accompaniment** Take in lesser-known compositions inside a frescoed pleasure palace at Palazzetto Bru Zane (p100), opera among Tiepolos at Scuola Grande di San Giovanni Evangelista (p100), or a baroque sonata at the ever-elegant Scuola Grande di San Rocco (p86).

Getting There & Away

➡ **Vaporetto** Most *vaporetti* call at Piazzale Roma or Ferrovia at the northwest corner of Santa Croce. In San Polo, lines 1 and N service Rialto-Mercato, as well as Rialto (on the San Marco side of the Rialto Bridge). Both lines also stop at Riva de Biasio, San Stae, San Silvestro and San Tomà.

Lonely Planet's Top Tip

Many of Venice's best restaurants, artisan studios and *bacari* (bars) are in the backstreets of San Polo and Santa Croce – if you can find them. This is the easiest area in which to get lost, so allow extra time if you have dinner reservations or a powerful thirst. If totally lost, follow the flow of foot traffic toward yellow Rialto or Ferrovia signs or red-and-white Scuola Grande di San Rocco signs, or head to central Campo San Polo.

SAN POLO & SANTA CROCE

✖ Best Places to Eat

➡ All'Arco (p95)
➡ Antiche Carampane (p97)
➡ Osteria Trefanti (p97)
➡ Dai Zemei (p95)

For reviews, see p95.➡

🍷 Best Places to Drink

➡ Al Prosecco (p98)
➡ Al Mercà (p98)
➡ Bacareto Da Lele (p99)
➡ Cantina Do Spade (p99)

For reviews, see p98.➡

⊙ Best Artisanal Finds

➡ Cárte (p100)
➡ Gilberto Penzo (p100)
➡ Veneziastampa (p102)
➡ VizioVirtù (p101)

For reviews, see p100.➡

You'll swear the paint is still fresh on the 50 action-packed Tintorettos completed between 1575 and 1587 for the Scuola Grande di San Rocco, dedicated to the patron saint of the plague-stricken. While the 1575–77 plague claimed one-third of Venice's residents, Tintoretto painted nail-biting scenes of looming despair and last-minute redemption, illuminating a survivor's struggle with breathtaking urgency.

Assembly Hall

Downstairs in the assembly hall, Tintoretto steals the scene with the story of the Virgin Mary, starting on the left wall with *Annunciation,* where the angel sneaks up on Mary at her sewing table through a broken door. Tintoretto shows a light touch in *Presentation at the Temple,* where the infant Mary is steadied on her feet by a cheerleading cherub.

Tintoretto's Virgin cycle ends with *Ascension* opposite; it's a dark and cataclysmic work, compared with Titian's glowing version at I Frari. From spring to late autumn, the artworks provide a bewitching backdrop to top-notch **concerts** of baroque music (ask at the counter or check the website for details).

Sala Grande Superiore

Take the grand **Scarpagnino staircase** to the Sala Grande Superiore, where you may be seized with a powerful instinct to duck, given all the action in the **Old Testament ceiling scenes** – you can almost hear the swoop! overhead as a winged angel dives to nourish the ailing prophet in *Elijah Fed by an Angel.* Grab a mirror to avoid the otherwise inevitable neck strain as you follow dramatic, super-heroic gestures through these ceiling panels. Mercy from above is

DON'T MISS...

➡ *Ascension*

➡ Scarpagnino staircase

➡ *Elijah Fed by an Angel*

➡ New Testament wall scenes

➡ Francesco Pianta's sculpture of Tintoretto

➡ St Roch in Glory ceiling

PRACTICALITIES

➡ Map p274, A6

➡ ☏041 523 48 64

➡ www.scuolagrande sanrocco.it

➡ Campo San Rocco 3052, San Polo

➡ adult/reduced €10/8

➡ ◷9.30am-5.30pm, Tesoro to 5.15pm

➡ 🚤San Tomà

a recurring theme, with Daniel's salvation by angels, the miraculous fall of manna in the desert, and Elisha distributing bread to the hungry

Tintoretto's **New Testament wall scenes** read like a modern graphic novel, with eerie lightning-bolt illumination striking his protagonists against the backdrop of the Black Death. Scenes from Christ's life aren't in chronological order: birth and baptism are followed by resurrection. The drama builds as background characters disappear into increasingly dark canvases, until an X-shaped black void looms at the centre of *Agony in the Garden*.

When Tintoretto painted these works, Venice's outlook was grim indeed: the plague had just taken 50,000 Venetians, including the great colourist Titian, and the cause of and cure for the bubonic plague would not be discovered for centuries. By focusing his talents on dynamic lines instead of Titianesque colour, Tintoretto creates a shockingly modern, moving parable for epidemics through the ages. A portrait of the artist with his paintbrushes is captured in Francesco Pianta's 17th-century carved-wood **sculpture**, third from the right beneath Tintoretto's New Testament masterpieces. Titian's own work – along with paintings by fellow Venetian A-listers Giorgione and Tiepolo – is also on show here, on the handful of easels dotting the space.

Sala Albergo

The New Testament cycle ends with the *Crucifixion* in the Sala Albergo, where things suddenly begin to look up – literally. Every Venetian artist who'd survived the plague wanted the commission to paint this building, so Tintoretto cheated a little. Instead of producing sketches like his rival Paolo Veronese, he painted this magnificent *tondo* (ceiling panel) and dedicated it to the saint, knowing that such a gift couldn't be refused, or matched by other artists.

The Sala Albergo is crowned by Tintoretto's restored *St Roch in Glory*, surrounded by representations of the four seasons and the saving graces of Felicity, Generosity, Faith and Hope. The angels are panting from their efforts at salvation, and feeble Hope is propped up on one elbow – still reeling from the tragedy of the Black Death, but miraculously alive.

Tesoro

After a century of closure, the Scuola's Tesoro (Treasury) is open to visitors. Through a side door in the Sala Superiore, climb to the landing to see unexpected multicultural marvels, including 13th-century lustreware from Iran and a 1720–27 chinoiserie tea set. Upstairs, pass through heavy bolted doors to see the jewel of San Rocco: an enchanting candlestick made from a branch of coral.

AN INTERFAITH EFFORT AGAINST THE PLAGUE

While the Black Death ravaged the rest of Europe, Venice mounted an interfaith effort against it. The city dedicated a church and *scuola* (religious confraternity) to San Rocco, where Venetians could pray for deliverance from the disease while also consulting resident Jewish and Muslim doctors about preventative measures. Venice established the world's first quarantine, with inspections and 40-day waiting periods for incoming ships at Lazaretto. Venice's forward-thinking, inclusive approach created artistic masterpieces that provide comfort to the afflicted and bereaved to this day, and set a public-health standard that has saved countless lives down the centuries.

Scarpagnino's uplifting, proto-baroque facade sees veined marble frame windows and doors, figures leaning out from atop the capitals, and flowering garlands adorning pillars as welcome signs of life post-plague. Bartolomeo Bon began the *scuola* in 1517, and at least three other architects were called in to finish the work by 1588.

TOP SIGHT I FRARI (CHIESA DI SANTA MARIA GLORIOSA DEI FRARI)

As you've no doubt heard, there's a Titian – make that *the* Titian – altarpiece at I Frari. But the 14th-century Italian-brick Gothic cathedral is itself a towering achievement, with intricate marquetry choir stalls, a rare Bellini, and an eerie Longhena funeral monument. While Canova's white-marble tomb seems permanently moonlit, Titian's *Assunta* seems to shed its own sunlight.

Assunta

Visitors are inexorably drawn to the front of this cavernous Gothic church by a petite altarpiece that seems to glow from within. This is Titian's 1518 *Assunta* (Ascension), capturing the split second the radiant Madonna reaches heavenward, finds her footing on a cloud, and escapes this mortal coil in a dramatic swirl of Titian-red robes. According to local lore, one glimpse of the Madonna's wrist slipping from her cloak has led many monks to recant their vows over the centuries.

Both inside and outside the painting, onlookers gasp and point at the glorious, glowing sight. Titian outdid himself here, upstaging his own **1526 Pesaro altarpiece** – a dreamlike composite family portrait of the Holy Family with the Venetian Pesaro family.

Other Masterpieces

As though this weren't quite enough artistic achievement for one church or planet, there's puzzlework marquetry worthy of MC Escher in the **coro** (choir stalls), Bellini's achingly sweet and startlingly 3D *Madonna with Child* triptych in the **sacristy**, and Bartolomeo Vivarini's *St Mark Enthroned*, showing the fluffy-bearded saint serenaded by an angelic orchestra in the **Capella Corner**.

In the middle of the nave, Baldassare Longhena's **Doge Pesaro funereal monument** is hoisted by four burly, black-marble figures bursting from ragged white clothes like Invincible Hulks. Bringing up the rear are disconsolate mourners dabbing at their eyes with the hems of their cloaks on Canova's marble **pyramid mausoleum**, originally intended as a monument to Titian. The great painter was lost to the plague at the age of 90 in 1576, but legend has it that, in light of his artistic contributions here, Venice's strict rules of quarantine were bent to allow Titian's burial near his masterpiece.

Architecture

Built of modest brick rather than stone for the Franciscans in the 14th and 15th centuries, the Frari has none of the flying buttresses, pinnacles and gargoyles typical of international Gothic – but its vaulted ceilings and broad, triple-nave, Latin-cross floor plan give this cathedral a grandeur befitting the masterpieces it contains.

The facade facing the canal has delicate scalloping under the roofline, contrasting red-and-white mouldings around windows and arches, and a repeating circle motif of *oculi* (porthole windows) around a high rosette window. The tall bell tower has managed to remain upright since 1386 – a rare feat, given the shifting *barene* (shoals) of Venice.

DON'T MISS...

➡ Titian's *Assunta*
➡ Titian's Pesaro altarpiece
➡ Coro
➡ Bellini's *Madonna with Child*
➡ Vivarini's *St Mark Enthroned*
➡ Canova's pyramid mausoleum

PRACTICALITIES

➡ Basilica di Santa Maria Gloriosa dei Frari
➡ Map p274, B6
➡ Campo dei Frari, San Polo 3072
➡ adult/reduced €3/1.50
➡ ⏱9am-6pm Mon-Sat, 1-6pm Sun
➡ 🚊San Tomà

◉ SIGHTS

SCUOLA GRANDE DI SAN ROCCO   MUSEUM
See p86.

I FRARI   CHURCH
See p88.

PONTE DI RIALTO   BRIDGE
Map p268 (🛥Rialto-Mercato) A superb feat of engineering, Antonio da Ponte's 1592 Istrian stone span took three years and 250,000 gold ducats to construct. Adorned with stone reliefs depicting St Mark, St Theodore and the Annunciation, the bridge crosses the Grand Canal at its narrowest point, connecting the neighbourhoods of San Polo and San Marco. Interestingly, it was da Conte's own nephew, Antonio Contino, who designed the city's other iconic bridge, the Ponte dei Sospiri (Bridge of Sighs).

When crowds of shutterbugs clear out around sunset, the bridge's south side offers a romantic view of black gondolas pulling up to golden Grand Canal *palazzi* (mansions).

IL GOBBO   MONUMENT
Map p274 (🛥Rialto-Mercato) Rubbed for luck for centuries, the 1541 statue *Il Gobbo* (The Hunchback) is now protected by an iron railing. *Il Gobbo* served as a podium for official proclamations and punishments: those guilty of misdemeanours were forced to run a gauntlet of jeering citizens from Piazza San Marco to the Rialto. The minute they touched *Il Gobbo*, their punishment was complete.

CHIESA DI SAN GIOVANNI ELEMOSINARIO   CHURCH
Map p274 (Ruga Vecchia di San Giovanni 477, San Polo; admission €3, or with Chorus Pass free; ⊘10am-5pm Mon-Sat; 🛥Rialto-Mercato) Hunkering modestly behind skimpy T-shirt kiosks is this soaring Renaissance brick church, built by Scarpagnino after a disastrous fire in 1514 destroyed much of the Rialto area. Cross the darkened threshhold to witness flashes of Renaissance genius: Titian's tender *St John the Almsgiver* (freshly restored and returned from the Accademia) and gloriously restored dome frescoes of frolicking angels by Pordenone.

FONDAZIONE PRADA   MUSEUM
Map p274 (Ca' Corner; 🕿041 810 91 61; www.fondazioneprada.org; Calle de Ca' Corner 2215, Santa Croce; adult/child €10/free; ⊘hours vary; 🛥San Stae) This stately Grand Canal palace – designed by Domenico Rossi and completed in

SAN POLO & SANTA CROCE SIGHTS

TOP SIGHT
RIALTO MARKET

Before there was a bridge at the Rialto or palaces along the Grand Canal, there was a **Pescaria** (Fish Market; Map p274; Rialto; ⊘7am-2pm Tue-Sun; 🛥Rialto) and a produce market. So loyal are locals to their 700-year-old market that talk of opening a larger, more convenient mainland fish market was swiftly crushed.

Pescaria fishmongers call out today's catch: from glistening mountains of *moscardini* (baby octopus) to tiny *moeche* (soft-shell crabs). Sustainable fishing practices are not a new idea at the Pescaria; marble plaques show regulations set centuries ago for the minimum allowable sizes for lagoon fish. Seafood tagged '*Nostrana*' is locally sourced, and the very best of it is sold at the stall of **Marco Bergamasco** (Map p274; 🕿041 522 53 54; Calle de le Beccarie, Rialto Market; ⊘7.30am-noon Tue-Sat), whose clients include Venice's Michelin-starred restaurants.

Veneto *verdure* (vegetables) intrigue with their otherworldy forms, among them Sant'Erasmo *castraure* (baby artichokes) and white Bassano asparagus. In the winter, look out for prized *rosa di Gorizia*, a rose-shaped chicory specimen, often eaten raw with honey, vinegar and pancetta in its native region Friuli Venezia Giulia.

Tuesday and Friday are the best days to visit.

DON'T MISS...
➡ Lagoon seafood displays
➡ Chanted boasts about local produce at bargain prices
➡ Produce barges by Grand Canal docks
➡ Veneto speciality produce
➡ Seasonal fruit

PRACTICALITIES
➡ Map p274, G3
➡ 🕿041 296 06 58
➡ ⊘7am-2pm, Pescaria closed Mon
➡ 🛥Rialto-Mercato

1728 – has been commandeered by Fondazione Prada, but you won't necessarily find handbags here. Instead Ca' Corner della Regina is now the setting for slick temporary exhibitions that explore the art and avant-garde that shape contemporary visual sensibilities. Frescoes on the *palazzo*'s *piano nobile* (main floor) depict Caterina Cornaro, Queen of Cyprus, born in a Gothic building on this very site in 1454.

CA' PESARO
MUSEUM

Map p274 (Galleria Internazionale d'Arte Moderna e Museo d'Arte Orientale; ☑041 72 11 27; www. visitmuve.it; Fondamenta di Ca' Pesaro 2070, Santa Croce; adult/reduced €10.50/8; ⊘10am-6pm Tue-Sun summer, to 5pm winter; ⓢSan Stae) Like a Carnevale costume built for two, the stately exterior of this Baldassare Longhena–designed 1710 *palazzo* hides two intriguing museums: **Galleria Internazionale d'Arte Moderna** and **Museo d'Arte Orientale**. While the former includes art showcased at the Venice Biennale, the latter holds treasures from Prince Enrico di Borbone's epic 1887–89 souvenir-shopping spree across Asia.

The Galleria Internazionale d'Arte Moderna spans numerous art movements of the 19th and 20th centuries, including the Macchiaioli, Expressionists and Surrealists. The 1961 De Lisi Bequest added Kandinskys and Morandis to the modernist mix of de Chiricos, Mirós and Moores, plus radical abstracts by postwar Venetian artists Giuseppe Santomaso and Emilio Vedova.

Collection highlights include Telemaco Signorini's quietly unsettling *The Room of the Disturbed at the Bonifacio in Florence* (1865), Gustav Klimt's 1909 *Judith II (Salome)*, Marc Chagall's *Rabbi of Vitebsk* (1914–22), and Arturo Martini's anxiety-ridden bronze *The Sprinter* (1935).

Climb the creaky attic stairs of the Museo d'Arte Orientale past a phalanx of samurai warriors guarding a princely collection of Asian travel mementos. Prince Enrico di Borbone reached Japan when Edo art was discounted in favour of modern Meiji, and Edo-era netsukes, screens and a lacquerware palanquin are standouts in his collection of 30,000 objets d'art. Around three-quarters of the collection is Japanese, the remaining quarter including a small collection of 12th- to 15th-century Islamic ceramic and an intricately carved Chinese chess set from the 18th century.

CHIESA DI SAN STAE
CHURCH

Map p274 (www.chorusvenezia.org; Campo San Stae 1981, Santa Croce; admission €3, or with Chorus Pass free; ⊘10am-5pm Mon-Sat; ⓢSan Stae) English painter William Turner painted San Stae obsessively, capturing early-morning Grand Canal mists swirling around the angels gracing its Palladian facade. The church was founded in 966 but finished in 1709, and though the interiors are surprisingly sparse for a baroque edifice, Giambattista Tiepolo's *The Martyrdom of St Bartholomew* and Sebastiano Ricci's *The Liberation of St Peter* are grace notes.

THE OTHER RIALTO MARKET: PONTE DELLE TETTE

No one remembers the original name of **Ponte delle Tette** (Map p274; ⓢSan Silvestro), known since the 15th century as 'Tits Bridge'. Back in those days, shadowy porticos around this bridge sheltered a designated red-light zone where neighbourhood prostitutes were encouraged to display their wares in windows instead of taking their marketing campaigns to the streets in their platform shoes. Between clients, the most ambitious working girls might be found studying: for educated conversation, *cortigiane* (courtesans) might charge 60 times the going rates for basic services from average prostitutes.

Church authorities and French dignitaries repeatedly professed dismay at Venice's lax attitudes towards prostitution, but Venice's idea of a crackdown was to prevent women prostitutes from luring clients by cross-dressing (aka false advertising) and to ban prostitutes from riding in two-oared boats – lucky that gondolas only require one oar. Fees were set by the state and posted in Rialto brothels (soap cost extra), and the rates of high-end *cortigiane* were published in catalogues extolling their various merits. The height of platform shoes was limited to a staggering 30cm by sumptuary laws intended to distinguish socialites from *cortigiane*, with little success.

PALAZZO MOCENIGO
MUSEUM

Map p274 (☏041 72 17 98; http://mocenigo.visit muve.it; Salizada San Stae 1992, Santa Croce; adult/reduced €8.50/6; ⊗10am-5pm Tue-Sun summer, to 4pm winter; ⛴San Stae) Venice received a dazzling addition to its property portfolio in 1945 when Count Alvise Nicolò Mocenigo bequeathed his family's 17th-century waterfront *palazzo* to the city. While the ground floor hosts temporary exhibitions, the *piano nobile* is where you'll find a dashing collection of historic fashion, from duchess *andrienne* (hip-extending dresses) to exquisitely embroidered silk waistcoats. Adding to the glamour and intrigue is an exhibition dedicated to the art of fragrance; an ode to Venice's 16th-century status as Europe's capital of perfume.

Palazzo Mocenigo's opulent, chandelier-graced rooms look pretty much as they did at 18th-century A-list parties. Yet, even when flirting shamelessly under Jacopo Guarana's 1787 *Allegory of Nuptial Bliss* ceiling in the Green Living Room, wise guests minded their tongues. The Mocenigos reported philosopher and sometime houseguest Giordano Bruno for heresy to the Inquisition, which subsequently tortured and burned the betrayed philosopher at the stake in Rome.

MUSEO DI STORIA NATURALE DI VENEZIA
MUSEUM

Map p274 (Fondaco dei Turchi; ☏041 275 02 06; www.visitmuve.it; Salizada del Fontego dei Turchi 1730, Santa Croce; adult/reduced €8/5.50; ⊗10am-6pm Tue-Sun Jun-Oct, 9am-5pm Tue-Fri & 10am-6pm Sat & Sun Nov-May; ⛴San Stae) Never mind the doge: insatiable curiosity rules Venice, and inside the Museo di Storia Naturale (Museum of Natural History) it runs wild. The adventure begins upstairs with dinosaurs and prehistoric crocodiles, then dashes through evolution to Venice's great age of exploration, when adventurers like Marco Polo fetched peculiar specimens from distant lands.

Outstare the only complete ouransaurus skeleton found to date, a macabre menagerie of colonial trophies, as well as a 19th-century *wunderkammer* (cabinet of curiosities) housing a pair of two-headed calves. Although the museum's grand finale downstairs is comparatively anti-climatic – a fish tank of Venetian coastal specimens bubbling for attention – it does offer you a close-up glimpse of the enormous dugout canoe moored at the water door.

TOUR THE ULTIMATE WALK-IN WARDROBE

Fashion alert: by popular demand, **Palazzo Mocenigo** now opens its secret attic storeroom the last Friday of every month for fascinating tours through fashion history. Costume historians lead up to 12 people into the ultimate walk-in closet, and open cupboards to reveal 1700s cleavage-revealing, nude-coloured silk gowns, men's 1600s embroidered peacock frock-coats with exaggerated hips, and other daring fashions too delicate for permanent display. Reserve ahead for 11am and 2pm tours in Italian and English (☏041 270 03 70; admission €12).

Alongside the exit staircase you'll notice marble heraldic symbols of kissing doves and knotted-tail dogs, dating from the building's history as a ducal palace and international trading house. The dukes of Ferrara had the run of this 12th-century mansion until they were elbowed aside in 1621 to make room for Venice's most important trading partner: Turkey.

Known as the Fondaco dei Turchi (Turkish Trading House), the building remained rented out to the Turks until 1858. Afterwards, a disastrous renovation indulged 19th-century architectural fancies, including odd crenellations that made the gracious Gothic building resemble a prison. Luckily, the renovation spared the courtyard and charming back garden, which is open during museum hours and ideal for picnics.

CHIESA DI SAN GIACOMO DELL'ORIO
CHURCH

Map p274 (www.chorusvenezia.org; Campo San Giacomo dell'Orio 1457, Santa Croce; admission €3, or with Chorus Pass free; ⊗10am-5pm Mon-Sat; ⛴Riva de Biasio) La Serenissima seems as serene as ever inside the cool gloom of this Romanesque church, founded in the 9th to 10th centuries and completed in Latin-cross form by 1225 with chapels bubbling along the edges. Notable 14th- to 18th-century artworks include luminous **sacristy paintings** by Palma Il Giovane, a rare Lorenzo Lotto *Madonna with Child and Saints*, and an exceptional Veronese crucifix.

Secrets of the Calli

Yellow signs point the way to major sights, but the secret to any Venetian adventure is: *ignore them*. That *calle* (backstreet) behind the thoroughfare leads to a world of artisan studios, backstreet *bacari* (bars) and hidden *campi* (squares).

Campo San Polo to San Giacomo dell'Orio

Take Calle del Scalater past a couple of artisan studios to hidden Campiello Sant'Agostin for draught beer and dramatic glass jewellery; cross the bridge to join happy hour and tag games alongside medieval San Giacomo dell'Orio.

Campo Bandiera e Moro to Campo San Giovanni e Paolo

Head north of Riva degli Schiavoni through neighbourly Campo Bandiera and along studio-lined Salizada San Antonin. Then zigzag up narrow *fondamente* and *calli* to emerge on Barbaria de le Tole, where bars flank the route to sundowners in the shadow of stunning Zanipolo.

Rialto Market to Museo di Storia Naturale

Gather picnic supplies at Rialto Market, then *campo*-hop from nearby Campo delle Beccarie through sunny Campo San Cassian to artisan studio–dotted Campo Santa Maria Domini; then follow wiggling, sometimes shoulder-width *calli* to Museo di Storia Naturale for your garden picnic

1. A Castello (p117) laneway 2. Calle Larga, Santa Croce (p84)
3. Chiesa di Santa Maria Formosa (p124)

SHAKESPEARE'S VENICE

There is much debate about whether Shakespeare ever visited Italy, but his Italian plays are full of local knowledge. Venetian writer, architect and presenter Francesco da Mosto shares his thoughts on the Bard and his links to La Serenissima:

'The Bard set *Othello* in Venice, and *The Merchant of Venice* mentions the Rialto Market area several times. He even talked about gondolas and 'the tranect', which could refer to the *traghetto* ferry, which transported people from Venice to the mainland. If he did visit, Shakespeare would have spent his time wandering the streets, eavesdropping on people's conversations and observing the goings-on in shops and at the market. A walk to the Rialto is certainly evocative of that time.

Across in San Marco, the Palazzo Ducale, with its magnificent Gothic facades and huge council hall, is probably what Shakespeare had in mind as the setting for the final courtroom scene in *The Merchant of Venice*, while the two bronze figures on top of the Torre dell'Orologio (clock tower) in Piazza San Marco are known as 'i Mori', or 'the Moors', which is a key reference in *Othello*.'

Don't miss Gaetano Zompini's macabre *Miracle of the Virgin*, which shows a rabble-rouser rudely interrupting the Virgin's funeral procession, only to have his hands miraculously fall off when he touches her coffin. Architectural quirks include decorative pillars, a 14th-century *carena di nave* (ship's keel) ceiling and a Lombard pulpit perched atop a 6th-century Byzantine green-marble column.

SCUOLA GRANDE DI SAN GIOVANNI EVANGELISTA   HISTORIC BUILDING

Map p274 (☑041 71 82 34; www.scuolasangiovanni.it; Campiello della Scuola 2454, San Polo; scuola & church adult/reduced €8/5; ⊙hours vary; ☱Ferrovia) Flagellants founded this confraternity in 1261, and it served as social club to the Council of Ten, Venice's dreaded secret service. Political power had obvious perks: Pietro Lombardo's 1481 triumphal entry arch, a Codussi-designed double staircase, and a 1729 1st-floor meeting hall designed by Giorgio Massari and decorated by Giandomenico Tiepolo, who was obliged to finish contracts signed by his father.

Bellini and Titian turned out world-class works for the *scuola* that have since been moved to the Gallerie dell'Accademia – but Palma Il Giovane's works still illuminate the Sala d'Albergo, and Pietro Longhi's wriggling baby Jesus is magnetic in *Adoration of the Wise Men*. The confraternity was suppressed by Napoleon, and today the *scuola* hosts conferences and concerts, opening to the public when not booked.

Across the street, the deconsecrated **Chiesa di San Giovanni Evangelista** houses a Tintoretto *Crucifixion*, and the adjoining private chapel, founded by the Badoer family in 970, features Pietro Vecchia's painting of St John the Evangelist holding a pen, eagerly awaiting dictation from God.

CHIESA DI SAN ROCCO   CHURCH

Map p274 (☑041 523 48 64; Campo San Rocco 3053, San Polo; ⊙9.30am-5.30pm; ☱San Tomà) **FREE** Originally built in 1489–1508, Bartolomeo Bon's creation received a baroque facelift in 1765–71, which included a grand portal flanked by Giovanni Marchiori statues. Bon's rose window was moved to the side of the church, near the architect's original side door. Inside the church's Sala dell'Albergo are a couple of comparatively quiet Tintorettos, including *San Rocco Healing the Animals*.

CASA DI CARLO GOLDONI   MUSEUM

Map p274 (☑041 275 93 25; www.visitmuve.it; Calle dei Nomboli 2794, San Polo; adult/reduced €5.50/4, or with Museum Pass free; ⊙10am-5pm Thu-Tue summer, to 4pm winter; ☱San Tomà) Venetian playwright Carlo Goldoni (1707–93) mastered second and third acts: he was a doctor's apprentice before switching to law, which proved handy when an *opera buffa* (comic opera) didn't sell. But as the 1st-floor display at his birthplace explains, Goldoni had the last laugh with his social satires. The real highlight here is an **18th-century puppet theatre**.

CHIESA DI SAN POLO   CHURCH

Map p274 (www.chorusvenezia.org; Campo San Polo 2118, San Polo; admission €3, or with Chorus Pass free; ⊙10am-5pm Mon-Sat; ☱San Tomà) Travellers pass this modest 9th-century

Byzantine brick church without guessing that major dramas unfold inside. Under the *carena di nave* ceiling, Tintoretto's *Last Supper* shows apostles alarmed by Jesus' announcement that one of them will betray him. Giandomenico Tiepolo's *Stations of the Cross* sacristy cycle shows onlookers tormenting Jesus, who leaps triumphantly from his tomb in the ceiling panel.

EATING

★ALL'ARCO   VENETIAN €

Map p274 (☑041 520 56 66; Calle dell'Ochialer 436, San Polo; cicheti from €1.50; ⓧ8am-8pm Wed-Fri, to 3pm Mon, Tue & Sat; ⬤Rialto-Mercato) Search out this authentic neighbourhood *osteria* (casual tavern) for some of the best *cicheti* (bar snacks) in town. Armed with ingredients from the nearby Rialto market, father–son team Francesco and Matteo serve miniature masterpieces such as *cannocchia* (mantis shrimp) with pumpkin and roe, and *otrega crudo* (raw butterfish) with mint-and-olive-oil marinade.

Even with copious *prosecco,* hardly any meal here tops €20 or falls short of five stars.

★DAI ZEMEI   VENETIAN, CICHETI €

Map p274 (☑041 520 85 46; www.ostariadaize mei.it; Ruga Vecchia San Giovanni 1045, San Polo; cicheti from €1.50; ⓧ8.30am-8.30pm Mon-Sat, to 7pm Sun; ⬤San Silvestro) Running this closet-sized *cicheti* counter are *zemei* (twins) Franco and Giovanni, who serve loyal regulars small meals with outsized imagination: gorgonzola lavished with *peperoncino* (chilli) marmalade, duck breast drizzled with truffle oil, or chicory paired with leek and marinated anchovies. A gourmet bargain for inspired bites and impeccable wines – try a crisp Nosiola or invigorating Prosecco Brut.

AL PONTE STORTO   VENETIAN, CICHETI €

Map p274 (☑041 528 21 44; www.alponte storto.com; Calle del Ponte Storto 1278, San Polo; cicheti from €1, meals €33; ⓧ10.30am-3pm & 6-10pm Tue-Sun; ☎; ⬤San Silvestro) Once an anarchist clubhouse, intimate, art-slung 'At The Crooked Bridge' serves up scrumptious *cicheti*, whether it's radicchio, pancetta and Brie quiche or the osteria's famed *polpette* (meatballs). For a more substantial feed, plonk yourself down at a table and tuck

into house favourites like *pappardelle con scampi e radicchio* (pasta with prawns and chicory). In the warmer months, request one of the two canalside tables.

IL VIZIETTO   CICHETI, SANDWICHES €

Map p274 (Campo San Stin 2532; cicheti €1.50, sandwiches €4-5; ⓧ9am-midnight Tue-Sun summer, 7.30am-10pm Tue-Thu & Sun, to midnight Fri & Sat winter; ☎; ⬤San Tomà) Dario Colla's square-side bar is a hit with peckish locals, who graze and gossip over generous, seasonal *cicheti* like silky Friulian *lardo* (lard) with truffle-scented mushroom pâté. The grilled focaccias and *piadine* (Italian flat-bread sandwiches) are just as lip-smackingly good, stuffed with combos like cherry tomatoes, ricotta, olive tapenade, rucola and grilled vegetables. Belly full, linger on the square with a glass of Triveneto vino.

AL BACCO FELICE   PIZZA, ITALIAN €

Map p277 (☑041 528 77 94; Calle dei Amai 197e, Santa Croce; pizza €5-20, meals €30; ⓧ11.30am-midnight; ⬤Piazzale Roma) Paper placemats, pop tunes on the radio, and glowing customer feedback plastered up the wall: Al Bacco sets a casual, convivial scene for decent, thin-crust pizzas, solid pasta dishes, and unfussy classic mains like veal scaloppine. Pizzas start at a bargain €5, making it an especially popular spot for students and families on a budget.

SNACK BAR AI NOMBOLI   SANDWICHES €

Map p274 (☑041 523 09 95; Rio Terà dei Nomboli 271c, San Polo; sandwiches €2, panini €6; ⓧ7am-8.30pm Mon-Fri, 7am-3pm Sat; ☎; ⬤San Tomà) This snappy Venetian comeback to McDonald's is never short of local professors, labourers and clued-in out-of-towners. Crusty rolls are packed with local cheeses, fresh greens, roast vegetables, salami, prosciutto and roast beef, and served at an antique marble lunch counter. Beyond standard mayo, condiments range from spicy mustard to wild nettle sauce. Cheap, filling and scrumptious.

OSTERIA MOCENIGO   VENETIAN €

Map p274 (☑041 523 17 03; Salizada San Stae 1919, Santa Croce; meals €25; ⓧnoon-3pm & 7-10.30pm; ☎☉; ⬤San Stae) Times and dining habits have changed since doges strained waistcoat buttons at neighbouring Palazzo Mocenigo: warm, homely Osteria Mocenigo offers casual lunches and dinners of dishes like ravioli with radicchio and

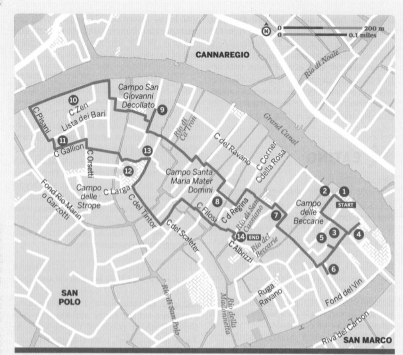

Neighbourhood Walk
Venice Gourmet Crawl

START RIALTO MARKET
END ANTICHE CARAMPANE
LENGTH 2.9KM, TWO HOURS

A trip through gourmet history starts where great Venetian meals have begun for centuries: **1 Rialto Market** (p89). Under the roof of the **2 Pescaria** (p89), fishmongers arrange the day's catch atop hillocks of ice.

Around the corner, glimpse the trade-route treasures that made Venice's fortune at **3 Drogheria Mascari** (p101), where fragrant spices mix it with artisanal local condiments and fine wines. Make a quick detour for **4 Casa del Parmigiano** (p104), a historic deli laden with harder-to-find cheeses and mouthwatering cured meats. Appetite piqued, duck into **5 All'Arco** (p95) for some of the city's best *cicheti* – ask for *una fantasia* (a fantasy), and father–son chefs Francesco and Matteo will invent a dish with ingredients you just saw at the market.

Stop for an aromatic espresso at specialist coffee peddler **6 Caffè del Doge** (p99),

then wander northwest to **7 Cárte** (p100) to browse recipe albums and cocktail rings in marble paper, and over a couple of bridges until you smell the ink drying on letterpress menus (also sold blank for swanky dinner parties) at **8 Veneziastampa** (p102).

Learn the scientific names of the lagoon creatures you just saw at the market at **9 Museo di Storia Naturale di Venezia** (p91). Walk a sunny stretch of Grand Canal along **10 Riva de Biasio**, allegedly named for 16th-century butcher Biagio (Biasio) Cargnio, whose sausages contained a special ingredient: children. When found out, Biasio was drawn and quartered.

Thankfully, there are no questionable ingredients in the organic gelato at standout **11 Alaska Gelateria** (p97). Grab a scoop or two and lick your way across to **12 Campo San Giacomo dell'Orio**, where natural-process *prosecco* awaits at **13 Al Prosecco** (p98) – just don't be late for dinner at much-loved **14 Antiche Carampane** (p97), or some other diner may nab the last bowl of gnocchi.

whitefish, and grilled meats. A single dish here makes a satisfying meal, with Veneto wine by the glass.

ANTICO FORNO
PIZZA €

Map p274 (☑041 520 41 10; Ruga Rialto 973, San Polo; pizza slices from €2.50; ⏰11am-10pm; 🚇; 🚤San Silvestro) The counter at this hole-in-the-wall take-away is a sea of oven-fresh pizza perfection of both the thin- and thick-crust varieties. Join the queue for staples like margherita or more imaginative pairings such as fresh ricotta with spinach and tomato. Two slices make for a cheap and satisfying lunch on the go.

⭐ALASKA GELATERIA
GELATERIA €

Map p274 (☑041 71 52 11; Calle Larga dei Bari 1159, Santa Croce; gelato from €1.50; ⏰11am-10pm; 🚼; 🚤Riva de Biasio) 🌱 Outlandish organic artisanal gelato. Enjoy a Slow Food scoop of house-roasted local pistachio, or two of the tangy Sicilian lemon with vaguely minty Sant'Erasmo *carciofi*. Or perhaps you're more a star anise, cardamom or green tea kind of gelatista? Even vegans are spoiled for choice of flavours, including watermelon and rose.

PASTICCERIA RIZZARDINI
PASTRIES €

Map p274 (☑041 522 38 35; Campiello dei Meloni 1415, San Polo; pastries €1.30-4; ⏰7am-8pm Mon & Wed-Sat, from 7.30am Sun; 🚤San Silvestro) 'From 1742' boasts this corner bakery, whose reputation for *krapfen* (cream puffs), strudel and doughnuts has survived many an *acqua alta* – record flood levels are marked by the door. Stop by any time for reliable espresso, *spritz* and *pallone di Casanova* (Casanova's balls) biscuits – but act fast if you want that last slice of tiramisu.

⭐OSTERIA TREFANTI
VENETIAN €€

Map p274 (☑041 520 17 89; www.osteriatrefanti.it; Fondamenta Garzotti 888, Santa Croce; meals €40; ⏰noon-2.30pm & 7-10.30pm Tue-Sat, noon-2.45pm Sun; 🚇; 🚤Riva de Biasio) 🌱 La Serenissima's spice trade lives on at simple, elegant Trefanti, where a vibrant dish of marinated prawns, hazelnuts, berries and caramel might get an intriguing kick from garam masala. Furnished with old pews and recycled copper lamps, it's the domain of the young and competent Sam Metcalfe and Umberto Slongo, whose passion for quality extends to a small, beautifully curated selection of local and organic wines.

The space is small and deservedly popular, so book ahead, especially later in the week.

⭐ANTICHE CARAMPANE
VENETIAN €€

Map p274 (☑041 524 01 65; www.antichecarampane.com; Rio Terà delle Carampane 1911, San Polo; meals €30-45; ⏰12.45-2.30pm & 7.30-10.30pm Tue-Sat; 🚤San Stae) Hidden in the once-shady lanes behind Ponte delle Tette, this culinary indulgence is a trick to find. Once you do, say goodbye to soggy lasagne and hello to a market-driven menu of silky *crudi* (raw fish/seafood), surprisingly light *fritto misto* (fried seafood) and *caramote* prawn salad with seasonal vegetables. Never short of a smart, convivial crowd, it's a good idea to book ahead.

ANTICA BESSETA
VENETIAN €€

Map p274 (☑041 72 16 87; www.anticabesseta.it in Italian; Salizada de Cà Zusto 1395; meals €35; ⏰noon-2.30pm & 7-10.30pm; 🚇; 🚤Riva de Biasio) Wood panelling and fresh flowers set the scene at this veteran trattoria, known for giving contemporary verve to regional classics. The *delizie di pesce dell'Adriatico* – a tasting plate which might see seared scallops served with a brandy and asparagus salsa – makes for a stimulating prologue to dishes like almond-crusted turbot with artichokes and cherry tomatoes.

Dapper owner Gigi Cassan is a trained sommelier, a fact reflected in the inspired wine list.

OSTERIA LA ZUCCA
MODERN ITALIAN €€

Map p274 (☑041 524 15 70; www.lazucca.it; Calle del Tentor 1762, Santa Croce; meals €35; ⏰12.30-2.30pm & 7-10.30pm Mon-Sat; 🚤San Stae) With its menu of seasonal vegetarian creations and classic meat dishes, this cosy, woody restaurant consistently hits the mark. Herbs and spices are used to great effect in dishes such as cinnamon-tinged pumpkin flan and lamb with dill and pecorino. The small interior can get toasty, so reserve canalside seats in summer.

RISTORANTE RIBOT
VENETIAN €€

Map p277 (☑041 524 24 86; www.ristoranteribot.com; Fondamenta Minotto 160; meals €32; ⏰noon-2.30pm & 7-10.30pm Mon-Fri, 7-10.30pm Sat; 🚤Piazzale Roma) While linen on the tables, cookbooks and bottles on the shelves, and the day's menu written on a single sheet of paper – friendly Ribot is a sound bet for a fresh, flavoursome regional feed.

A DECLINING POPULATION

Between 1563 and 1951 Venice's population hovered between 105,000 and 175,000 people, even taking into account the plague. By February 2015 that figure had declined to 56,282 as residents increasingly abandon the city and its diminishing amenities for the mainland.

Dishes span surf and turf, from a simple, well-balanced *impepata di cozze* (mussels with pepper and white wine) to a remarkably delicate *fegato alla veneziana* (Venetian-style calves' liver).

There's courtyard seating in the summer months, and a well-stocked cellar with around 500 wines.

TRATTORIA DA IGNAZIO
VENETIAN, SEAFOOD €€

Map p274 (☑041 523 48 52; www.trattoriada ignazio.com; Calle dei Saoneri 2749, San Polo; meals €25-30; ⊙noon-3pm & 7-10pm Sun-Fri; ⏅; ⓢSan Tomà) Dapper white-jacketed waiters serve pristine grilled lagoon fish, fresh pasta and desserts made in-house ('of course') with a proud flourish, on tables bedecked with yellow linen. On cloudy days, homemade crab pasta with a bright Lugana white wine make a fine substitute for sunshine. On sunny days and warm nights, the neighbourhood converges beneath the garden's grape arbour.

FRARY'S
MIDDLE EASTERN, MEDITERRANEAN €€

Map p274 (☑041 72 00 50; www.frarys.it; Fondamenta dei Frari 2558, San Polo; meals €25, 2-course weekday lunch €12; ⊙noon-3pm & 6-10.30pm; ☎⏅; ⓢSan Tomà) Spice things up at Frary's, a bohemian-spirited bolthole serving up classics from Morocco to the UAE. The antipasto platter might pair Greek *hortopita* (filo pastry stuffed with cheese and vegetables) with Kurdish *kubbe* (fried rice ball stuffed with spiced ground meat), while the fragrant mains include classic moussaka and spicy Jordanian rice dish *maglu'ba*. The menu includes vegan and gluten-free options.

If she's 'in the zone', owner Federica might even read your future in the bottom of your coffee cup.

MURO
PIZZA, ITALIAN €€

Map p274 (☑041 524 16 28; www.murovenezia. com; Campiello dello Spezier 2048; pizza €7-15, meals €35; ⊙noon-3pm & 7-10.30pm; ⓢSan Stae) Contemporary and relaxed, versatile Muro plays the role of both restaurant and pizzeria. Tuck into inventive pizzas and seasonal salads, or linger over fresh, flavourpacked dishes like *zuppa di pesce* (fish soup). Carnivores are especially well catered for, with no shortage of grilled meats and a succulent tartare to boot.

BIRRARIA LA CORTE
PIZZA €€

Map p274 (☑041 275 05 70; Campo San Polo 2168, San Polo; pizzas €7-14, meals €35; ⊙noon-3pm & 6-10.30pm; ☎; ⓢSan Tomà) This onetime bull stable became a brewery in the 19th century to keep Venice's Austrian occupiers occupied, and beer and beef remain reliable bets. There's also pizza and much coveted piazza-side seating.

DRINKING & NIGHTLIFE

★AL PROSECCO
WINE BAR

Map p274 (☑041 524 02 22; www.alprosecco. com; Campo San Giacomo dell'Orio, Santa Croce 1503; ⊙10am-8pm; ⓢSan Stae) 🍷 The urge to toast sunsets in Venice's loveliest *campo* is only natural – and so is the wine at Al Prosecco. This forward-thinking bar specialises in *vini naturi* (natural-process wines) – organic, biodynamic, wild-yeast fermented – from enlightened Italian winemakers like Cinque Campi and Azienda Agricola Barichel. So order a glass of unfiltered 'cloudy' prosecco and toast to the good things in life.

★AL MERCÀ
WINE BAR

Map p274 (Campo Cesare Battisti 213, San Polo; ⊙10am-2.30pm & 6-9pm Mon-Thu, to 9.30pm Fri & Sat; ⓢRialto) Discerning drinkers throng to this cupboard-sized counter on a Rialto market square to sip on top-notch *prosecco* and DOC wines by the glass (from €2). Edibles usually include meatballs and mini *panini* (from €1), proudly made using super-fresh ingredients.

DO MORI
WINE BAR

Map p274 (☑041 522 54 01; Sotoportego dei do Mori 429; ⊙8am-2pm & 4.30-7.30pm Mon-Sat; ⓢRialto) You'll feel like you've stepped into a

Rembrandt painting at venerable Do Mori, a dark, rustic bar with roots in the 15th century. Under gleaming, gargantuan copper pots, nostalgists swill from around 40 wines by the glass, or slurp *prosecco* from old-school champagne saucers. Peckish? Bar bites include pickled onions with anchovies, succulent *polpette* (meat balls) and slices of pecorino.

★CANTINA DO SPADE   BAR

Map p274 (☎041 521 05 83; www.cantinado spade.com; Calle delle Do Spade 860, San Polo; ⊙10am-3pm & 6-10pm; 🐾; 🚊Rialto) Famously mentioned in Casanova's memoirs, cosy, brick-lined 'Two Spades' continues to keep Venice in good spirits with its bargain Tri-Veneto wines and young, laid-back management. Come early for market-fresh *fritture* (batter-fried seafood) or linger longer with satisfying, sit-down dishes like *bigoli in salsa* (pasta in anchovy and onion sauce).

★BACARETO DA LELE   BAR

Map p277 (Campo dei Tolentini 183, Santa Croce; ⊙6am-8pm Mon-Fri, to 2pm Sat; 🚊Piazzale Roma) Pocket-sized Da Lele is never short of uni students and workers, stopping for a cheap, stand-up *ombra* (from €0.60) on their way to and from the train station. Scan the blackboard for the day's wines and pair them with bite-sized *panini* (€1), stuffed with freshly shaved cured meats and combos like pancetta and artichoke. The place closes for much of August.

OSTERIA DA FILO   CAFE, BAR

Map p274 (Hosteria alla Poppa; ☎041 524 65 54; Calle delle Oche, Santa Croce; ⊙5-11pm; 🐾; 🚊Riva de Biasio) A living room where drinks are served, Hosteria alla Poppa comes complete with creaky sofas, free wi-fi, abandoned novels and the odd live music gig. Service is brusque, but drinks are cheap and the Mediterranean tapas tasty.

CAFFÈ DEI FRARI   CAFE, BAR

Map p274 (☎041 524 18 77; Fondamenta dei Frari 2564, San Polo; ⊙9am-9pm Wed-Sun; 🚊San Tomà) Take your (admittedly expensive) espresso with a heaping of history at this century-old carved wooden bar, or recover from the sensory overload of I Frari with a sandwich, a glass of wine and easy conversation at the dinky indoor cafe tables downstairs or on the Liberty-style wrought-iron balcony upstairs. The bar can close at around 4pm on Sundays in winter.

TAVERNA DA BAFFO   OSTERIA

Map p274 (☎041 524 20 61; www.tavernada baffo.com; Campiello Sant'Agostin 2346, Santa Croce; ⊙11am-11pm; 🐾; 🚊San Tomà) This *osteria*, named for Casanova's licentious poet pal Giorgio Baffo, is actually a converted chapel, stripped to its naked brick walls. With strong *spritz,* draught beer and tasty house wines, there may be impromptu poetry from the *campo* crowd by night's end. Arrive early at summer happy hours to claim outdoor tables, *bruschetta* orders and the bartender's attention.

BARCOLLO   BAR

Map p274 (☎041 522 81 58; Campo Cesare Battista 219, San Polo; ⊙7.30am-12.30am Mon-Thu, to 2am Fri & Sat, 10am-midnight Sun; 🐾; 🚊Rialto) Its name might mean stagger, but there's more to contemporary, light-filled Barcollo than hardy cocktail sessions and Friday night DJ sets. Just steps away from Rialto Market, the cafe-bar makes for a handy daytime pitstop, with everything from OJ and coffee, to brioche, muffins and *arancini* (rice balls). If the thought of staggering does appeal, no doubt the €1 house wine will help you on your way.

CAFFÈ DEL DOGE   CAFE

Map p274 (☎041 522 77 87; www.caffedeldoge. com; Calle dei Cinque 609, San Polo; ⊙7am-7pm; 🚊San Silvestro) Sniff your way to the affable Doge, where dedicated drinkers slurp their way through the menu of speciality imported coffees from Ethiopia to Guatemala, all

> ### ❶ GUIDED BAR CRAWLS
>
> Why drink alone? To help visitors navigate Venice's vast *cicheti* (bar snacks) repertoire and confusing backstreets, **Venice Urban Adventures** (Map p278; ☎348 980 85 66; www.veniceurbanadventures.com; cicheti tour €77; ⊙tours 11.30am & 5.30pm Mon-Sat) offers intimate tours of happy-hour hot spots led by knowledgable, enthusiastic, English-speaking local foodies. Tours run €77 per person (with up to 12 participants), covering *ombre* (wine by the glass) and *cicheti* in five (yes, five) *bacari* (bars) and a tipsy Rialto gondola crossing (weather permitting). Departure points vary seasonally; consult website.

SAN POLO & SANTA CROCE DRINKING & NIGHTLIFE

roasted on the premises. If you're feel especially inspired, you can even pick up a coffee percolator. Add a block of chocolate and you have yourself the perfect pick-me-up.

☆ ENTERTAINMENT

★**PALAZETTO BRU ZANE**　CLASSICAL MUSIC

Map p274 (Centre du Musique Romantique Française; 📞041 521 10 05; www.bru-zane.com; Palazetto Bru Zane 2368, San Polo; adult/reduced €15/5; ⊙box office 2.30-5.30pm Mon-Fri, closed late Jul–mid-Aug; 🚉San Tomà) Pleasure palaces don't get more romantic than Palazetto Bru Zane on concert nights, when exquisite harmonies tickle Sebastiano Ricci angels tumbling across stucco-frosted ceilings. Multi-year restorations returned the 1695–97 Casino Zane's 100-seat music room to its original function, attracting world-class musicians to enjoy its acoustics from late September to mid-May.

Free guided tours of the building run on Thursdays (in Italian/French/English 2.30pm/3pm/3.30pm), with the added offer of discounted €12 concert tickets.

CASA DEL CINEMA　CINEMA

Map p274 (Videoteca Pasinetti; 📞041 524 13 20; www.comune.venezia.it/cinema; Salizada San Stae 1990, Santa Croce; adult/reduced €7.50/7; ⊙shows afternoon Mon-Sat; 🚉San Stae) Venice's public film archive shows art films in a modern 50-seat, wood-beamed screening room inside Palazzo Mocenigo. Original-language classics are shown Monday and Thursday, while first-run independent films are screened on Friday; check online for pre-release previews and revivals with introductions by directors, actors and scholars.

SCUOLA GRANDE DI SAN GIOVANNI EVANGELISTA　OPERA

Map p274 (📞041 426 65 59; www.scuolasangiovanni.it; Campiello della Scuola 2454, Santa Croce; adult/reduced from €30/25; 🚉San Tomà) Drama comes with the scenery when Italian opera favourites – Puccini's *Tosca*, Verdi's *La Traviata*, Rossini's *Il Barbiere di Seviglia* – are performed in the lavish hall where Venice's secretive Council of Ten socialised. Stage sets can't compare to the Scuola: sweep up Mauro Codussi's 15th-century staircase into Giorgio Massari's

1729 hall, and take your seat amid Giandomenico Tiepolo paintings.

🛍 SHOPPING

★**CÁRTE**　HANDICRAFTS

Map p274 (📞320 0248776; www.cartevenezia.it; Calle dei Cristi 1731, San Polo; ⊙11am-5.30pm; 🚉Rialto-Mercato) Venice's shimmering lagoon echoes in marbled-paper earrings and artist's portfolios, thanks to the steady hands and restless imagination of *carta marmorizzata* (marbled-paper) *maestra* Rosanna Corrò. After years restoring ancient Venetian books, Rosanna began creating her original, bookish beauties: tubular statement necklaces, op-art jewellery boxes, one-of-a-kind contemporary handbags, even wedding albums.

★**GILBERTO PENZO**　HANDICRAFTS

Map p274 (📞041 71 93 72; www.veniceboats.com; Calle 2 dei Saoneri 2681, San Polo; ⊙9am-12.30pm & 3-6pm Mon-Sat; ♿; 🚉San Tomà) Yes, you actually can take a gondola home in your pocket. Anyone fascinated by the models at Museo Storico Navale (p128) will go wild here, amid handmade wooden models of all kinds of Venetian boats, including some that are seaworthy (or at least bathtub worthy). Signor Penzo also creates kits, so crafty types and kids can have a crack at it themselves.

I VETRI A LUME DI AMADI　GLASS

Map p274 (📞041 523 80 89; Calle Saoneri 2747, San Polo; ⊙10am-1pm & 2.30-6pm Mon-Sat; 🚉San Tomà) Glass menageries don't get more fascinating than the one created before your eyes by Signor Amadi. Fierce little glass crabs approach pink-tipped coral, and glass peas spill from a speckled pea pod. You might be tempted to swat at eerily lifelike glass mosquitoes or (gently) prod a snapping pelican. Venetian pets at their low-maintenance best.

DECLARE　ACCESSORIES

Map p274 (📞041 822 32 27; www.declareindependence.it; Calle Seconda dei Saoneri 2671, San Polo; ⊙10.30am-7.30pm; 🚉San Tomà) Declare's sleek black fitout provides a dramatic backdrop for Emanuel Cestaro's and Omar Pavanello's boldly hued, contemporary leathergoods. Made by artisans using full-grain Tuscan leather, these coveted, butter-soft creations include origami-inspired wallets, slinky clutch purses and totes, as well as effortlessly stylish duffle and messenger bags. You'll find a second branch in **San Marco** (Map p268; ☑041 522 55 59; www.declareindependence.it; Calle della Mandola 3801; ☺10.30am-7.30pm; ☻Sant'Angelo).

VIZIOVIRTÙ   FOOD

Map p274 (☑041 275 01 49; www.viziovirtu.com; Calle del Campaniel 2898a, San Polo; ☺10am-1pm & 1.30-7.30pm, closed Sun Jun-Aug; ☻Ca' Rezzonico) Work your way through Venice's most decadent vices at this Willy Wonka-esque chocolatier, whose whisker-licking edibles include plague-doctor's masks. Ganache-filled chocolates come in a five-course meal of flavours, from barolo wine, pink pepper and balsamic vinegar, to wild fennel and Earl Grey.

DAMOCLE EDIZIONI   BOOKS

Map p274 (☑346 8345720; www.edizionidamocle.com; Calle Perdon 1311, San Polo; ☺10am-1pm & 3-7pm Mon-Fri; ☻San Silvestro) Pocket-sized Damocle is both a bookshop and publisher, translating literary greats like Oscar Wilde and Luigi Pirandello, as well as showcasing emerging writing talent, from contemporary Chinese poets to Spanish writer Luna Miguel. Most of Damocle's creations are bilingual (including books in English) and many feature beautiful artwork created through collaborations with local and foreign artists.

OH MY BLUE   JEWELLERY, HANDICRAFTS

Map p274 (☑041 243 57 41; www.ohmyblue.it; Campo San Tomà 2865, San Polo; ☺10am-7.30pm; ☻San Tomà) In her white-on-white gallery, switched-on Elena Rizzi showcases edgy, show-stopping jewellery, accessories and decorative objects from both local and international talent like Elena Camilla Bertellotti, Ana Hagopian and Yoko Takirai. Expect anything from quartz rings and paper necklaces, to sculptural bags and ceramics.

PIED À TERRE   SHOES

Map p274 (☑041 528 55 13; www.piedaterre-venice.com; Sotoportego degli Oresi 60, San Polo; ☺10am-12.30pm & 2.30-7.30pm; ☻Rialto) Rialto courtesans and their 30cm-high platform shoes are long gone, but Venetian slippers stay stylish. Pied à Terre's colourful *furlane* (slippers) are handcrafted with recycled bicycle-tyre treads, ideal for finding your footing on a gondola. Choose from velvet, brocade or raw silk in vibrant shades of lemon and ruby, with optional piping. Don't see your size? Shoes can be custom made and shipped.

ALBERTO SARRIA MASKS   HANDICRAFTS

Map p274 (☑041 520 72 78; www.masksvenice.com; San Polo 777, Santa Croce; ☺10am-7pm; ☻San Stae) Go Gaga or channel Casanova at this atelier, dedicated to the art of masquerade for over 30 years. Sarria's *commedia dell'arte* masks are worn by theatre companies from Argentina to Osaka – ominous burnished black leather for dramatic leads, harlequin-chequered *cartapesta* (papier-mâché) for comic foils, starting from around €20. Beyond the masks is a cast of one-of-a-kind marionettes, ready to take their first steps.

DROGHERIA MASCARI   FOOD, WINE

Map p274 (☑041 522 97 62; www.imascari.com; Ruga degli Spezieri 381, San Polo; ☺8am-1pm & 4-7.30pm Mon, Tue & Thu-Sat, 8am-1pm Wed; ☻Rialto) Ziggurats of cayenne, leaning towers of star anise and chorus lines of olive oils draw awestruck foodies to Drogheria Mascari's windows. Indoors, chefs clutch truffle jars like holy relics, kids ogle candy in copper-lidded jars and dazed gourmands confront 50 different aromatic honeys. For small-production Italian vino – including Veneto cult producers like Giuseppe Quintarelli – don't miss the backroom *cantina*, home to around 1000 wines.

MICHELA PAVAN GALLERY   JEWELLERY, ARTS

Map p274 (☑041 523 70 46; www.galleriamichelapavan.it; Rio Terà Secondo 2279, San Polo; ☺10am-7pm; ☻San Stae) This beautifully curated gallery serves as a platform for highly talented, emerging jewellery designers. While the line-up changes every two to three months, the underlying theme remains the same – design inspired by history or nature (think bronze rings inspired by ancient Etruscan culture). The space also exhibits conversation-sparking sculpture and painting, in which contemporary themes might merge with Renaissance techniques.

DIETROLANGOLO   ACCESSORIES

Map p274 (☑041 524 30 71; www.dietrolangolo2657.com; Calle Seconda dei Saoneri 2657, San Polo; ☺10am-7.30pm; ☻San Tomà) On a backstreet behind I Frari, Dietrolangolo

TALK, EAT, LIVE ITALIAN

You see a rental sign on a palace door and you start daydreaming: morning banter with the market *fruttivendoli* (greengrocers), lunchtime gossip with the neighbours at your local *bacaro* (hole-in-the-wall bar), perhaps an evening *ti amo* at a candlelit, canalside restaurant. There's no doubt that a grasp of Italian will enrich your experience of Venice, from casual bar chats to a richer understanding of the city's culture and nuances.

If you're itching for a deeper Venetian connection, consider signing up for a language course with **Venice Italian School** (p246). Not only is the school run by Venetian locals Diego and Lucia Cattaneo, it uses the broader classroom of Venice to draw out its students' burgeoning language skills.

Classes take place in the family house on Campo San Stin, where their biscuit-bearing father also bears cheery Italian salutations. In the afternoon keener students convene in church clubrooms, or opt for an afternoon practising the imperative at the local *voga* (Venetian-style rowing) club.

Art curators wanting to cut a *bella figura* at the Biennale may take lunchtime lessons in a local restaurant; food and wine junkies indulge in real-world tastings in local *bacari* where successful pronunciation brings platters of unusual *cicheti* and glasses of limited-production wines. Best of all is the cooking class in Mariagrazia's gorgeous *palazzo* (mansion), where students are challenged to make fresh pasta, navigating kitchen utensils and foreign ingredients. The reward for star students: one of the most delicious and convivial meals you'll share in town.

All the courses are bespoke and can be organised for individuals, groups or families. Cultural classes learning *voga*, cheese tasting or cooking can be booked independently and are open to outsiders. And if that wasn't enough, the school can also help arrange well-priced accommodation.

stocks affordable, original design pieces by young and innovative talent from Italy and beyond. On any given visit you might find reversible handbags and foldable gumboots, to architectural jewellery and street-art–inspired tees.

FRANCO FURLANETTO
HANDICRAFTS

Map p274 (☑041 520 95 44; www.ffurlanetto. com; Calle delle Nomboli 2768, San Polo; ◷10am-6pm Mon-Fri, to 5pm Sat; ☷San Tomà) Masks and violins inspire maestro Franco's sleek, original designs for *forcole* (gondola oarlocks) and *remi* (oars), hand-carved on site from blocks of walnut, cherry and pear wood. There's a science to each creation, perfectly weighted and angled to propel a vessel forward, but also a delicate art. For its sculptural finesse, Franco's work has been shown in New York's Metropolitan Museum of Art.

ANATEMA
FASHION, ACCESSORIES

Map p274 (☑041 524 22 21; www.anatema.it; Rio Terà 2603, San Polo; ◷10am-1.30pm & 3-7.30pm; ☷San Tomà) Add a Venetian eye for colour to a Japanese flair for sculptural fashion, and here you have it: teal Italian mohair tube scarves that float around the collarbone like clouds, and pleated Thai and Italian silk shawls and bags in shimmering *cangiante* (dual-toned) shades worthy of a Milan runway. The Venetian–Japanese design duo behind Anatema brings out new collections each season, from sunhats to wool-felt brooches.

VENEZIASTAMPA
HANDICRAFTS

Map p274 (☑041 71 54 55; www.veneziastampa. com; Campo Santa Maria Mater Domini 2173, Santa Croce; ◷8.15am-1pm & 2.30-7pm Mon-Fri, 9.30am-5pm Sat; ☷San Stae) Mornings are best to catch the 1930s Heidelberg machine in action – but whenever you arrive, you'll find mementos hot off the proverbial press. Veneziastampa recalls more elegant times, when postcards were gorgeously lithographed and Casanovas invited dates upstairs to 'look at my etchings'. Pick your signature symbols – meteors, faucets, trapeze artists – for original bookplates and cards.

GMEINER
SHOES

Map p274 (☑338 8962189; www.gabriele gmeiner.com; Campiello del Sol 951, San Polo; ◷by appointment 10am-1pm & 3-7pm Mon-Fri;

Rialto-Mercato) Paris, London, Venice: Gabriele Gmeiner honed her shoemaking craft at Hermès and John Lobb, and today jetsetters fly to Venice just for her ultrasleek Oxfords with hidden 'bent' seams and minutely handstiched brogues, made to measure for men and women (around €3000, including hand-carved wooden last).

NERODISEPPIA   GIFTS

Map p274 (☏041 865 18 89; www.nerodisep piavenezia.com; Calle Larga dei Bari 968, Santa Croce; ☺11am-1pm & 3.30-7.30pm Mon, Tue & Thu-Sat; ⛴Ferrovia) Collective gallery Nerodiseppia ditches baroque glitz for emerging Venetian and Italian design talent. Uncover anything from graphic tees and two-toned leather satchels, to recycled leather notebooks and asymmetrical, boiled-wool coats. The space doubles as an alt-culture hub, hosting art openings, CD release parties and DJ sets – check the Facebook page for upcoming events.

LABERINTHO   JEWELLERY

Map p274 (☏041 71 00 17; www.laberintho.it; Calle del Scaleter 2236, San Polo; ☺10am-12.30pm & 3-7pm Tue-Sat; ⛴San Stae) A token jewel in the window is a tantalising hint of the custom jewellery this versatile goldsmiths' atelier can create for you, with original designs that nod at Venice's seafaring, Byzantine past: a nautilus-inspired ring inset with opal and turquoise mosaic, a square gold bracelet inlaid with ebony, a necklace of Murano glass seascapes that float on the collarbone like islands...

SCRIBA   ARTS

Map p274 (☏041 523 67 28; Campo dei Frari 3030, San Polo; ☺10am-6pm; ⛴San Tomà) Right behind I Frari, Scriba stocks beautiful lithographs of Venice for around €30, as well as original artwork, photography and old maps. Run by Marina Bertoldini and her husband Fabio, the gallery works with artists from Venice's Accademia di Belle Arti and Florence's Accademia D'Arte, making it a good place to discover local and emerging artists.

SABBIE E NEBBIE   GIFTS

Map p274 (☏041 71 90 73; www.sabbie nebbie.com; Calle dei Nomboli 2768a, San Polo; ☺10am-12.30pm & 4-7.30pm Mon-Sat; ⛴San Tomà) East–West trade-route trends begin here, with chic cast-iron teapots, Japanese-

textile patchwork totes, and Orient-inspired ceramics by Rita Menardi. Trained in design and graphics, owner Maria Teresa Laghi has a sharp eye for beautiful, unique and inspiring objects, making her shop especially popular with discerning locals.

IL PAVONE DI PAOLO PELOSIN   HANDICRAFTS

Map p274 (☏041 522 42 96; Campiello dei Meoni 1478, San Polo; ☺9.30am-2pm & 2.45-7pm Thu-Tue; ⛴San Silvestro) Consider Paolo's hand-bound marbled-paper journals and photo albums a challenge: now it's up to you to create Venice memories worthy of such inspired workmanship. Recipe books are covered in violet and gold feather patterns, rippled blue sketchbooks inspire seascapes, and paper-wrapped pens seem to catch fire with flickers of orange and red.

FARMACIA BURATI   BEAUTY

Map p274 (☏041 522 35 27; www.farmaciabu rati.it; Campo San Polo 2012; ☺9am-1pm & 3.30-7.30pm Mon-Fri, 9am-12.45pm Sat; ⛴San Tomà) When you start feeling the effects of all those *spritz* sessions, pick up some healing herbs at this vintage pharmacy. Adorned with 19th-century woodwork and mosaics, it peddles an impressive range of herbal teas, designed to target a range of ailments. A small range of cosmetics includes deeply moisturising lotions made using argan oil.

CAMPIELLO CA' ZEN   ANTIQUES

Map p274 (☏329 4011625, 041 71 48 71; www. campiellocazen.com; Campiello Zen 2581, San Polo; ☺9am-1pm & 3-7pm Mon-Sat; ⛴San Tomà) Antique Murano glass lamps are the last thing you'd want to cram into your luggage – or so you thought before you saw the 1940s Salviati silver chandelier and the rare ultra-mod red Seguso lamp. That golden Venini goblet seems safe to admire, but here's a dangerous thought: they ship.

MILLE E UNA NOTA   MUSIC

Map p274 (☏041 523 18 22; Calle di Mezzo 1235, San Polo; ☺9.30am-1pm & 3-7.30pm Mon-Sat; ⛴San Tomà) The same thought occurs to almost everyone after hearing a concert in Venice: is it too late to take up an instrument? The easiest would be harmonica or recorder, and Mille e Una Nota has impressive vintage and modern ones from the Italian Alps. If you're feeling ambitious, you can pick up Albinoni sheet music and a lute, too.

SAN POLO & SANTA CROCE SHOPPING

SAN POLO & SANTA CROCE SHOPPING

MURRA
HANDICRAFTS

Map p274 (☑041 523 40 30; Ruga degli Speziali 299, San Polo; ☺10am-7.30pm; ☷Rialto-Mercato) Hot copper and extremely careful handling are the secrets to the embossed leather designs gracing journals, handbags and wallets in artisan Raffaella Murra's atelier. Choose from unique jewellery pieces, satchels detailed with Murano glass or leather roses, hand-sewn journals filled with artisanal Amalfi Coast paper, or a Venetian mask *sans* the kitsch factor.

IL BAULE BLU
VINTAGE

Map p274 (☑041 71 94 48; Campo San Tomà 2916a, San Polo; ☺10.30am-12.30pm & 4-7.30pm Mon-Sat; ☷; ☷San Tomà) A curiosity cabinet of elusive treasures where you can expect to stumble across anything from 1970s bubble sunglasses and vintage Murano *murrine* (glass beads), to vintage Italian coats and frocks in good condition. If travel has proved tough on your kid's favourite toy, first aid and kind words will be administered at the in-house **teddy hospital**.

OTTICA VASCELLARI
ACCESSORIES

Map p274 (☑041 522 93 88; www.otticavascellari.it; Ruga Rialto 1030, San Polo; ☺9am-12.30pm & 3-7.30pm Mon-Sat, closed Mon winter; ☷San Silvestro) ✐ Second-generation opticians and first-class stylists, here the Vascellari family intuit eyewear needs with a glance at your prescription and a long look to assess your face shape and personal style. Angular features demand Vascellari's architectural eyewear with hand-finished two-tone laminates, while delicate features are set off with sleek specs of eco-friendly cotton-resin – all for less than mass-market brands.

CASA DEL PARMIGIANO
FOOD

Map p274 (☑041 520 65 25; www.aliani-casadelparmigiano.it; Campo Cesare Battisti 214; ☺8am-1.30pm Mon-Wed, to 7.30pm Thu-Sat; ☷Rialto) Set suitably beside the appetite-piquing Rialto Market (p89), cheery Casa del Parmigiano heaves with coveted cheeses like potent *parmigiano reggiano* aged three years, to rare, local Asiago Stravecchio di Malga. All are kept good company by fragrant cured meats, *baccalà* (cod) and trays of marinated Sicilian olives. Drooling yet?

GIUSEPPE TINTI
GLASS

Map p274 (☑041 524 12 57; www.tintimuranoglass.com; Campo San Cassian 2343, Santa Croce; ☺9am-7.30pm; ☷Rialto-Mercato) Watch Giuseppe turn molten glass into a colourful, cartoon-like fish with a blowtorch and very steady hands. The results are all around you in this tiny, packed corner bolthole: highly portable, affordable souvenirs, including elegant glass-bead necklaces infused with white and yellow gold, stackable glass-band rings, colourful bottle stoppers, and playful glass magnets.

LA MARGHERITA
HANDICRAFTS

Map p274 (☑393 2100272; www.lamargheritavenezia.com; Campo San Cassian 2345, Santa Croce; ☺10am-7pm Mon-Fri, to 2pm Sat; ☷; ☷Rialto-Mercato) The charm of Venice is captured in a squiggle of Gothic archways by Margherita Rossetto, a cartoonist who also applies her graphic talents to ceramics at this studio. Hand-drawn cards feature Venetian signoras leaning over ironwork balconies, kitchen tiles feature cats sunning on Gothic windowsills, and grinning fish greet diners with a knowing wink on oval fish platters.

MARE DI CARTA
BOOKS

Map p277 (☑041 71 63 04; www.maredicarta.com; Fondamenta dei Tolentini 222, Santa Croce; ☺9am-1pm & 3.30-7.30pm Mon-Fri, 9am-12.30pm & 3-7.30pm Sat; ☷Ferrovia) Sailors, pirates and armchair seafarers should navigate to this canalside storefront, which stocks every maritime map and sailor's-knot manual needed for lagoon exploration, boat upkeep and sealife spotting. If you're considering a sailing, kayaking or diving course or tour – who wouldn't after a few days on the lagoon? – stop here for information.

RIALTO BIOCENTER
FOOD & DRINK

Map p274 (☑041 523 95 15; www.rialtobiocenter.it; Calle della Regina, Santa Croce 2264; ☺8.30am-8pm Mon-Sat; ☷San Stae) ✐ For organic edibles from baby food to biscuits plus sustainably produced wines, pop into Rialto Biocenter, an easy walk to the west of Rialto Market.

Cannaregio

Neighbourhood Top Five

① Exploring the **Ghetto** (p107), the historic island home of Venice's Jewish community that offered refuge from the Inquisition and sparked a Renaissance in thought.

② Discovering the chapel that marked a turning point in art history: **Chiesa di Santa Maria dei Miracoli** (p109).

③ Paying respects to the patron saint of travellers and the genius of Tintoretto at **Chiesa della Madonna dell'Orto** (p109).

④ Finding Grand Canal photo ops and stolen masterpieces at glorious Venetian Gothic **Ca' d'Oro** (p110).

⑤ Munching *cicheti* (bar snacks) during a backstreet bar crawl led by **Cook in Venice** (p113).

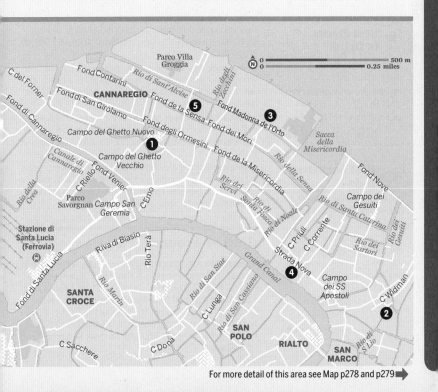

For more detail of this area see Map p278 and p279 ➡

Lonely Planet's Top Tip

Napoleon created the wide pedestrian boulevard that links the train station to the Rialto, and it's a lot like a highway, with rush-hour pedestrian traffic, and fast food and chain stores. But one of Venice's most scenic walks runs parallel to it, along the sunny *fondamenta* (canal bank) running north of the Ghetto and along the lagoon on the Fondamenta Nouve.

✖ Best Places to Eat

➡ Da Rioba (p112)

➡ Dalla Marisa (p111)

➡ Osteria Boccadoro (p112)

➡ Cantina Aziende Agricole (p110)

For reviews, see p110.➡

☕ Best Places to Drink

➡ Vino Vero (p112)

➡ Al Timon (p113)

➡ Torrefazione Cannaregio (p112)

➡ La Cantina (p111)

For reviews, see p112.➡

◉ Best Backstreet Buys

➡ Hand-stamped calling cards at Gianni Basso. (p114)

➡ Vintage *murrine* necklaces from Atelier Leonardo (p115)

➡ Glass bugs from Vittorio Costantini (p115)

➡ Micro-mosaics from Orsoni Mosaici (p116)

For reviews, see p114.➡

CANNAREGIO

Explore Cannaregio

Cannaregio doesn't have the sex appeal of San Marco, the youth of Dorsoduro or the working-class attitude of Castello. Rather, it's a well-balanced residential neighbourhood of unpretentious, patrician *palazzi* (mansions), picturesque canals and quiet *campi* (squares). Like a middle-aged, hipster aunt, it also has an enviable address book of some of the city's best bars, restaurants and shops.

Settled in the 15th-century when Renaissance town planning was taking effect, Cannaregio is less of a maze than the medieval Rialto, its numerous canals cut in straight lines with broad, pedestrian-friendly *fondamente* (canal banks). The Strada Nova, laid in 1871, slices right through the neighbourhood. From this pedestrian highway you can reach most of the area's sights: the churches of Miracoli and Gesuiti, the Jewish Ghetto with its historically important synagogues and the impressive Gothic gallery of Ca' d'Oro. Come evening and you'll appreciate Cannaregio's understated charms even more, as locals flock to sun-soaked bars and canalside restaurants along the Cannaregio, Ormesini and Sensa canals.

Local Life

➡**Canalside dining** Romance comes naturally to candlelit tables reflected in the canal at Dalla Marisa (p111), Da Rioba (p112), Anice Stellato (p112) and Osteria l'Orto dei Mori (p111).

➡**Shopping secrets** Campo Santa Maria Nova hosts a monthly outdoor antiques market (p115) from spring to autumn, but you'll also find artisans, fashion and gifts galore.

➡**Serious about beer** Sightseers craving craft beers will find Venice's best brews at Il Santo Bevitore (p113), Agli Ormesini (p113) and Cantina Aziende Agricole (p110).

➡**Neighbourhood nightlife** Cannaregio's timeless calm is broken at night by modern music acts at Al Timon (p113), Al Parlamento (p113), Paradiso Perduto (p114) and Teatro Fondamenta Nuove (p114).

Getting Around

➡**Vaporetto** After the busy Ferrovia stop, there are two more Grand Canal stops in Cannaregio: San Marcuola (lines 1, 82 and N) and Ca' d'Oro (1 and N). Lines 4.1, 4.2, 5.1 and 5.2 head from Ferrovia into the Canale di Cannaregio and onwards to Fondamenta Nuove. Ferries head from Fondamenta Nuove to the northern islands, including San Michele, Murano, Burano, Le Vignole and Sant'Erasmo.

TOP SIGHT
THE GHETTO

This Cannaregio corner once housed Venice's *ghetto* (foundry) – but its role as Venice's designated Jewish quarter from the 16th to 18th centuries gave the word a whole new meaning. In accordance with the Venetian Republic's 1516 decree, Jewish artisans and lenders stocked and funded Venice's commercial enterprises by day, while at night and on Christian holidays they were restricted to the gated island of Ghetto Nuovo.

DON'T MISS...

➡ Campo del Ghetto Nuovo

➡ Synagogue tour

➡ Museo Ebraico

➡ 1704 Ghetto decree

➡ 1943 memorial

PRACTICALITIES

➡ Map p278, C2

➡ ☑041 715 359

➡ Campo del Ghetto Nuovo

➡ adult/reduced synagogue tour incl museum admission €10/8

➡ ⏱10.30am-5pm Sun-Fri

➡ 🚤Guglie

Campo del Ghetto Nuovo

Unlike most European cities of the era, pragmatic Venice granted Jewish communities the right to practise certain professions key to the city's livelihood, including medicine, trade, banking, fashion and publishing. When the Inquisition forced Jewish communities out of Spain, many fled to Venice. There were Jews in the city from the 12th century onwards, although it wasn't until 1516 that they were segregated in the ghetto and subject to a strict sunset curfew.

As new inhabitants crowded in, upper storeys were added to houses, creating mini-high rises. But while the ghetto was created as an act of segregation, over time it became a refuge in which Jewish culture and ideas thrived. It was the principle site of Hebrew publishing in Europe, Christians flocked to the Italian sermons of learned rabbi Leon da Modena, as well as rowdy Purim plays, and ghetto literary salons attracted leading thinkers of all faiths.

When Napoleon conquered the Republic in 1797, the restrictions pertaining to the ghetto were abolished and Ghetto residents gained standing as Venetian citizens. However, Mussolini's 1938 Racial Laws revived 16th-century discrimination, and in 1943 most Jewish Venetians were deported to concentration camps. As a memorial on the northeast end of the *campo* notes, only 37 returned. Today few of Venice's 500-person Jewish community actually live in the Ghetto, but their children come to the *campo* to play, surrounded by the Ghetto's living legacy of bookshops, art galleries and religious institutions.

Synagogues

As you enter Campo del Ghetto Nuovo, look up: atop private apartments is the wooden cupola of the 1575 **Schola Italiana** (Italian Synagogue; Map p278). The Italians were the poorest in the Ghetto, and their synagogue is starkly beautiful, with elegantly carved woodwork.

Recognisable from the square by its five long windows, the **Schola Tedesca** (German Synagogue) has been the spiritual home of Venice's Ashkenazi community since 1528. By 16th-century Venetian law, only the German Jewish community could lend money, and the success of this trade shows in the handsome decor. The baroque pulpit and carved benches downstairs are topped by a gilded, elliptical women's gallery, modelled after a Venetian opera balcony.

Above the Schola Tedesca in the corner of the *campo*, you'll spot the wooden cupola of **Schola Canton** (the Corner or French Synagogue; Map p278), built c 1531 with gilded rococo interiors added in the 18th century. Though European synagogues typically avoid figurative imagery, this little synagogue makes an exception to the rule with eight charming landscapes inspired by Biblical parables.

Over the bridge in **Campo del Ghetto Vecchio**, refugees from Portugal and Spain raised two synagogues considered among the most elegant in northern Italy, with renovated 17th-century interiors often attributed to Baldassare Longhena. The **Schola Levantina** (Levantine Synagogue; Map p278) has a magnificent 17th-century woodworked pulpit, while

GHETTO RULES

On the wall at No 1131 Calle del Ghetto Vecchio, an official 1704 decree of the Republic forbids Jews converted to Christianity entry into the Ghetto, punishable by 'the rope [hanging], prison, galleys, flogging...and other greater punishments, depending on the judgment of their excellencies (the Executors Against Blasphemy)'.

Despite a 10-year censorship order issued by the church in Rome in 1553, Jewish Venetian publishers contributed hundreds of titles popularising new Renaissance ideas on humanist philosophy, medicine and religion – including the first printed Qur'an.

For more information about the Ghetto, contact the **Jewish Community Centre** (Map p278; ☑041 523 75 65; www.jvenice.org; Ghetto Vecchio; ☺9.30am-5pm Mon-Fri)

SIGHTS

THE GHETTO
JEWISH

See p107.

BANCO ROSSO
HISTORIC BUILDING

Map p278 (☑041 74 03 17; www.bancorosso.org; Campo del Ghetto Nuovo 2912; adult/reduced €2/1.50; ⏱10am-6.30pm May-Sep, to 5pm Oct-Apr; ⛴Guglie) Within the Venetian economy, one of the traditional functions of the Jewish community was to provide cut-rate pawnbroking services – theoretically to the poor, although the well-to-do frequently made use of the service. Of the three, original 'banks' in the Ghetto, the Red Bench is the only one to survive. Inside, a fascinating documentary describes how Jewish moneylenders laid the foundations for the modern banking system and gave us expressions such as bankruptcy and 'in the red'.

CAMPO DEI MORI
PIAZZA

Map p278 (Campo dei Mori; ⛴Madonna dell'Orto) A gent in an outsized turban called Sior Rioba has been hanging out at the corner of Calle dei Mori since the Middle Ages. This is one of four such figures ringing the Campo dei Mori (Square of the Moors) – a misnomer, since these statues are believed to represent the Greek Mastelli family, 12th-century merchants from Morea. The Mastelli brothers became notorious for their eager participation in Doge Dandolo's sacking of Constantinople and, according to legend, Mary Magdalene herself turned them into stone.

★CHIESA DELLA MADONNA DELL'ORTO
CHURCH

Map p278 (Campo della Madonna dell'Orto 3520; admission €2.50; ⏱10am-5pm Mon-Sat; ⛴Madonna dell'Orto) This elegantly spare 1365 brick Gothic cathedral dedicated to the patron saint of travellers remains one of Venice's best kept secrets. It was the parish church of Venetian Renaissance painter Tintoretto, who is buried here in the corner chapel. He saved two of his finest works for the apse: *Presentation of the Virgin in the Temple* and his 1546 *Last Judgement*, where lost souls attempt to hold back a teal tidal wave while an angel rescues one last person from the ultimate *acqua alta* (high tide).

Madonna dell'Orto also had a Bellini masterpiece that was stolen in 1993 – note the empty space in the side chapel.

CANNAREGIO SIGHTS

◉ TOP SIGHT
CHIESA DI SANTA MARIA DEI MIRACOLI

When Nicolò di Pietro's Madonna icon started miraculously weeping in its outdoor shrine around 1480, crowd control became impossible. With pooled resources and marble scavenged from San Marco slag-heaps, neighbours built this chapel (1481–89) to house the painting. Pietro and Tullio Lombardo's miraculous design dropped grandiose Gothic in favour of human-scale harmonies, introducing Renaissance architecture to Venice.

The father–son team creatively repurposed **polychrome marbles** plundered from Egypt to Syria from the sides of Basilica di San Marco. Note the fine scrollwork capitals, and Venetian fish-scale patterns framing veined-marble panels.

The lofty vaulted interior and domed apse seem effortless, but they're marvels of Renaissance engineering, achieved without the Gothic gimmick of buttressing. Look closely at the **chancel staircase** – there are angels and mermaids carved right into the railings by Tullio Lombardo. In a prime example of Renaissance humanism, Pier Maria Pennacchi filled each of the 50 wooden **coffered ceiling panels** with a bright-eyed portrait of a saint or prophet dressed as a contemporary Venetian, like a class photo in a school yearbook.

DON'T MISS...

➜ Pietro Lombardo's Renaissance design
➜ Tullio Lombardo's chancel staircase
➜ Pier Maria Pennacchi's 50 saints on the ceiling
➜ Nicolò di Pietro's Madonna

PRACTICALITIES

➜ Map p278, H5
➜ Campo dei Miracoli 6074
➜ admission €2.50
➜ ⏱10am-5pm Mon-Sat
➜ ⛴Fondamenta Nuove

ARZANÀ
HISTORIC BUILDING

Map p278 (www.arzana.org; Calle delle Pignatte 1936/d; entry by donation; ⛴San Marcuola) Housed in one of Cannaregio's last remaining *squeri* (boatyards) is a fascinating collection of 50 historic boats and their endlessly varied trimmings, saved from destruction by enthusiastic non-profit Arzanà. The yard isn't open to the public on a regular basis, but visits can be arranged in advance by email. Donations are used for the maintenance of the boats and museum collection.

SPEZIERIA ANTICA SANTA FOSCA
HISTORIC SITE

Map p278 (☑041 720 600; Campo Santa Fosca 2234a; ⊘9am-12.30pm & 3-7.30pm Mon-Fri, 9am-12.45pm Sat; ⛴Ca' d'Oro) **FREE** This perfectly preserved 17th-century *spezieria* (pharmacy) illustrates how Venetian medical advice was dispensed three centuries ago, with curatives in antique maiolica jars lined up on hand-carved walnut shelves. The ornately panelled room is richly decorated with etchings of wise doctors hanging beneath a gilded wood-beam ceiling in the style of Sansovino.

The room is now home to bespoke perfumery, **The Merchant of Venice**, where you can buy gauzy golden bags of Byzantium Saffron pot pourri and signature historic fragrances in handblown Murano glass bottles.

CA' D'ORO
MUSEUM

Map p278 (☑041 520 03 45; www.cadoro.org; Calle di Ca' d'Oro 3932; adult/reduced €9.50/6.50; ⊘8.15am-2pm Mon, 8.15am-7.15pm Tue-Sun; ⛴Ca' d'Oro) Along the Grand Canal, you can't miss 15th-century Ca' d'Oro's lacy **arcaded Gothic facade**, resplendent even without the original gold-leaf details that gave the palace its name (Golden House). Baron Franchetti donated to Venice this treasure-box palace packed with masterpieces displayed upstairs in **Galleria Franchetti**, alongside Renaissance wonders plundered from Veneto churches during Napoleon's conquest of Italy.

Napoleon had excellent taste in souvenirs, including bronzes, tapestries, paintings and sculpture ripped (sometimes literally) from church altars. Most were warehoused at Milan's Brera Museum as Napoleonic war trophies until they were reclaimed by Venice for display here. Collection highlights include Titian's flushed, smouldering *Venus at the Mirror* (c 1550); Mantegna's arrow-riddled *St Sebastian*;

and Pietro Lombardo's chubby-kneed Jesus leaning on his mother, in glistening Carrara marble that actually looks soft.

Step outside onto Ca' d'Oro's **double-decker loggie** (balconies), where Grand Canal views framed by Gothic arcades make the city's most irresistible photo op.

I GESUITI
CHURCH

Map p278 (Santa Maria Assunta; ☑041 528 65 79; Salizada dei Specchieri 4880; ⊘10am-noon & 3.30-5.30pm; ⛴Fondamenta Nuove) **FREE** Giddily over the top even by rococo standards, this glitzy 18th-century Jesuit church is difficult to take in all at once, with a staggering spaceship of a **pulpit**, white-and-green intarsia (inlaid marble) walls that look like a version of Venetian flocked wallpaper, and a faux-marble carpet spilling down the altar stairs. While the ceiling is a riot of gold-and-white stuccowork, gravity is provided by Titian's uncharacteristically gloomy *Martyrdom of St Lawrence*, on the left as you enter the church. In the sacristy are 21 superior works by Palma Giovane celebrating the Eucharist.

✗ EATING

★CANTINA AZIENDE AGRICOLE
VENETIAN, CICHETI €

Map p278 (Rio Tera Farsetti; meals €15-25, cicheti €1-3; ⊘9am-1.30pm & 5-10pm Mon-Sat; ⛴San Marcuola) For 35 years Roberto di Berti and his sister Sabrina have been running this *bacaro* (bar/eatery), serving an impressive array of local wine to a loyal group of customers who treat the place much like a social club. Join them for a glass of chilled red Raboso and heaped platters of *lardo* (cured pork fat), Fossa cheese drizzled with honey and delicious deep-fried pumpkin.

If you're still hungry, order the homemade pasta with boar *ragu* and be surprised by a bill of under €25.

OSTERIA DA ALBERTO
VENETIAN €

Map p278 (☑041 523 81 53; Calle Larga Giacinto Gallina 5401; meals €15-25; ⊘noon-3pm & 6-11pm Mon-Sat; ⛴Fondamenta Nuove) All the makings of a true Venetian *osteria* (casual tavern) – hidden location, casks of wine, chandeliers that look like medieval torture devices – plus fair prices on spaghetti *alla busara* (with shrimp sauce), seasonal *cicheti* (bar snacks), crispy Venetian seafood fry, and silky panna cotta with strawberries. Call ahead, because the kitchen closes early when the joint's not jumping.

GELATERIA CA' D'ORO
GELATERIA €

Map p278 (☑041 522 89 82; Strada Nuova 4273; gelato €2-4.50; ☺11am-8pm; ▓; ☺Ca' d'Oro) Foot traffic stops here, for slow-food flavours – Sorrento lemon and Bronte pistachio, anyone? – are artisanally made in-house daily. For a summer pick-me-up, try the *granita di caffè con panna* (coffee-flavoured shaved ice with whipped cream).

PANIFICIO VOLPE GIOVANNI
BAKERY €

Map p278 (☑041 71 51 78; Ghetto Vecchio 1143; pastries €1.50-3; ☺7am-7.30pm Sun-Fri; ☺Guglie) Aside from unleavened pumpkin-and-radicchio bread, you can try unusual treats such as crumbly almond *impade* (sweet pastry sticks flavoured with ground almonds) and *orecchiette di Amman* (little ears of Amman), ear-shaped pastries stuffed with chocolate.

PASTICCERIA DAL MAS
PASTRIES €

Map p278 (☑041 71 51 01; Rio Terà Lista di Spagna 150a; pastries €0.90-1.70; ☺7am-6pm; ☑; ☺Ferrovia) Early departures and commuter cravings call for flaky pastries near the train station, devoured warm with a *macchiatone* (espresso generously stained with milk). Reliable bets include apple turnovers, *krapfen* (doughnuts) and the classic *cornetto* (croissant).

★LA CANTINA
VENETIAN, CICHETI €€

Map p278 (☑041 522 82 58; Campo San Felice 3689; cicheti €2.50-5, meals €25-40; ☺11am-11pm Mon-Sat; ☺Ca' d'Oro) Talk about slow food: grab a stool and local Morgana beer while you await seasonal *bruschette* (made to order) and hearty bean soup. Seafood platters require larger appetites and deeper pockets – market price varies, so ask the day's rate – but mullet with roast potatoes, *scampi crudi* (Venetian-style sweet-prawn sushi) and corn-breaded fried anchovies are worthy investments.

OSTERIA L'ORTO DEI MORI
MODERN ITALIAN €€

Map p278 (☑041 524 36 77; www.osteriaortodeimori.com; Campo dei Mori 3386; meals €25-45; ☺12.30-3.30pm & 7.30pm-midnight Wed-Mon; ☺Madonna dell'Orto) Not since Tintoretto lived next door has this neighbourhood seen so much action, thanks to this bustling *osteria* (casual tavern). Sicilian chef Lorenzo makes fresh surf-and-turf pasta daily, including squid atop spinach *tagliolini* and pasta with zucchini blossoms and scampi. Upbeat staff and fish-shaped lamps set a playful mood, and you'll be handed *prosecco* to help you endure waits for tables.

AI PROMESSI SPOSI
VENETIAN €€

Map p278 (☑041 241 27 47; Calle d'Oca 4367; meals €25-35; ☺11.30am-3pm & 6.30-11.30pm Thu-Sun & Tue, 6.30-11.30pm Mon & Wed; ☺Ca' d'Oro) Bantering Venetians thronging the bar are the only permanent fixtures at this neighbourhood *osteria*, where handwritten menus created daily feature fresh Venetian seafood and Veneto meats at excellent prices. Seasonal standouts include *seppie in umido* (cuttlefish in rich tomato sauce) and housemade tagliatelle with *anatra* (wild duck), but pace yourself for cloudlike tiramisu and elegant chocolate torte.

ALLE DUE GONDOLETTE
VENETIAN €€

Map p278 (☑041 71 75 23; www.alleduegondolette.com; Fondamente Coletti 3016; meals €15-25; ☺noon-2.30pm Mon-Thu, noon-2.30pm

---

LOCAL KNOWLEDGE

DALLA MARISA

At the Cannaregio institution **Dalla Marisa** (Map p278; ☑041 72 02 11; Fondamenta di San Giobbe 652b, Cannaregio; set menus lunch/dinner €15/35; ☺noon-3pm daily & 7-11pm Tue & Thu-Sat; ☺Crea), you'll be seated where there's room and get no menu – you'll have whatever Marisa's cooking. And you'll like it. Lunches are a bargain at €15 for a first, main, side, wine, water and coffee – pace yourself through prawn risotto to finish steak and grilled zucchini, or Marisa will jokingly scold you over coffee.

For dinner, you will be informed whether the absurdly abundant menu is meat- or fish-based when you book (ample house wine is included in the fixed price). Fish night (usually Tuesday) brings hauls of lagoon seafood grilled, fried and perched atop pasta and arugula, while meaty menus often feature Marisa's *fegato alla veneziana* (Venetian calf's liver) to send Venetian regulars into raptures. Advance reservations and pre-meal fasting advised. No credit cards.

& 7-10.30pm Fri & Sat; ⊕Madonna dell'Orto) On Friday it's worth walking the extra mile to this working class diner for its generous servings of *baccalà* (cod), either creamed with olive oil, lemon and parsley or *alla Vicentina* (braised with onions, anchovies and milk). Despite the '70s-style mint-coloured walls, the cooking here is bang up-to-date, including highlights such as pork in plum sauce and persimmon mousse with pistachios.

TRATTORIA DA BEPI GIÀ "54"   VENETIAN €€

Map p278 (☑041 528 50 31; www.dabepi.it; Campo SS Apostoli 4550; meals €30-40; ☺noon-2.30pm & 7-10pm Fri-Wed; ⊛Ca' d'Oro) Da Bepi is a traditional trattoria in the very best sense. The interior is a warm, wood-panelled cocoon, the service is efficient and friendly, and host Loris has been welcoming loyal locals and curious culinary travellers for years. Take their advice on the classic Venetian menu and order sweet, steamed spider crabs, briny razor clams, grilled turbot with artichokes and, for once, a tiramisu that doesn't disappoint.

OSTERIA ALLA VEDOVA   VENETIAN, CICHETI €€

Map p278 (☑041 528 53 24; Calle del Pistor 3912; cicheti €1-3.50, meals €15-40; ☺11.30am-2:30pm & 6.30-10.30pm Mon-Wed, Fri & Sat, 6.30-10.30pm Sun; ⊛Ca' d'Oro) Culinary convictions run deep here at one of Venice's oldest *osterie*, so you won't find *spritz* or coffee on the menu, or pay more than €1 to snack on a Venetian meatball. Enjoy superior seasonal *cicheti* and *ombre* (wine by the glass) with the local crowd at the bar, or call ahead for brusque table service and strictly authentic Venetian tripe or clam pasta.

★DA RIOBA   MODERN ITALIAN €€€

Map p278 (☑041 524 43 79; www.darioba.com; Fondamenta della Misericordia 2553; meals €45-60; ☺12.30-2.30pm & 7.30-11pm Tue-Sun; ⊛San Marcuola) Taking the lead with interesting spices and herbs pulled from the family's Sant'Erasmo farm, da Rioba's inventive kitchen turns out exquisite plates as colourful and creative as the artwork on the walls. This is prime date-night territory. In winter, enjoy goose carpaccio with dried fruits in the cosy woodbeamed interior, and in summer sit canalside with a plate of pretty fish fillet 'flowers' marinated in aromatic herbs. Reservations recommended.

★OSTERIA BOCCADORO   VENETIAN €€€

Map p278 (☑041 521 10 21; www.boccadoroven ezia.it; Campiello Widmann 5405a; meals €40-55; ☺noon-3pm & 7-10pm Tue-Sun; ⊛Fondamenta Nuove) Birds sweetly singing in this *campo* are probably angling for your leftovers, but they don't stand a chance. Chef-owner Luciano's creative *crudi* (raw seafood) are two-bite delights – tuna with blood orange, sweet prawn atop tart green apple – and cloudlike gnocchi topped with spider crab are gone entirely too soon. Save room for luxuriant mousse with six kinds of chocolate.

ANICE STELLATO   VENETIAN €€€

Map p278 (☑041 72 07 44; www.osterianice stellato.com; Fondamenta della Sensa 3272; bar snacks €13.50, meals €45-50; ☺10.30am-3.30pm & 6.30pm-midnight Wed-Sun; ⊛Madonna dell'Orto) 🖉 Tin lamps, unadorned rustic tables and a small wooden bar set the scene for quality seafood at this excellent canalside *bacaro* (bar). Munch on barside *cicheti* or go for the à la carte menu and swoon over juicy scampi in *saor* (vinegar marinade) and grilled tuna. Reservations recommended.

🍷 DRINKING & NIGHTLIFE

★VINO VERO   WINE BAR

Map p278 (☑041 275 00 44; Fondamenta della Misericordia 2497; ☺6pm-midnight Mon, 11am-midnight Tue-Sun; ⊛Ca' d'Oro) Lining the exposed brick walls of Matteo Bartoli's superior local wine bar are interesting small production wines, including a great selection of natural and biodynamic labels. The *cicheti*, too, are deliciously varied: wild boar sausage with aubergine, gorgonzola drizzled with honey or creamy baba ganoush topped with prosciutto.

★TORREFAZIONE CANNAREGIO   CAFE

Map p278 (☑041 71 63 71; www.torrefazione cannaregio.it; Rio Terà San Leonardo 1337; ☺7am-7pm; ⊛Guglie) Venetians can't catch a train without a pit stop at this aromatic shopfront lined with brass-knobbed coffee bins. Since 1930, Venice's Marchi family has been importing specialty beans, roasted fresh daily in a washtub-size roaster behind the marble bar and ground to order. Try *noxea*, espresso made with coffee beans roasted with fresh hazelnuts.

FURTHER ADVENTURES IN WINE & CICHETI

Prosecco, soave and Amarone aren't the only wines in town. Expand your happy-hour options with an immersion experience in Veneto wines led by an English-speaking sommelier from **Venetian Vine** (www.venetianvine.com; tastings per person €75). Tasting sessions are held at **La Cantina** (p111), in Cannaregio, and **Estro** (p81) in Dorsoduro. Nan, who hosts the tastings, is also a dab hand at Venetian Voga and is one of the tutors at **Row Venice** (p154). The brave (or the foolhardy) may be tempted to try her **Cichetto Row**: a gentle 2½-hour row between canalside bars (www.rowvenice. com; €240 for two people).

Landlubbers in search of a good backstreet *bacaro* (bar) crawl, should opt for fun and informed *cicheti* (bar snack) tours with Venetian home cook Monica Cesarato from **Cook in Venice** (www.cookinvenice.com; tours €35-60, courses €140-225). She'll ply you with more wine, *cicheti* and anecdotes than is seemly for one night and you'll no doubt end the evening toasting Venice with grappa-soaked grapes and chocolate 'salami'.

★ **AL TIMON**　　　　WINE BAR
Map p278 (☑041 524 60 66; Fondamenta degli Ormesini 2754; ☺11am-1am Thu-Tue & 6pm-1am Wed; ⓢSan Marcuola) Find a spot on the boat moored out front along the canal and watch the motley parade of drinkers and dreamers arrive for seafood *crostini* (open-face sandwiches) and quality organic and DOC wines by the *ombra* (half-glass of wine) or carafe. Folk singers play sets canalside when the weather obliges; when it's cold, regulars scoot over to make room for newcomers at indoor tables.

EL SBARLEFO　　　　BAR
Map p278 (☑041 523 30 84; Salizzada del Pistor 4556c; ☺10am-11pm; ⓢCa' d'Oro) You'll probably notice a stream of hip Venetians nipping in and out of Andrea and Alessandro's stylish bar. They know what's good for them: a mellow jazz soundtrack, excellent wines from the Veneto, Friuli and Trentino, and superb *cicheti* of spicy pimientos stuffed with tuna, baby cuttlefish drizzled with pesto and tiny pink *moscardini* (octopi) on cocktail sticks.

AL PARLAMENTO　　　　CAFE, BAR
Map p278 (☑041 244 02 14; Fondamenta Savorgnan 511; ☺8am-midnight Mon-Fri, 6pm-midnight Sat & Sun; ⓢCrea) Entire university careers and international romances are owed to Al Parlamento's powerful espresso, 6pm-to-9pm happy-hour cocktails and excellent overstuffed *tramezzini* (triangular, stacked sandwiches). When they warn you the ham, chicory and pepper-spread *tramezzino* is *picante* (spicy), you'd best pre-order that mojito. Thursday brings live music at 9pm,

and weekends you'll be talking over DJ sets unless you claim canalside seating early.

IL SANTO BEVITORE　　　　PUB
Map p278 (☑335 841 57 71; www.ilsantobevitorepub.com; Calle Zancani 2393a; ☺8am-midnight Mon-Sat; ⓢCa' d'Oro) San Marco has its glittering cathedral, but beer lovers prefer pilgrimages to this shrine of the 'Holy Drinker' for 20 brews on tap, including Trappist ales and seasonal stouts. The faithful receive canalside seating, footy matches on TV, free afternoon internet access, a saintly *spritz*, and the occasional live concert (pop rock, jazz funk and blues bands are perennial favourites).

MQ10　　　　CAFE, BAR
Map p278 (☑041 71 32 41; Fondamenta di Cannaregio; sandwiches €4-5, mains €9; ☺8am-midnight) Basking in a sunny spot that overlooks the busy Canale di Cannaregio is chic '10 metres squared'. In the modern, monochrome interior, barman Giuliano mixes fresh fruit mojitos and flame-coloured *spritz* that contrast nicely with the all-white decor. Salads, *panini* and platters of mixed salami and cheese help keep canalside seats full throughout the day.

AGLI ORMESINI　　　　PUB
Map p278 (Da Aldo; ☑041 71 58 34; Fondamenta degli Ormesini 2710; ☺8pm-1am Mon-Sat; ⓢMadonna dell'Orto) While the rest of Venice is awash in wine, Ormesini offers more than 100 brews, including reasonably priced bottles of specialty craft ales and local Birra Venezia. The cheery, beery scene often spills into the street – but keep it down, or the neighbours will get testy.

CANNAREGIO DRINKING & NIGHTLIFE

DODO CAFFÈ CAFE, BAR

Map p278 (☑041 71 59 05; www.dodocaffe.it; Fondamenta degli Ormesini 2845; ☺7am-9pm; ⊠San Marcuola) For sunsets as rosy as your *aperol spritz* arrive early to snag canalside seating at this local favourite. Dodo and barmaid Cristina offer a warm welcome to strangers along with generously stuffed *panini* and *tramezzini*.

UN MONDO DI VINO BAR

Map p278 (☑041 521 10 93; Salizada San Canciano 5984a; ☺11am-3pm & 5.30-11pm Tue-Sun; ⊠Rialto) Get here early for first crack at marinated artichokes and *sarde in saor* (sardines in tangy onion marinade), and to claim a few square inches of ledge for your plate and wineglass. There are 45 wines offered by the glass here, with prices ranging from €1.50 to €5, so take a chance on a freak blend or obscure varietal.

⭐ ENTERTAINMENT

TEATRO
FONDAMENTA NUOVE THEATRE, DANCE

Map p278 (☑041 522 44 98; www.teatrofondamentanuove.it; Fondamenta Nuove 5013; tickets €2.50-15; ⊠Fondamenta Nuove) Expect the unexpected in Cannaregio's experimental corner: dances inspired by water and arithmetic, new American cellists and long-lost Kyrgyz composers, Egyptian performance-art premieres in collaboration with Palazzo Grassi, and a steady stream of acclaimed artists from Brazil to Finland playing to a full house of 200.

TEATRO MALIBRAN THEATRE

Map p278 (☑041 965 19 75; www.teatrolafenice.it; Calle del Teatro 5873; ⊠Rialto) This diminutive 17th-century theatre was built over the ruins of Marco Polo's *palazzo* (mansion). It now shares a classical music, opera and ballet program with La Fenice, as well as hosting an intimate chamber-music season.

CASINÒ DI VENEZIA CASINO

Map p278 (Palazzo Vendramin-Calergi; ☑041 529 71 11; www.casinovenezia.it; Palazzo Vendramin-Calergi 2040; admission €5, with €10 gaming-token purchase free; ☺11am-2.45am Sun-Thu, to 3.15am Sat; ⊠San Marcuola) Fortunes have been won and lost inside this palatial casino since the 16th century. Slots open at 11am; to take on gaming tables, arrive after 3.30pm (or 4pm mid-June to August) wear-

ing your jacket and poker face. Ask your hotel concierge for free-admission coupons, and take the casino's free water-taxi ride from Piazzale Roma – bargains, unless you count your losses. You must be at least 18 to enter the casino.

Richard Wagner survived the 20-year effort of composing his stormy Ring cycle only to expire here in 1883. His suite – filled with musical scores and Wagner memorabilia – can be visited by **pre-booked tours** (arwv@libero.it; ☺10.30am Tue & Sat, 2.30pm Thu).

PARADISO PERDUTO LIVE MUSIC

Map p278 (☑041 72 05 81; http://ilparadisoperduto.com; Fondamenta della Misericordia 2540; ☺6pm-midnight Mon, noon-midnight Thu, 11am-1am Fri-Sun; ⊠Madonna dell'Orto) 'Paradise Lost' is a find for anyone craving a cold beer canalside on a hot summer's night, with a regular round of live-music acts. Over the past 25 years, troubadour Vinicio Capossela, Italian jazz great Massimo Urbani and Keith Richards have played the small stage at the Paradiso. On Monday, jam sessions alternate with local art openings.

CINEMA GIORGIONE
MOVIE D'ESSAI CINEMA

Map p278 (☑041 522 62 98; Rio Terà di Franceschi 4612; adult/student €7.50/6; ☺Wed-Mon; ▣; ⊠Fondamenta Nuove) Screenings of international film-festival winners, recently restored classics and family-friendly animation share top billing at this modern cinema in the heart of Venice. There are two screens (one tiny) and two or three screenings a day (usually 5.30pm and 7.30pm, occasionally also 9.30pm), plus matinees on Sunday.

🔒 SHOPPING

⭐**GIANNI BASSO** ARTISANAL, PRINTER

Map p278 (☑041 523 46 81; Calle del Fumo 5306; ☺9am-1pm & 2-6pm Mon-Fri, 9am-noon Sat; ⊠Fondamenta Nuove) Gianni Basso doesn't advertise his letterpressing services: the clever calling cards crowding his studio window do the trick. Restaurant critic Gale Greene's title is framed by a knife and fork, and Hugh Grant's moniker appears next to a surprisingly tame lion. Bring cash to commission business cards, ex-libris, menus or invitations, and trust Signor Basso to deliver via post.

★ATELIER LEONARDO   JEWELLERY

Map p278 (Rio Terà San Leonardo 1703; ⛴San Marcuola) Set out like a fine art showroom, Atelier Leonardo stocks jewellery from some of the very best Murano glass artists, many of whom rarely sell outside their own showrooms. Chalcedony pendants in opal glass by Antonio Vaccari and contemporary, statement necklaces by Igor Balbi are complemented by unique historical pieces, such as African murrine bead necklaces, so called as Venetian glass beads were widely traded throughout Africa for slaves, ivory and gold.

MERCANTINO DEI MIRACOLI   ANTIQUES

Map p278 (Campo Santa Maria Nova; ⊘9am-5pm usually last weekends Mar & Apr, 1st weekends May, Sep, Oct & Dec; ⛴Fondamente Nuove) From spring to autumn Campo Santa Maria Nova hosts a monthly outdoor antiques market packed with vintage treasures. Recent finds include 1930s Murano glass buttons, marbled silk shawls and 19th-century cameos, at moderate prices.

L'ARMADIO DI COCO   VINTAGE

Map p278 (⌀041 523 60 93; Campo Santa Maria Nova 6029/b; ⊘10.30am-7.30pm Tue-Sun, 2.30-7.30pm Mon; ⛴Rialto) For refined vintage threads from the '30s to the '80s, look no further than 'Coco's closet'. The passion project of fashion student Federica, the space was conceived as both a retail outlet and a studio where Federica designs and makes her own line of coats and clothes fashioned from upcycled fabrics. Other emerging designers also get rack space, making this a sure fire place to hunt out unique and affordable fashion pieces.

VITTORIO COSTANTINI   GLASS

Map p278 (⌀041 522 22 65; www.vittoriocostantini.com; Calle del Fumo 5311; ⊘9.30am-1pm & 2.15-5.30pm Mon-Fri; ⛴Fondamenta Nuove) Kids will be thrilled at the magical, miniature insects, butterflies, shells and birds that Vittorio Costantini fashions out of glass using a lampwork technique. The body of one of those iridescent beetles has 21 segments that need to be fused together with dazzling dexterity and speed. Prices range from €8 ladybirds to €150 for a fully feathered flamingo. Whatever you choose, this is a unique crystallised piece of the Venetian lagoon.

LOCAL KNOWLEDGE

CARNIVAL COSTUME HIRE

If you're wondering where Cinderella goes to find the perfect Carnival ball gown or Prince Charming his tux, look no further than **Nicolao Atelier** (Map p278; ⌀041 520 70 51; www.nicolao.com; Fondamenta della Misericordia 2590; ⊘9.15am-1pm & 2.15-6pm Mon-Fri; ⛴Madonna dell'Orto). In his past life, Stefano Nicolao was an actor and an assistant costumier before finding his true calling as a scholar and curator of historical fashion, over 10,000 pieces of which are now stored in his vast Cannaregio studio.

If you're anxious about the correct cut or whether silk damask suits you better than crinoline, have no fear, his knowledge is prodigious. No wonder he's the the best dressed star at the Regata Storica or that his shop is jam-packed with customers buying and renting costumes for Carnival. Out of festival season he does brisk business catering to theatres, opera houses and films worldwide. Incredible as it may seem everything, including that Cinderella dress sewn with hundreds of diamante crystals, is handmade.

LIBRERIA INTERNAZIONALE
MARCO POLO   BOOKS

Map p278 (⌀041 522 63 43; www.libreriamarcopolo.com; Calle del Teatro Malibran 5886a; ⊘9.30am-7.30pm Mon-Thu & Sat, 9.30am-11pm Fri, 11am-7pm Sun; ⛴Rialto) Everything you'd travel the world to find in an indie bookseller is right here in Venice: impassioned book recommendations from writerly staff, book exchanges for credit toward gorgeous limited-edition art books, used and new titles in English, and local manifestos such as Eye on Venice pamphlets *Dear Tourist* and *Misreading the Lagoon*. Meet here for writing workshops, author readings, and bookish flirtations.

BALDUCCI BORSE   SHOES, ACCESSORIES

Map p278 (⌀041 524 62 33; www.balducciborse.com; Rio Terà San Leonardo 1593; ⛴San Marcuola) Venice is not known for its leatherwork, but there's always an exception to the rule and Franco Balducci is it. Step through the door of his Cannaregio workshop and you can smell the quality of the

CANNAREGIO SHOPPING

SECRETS OF THE TRADE: CRAFT COURSES

As the ultimate merchant city, Venice has always been a creator and purveyor of luxury goods. To get an insight into this exclusive, creative world consider taking a course at one of the following Cannaregio workshops:

Orsoni Mosaici (Map p278; ✆041 244 00 02; www.orsoni.com; Via Cannaregio 1045; 3-day/1-/2-week course €500/780/1400; ⛴Guglie) Since 1888, Orsoni have been producing *smalti* (coloured opaque glass tiles) and gold-leaf mosaic to adorn some of the world's most beautiful buildings. Now you, too, can learn the 'divine art' on courses covering the basics, micro-mosaic or portraiture. Once you've honed your skills, you can purchase bags of rainbow-coloured *smalti* (€15 to €45 per kg) and set to work redecorating your home in the style of St Mark's basilica.

Fallani Venezia (Map p278; ✆041 523 57 72; www.fallanivenezia.com; Salizada Seriman 4875; 1-hour/half-/full-day courses €40/€100/€200; ♿; ⛴Fondamenta Nuove) Credited with transforming screenprinting from a medium of reproduction to an innovative and creative artistic technique, Fiorenzo Fallani's laboratory has hosted international artists such as Hans Richter, Janez Bernik and Hsiao Chin. Courses get you from printing your own t-shirt to more complex processes using different colours, acetates and frames. Even if you don't fancy taking a course, this is a great place to purchase original, art prints of Venice.

Bottega del Tintoretto (Map p278; ✆041 72 20 81; www.tintorettovenezia.it; Fondamenta dei Mori 3400; 5-day course incl lunch & materials €410; ⛴San Marcuola) During the 1500s Tintoretto operated a printmaking lab in the ground floor of his Cannaregio home. Revived and restored in 1985, the bottega once again offers artists a laboratory in which they can practise, while also running a series of courses in printmaking, bookbinding, watercolour, fresco and sculpture.

handpicked Tuscan hides that he fashions on the premises into glossy ankle- and knee-high boots. There's also a small selection of chic saddle bags, classic briefcases and slouchy shoulder bags.

VIRGINIA PREO CASHMERE　　FASHION

Map p278 (✆041 522 86 51; www.virginiapreo.com; Salizada San Giovanni Grisostomo 5800; ⊙10am-1.30pm & 2-7.30pm Mon-Sat; ⛴Rialto) Like an upmarket Uniqlo, Barbara Preo's luxe cashmere cardigans, tops, dresses and jackets come in an assortment of candy-coloured threads. You can thank her daughter, Virginia, after whom the brand is named, for the creative, contemporary styles which are perfectly attuned to the temperamental Venetian weather and the colours of the lagoon.

BRANDS　　ACCESSORIES

Map p278 (Fullspot; www.fullspot.it; San Geremia 314; ⊙10am-7.30pm; ⛴Ferrovia) Right in style and on the money, this Padua-based designer sells affordable, mix-and-match accessories: watch faces with interchangeable rubber wristbands and sleek silicon totebags with removeable handles. Try tone-on-tone with a lagoon-teal-blue face and band,

or high-contrast yellow-and-grey combos. Switch up totebags seasonally: flocked fuschia with white patent-leather handles works for winter, while orange with sailor's-rope handles just says summer.

ANTICHITÀ AL GHETTO　　ANTIQUES

Map p278 (✆041 524 45 92; Calle del Ghetto Vecchio 1133/4; ⊙9.30am-noon & 2.30-6pm Wed-Sat, 2.30-6pm Tue, 10am-1pm Sun; ⛴Guglie) Instead of souvenir T-shirts, this antique shop offers mementos of Venetian history: ancient maps of the canals, etchings of Venetian dandies daintily alighting from gondolas, and 18th-century cameos worn by the most fashionable ladies in the Ghetto.

DOLCEAMARO　　FOOD, WINE

Map p278 (✆041 523 87 08; Campo San Canciano 6051; ⊙10.30am-1.30pm & 4-8pm; ⛴Rialto) For the well-travelled foodie who's been there, eaten that, here's something original: a miniature platter of Italian cheeses and cured meats, made out of artisanal chocolate. Dolceamaro also stocks wines, speciality Veneto grappa (spirits), and other gourmet temptations, including aged balsamic vinegars and whole truffles.

Castello

Neighbourhood Top Five

1 Getting an insider's view during special events at the **Arsenale** (p119), the Venetian Republic's vast honeycomb of a shipyard and once the world's best-kept industrial secret.

2 Gawking at the sheer scale of **Zanipolo** (p121), a 14th-century church packed with master works of painting and sculpture.

3 Taking an early-morning stroll along **Riva degli Schiavoni** (p128), Castello's breathtaking waterfront promenade.

4 Taking a break from brick and marble amid the leafy byways of Napoleon's **Giardini Pubblici** (p122).

5 Basking in the golden glow of Carpaccio's paintings in the **Scuola di San Giorgio degli Schiavoni** (p123).

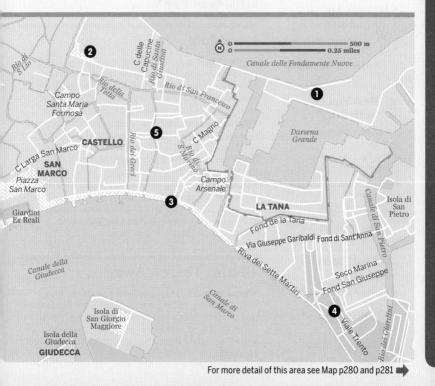

Lonely Planet's Top Tip

Venice is always best early in the morning or after the crowds thin in the evening. This is especially true of the Riva degli Schiavoni, which is packed from 11am to 7pm with day-trippers as cruises disgorge their madding crowds. But if you can get yourself out of bed, the seafront promenade is a magnificent and remarkably solitary spot for a morning constitutional. At the other end of the day, it is a stunning sundowner spot for views across the lagoon and back to San Marco.

✖ Best Places to Eat

➡ Trattoria Corte Sconta (p132)

➡ Alle Testiere (p132)

➡ Osteria Ruga di Jaffa (p130)

➡ CoVino (p131)

For reviews, see p130. ➡

🍷 Best Places to Drink

➡ La Serra dei Giardini (p132)

➡ Bar Terazza Danieli (p133)

➡ Enoteca Mascareta (p133)

➡ STRANI (p132)

For reviews, see p132. ➡

🔒 Best Places to Shop

➡ Atelier Alessandro Merlin (p134)

➡ Fabricharte (p134)

➡ Bragorà (p133)

➡ Al Campanil (p134)

For reviews, see p133. ➡

Explore Castello

Stretching eastwards from San Marco, Castello is the city's most sprawling neighbourhood and exploring its entirety in one day will test your walking shoes. Start with its most compelling sites – the masterfully grand Zanipolo church, Negroponte's rose-fringed Madonna in Chiesa di San Francesco della Vigna and Bellini's *Virgin Enthroned* in opulent Chiesa di San Zaccaria. All are within a stone's throw of San Marco and Rialto.

Moving east, you'll reach the engine of the city's seafaring might: the sprawling shipyards known simply as the Arsenale. While the Arsenale is only open for special events, the nearby Museo Storico Navale helps fill in the city's blockbuster maritime history. East of the Arsenale lie working-class neighbourhoods around Via Garibaldi. You're most likely to hear the Venetian dialect here, and it's a great place for an *aperitivo* (pre-dinner drink).

The Napoleonic gardens, the pavilion-dotted Giardini Pubblici and the Parco delle Rimembranze skirt the island's southern shore. The Giardini springs to life in summer months when Biennale events attract the global art world. In Castello's easternmost reaches, visit Venice's first cathedral on the island of San Pietro del Castello before returning at sunset along the Riva dei Partigiani for sweeping views of San Giorgio Maggiore and the Bacino di San Marco.

Local Life

➡**Artist Studios** Away from the main tourist areas, Castello's artisans are free to experiment. Don't miss Alessandro Merlin's (p134) *sgraffito* ceramics, Paolo Brandolisio's (p134) wood workshop and visits to artists' studios (p130) to discuss their work.

➡**Backstreet bacaro** Locals drop in all day for *cicheti* (bar snacks) at Bacaro Risorto (p133), Al Portego (p133) and STRANI (p132); while *gondolieri* prefer their breakfast *cornetto* (croissant) at Pasticceria Da Bonifacio (p131).

➡**Outdoor living** *Nonne* (grandmothers) gather for afternoon gossip while their young charges kick balls across Campo di Bandiera e Moro, Campo Zanipolo, the Giardini Pubblici (p122) and the Parco delle Rimembranze (p122) on Sant'Elena.

Getting There & Away

➡**Vaporetto** Line 1 makes all stops along the Riva degli Schiavoni, linking it with both Grand Canal stops and the Lido. Line 2 also heads up the Grand Canal. Lines 4.1, 4.2, 5.1 and 5.2 circle the outer perimeter of Venice, including stops along Riva degli Schiavoni and Giudecca.

TOP SIGHT
ARSENALE

Founded in 1104, the Arsenale quickly grew to become Europe's greatest naval installation and the largest productive complex in the world. Sustained by an enormous 10% of the city's income and employing up to 16,000 highly skilled *arsenolotti* (Arsenale workers), it was the very heart of Venice's mercantile and military power. A unique pre-industrial example of mass production, its centralised organisation, standardised processes and stringent quality control all anticipate the modern factory. Not only was the Arsenale capable of turning out a new galley in a single day, its 45-hectare (100-acre) physical footprint occupied 15% of the city. Even today, it is completely surrounded by 3.2km (2 miles) of crenellated walls.

At its peak, the Arsenale must have made an enormous impression, with its boiling black pitch, metalworking and timber cutting. Many streets in Castello are still named after its activities: Calle della Pece (pitch), del Piombo (lead), delle Ancore (anchors) and delle Vele (sails). Indeed, Dante used it as a model scene for hell in his *Divina Commedia* (Divine Comedy; Canto XXI, lines 7 to 21).

Perhaps the most revolutionary aspect of the Arsenale was that it used canals as moving assembly lines. The growing ship would move through the canals from one stage of construction to the next – a system that was not reproduced on such a scale until Henry Ford's 'revolutionary' car factory in the 20th century. As a result of this innovation, as many as 100 galleys could be in production at a single time. In addition, special consultants, such as Galileo, helped the Venetians rationalise production and build ships that could be equipped with increasingly powerful munitions. The treatise Galileo later wrote, drawing on his experience, is considered a seminal text of materials science.

The physical appearance of the yards was also a matter of prestige and cutting-edge design. At the core of the complex is the **Arsenale Vecchio** or Old Arsenal (Map p280;

DON'T MISS...

➡ Porta Magna
➡ Corderia
➡ Artigliere
➡ Gaggiandre

PRACTICALITIES

➡ Map p280, G2
➡ ☏041 274 82 09
➡ http://arsenale.comune.venezia.it
➡ admission prices vary
➡ ⊘only during events
➡ 🚤Celestia

BUCINTORO

Seven centuries before *Pimp My Ride*, there was the Bucintoro. The most lavish creation of the Arsenale, it was the doge's official galley. The most extravagant version was completed in 1727, and was entirely covered in gold leaf. It had seating for 90 people and required 168 oarsmen to manoeuvre. You can see a scale model in the Museo Storico Navale (p128), plus a few original details salvaged after Napoleonic troops burned it in 1798.

The work horse of the Venetian Lagoon was the *trabaccolo*, a type of lugger derived from a Byzantine cargo ship. It was used to transport coal, wood and Istrian stone as well as foodstuffs, and despite its large capacity, it was nimble and manoeuvrable in the canals. Il Nuovo Trionfo (☎335 623 33 28; www.ilnuovotrionfo.org) is the only remaining seaworthy trabaccolo in Venice, having been lovingly restored by Alfredo Zambon. It's often moored at the Punta della Dogana and is open to visitors. Check the website for details.

TOP SIGHT
ZANIPOLO

When the Dominicans began building Zanipolo in 1333 to rival the Franciscans' Basilica di Santa Maria Gloriosa dei Frari (p88), the church stirred passions more common to Serie A football than architecture. Both structures feature red-brick facades with high-contrast detailing in white stone. But since Zanipolo's facade remains unfinished, the Frari won a decisive early decision with its soaring grace and Titian's *Assunta* altarpiece. Over the centuries, Zanipolo has at least tied the score with its pantheon of ducal funerary monuments and the variety of its masterpieces.

Named after two minor martyrs of early Christian Rome, Santi Giovanni e Paolo – elided to San Zanipolo in Venetian dialect – the structure was designed to make worshippers feel small and reverential. Little can prepare you for its cavernous interior (90m by 38m) suffused by a soft pink glow.

Architecture

Built in classic Italian Gothic style, the basilica could accommodate virtually the entire population of 14th-century Castello. Its 33m-high nave is reinforced by a clever series of cross-beams – necessary because of Venice's water-logged soil. Typical of Italian Gothic and different from French Gothic, its exteriors and interiors have a barn-like simplicity. Rarest of all is the surviving 15th-century stained glass in the south transept. Created on Murano, it richly illuminates designs by Bartolomeo Vivarini and Girolamo Mocetto.

Tombs of the Doges

For centuries, Zanipolo was the site of doges' funerals, and the walls are punctuated by 25 of their lavish tombs. From Pietro Lombardo's three-tier monument celebrating the *Ages of Man* for Pietro Mocenigo (1406–76) to the Gothic tomb of Michele Morosini (1308–82) and Andrea Tirali's bombastic *Tomba dei Valier* (1708), they provide an overview of the stylistic development of Venetian art.

Bellini, Reni, Lorenzetti & Veronese

In 1867 a fire destroyed paintings by Tintoretto, Palma di Giovanni, Titian and Bellini. Anti-Catholic arson was suspected, but nothing was proved. A second Bellini polyptych, on the second altar in the right aisle, survived intact. Depicting *SS Vincent Ferrer, Christopher and Sebastian*, the work has a vivid sensuousness that was to become a hallmark of Venetian painting.

Guido Reni's *San Giuseppe* is a rare expression of holy bonding, with Joseph exchanging adoring looks with baby Jesus. The dome on the southwest end of the nave boasts Giambattista Lorenzetti's *Jesus the Navigator* – Jesus scans the skies like an anxious Venetian sea captain. In the **Cappella del Rosario**, Paolo Veronese's *Assunta* ceiling depicts the rosy Virgin ascending a staggering staircase to be crowned by cherubs.

DON'T MISS...

→ Giovanni Bellini's *SS Vincent Ferrer, Christopher and Sebastian*

→ Pietro Lombardo's tomb for Pietro Mocenigo

→ Guido Reni's *San Giuseppe*

→ Giambattista Lorenzetti's *Jesus the Navigator*

PRACTICALITIES

→ Chiesa dei SS Giovanni e Paolo

→ Map p280, B1

→ ☎ 041 523 59 13

→ www.basilicasantigiovanniepaolo.it

→ Campo Zanipolo

→ adult/reduced €2.50/1.25

→ ⏰9am-6pm Mon-Sat, noon-6pm Sun, tours in Eng 5.30pm Thu

→ 🚢Ospedale

TOP SIGHT
GIARDINI PUBBLICI

Venice's first public gardens were laid out between 1808 and 1812 on the orders of Napoleon, who decided the city needed a little breathing space. Never mind that an entire residential district had to be demolished or acres of swampland reclaimed. A winning combination of formal gardens and winding pathways, the park now stretches from Via Garibaldi, past the Garibaldi monument with its punk-haired lion, through the Napoleonic gardens and past the Biennale pavilions to Sant'Elena, making this the largest park in Venice.

DON'T MISS...
➜ Venezuelan Pavilion
➜ Austrian Pavilion
➜ Australian Pavilion
➜ La Serra

PRACTICALITIES
➜ Map p280, G6
➜ www.labiennale.org
➜ 🚲Giardini, Biennale

Biennale Pavilions

A large portion of the gardens is given over to the Biennale exhibition arena, hosting international art (odd years) and architecture (even years) events in 29 modernist pavilions, each allocated to a different nation. During the **Art Biennale's** June to September run, connoisseurs swarm national showcases ranging from Geza Rintel Maroti's 1909 Secessionist-era **Hungarian Pavilion** to the 2015 **Australian Pavilion**.

The pavilions tell a fascinating story of 20th-century architecture – not least because Venetian modernist master Carlo Scarpa contributed to the Biennale from 1948 to 1972, trying to make the best of Duilio Torres' Fascist 1932 Italian Pavilion (now the **Palazzo delle Esposizioni**). Scarpa is also responsible for the daring 1956 raw-concrete-and-glass **Venezuelan Pavilion** and the winsome, bug-shaped **Biglietteria** (Ticket Office). The newest pavilion in the garden (the first in 20 years) is the **Australian Pavilion**, a black granite box designed by starchitects Denton Corker Marshall. Hidden intriguingly amid the leafy foliage, it speaks of the imposition of European settlements on indigenous Australian lands. Note that the Biennale grounds are only open during Biennale events.

Monument to the Partisan Woman

Located purposefully in the lapping water off the Riva dei Sette Martiri – where seven Venetian partisans were shot and killed in 1944 – lies the 1200kg bronze figure of a **woman partisan** (Map p280; 🚲Giardini, Biennale). Sculpted by Augusto Murer, the figure reclines, exhausted it seems, on an arrangement of Istrian stone platforms designed by Scarpa to catch the eye as she appears and disappears beneath the rising and falling tide.

La Serra

In 1894 Napoleon's gardens were furnished with a fashionable iron-framed, greenhouse (p132), originally intended to house the palms used in Biennale events. It rapidly expanded into a community hub and a centre for propagation: many plants grown here went to adorn the municipal flowerbeds of the Lido and the ballrooms of aristocratic *palazzi* (mansions). Restored in 2010, it's now the location of a delightful cafe and hosts events and workshops from paper making to yoga.

Parco delle Rimembranze

At the eastern limit of the gardens, on the island of Sant'Elena, is this **memorial park** (Isola di Sant'Elena; 🚶; 🚲Sant'Elena) FREE. Planted with umbrella pines, each originally commemorating a fallen soldier of WWI, it's a tranquil spot with postcard views of the Bacino di San Marco. Families gather here to sit on the benches, roller skate around the rink and play on the slides and swings. Apart from providing a shady respite in a relentlessly urban environment, it offers a real slice of Venetian life.

SIGHTS

ARSENALE   HISTORIC BUILDING
See p119.

GIARDINI PUBBLICI   GARDENS
See p122.

ZANIPOLO   BASILICA
See p121.

**SCUOLA GRANDE
DI SAN MARCO**   NOTABLE BUILDING
Map p280 (Campo Zanipolo; ☒Ospedale) Instead of a simple Saturday father–son handyman project, sculptor Pietro Lombardo and his sons had something more ambitious in mind: a high-Renaissance polychrome marble facade for the most important confraternity in Venice. Mauro Codussi was brought in to put the finishing touches on this gem. Magnificent lions of St Mark prowl above the portals, while sculpted *trompe l'œil* perspectives beguile the eye. The *scuola* now serves as the main entrance to the Ospedale Civile, the city's public hospital.

**STATUE OF
BARTOLOMEO COLLEONI**   MONUMENT
Map p280 (Campo Zanipolo; ☒Ospedale) Bartolomeo Colleoni's galloping bronze equestrian statue is one of only two such public monuments in Venice – and an extraordinary example of early-Renaissance sculpture. It commemorates one of Venice's most loyal mercenary commanders. From 1448, Colleoni commanded armies for the Republic, though in true mercenary form he switched sides a couple of times when he felt he'd been stiffed on pay or promotions.

On his death in 1474, Colleoni bequeathed 216,000 gold and silver ducats to Venice, on one condition: that the city erect a commemorative statue to him in Piazza San Marco. Since not even a doge had ever won such pride of place in Venice, the Senate found a workaround, placing the monument in front of the Scuola Grande di San Marco instead. Sculpted by Florentine master Andrea del Verrocchio (1435–88), it is embellished with Colleoni's emblematic *coglioni* (cullions or testicles) – a typically crude Renaissance pun. You can spot them on the base, looking like emphatic quotation marks.

CASTELLO SIGHTS

TOP SIGHT **SCUOLA DI SAN GIORGIO DEGLI SCHIAVONI**

In the 15th century, Venice annexed Dalmatia – an area roughly corresponding to the former Yugoslavia – and large numbers of Dalmatians, known as Schiavoni, emigrated to Venice. In a testament to Venetian pluralism, they were granted their own *scuola* (religious confraternity) in 1451. Around 1500, they began building their headquarters, making the brilliant decision to hire Vittore Carpaccio (also of Dalmatian descent) to complete an extraordinary cycle of paintings of Dalmatia's patron saints George, Tryphone and Jerome.

Though Carpaccio never left Venice, his scenes with Dalmatian backdrops are minutely detailed. But the real brilliance of Carpaccio's imagined worlds are their engaging narrative power: St George charges a lizard-like dragon across a Libyan desert scattered with half-eaten corpses; St Jerome leads his tame-looking lion into a monastery, scattering friars like a flock of lagoon birds; and St Augustine, watched by his dog, is distracted from correspondence by a heavenly voice informing him of Jerome's death.

DON'T MISS...
- ➡ Carpaccio's *St George and the Dragon*
- ➡ Carpaccio's *St Jerome and the Lion*
- ➡ Carpaccio's *St Augustine in His Study*

PRACTICALITIES
- ➡ Map p280, C3
- ➡ ☑041 522 88 28
- ➡ Calle dei Furlani 3259a
- ➡ adult/reduced €5/3
- ➡ ⊙2.45-6pm Mon, 9.15am-1pm & 2.45-6pm Tue-Sat, 9.15am-1pm Sun
- ➡ ☒Pietà

OSPEDALETTO
CHURCH

Map p280 (☑041 271 90 12; www.scalabovolo.
org; Barbaria delle Tole 6691; guided visits for
groups €60; ⊙by reservation; 🚊Ospedale) This
Ruskin-baiting baroque affair, which the
celebrated art critic thought 'the most monstrous example of the Grotesque Renaissance...in Venice' was, like Vivaldi's **Pietà**
(Map p280; ☑041 522 11 20; www.chiesavivaldi.
it; Riva degli Schiavoni; adult/reduced €25/20;
⊙concerts 8.30pm; 🚊Pietà), famous for its
female musicians. The accomplished girls
came from the adjoining orphanage and
hospice, designed by Antonio Sardi, and
played amid the trumpeting angels of Baldassare Longhena's 1660s chapel, complete
with charming frescoed music room.

The complex is owned by IRE, a public
institution that runs homes for the elderly.
Reserve visits at least one week in advance.

CHIESA DI SAN LIO
CHURCH

Map p280 (Campo San Lio; donations appreciated;
⊙9am-noon; 🚊Rialto) **FREE** Giandomenico
Tiepolo sure did know how to light up a
room. Duck into the atmospheric gloom
of San Lio's baroque interior and, as your
eyes adjust, look up at Tiepolo's magnificent ceiling fresco, *The Glory of the Cross
and St Leon IX*. On your left by the main
door is Titian's *Apostle James the Great*, but
this church is better known for yet another
Venetian artist: the great *vedutista* (land-
scapist) Canaletto, who was baptised and
buried in this, his parish church.

CHIESA DI
SANTA MARIA FORMOSA
CHURCH

Map p280 (Campo Santa Maria Formosa 5267;
admission €3, or with Chorus Pass free; ⊙10am-
5pm Mon-Sat; 🚊Rialto, San Zaccaria) Originally
built from wood and thatched with straw,
in 842 Santa Maria Formosa was the first
church on the Rialto to be dedicated to the

LOCAL KNOWLEDGE

LOVERS ALLEY

Under the arch of the covered pas-
sageway **Sotoportego dei Preti** (Map
p280; 🚊Arsenale) is hidden a reddish,
heart-shaped stone about the size of
a hand. Local lore has it that couples
that touch it together will remain in
love forever. Not ready to commit just
yet? This is also a nice private spot for
a smooch.

Virgin Mary. Destroyed by fire in 1106, the
church was refashioned by Mauro Codussi
in 1492 with new baroque curves that make
good on its name – 'Shapely St Mary'. So
does Palma il Vecchio's polyptych of the
forceful-looking *St Barbara*, swathed in a
billowing red cape atop the Third Altar. It
is dedicated to the School of Shipbuilders,
of whom she is patron saint.

According to legend, the church's curious name was inspired by a vision of San
Magno, Bishop of Oderzo, although another, more likely, version of events claims the
name was confused with the address of a
comely courtesan, who lived on the square
in the 16th century. Certainly, Veronica
Franco (1546–91), one of Venice's most
famous courtesans and an accomplished
poetess, frequented literary salons at Ca'
Vernier opposite the church, and the stage-
set *campo* was a lively social hub.

PALAZZO GRIMANI
MUSEUM

Map p280 (☑041 520 03 45; www.palazzogrima
ni.org; Ramo Grimani 4858; adult/reduced €6/5;
⊙8.15am-2pm Mon, 8.15am-7.15pm Tue-Sun;
🚊San Zaccaria) The Grimani family built
their Renaissance *palazzo* to house an
extraordinary Graeco-Roman collection,
which was destined to become the basis
of the archaeological museum now housed
in the Museo Correr (p57). Unusually for
Venice, the palace has a Roman-style courtyard, which shed a flattering light on the
archaeological curiosities. These days, the
empty halls host temporary exhibitions,
though their bedazzling frescoed interiors
are reason enough to visit.

There is debate about who designed the
building. However, it's certain that Giovanni Grimani (1501–93) himself played a
large role in a design that consciously recalls the glories of ancient Rome. Grimani
also hired a dream team of fresco painters specialising in fanciful grotesques and
Pompeii-style mythological scenes. Francesco Salviati applied the glowing, Raphael-
style colours he'd used in Rome's Palazzo
Farnese, while Roman painter Giovanni
da Udine – considered among the brightest
pupils of Raphael and Giorgione – devoted
three rooms to the stories of Ovid.

The **Sala ai Fogliami** (Foliage Room) is
the most memorable room, though. Painted
by Mantovano, ceiling and walls are awash
with remarkably convincing plant and bird
life. They even include New World species
that had only recently been discovered by

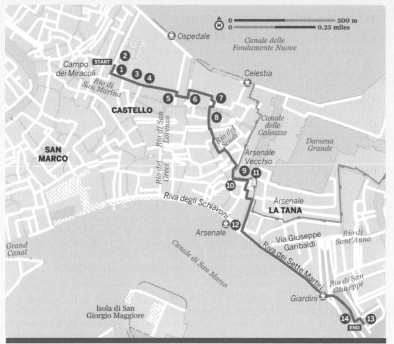

Neighbourhood Walk
Castello's Byways

Start in Campo Zanipolo, where you can't miss the **1 Bartolomeo Colleoni statue** (p123). Colleoni left the city a fortune on condition that the city erect a statue in his honour in Piazza San Marco. Venice bent the rules, erecting the statue in front of the **2 Scuola Grande di San Marco** (p123) instead. Next door are the imposing Gothic heights of the treasure-packed **3 Zanipolo** (p121).

A block east, pass the **4 Ospedaletto** (p124), an orphanage chapel designed by Palladio and Longhena. Continue to stroll east down Barbaria de le Tole, past bric-a-brac haven **5 Ballarin** (p135) and aross the canal in front of the **6 Liceo Scientifico**, with another fine Longhena facade.

Dog-leg left for Palladio's massive, classical **7 Chiesa di San Francesco della Vigna** (p128), home to a fine Bellini and

Antonio Negroponte's gorgeous *Virgin and Child Enthroned*.

Turn south, just over the Rio di San Francesco is the graffitied wall of **8 Laboratorio Occupato Morion** (p133), one of the few walls of grafitti in the city. Continue past Campo delle Gatte and enter a tight nest of alleys, once housing works of the **9 Arsenale** (p119), whose walls rear up ahead. Turn right at Campo de le Gorne and follow the walls round to **10 Chiesa di San Martino** (p128). To the right of its doorway is a *bocca di leoni* (mouth of the lion), in which Venetians slipped denunciations of their neighbours.

Keep following the Arsenale's walls until you reach the **11 Porta Magna** (Main Gate, p120), considered the city's earliest example of Renaissance architecture. From here, turn southeast onto the **12 Riva degli Schiavoni** (p128) and gawk at the views across the Bacino, before finishing your walk with a herbal tisane at **13 La Serra** (p132) or a *spritz* and lagoon-side seat at **14 Paradiso** (p133).

VENICE'S SECRET WEAPON: ARSENALOTTI

In an early version of the assembly line, ships built in the Arsenale progressed through sequenced design phases, each staffed by *arsenalotti* (Arsenale workers) specialised in a particular aspect of construction, ranging from hull assembly and pitch application through to sail rigging. Women specialised in sails; children started apprenticeships at age 10, and did their part twisting hemp into rope.

But this wasn't a low-paid, low-status job. The *arsenalotti* were well remunerated, with cradle-to-grave fringe benefits. This helped keep them remarkably faithful to the Republic, and throughout Venetian history, *arsenalotti* repeatedly proved both their loyalty and their brawn during periods of war and rebellion. Using their proven shipbuilding techniques, they also constructed the vast *carena di nave* (ship's keel) ceilings you see in Venetian churches and in the **Palazzo Ducale's Sala del Maggior Consiglio** (p53).

Job requirements for *arsenalotti* included manual dexterity, strength and silence. Even in raucous Castello *bacari* (old-style bars), *arsenalotti* remained carefully vague about the specifics of their workday, in an 'I could tell you, but then I'd have to kill you' kind of way. Shipbuilding processes were top secret, and industrial espionage was considered an act of high treason, punishable by exile or death. For centuries the crenellated walls of the Arsenale hid the feverish activity inside from view. Even outside the walls, the *arsenalotti* tended to stick to their own kind. They intermarried, and even had their own market gardens to reduce contact with the rest of the city.

Europeans, including two that would come to be staples of Venetian life: tobacco and corn.

PALAZZO QUERINI STAMPALIA   MUSEUM

Map p280 (🖉041 271 14 11; www.querinistampa lia.it; Campiello Querini Stampalia 5252; 🚤San Zaccaria, Rialto) In 1869 Conte Giovanni Querini Stampalia made a gift of his ancestral *palazzo* to the city on the forward-thinking condition that its 700-year-old library operate late-night openings. Downstairs, savvy drinkers take their *aperitivi* with a twist of high modernism in the Carlo Scarpa-designed **garden**, while the *palazzo*'s rotating contemporary shows add an element of the unexpected to the silk-draped salons upstairs.

Enter through the Botta-designed QShop to buy tickets for the **Museo della Fondazione Querini Stampalia** (Map p280; adult/reduced €10/8, Carlo Scarpa garden €8; 🕙10am-6pm Tue-Sun; 🚤San Zaccaria). Located in the duke's apartments, the museum reflects the 18th-century tastes and interests of the count: beneath the stuccoed ceilings you'll find rich furnishings and tapestries, Meissen and Sèvres porcelain, marble busts and some 400 paintings. Of these, many are dynastic portraits and conversation pieces, such as Alessandro and Pietro Longhi's genre scenes of masked balls, gambling dens and 18th-century bon vivants.

The clear standout in the collection is Giovanni Bellini's arresting *Presentation of Jesus at the Temple*, where the hapless child looks like a toddler mummy, standing up in tightly wrapped swaddling clothes. Other engaging pieces are the 39 winningly naïve *Scenes of Public Life in Venice* by Gabriele Bella (1730–99), which document scenes of the city and its customs during the period. Although rather crude in their realisation, the subject matter – a football game in Sant'Alvise, the frozen lagoon in 1708, the courtesans' race on the Rio de la Sensa – is fascinating.

MUSEO DIOCESANO DI VENEZIA   MUSEUM

Map p280 (🖉041 277 17 02; www.veneziaubc.org; Chiostro di Sant'Apollonia 4312; adult/reduced €5/2.50; 🕙10am-6pm Tue-Sun; 🚤San Zaccaria) Housed in a former Benedictine monastery dedicated to Sant'Apollonia, this museum has a fairly predictable collection of religious art and the occasional standout temporary show – but the exquisite Romanesque cloister is the sole example of the genre in Venice. The adjoining building was a church until 1906, and now houses exhibition spaces.

CHIESA DI SAN ZACCARIA   CHURCH

Map p280 (Campo San Zaccaria 4693; 🕙10am-noon & 4-6pm Mon-Sat, 4-6pm Sun; 🚤San Zaccaria) **FREE** When 15th-century Venetian girls showed more interest in sailors than saints, they were sent to the convent adjoining San Zaccaria. The wealth showered on the church by their grateful parents is evident. Masterpieces by Bellini, Titian, Tintoretto and Van Dyck crowd the walls. Bellini's altarpiece is such a treasure that Napoleon whisked it away to Paris for 20 years when he plundered the city in 1797.

To your right as you enter, the **Cappella di San Atanasio** (admission €1) holds Tintoretto's *Birth of St John the Baptist*, while Tiepolo depicts the Holy Family fleeing to Egypt in a typically Venetian boat. Both hang above magnificently crafted choir stalls. Behind this chapel you'll find the Gothic **Cappella di San Tarasio** (also called Cappella d'Oro or the Golden Chapel), with impressive Renaissance-style frescoes by Andrea del Castagno and Francesco da Faenza from the 1440s.

The star of the show is undoubtedly Giovanni Bellini's *Virgin Enthroned with Jesus, an Angel Musician and Saints* (1505), which glows like it's plugged into an outlet. Bellini was in his 70s when he painted it and had already been confronted by the first achievements of Giorgione (1477–1510), with his softer *sfumato* ('smokey') technique. Bellini's assimilation of the technique is clear in the shafts of sunlight that strike the saintly arrangement infusing it with a sense of devout spirituality.

MUSEO DELLE ICONE   MUSEUM
Map p280 (Museum of Icons; ☑041 522 65 81; www.istitutoellenico.org; Campiello dei Greci 3412; adult/reduced €4/2; ⊙9am-5pm; ⑤Pietà) Glowing colours and all-seeing eyes fill this treasure box of some 80 Greek icons made in 14th- to 17th-century Italy. Keep your own eye out for the expressive *San Giovanni Climaco,* which shows the saintly author

of a Greek spiritual guide distracted from his work by visions of souls diving into hell.

The museum goes by a confusing variety of names: it's also known as the 'Museo dei Dipinti Sacri Bizantini' (Museum of Holy Byzantine Paintings), and technically it's housed in the Istituto Ellenico (Hellenic Institute).

CHIESA DI SAN GIORGIO DEI GRECI   CHURCH
Map p280 (www.ortodossia.it; Campiello dei Greci 3412; ⊙9am-12.30pm & 2.30-4.30pm Mon & Wed-Sat, 9am-1pm Sun; ⑤Pietà) **FREE** Greek Orthodox refugees who fled to Venice from Turkey with the rise of the Ottoman Empire built a church here in 1536, with the aid of a special dispensation from Venice to collect taxes on incoming Greek ships. Nicknamed 'St George of the Greeks', the little church has an impressive iconostasis, and clouds of fine incense linger over services. The separate, slender **bell tower** was completed in 1603, though it began to lean right from the start. These days, it seems poised to dive into the canal on which the church sits.

Permission for the church was granted in the late 15th century in acknowledgement of the growing importance of the Greek community in the city, which at its peak numbered around 4000. Greek scholars contributed greatly to Venice's dominance in the printing trade, and thereby to its eminence as a seat of Renaissance learning.

While the exterior is classically Venetian, the interior is Orthodox in style: the aisleless nave is surrounded by dark, wooden stalls and there's a *matroneo* (women's gallery). All eyes, however, are drawn to the golden iconostasis with its 46 icons, the majority of which are the work of 16th-century Cretan artist Michael Danaskinàs. Other fabulous works by the Venetian school of

---

THE VENETIAN 'BURBS

At the easternmost reaches of Venice, Sant'Elena is the city's most far-flung island. Most of it, with the exception of the 12th-century church and monastery of the eponymous saint, was built upon reclaimed swampland dredged up in the process of creating shipping lanes in the early 20th century.

The island took on its current aspect during the 1920s, when it was developed as the city's newest residential area. Deliberately eschewing the Modernist trends of its time, the middle-class apartments are faithful copies of the city's aristocratic palaces, although they lack the quirks and elegant decay that define the rest of Venice.

Today Sant'Elena is a quiet residential quarter and a favourite destination for joggers, thanks to its shady byways and distinct lack of crowds.

icon painters can be found in the Museo delle Icone (p127).

LA PIETÀ
CHURCH

Map p280 (☎041 522 21 71; www.pietavenezia.org; Riva degli Schiavoni; admission €3, guided tour €10; ⊙9am-5pm Sat & Sun, tours noon Tue-Fri; ◉Pietà) Originally called Chiesa di Santa Maria della Visitazione but fondly nicknamed La Pietà, this harmonious church designed by Giorgio Massari is known for its association with the composer Vivaldi, who was concertmaster here in the early 18th century. Though the current church was built after Vivaldi's death, its acoustic-friendly oval shape honours his memory, and it is still used as a concert hall.

CHIESA DI SAN FRANCESCO DELLA VIGNA
CHURCH

Map p280 (Campo San Francesco della Vigna 2786; ⊙8.30am-12.30pm & 3-7pm; ◉Celestia) FREE Designed and built by Jacopo Sansovino, with a facade by Palladio, this enchanting Franciscan church is one of Venice's most underappreciated attractions. The Madonna positively glows in Bellini's 1507 *Madonna and Saints* in the **Cappella Santa**, just off the flower-carpeted **cloister**, while swimming angels and strutting birds steal the scene in delightful *Virgin Enthroned* (c 1460–70) by Antonio da Negroponte. Bring €0.20 to illuminate them.

Palladio and the Madonna are tough acts to follow, but father–son sculptors Pietro and Tullio Lombardo make their own mark with their 15th-century marble reliefs that recount the lives of Christ and an assortment of saints. Housed in the **Cappella Giustiniani**, just left of the altar, they are storytelling triumphs. Breezes seem to ripple through carved-marble trees, and life-like lions seem prepared to pounce right off the wall.

Out the back, the bell tower looks like the long-lost twin of the Campanile di San Marco and, facing north, a couple of steps leading to a portico of classical columns make the *campo* look like a proper ancient-Roman *agora* (market place). This makes a sociable setting for Venice's best annual block party, the **Festa di Francesco della Vigna**, with wine and rustic fare served up in the stately shadow of Palladio; it's usually held the third week in June.

CHIESA DI SAN GIOVANNI IN BRAGORA
CHURCH

Map p280 (Campo Bandiera e Moro 3790; ⊙9-11am & 3.30-5pm Mon-Sat, 9.30-noon Sun; ◉Arsenale) FREE This serene, 15th-century brick church harmonises Gothic and Renaissance styles with remarkable ease, setting the tone for a young Antonio Vivaldi, who was baptised here. Look for Bartolomeo Vivarini's 1478 *Enthroned Madonna with St Andrew and John the Baptist,* which shows the Madonna bouncing a delighted baby Jesus on her knee.

Bartolomeo's nephew Alvise depicts Jesus in later years in his splendidly restored 1494 *Saviour Blessing,* in which Christ has a cloudlike beard and eyes that seem to follow you around the room.

RIVA DEGLI SCHIAVONI
PROMENADE

Map p280 (◉San Zaccaria) Stretching west from San Marco, this paved boardwalk is one of the world's great promenades. *Schiavoni* (literally, 'Slavs') refers to the fishermen from Dalmatia who arrived in Venice in medieval times and found this a handy spot for casting their nets. For centuries, vessels would dock and disembark here, the waterfront a Babel of languages, as traders, dignitaries and sailors arrived from ports around the Mediterranean and beyond.

CHIESA DI SAN MARTINO
CHURCH

Map p280 (Campo San Martino 2298; ⊙11am-noon & 5-6.30pm Mon-Sat, 10.30am-12.30pm Sun; ◉Arsenale) FREE The neighbourhood church of San Martino is named after St Martin of Tours (AD 316–97), a Hungarian priest and the first Christian saint to die a natural death rather than suffer some irksome martyrdom. Inside, Sansovino's Greek-cross interior is lined with eight chapels and topped by a *trompe l'œil* ceiling by Domenico Bruni. Palma di Giovane's canvases of Jesus being flogged and then marched towards Calvary are tucked out of sight in the choir stalls.

To the right of the church is the former **Scuola di San Martino**, where secondhand sales are sometimes held.

MUSEO STORICO NAVALE
MUSEUM

Map p280 (☎041 244 13 99; Riva San Biagio 2148; adult/reduced €5/3.50; ⊙8.45am-1.30pm Mon-Thu, 8.45am-5.30pm Fri & Sat, 10am-5.30pm Sun; ◉; ◉Arsenale) Maritime madness spans 42 rooms at this museum of Venice's seafaring

LOCAL KNOWLEDGE

ART BIENNALE: A LOCAL'S GUIDE

Experienced art curators and event planners, Luca Berta and Francesca Giubilei are the creative force behind **VeniceArtFactory** (www.veniceartfactory.org). Their mission is simple: make more art happen in Venice and facilitate interesting and creative connections between artists and new audiences. Aside from organising multiple **Biennale** (p39) exhibits and events, they arrange unique tours in a range of Venetian **artist studios** (p130).

If you only have a weekend The Biennale has two main venues, the **Giardini Pubblici** (p122) and the **Arsenale** (p119), but visiting them in the same day can be as overwhelming as a full day at the Louvre. Instead focus on one of the main venues each morning, then spend the afternoon exploring collateral events in other parts of the city.

Beating the crowds The preview week of Art Biennale (three to four days before the public opening) is a must for artists, curators, gallerists and collectors. For those interested in enjoying the exhibitions, any time after the crowded first two weeks is best, although July and August are hot months in the city. Early November, just before the Biennale's closing, also offers a perfect combination of low season prices, mild weather and minimal crowds.

For the glamour of it all During the vernissage, the art world descends on Venice filling the *campi* (squares) and *calli* (streets) with gossiping groups and drawing celebrities to glamorous preview parties. Hotel bars at the Palazzina G, Bauer Hotel and Metropole are favourite hangouts, as is the **Il Piccolo Mondo** (Map p272; ☑041 520 03 71; Calle Contarini-Corfù 1056/A; ☺10.30pm-4am; ⏃Accademia) club in Dorsoduro.

Refuelling Close to the Biennale You'll find authentic Venetian cuisine at **Il Nuovo Galeon** (p131), contemporary fine dining at **CoVino** (p131), excellent *porchetta* and radicchio *panini* at **STRANI** (p132) and vegetarian take-out at **Le Spighe** (p131).

Treasure hunting One of the biggest thrills of the Biennale is discovering hidden corners of Venice while hunting down some of the 90 collateral exhibits. Pick up a map at the ticket office and get busy exploring private *palazzi* (mansions), artisan workshops, old factories and normally inaccessible churches.

Favourite far-flung venue Try **Spazio Punch** (p140), the former beer-brewing plant on the island of Giudecca.

history, featuring scale models of Venetian-built vessels as well as Peggy Guggenheim's not-so-minimalist gondola. On the ground floor, 'the barn', you'll find sprawling galleries of fearsome weaponry and 17th-century dioramas of forts and ports. Upstairs you can gawk at a sumptuous model of the *bucintoro*, the doge's gilded ceremonial barge, destroyed by Napoleonic troops in 1798.

Although the minutiae of some of the exhibits will mostly be of interest to enthusiasts and specialists, the display illustrates the incredible span of Venetian power across the Adriatic and Mediterranean over the centuries. In addition, the 2nd floor covers Italian naval history and memorabilia, from unification to the present day, and on the 3rd floor is a room devoted to gondolas, including Peggy Guggenheim's pimped-up ride.

The ticket also gets you entrance to the **Padiglione delle Navi** (Ships Pavilion; Map p280; Fondamenta della Madonna; admission incl museum €5; ☺2pm & 3.30pm Sat, 11am, 12.30pm, 2pm & 3.30pm Sun; ⏃Arsenale), though at writing it was only open at timed slots on the weekends. Of the many boats on display here, the most eye-catching is the **Scalé Reale**, an early-19th-century ceremonial vessel used to ferry King Vittorio Emanuele to Piazza San Marco in 1866 when Venice joined the nascent Kingdom of Italy. The ship last set sail in 1959, when it brought the body of the Venetian Pope Pius X to rest at the Basilica di San Marco.

VENICE IN A BOTTLE   GALLERY

Map p280 (☑349 779 93 85, 328 658 38 71; www.veniceinabottle.com; Via Garibaldi 1794; ☺10am-7pm Tue-Sat; ⏃Arsenale) This contemporary glass gallery works with young, Venetian

ARTIST STUDIO TOURS

Venice is a city built on art as much as it is a city built on water. Visitors soon realise that canals are just brief interruptions between artworks in this Unesco World Heritage site.

Understandably, it's easy to feel overwhelmed by all these masterpieces. After all, what does it all mean? How should you feel looking at Maurizio Cattelan's taxidermied horse with its head jammed in the wall of the Punta della Dogana? And why was Titian so possessed when painting the Salute's *Pietà* that he smeared the paint on the canvas with his hands?

Some of these questions are best answered by the artists who continue to work in Venice today. During VeniceArtFactory's **Studio Tours** (Map p280; ☑349 779 93 85, 328 658 38 71; www.veniceartfactory.org; Via Garibaldi 1794; 2-person tour €180, additional adult/student €40/20; ☒Arsenale) you can sit down to breakfast or share an aperitif with painters, sculptors and engravers in their studios and homes, view their works in progress and ask them what it's all about. Where do they find their inspiration? Who commissions their work? What motivates them? And, what are they trying to communicate? It's a fascinating insight into what it's like to be an artist in the world's most artful city.

and international designers and scientists on cutting-edge, experimental glass projects which continue to push the boundaries of Murano's glass masters. It can also arrange a unique dining experience in a Murano furnace, hosted by its network of collaborating designers.

CATTEDRALE DI
SAN PIETRO DI CASTELLO   CHURCH
Map p280 (Campo San Pietro 2787; admission €3, or with Chorus Pass free; ☺10am-5pm Mon-Sat; ☒San Pietro) This sleepy church on the far-flung island of San Pietro served as Venice's cathedral from 1451 to 1807. An almost-but-not-quite Palladio design with a white **bell tower** of Istrian stone by Codussi, its expansive 54m **dome** rivals Michelangelo's at the Vatican in width (though not height). The most intriguing piece inside the church is **St Peter's Throne**, which according to legend was used by the Apostle Peter in Antioch and once hid the Holy Grail.

While the story has all the makings of an *Indiana Jones* sequel, sadly there's very little truth to it: the intricately carved stone back is in fact made from a scavenged Muslim tombstone that postdates the Apostle's death by many centuries. Still, it seems a fitting tale for such a historic location, given that the island of San Pietro (originally known as Olivolo) was among the first to be inhabited in Venice, and the original church here was the seat of a bishopric as early as 775.

🍴 EATING

★**OSTERIA RUGA DI JAFFA**   OSTERIA €
Map p280 (Ruga Giuffa 4864; meals €20-25; ☺8am-11pm) Hiding in plain sight on the busy Ruga Giuffa is this excellent *osteria* (casual tavern). You should be able to spot it by the *gondolieri* packing out the tables at lunch time. They may not appreciate the vase of blooming hydrangeas on the bar or the artsy Murano wall lamps, but they thoroughly approve of the select menu of house-made pastas and succulent over-roast pork soaked in its own savoury juices.

ALLA BASILICA   ITALIAN €
Map p280 (☑041 522 05 24; www.allabasilicavenezia.it; Calle degli Albanesi 4255; meals €14-20; ☺noon-3pm Tue-Sun; ☒San Zaccaria) Continuing the long tradition of welcoming travellers to Venice, the Diocese of Venice lays on a hearty €14 lunch menu in this canteen-style restaurant. Never mind the glaring lighting and the lack of homely decor, the food is home-cooked and surprisingly good. When we visited there was grilled blue shark and lamb *quadrelli* (square-shaped pasta) scattered with fresh herbs.

DIDOVICH   BAKERY, DELI €
Map p280 (☑041 523 00 17; Camp di Santa Marina 5908; pastries €1.10, mains €7-10; ☺7am-8pm Mon-Sat; ☒Rialto) With outside seating on pretty Campo Santa Marina, Didovich is an ideal breakfast and light-lunch spot. It specialises in miniature-sized pastries, which

means you can try a selection of chocolate or flaky almond croissants and *fritelle* (fried dough) filled with alcohol-infused *zabaione* (cream). At lunch time, sweets change to savouries with an option to take out portions of homemade pasta dishes or meat and tuna *polpette* (meat- or fishballs).

PASTICCERIA DA BONIFACIO PASTRIES €
Map p280 (☑041 522 75 07; Calle degli Albanesi 4237; pastries €1.50-4; ☺7am-8pm Fri-Wed; ◉San Zaccaria) Pastry awards line the wall in this tiny bakery where gondoliers and Venetian housewives flock to devour the buttery, just-baked sweetness of almond croissants and take-home boxes of Venetian specialities such as *zaletti* (cornmeal biscuits with sultanas). As afternoon wanes, the bakery turns into a makeshift bar as locals pop in for the signature *spritz* and *mammalucchi* (deep-fried batter balls with candied fruit).

LE SPIGHE VEGETARIAN €
Map p280 (☑041 523 81 73; Via Garibaldi 1341; meals €10-15; ☺9.30am-2pm & 5.30-7.30pm Mon-Sat; ✈; ◉Giardini) All vegetarian, all organic and vegan-friendly, Doriana's tiny eatery offers quick but delicious dishes based on seasonal produce, from crunchy fennel salads to delicious potato-and-squash pies. And the vegan chocolate cake tastes divine, whatever its other virtues might be.

TRATTORIA ALLA RAMPA VENETIAN €
Map p280 (☑041 528 53 65; Via Garibaldi 1135; meals €12-22; ☺noon-2pm Mon-Fri; ◉Giardini) Hidden behind a little working-class bar is a low-slung dining room serving up some of Venice's heartiest lunch specials. A largely male, Venetian crowd tucks in hungrily to generous portions of roasted meat and fish, accompanied by seasonal vegetables and plentiful hunks of bread to sop up the sauces – all for €13.

CIP CIAP PIZZA €
Map p280 (☑041 523 6621; Calle del Mondo Novo 5799a; pizza per kilo €12; ☺10am-9pm; ✈; ◉Rialto) The cooks at this to-go pizza joint (where slices and pies are sold by weight) take their job seriously enough to dress in traditional chef's whites, and their thick-crust pizzas are a cut above the competition, thanks to fresh, high-quality ingredients. If you can snag one of the half-dozen stools, you'll even get a canal view thrown in with your meal.

★ IL GIARDINETTO - DA SEVERINO VENETIAN €€
Map p280 (☑041 528 53 32; www.algiardinetto. it; Salizada Zorzi 4928; meals €40; ☺noon-3pm & 7-10pm Fri-Wed Feb-Dec; ◉San Zaccaria) Date nights and spring feasts of *primizie della primavera* (the first spring vegetables) don't come better than sitting in a sea of greenery beneath Il Giardinetto's vine-covered courtyard. For over 60 years the Bastianello-Parmesan family have run this restaurant in the former chapel of the 15th-century Palazzo Zorzi. Over those years they've perfected delightfully light lunches of lagoon salads and fresh crab pasta, plus a naughty *zuppa inglese* (trifle).

★ COVINO VENETIAN €€
Map p280 (☑041 241 27 05; www.covinovenezia. com; Calle del Pestrin 3829a; three-course menu €36; ☺noon-2.30pm & 7-11pm Thu-Sun, 7-11pm Mon) Tiny CoVino has only 14 covers but demonstrates bags of ambition in its inventive, seasonal menu inspired by the Venetian terroir. Specialty products, such as Bronte pistachios and Bra sausages, are selected from Slow Food Presidio producers, and wines focus on natural and biodynamic varieties. Chef Dimitri works like an origami artist in the tiniest of kitchens, while host Andrea choreographs the convivial atmosphere in the restaurant like a pro.

Only the set menu is available at dinner, but there's an à la carte selection at lunch time. Bookings essential.

IL NUOVO GALEON VENETIAN €€
Map p280 (☑041 520 46 56; www.ilnuovogaleon. com; Via Garibaldi 1309; meals €30-40; ☺noon-3pm & 7-10pm Wed-Mon; ◉Arsenale, Giardini) With half the hull of a boat for a bar and daily hauls of lagoon goodies, you can be sure of simple but excellent Venetian seafood at this Castello institution. The mixed shellfish soup packs a powerful flavour punch and is chock full of clams and mussels. For *secondi*, aside from the typical Venetian cuttlefish, there's tuna 'Livorno style' and a very good sole meunière.

ALLA RIVETTA VENETIAN €€
Map p280 (☑041 528 73 02; Salizada San Provolo 4625; meals €20-25; ☺noon-2.30pm & 7-10.30pm Tue-Sun; ◉San Zaccaria) Tucked behind the Ponte San Provolo, this trattoria hums with the chatter of contented diners even in the dead of winter. It is staffed by a clutch of senior waiters in jovial red gilets,

who'll dispense free nibbles and a glass of strawberry wine as you wait for your table. Then they'll cordially serve you platters of lagoon fare: raw seafood antipasti, pasta with clams and *fritto misto* (mixed fried seafood).

★TRATTORIA
CORTE SCONTA   MODERN VENETIAN €€€

Map p280 (✆041 522 70 24; Calle del Pestrin 3886; meals €50-65; ◷12.30-2.30pm & 7-9.30pm Tue-Sat, closed Jan & Aug; ⚓Arsenale) Well-informed visitors and celebrating locals seek out this vine-covered *corte sconta* (hidden courtyard) for its trademark seafood antipasti and imaginative house-made pasta. Inventive flavour pairings transform the classics: clams zing with the hot, citrus-like taste of ginger; prawn and courgette linguine is recast with an earthy dash of saffron; and the roast eel loops like the Brenta River in a drizzle of balsamic reduction.

The evolving wine list features a notable selection of organic and biodynamic wines.

OSTERIA DI
SANTA MARINA   MODERN VENETIAN €€€

Map p280 (✆041 528 52 39; www.osteriadisanta marina.com; Campo Santa Marina 5911; meals €65, tasting menus €75-80; ◷12.30-2.30pm & 7.30-10pm Tue-Sat, 7.30-10pm Mon; ⚓Rialto) Don't be fooled by the casual piazza seating: this restaurant is saving up all the drama for your plate. Each course of the €75 tasting menu brings two bites of reinvented local fare – a prawn in a nest of shaved red pepper, artichoke and soft-shelled crab with squash *saor* marinade – while home-made pastas marry surprising flavours such as the shrimp and chestnut ravioli.

Bookings are essential and in busy periods you're required to reconfirm – otherwise you'll likely face the cold shoulder of the wait staff.

★ALLE TESTIERE   VENETIAN €€€

Map p280 (✆041 522 72 20; www.osterialletes tiere.it; Calle del Mondo Novo 5801; meals €50-60; ◷12.30-3pm & 7-11pm Tue-Sat) Make a reservation for one of the two evening sittings and come prepared for one of Bruno Gavagnin's seafood feasts. If you're lucky, you may get a plate of sweet, sci-fi-looking mantis shrimps, a gazpacho of grilled *moscardini* (little octopus) or langoustines from the lagoon. Subtle spices such as ginger, cinnamon and orange zest recall Venice's trading

past with the East; and there are also wines from the house vineyard.

AL COVO   VENETIAN €€€

Map p280 (✆041 522 38 12; www.ristoranteal covo.com; Campiello della Pescaria 3968; meals €55-80; ◷12.45-2pm & 7.30-10pm Fri-Tue; ⚓Arsenale) For years Diane Rankin and Cesare Benelli have dedicated themselves to the preservation of heritage products and lagoon recipes, which has placed them firmly on the gourmet map. Only the freshest seasonal fish gets the Covo treatment, accompanied by artichokes, aubergines, *cipollini* onions and mushrooms from the lagoon larders of Sant'Erasmus, Vignole, Treporti and Cavallino. Meat, too, is carefully sourced and much of it is Slow Food accredited, too.

Prices are offset by reasonably priced, limited-production wine.

🍷 DRINKING & NIGHTLIFE

★STRANI   BAR

Map p280 (✆041 099 14 34; www.straninvenice. it; Via Garibaldi 1582; cicheti & sandwiches €1.80-€4; ◷7.30am-1am; ⚓Arsenale) There's always a party on at STRANI thanks to its excellent selection of beers on tap, well-priced glasses of DOC Veneto wines and platters of *sopressa* (soft salami) and salami that deserve to be tasted for their flavoursome quality. Fragrant flatbreads, heaped bruschetta of *porchetta* and radicchio, and a plethora of *cicheti* keep drinkers fuelled for late-night jam sessions with the locals.

★LA SERRA DEI GIARDINI   CAFE

Map p280 (✆041 296 03 60; www.serradeigiardi ni.org; Viale Giuseppe Garibaldi 1254; snacks €4-15; ◷10am-9.30pm summer, 11am-8pm Mon-Thu & 10am-9pm Fri & Sat winter; ☎♿; ⚓Giardini) Order a herbal tisane or the signature pear bellini and sit back amid the hothouse flowers in Napoleon's fabulous greenhouse. Cathedral-like windows look out onto the tranquil greenery of the public gardens, while upstairs workshops in painting and gardening are hosted on the suspended mezzanine. Light snacks and homemade cakes are also available alongside unique micro-brews and Lurisia sodas flavoured with Slow Food Presidia products.

ROSA SALVA CAFE

Map p280 (☑041 522 79 49; www.rosasalva.it; Campo Zanipolo; pastries & sandwiches €1.50-5; ☺7.30am-8.30pm Thu-Tue; ⛴Fondamente Nove) For over a century, Rosa Salva has been serving tea, pastries, ice-creams and *babà* (a type of cake) to the passing trade on Campo Zanipolo. Founder Antonio Salva was pastry chef to the royal household in 1879 and the tradition of excellence endures. Inside the 1930s throwback interior, ladies take *tramezzini* (triangular, stacked sandwiches) and trays of *tè con limone* at marble-topped tables, while outside sunseekers swirl the ice in their cocktails and children slurp ice-creams from the gelato bar.

AL PORTEGO BAR

Map p280 (☑041 522 90 38; Calle de la Malvasia 6015; cicheti €1.50-3; ☺noon-3pm & 6-10pm; ⛴Rialto) Beneath the portico that gives this *bacaro* (bar/eatery) its name is a walk-in closet that somehow manages to distribute wine and *cicheti* to the overflowing crowd of young Venetians in approximate order of arrival. Wine is cheap (€2 to €3) and plentiful, and the bar groans with classic nibbles. If that's not enough, make a dash for one of the five tables round the back where enormous plates of *fritto misto* (fried seafood) and pasta with scampi are served.

★ENOTECA MASCARETA WINE BAR

Map p280 (☑041 523 07 44; Calle Lunga Santa Maria Formosa 5138; ☺7pm-2am Fri-Tue; ⛴Ospedale) Oenophiles love this traditional *enoteca* (wine bar) for its stellar wines by the glass – including big Amarones and cloudily organic *prosecco*, one of them made by owner Mauro. If you're hungry, the excellent *taier misto* (platters of cured meats and cheeses) could pass for a light meal for two – all for €15.

★BAR TERAZZA DANIELI BAR

Map p280 (☑041 522 64 80; www.starwood hotels.com; Riva degli Schiavoni 4196; cocktails €18-22; ☺3-6.30pm mid-Apr–Oct; ⛴San Zaccaria) Gondolas glide in to dock along the quay, while across the lagoon the white-marble edifice of Palladio's San Giorgio Maggiore turns from gold to pink in the waters of the canal: the late-afternoon scene from the Hotel Danieli's top-floor balcony bar definitely calls for a toast. Linger over a *spritz* (€10) or cocktail – preferably the sunset-tinted signature Danieli cocktail of gin, apricot and orange juices, and a splash of grenadine.

BACARO RISORTO BAR

Map p280 (Campo San Provolo 4700; cicheti €1.50-4; ☺9am-9pm Mon-Sat; ⛴San Zaccaria) Just a footbridge from San Marco, this shoebox of a corner bar overflowing with happy drinkers offers quality wines and abundant *cicheti*, including *crostini* heaped with *sarde in saòr* (grilled sardines in a sweet-and-sour sauce), soft cheeses and melon tightly swaddled in prosciutto. Note that opening times are 'flexible.'

PARADISO CAFE

Map p280 (☑041 241 39 72; Giardini della Biennale 1260; ☺9am-7pm, later during Biennale; ⛴Biennale) This cheery yellow mini-*palazzo* is fuelled by a steady stream of coffee and cocktails that cost less than you'd expect given the designer chairs, waterfront terrace and lack of competition – this is the only cafe within reach of anyone in stilettos at the Biennale.

☆ ENTERTAINMENT

LABORATORIO OCCUPATO MORION CULTURAL CENTRE

Map p280 (lab.morion@gmail.com; Salizada San Francesco 2951; ⛴Celestia) When not busy staging environmental protests or avant-garde performance art, this counterculture social centre throws one hell of a dance party, with performances by bands from around the Veneto. Events are announced via wheat-paste posters thrown up around town and on its Facebook page (www.face book.com/laboratoriooccupatomorion).

🔒 SHOPPING

★BRAGORÀ ACCESSORIES, CRAFTS

Map p280 (☑041 319 08 64; www.bragora. it; Salizada Sant'Antonin 3496; ☺9am-1pm & 3-6pm Mon-Fri; ⛴San Zaccaria) Aiming to bring some contemporary cool to Castello, Bragorà is a multipurpose space: part shop, service centre and cultural hub. Its upcycled products include beach bags sewn out of boat sails, toy gondolas fashioned from drink cans, belts made from bike tyres and jewellery crafted from upcycled springs. In the back, you can print your own T-shirt or poster, and there's a useful internet point

VENETIAN ROAD RULES

Even though there are no cars in Venice, some pedestrian traffic rules apply:

➡ **Walk single file and keep right** along narrow streets to let people pass in either direction, and make way for anyone who says *permesso* (excuse me) – usually a local rushing to or from work or school.

➡ **Pull over to the side** if you want to check out a shop window or snap a photo, but don't linger for long: this is the pedestrian equivalent of double-parking your car.

➡ **Keep moving on smaller bridges**, where stalled shutterbugs can cause traffic jams. But feel free to snap away on the Rialto and Accademia bridges – everyone loves photographing these Grand Canal views, including locals.

➡ **Offer to lend a hand** if you see someone struggling with a stroller or heavy bag on a bridge, and you may earn a grateful *grazie!*

and a good supply of tech devices if you've left home without that adaptor.

As a community hub, it sometimes hosts comedy nights or workshops with the artists whose products they stock. Check out www.facebook.com/bragora for details.

★**FABRICHARTE** CRAFTS

Map p280 (☑041 200 67 43; www.fabricharte.org; Calle del Cafetier 6477/Z; ☺11am-7pm Mon-Sat; ☑Fondamente Nove) Stacks of handbound books, picture frames, trays and keepsake boxes all covered in delightful, handstamped papers make the the window of Andreatta Andrea's workshop look like Christmas. He apprenticed at the legendary Piazzesi and now offers a unique service in Venice: bring him any well-loved book and he can rebind it for you in any of the available Raimondini papers in a day or two. He also fashions gift-worthy sketch pads, composition books and can transform paperbacks into hardbacks.

Worldwide shipping and online ordering is available.

★**PAOLO BRANDOLISIO** CRAFTS

Map p280 (☑041 522 41 55; www.paolobrandolisio.altervista.org; Sotoportego Corte Rota 4725; ☺hours vary; ☑San Zaccaria) Beneath all the marble, gilding and lacquering, Venice is a city of wood long supported by its carpenters, caulkers, oarmakers and gilders. Master woodcarver Paolo Brandolisio continues the traditions, crafting the sinuous rowlock (*forcola*) that supports the gondolier's oar. Made of walnut or cherry wood, each one is crafted specifically for boat and gondolier. Miniature replicas, which make great gifts, are on sale in the workroom.

QSHOP ARTS, HOMEWARES

Map p280 (Campiello Querini Stampalia 5252; ☺10am-5.30pm Tue-Sun; ☑Rialto, San Zaccaria) Aside from its sumptuous range of art and design books, the shop of the Querini Stampalia Foundation offers a highly curated selection of glass, jewellery, household items, silverware and textiles. Pieces from design greats such as Carlo Scarpa, Carlo Moretti and San Lorenzo sit beside the work of emerging talents such as Clamour Glamour bracelets, Ichendorf ceramics and Andreina Brengola's upcycled jewellery made out of springs.

★**ATELIER ALESSANDRO MERLIN** HOMEWARES

Map p280 (☑041 522 58 95; Calle del Pestrin 3876; ☺10am-noon & 3-7pm Mon-Thu & Sat, 3-7pm Fri & Sun; ☑Arsenale) Enjoy your breakfast in the nude, on a horse or atop a jellyfish – Alessandro Merlin paints them all on striking black and white cappuccino cups and saucers. His expressive characters are modern, but the *sgraffito* technique he uses on some of his work dates back to Roman times: designs are scratched white lines against a black background.

★**AL CAMPANIL** JEWELLERY

Map p280 (☑041 523 57 34; Calle Lunga Santa Maria Formosa 5184; ☺9.30am-12.30pm & 3.30-7.30pm Mon-Sat; ☑Ospedale, San Zaccaria) Utilising traditional Murano techniques and materials, including oxides and resins, Sabina Melinato conjures up contemporary glass and costume jewellery. Her deco-inspired glass pendants are so highly polished they look like lacquerwork – just what you'd expect from a teacher at Murano's International School of Glass.

GIOVANNA ZANELLA — SHOES

Map p280 (☑041 523 55 00; www.giovannaz anella.it; Calle Carminati 5641; ⊙1.30-8pm Mon-Sat; ☑Rialto) Woven, sculpted and crested like lagoon birds, Zanella's shoes practically demand that red carpets unfurl before you. The Venetian designer custom-makes shoes, so the answer is always: yes, you can get those peep-toe numbers in yellow and grey, size 12, extra narrow. Closed last two weeks of August.

KALIMALA CUOIERIA — SHOES, ACCESSORIES

Map p280 (☑041 528 35 96; www.kalimala. it; Salizada San Lio 5387; ⊙9.30am-7.30pm Mon-Sat, 10.30am-7.30pm Sun; ☑Rialto) Sleek, supple belts with brushed-steel buckles, modern satchels, man-bags and knee-high red boots: Kalimala makes beautiful leather goods in practical, modern styles. Shoes, sandals and gloves are crafted from vegetable-cured cow hide and dyed in a mix of earthy tones and vibrant lapis blues. Given the natural tanning and top-flight leather, the prices are remarkably reasonable, with handmade shoes starting at €100.

BALLARIN — ANTIQUES

Map p280 (☑347 779 24 92; Calle del Cafetier 6482; ⊙10am-1pm & 4.30-7.30pm Mon-Sat; ☑Ospedale) If you're looking for something distinctively Venetian, join bargain-hunters in Valter Ballarin's Aladdin's cave. An old-fashioned dealer and artisan restorer, Valter has a knack for tracking down period furnishings, hand-painted glassware, prints, books, toys and lamps. The best souvenir, though, is a handful of colourful, hand-blown glass flowers from dismembered Murano chandeliers.

BANCO LOTTO 10 — FASHION, ACCESSORIES

Map p280 (☑041 522 14 39; Salizada da Sant'Antonin 3478a; ⊙10am-7pm Tue-Sat; ☑Pietà) Prison orange is out and plum silk velvet is in at this nonprofit boutique, whose hand-sewn fashions are the fruit of a retraining program at the women's prison on Giudecca. Designed and made by inmates, the smartly tailored jackets (€80 to €140) and handbags often incorporate opulent silks, velvets and tapestry donated by Fortuny and Bevilacqua. Even La Fenice has dressed its divas in Banco Lotto ensembles.

Volunteers run the boutique and purchases fund the women prisoners' continuing career training and reintegration into the community after their release.

SPORTS & ACTIVITIES

★YOGA VENEZIA — YOGA

Map p280 (☑346 795 59 84; www.yogavenezia. com; La Serra dei Giardini, Viale Garibaldi 1254a; one/five sessions €15/50; ☑Giardini) Drop in to Napoleon's plant-filled greenhouse during the evening and you'll find stressed out hotel workers, gap-year students and Biennale curators striking yoga poses amid the greenery. Californian Julia Curtis has over 18 years of practice behind her and teaches classes in Hatha, Vinyasa and Anusara styles. Classes cater to adults and children from 6 to 12 years old, although you may get hooked and want to join Julia on her yoga art tours or in Giudecca's gorgeous gardens (p146). See the website for details of classes.

SUP IN VENICE — WATER SPORTS

(☑339 565 92 40; www.supinvenice.com; per person 2-/4-person groups €70/50; ⊙summer) Eliana Argine is a passionate paddler and a trained Venetian tour guide, so it made sense to combine the two in this unique stand-up paddleboard tour. Available to confident paddlers over the age of 14, the two-hour tours weave through the quieter canals of Castello and Cannaregio with Eliana pointing out fascinating details about the city that can only be appreciated from the water.

Safety is paramount and all paddlers are required to sign up to FISURF (www.fisurf. net; membership €10), which provides full insurance.

REALI WELLNESS SPA — SPA

Map p280 (☑041 241 59 16; www.hotelaireali.com; Campo della Fava 5527; ⊙10am-9pm; ☑Rialto) In this surprisingly spa-starved city, the Reali offers a sanctuary of Asian-inspired wellness. Instead of being banished to the basement as is usually the case, the Reali's spa is on the top floor where light floods into the Turkish bath and soothes you in your 'emotional' shower. Treatments cover a range of Thai massages (€60 to €100) and beauty treatments (€30 to €115) and are good value compared with treatments at the Bauer and Cipriani.

Giudecca, Lido & the Southern Islands

GIUDECCA | ISOLA DI SAN SERVOLO | ISOLA DI SAN LAZZARO DEGLI ARMENI | LIDO DI VENEZIA | PELLESTRINA

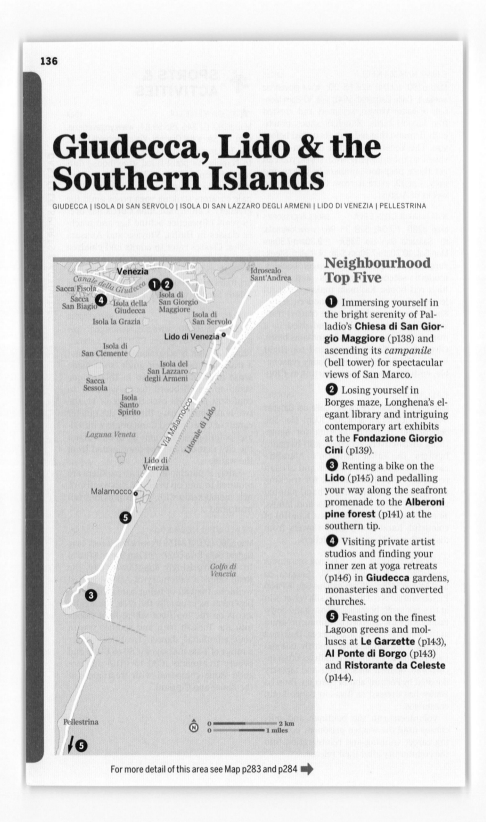

Neighbourhood Top Five

❶ Immersing yourself in the bright serenity of Palladio's **Chiesa di San Giorgio Maggiore** (p138) and ascending its *campanile* (bell tower) for spectacular views of San Marco.

❷ Losing yourself in Borges maze, Longhena's elegant library and intriguing contemporary art exhibits at the **Fondazione Giorgio Cini** (p139).

❸ Renting a bike on the **Lido** (p145) and pedalling your way along the seafront promenade to the **Alberoni pine forest** (p141) at the southern tip.

❹ Visiting private artist studios and finding your inner zen at yoga retreats (p146) in **Giudecca** gardens, monasteries and converted churches.

❺ Feasting on the finest Lagoon greens and molluscs at **Le Garzette** (p143), **Al Ponte di Borgo** (p143) and **Ristorante da Celeste** (p144).

For more detail of this area see Map p283 and p284 ➡

Explore Giudecca, Lido & the Southern Islands

Other cities have suburban sprawl; Venice has medieval monasteries floating in teal-blue waters. To the south, the seaward side of the lagoon is sheltered from the Adriatic by the Lido, for centuries the beach and bastion of the city. In the 19th century, it found a new lease of life as a bathing resort and a place of welcome natural beauty after the urban rigours of the Rialto. It's a quick 15 to 20 minute boat ride from San Marco, although many people decamp here for weeks in the summer.

Smaller islands dot the foreground of remarkable views back to San Marco: Sacca Sessola, San Lazzaro degli Armeni, San Servolo and San Giorgio Maggiore. In the past they served the Republic well as quarantine islands, convents and mental asylums.

In the shadow of San Giorgio Maggiore lies La Giudecca, Venice's unofficial seventh *sestiere* (district). It was once an aristocratic retreat and later the city's industrial centre. You can easily visit both islands in half a day – weekends are best, when you can also visit the Fondazione Giorgio Cini.

Note that many island restaurants close from November to March, especially on the Lido.

Local Life

➡ **Cicheti hot spots** Join artists and rough-and-ready locals for generous *cicheti* (bar snacks) at La Palanca (p142), Lepanto (p144), Da Cri Cri e Tendina (p144) and al Mercà (p143).

➡ **Island pastimes** Join weekending locals on the Lido golf course, at summer surf club or striking a pose in Venice's most scenic gym with Yoga Venezia (p146).

➡ **Off-the-beaten-track beaches** Pack a picnic and head for the dunefields of Alberoni (p141), and enjoy the winter sun with Lido families at the *spiaggia comunale* (public beach) and Pachuka beach (p144).

Getting There & Away

➡ **Vaporetto Giudecca** *Vaporetto* lines 2, 4.1, 4.2 and N (night) serve Giudecca from San Marco or Dorsoduro.

➡ **Vaporetto San Giorgio Maggiore** Line 2 leaves from San Zaccaria.

➡ **Vaporetto Lido** Lines 1, 5.1 and 5.2 connect the Lido with all major stops in Venice. Line 6 is a fast service to the train station.

➡ **Vaporetto San Servolo & San Lazzaro** Line 20 from San Zaccaria serves both islands.

Lonely Planet's Top Tip

Instead of braving the lines at San Marco's *campanile* (bell tower), seek out San Giorgio Maggiore's *campanile*, which offers comparable views for a fraction of the wait time.

✕ Best Places to Eat

➡ Trattoria Altanella (p142)
➡ La Favorita (p143)
➡ Le Garzette (p143)
➡ Al Ponte di Borgo (p143)
➡ Ristorante Da Celeste (p144)

For reviews, see p142.➡

⬤ Best Places to Drink

➡ Skyline Rooftop Bar (p144)
➡ Harry's Dolci (p143)
➡ Pachuka (p144)
➡ Villa Laguna (p144)

For reviews, see p144.➡

🔒 Best Places to Shop

➡ Fortuny Tessuti Artistici (p145)
➡ CartaVenezia (p145)
➡ Monastero di San Lazzaro degli Armeni (p140)
➡ Laura Mirè Design (p145)

For reviews, see p145.➡

Most visitors only see San Giorgio across the water. It's quite a view – Palladio chose the white Istrian stone to stand out against the blue lagoon waters, and set it at an angle to create visual drama while also ensuring that it catches the sun all afternoon.

Palladio's Facade

Palladio's radical 15th-century facade gracefully solved the problem bedevilling Renaissance church design: how to graft a triangular, classical pediment onto a Christian church, with its high, central nave and lower side aisles. Palladio's solution: use one pediment to crown the nave, and a lower, half-pediment to span both side aisles. The two interlock with rhythmic harmony, while prominent three-quarter columns, deeply incised capitals and sculptural niches create depth with clever shadow-play. Above the facade rises a brick *campanile* with a conical copper spire and a cap of Istrian stone, from where you can catch a unique view back across the lagoon to San Marco.

Church Interior & Tintorettos

Likewise, the interior is an uncanny combination of brightness and serenity. Sunlight enters through high thermal windows and is then diffused by acres of white stucco. Floors inlaid with black, white and red stone draw the eye toward the altar. With its rigorous application of classical motifs, it's reminiscent of a Roman theatre.

Two outstanding late works by Tintoretto flank the church's altar. On one side hangs his *Fall of Manna*; on the other side, *Last Supper* depicts Christ and his apostles in a scene that looks suspiciously like a 16th-century Venetian tavern. Nearby, in the Cappella dei Morti, hangs Tintoretto's last work, the moving *Deposition of Christ*.

DON'T MISS...

→ Tintoretto's *Fall of Manna* and *Last Supper*

→ Views from the 60m-high bell tower

PRACTICALITIES

→ Map p283, E2

→ ☏ 041 522 78 27

→ Isola di San Giorgio Maggiore

→ bell tower adult/reduced €6/4

→ ⊙9.30am-12.30pm & 2.30-6.30pm Mon-Sat, 2-6.30pm Sun

→ 🚤San Giorgio Maggiore

SIGHTS & ACTIVITIES

Giudecca

Giudecca's disputed history begins with its name. The name comes not from its one-time Jewish inhabitants (the Italian word for Jews is *ebrei*), but from the Venetian *zudega*, meaning 'the judged' – referring to rebel aristocratic families banished here during the 9th century.

Michelangelo fled here from Florence in 1529, though by the time he arrived, the aristocratic Dandolos, Mocenigos and Vendramins had transformed the island from a prison into a neighbourhood of garden villas. When the nobles headed inland in the 18th century to build villas along the Riviera Brenta, Giudecca's gardens gave way to factories, tenements and military barracks.

In recent years, these large abandoned spaces have attracted a new set of exiles – artists who can no longer afford rents in central Venice. Today, SS Cosma e Damiano, first a church and then a factory, has live-work loft spaces, while a munitions depot is now the cutting-edge Teatro Junghans (p144).

CHIESA DELLE ZITELLE
CHURCH

Map p283 (✆041 260 19 74; Fondamenta delle Zitelle; ☉mass 10am-noon Sun; ⚢Zitelle) Designed by Palladio in the late 16th century, the Chiesa di Santa Maria della Presentazione, known as the Zitelle, was a church and hospice for orphans and poor young women (*zitelle* is old local slang for 'old maids'). The doors are rarely open, but you can get a spa treatment in the adjoining convent and sleep in the orphanage. The luxury Bauer Palladio Hotel & Spa (www.palladiohotel spa.com) has creatively tweaked the original structure without altering Palladio's blueprint or the original cloister garden.

★CASA DEI TRE OCI
CULTURAL CENTRE

Map p283 (✆041 241 23 32; www.treoci.org; Fondamente de la Croce 43; exhibits €5; ☉10am-6pm Wed-Mon; ⚢Zitelle) FREE Acquired by the Fondazione di Venezia in 2000, this fanciful neo-Gothic house was once the home of early-20th-century artist and photographer Mario de Maria, who conceived its distinctive brick facade with its three arched windows (its namesake 'eyes') in 1910. Now

GIUDECCA, LIDO & THE SOUTHERN ISLANDS SIGHTS & ACTIVITIES

TOP SIGHT
FONDAZIONE GIORGIO CINI

In 1951, industrialist and art patron Vittorio Cini – a survivor of Dachau – acquired the monastery of San Giorgio and restored it in memory of his son, Giorgio Cini. The rehabilitated complex, now home to Cini's cultural foundation, is an architectural treasure incorporating a **refectory** and **cloister** by Palladio, and Baldassare Longhena's **monumental staircase** and 17th-century **library**. Veronese's *Wedding Feast at Cana* once hung in Palladio's refectory, but was removed by Napoleon in 1797 and sent to the Louvre.

Today, in the **Branca Centre**, the foundation continues the Benedictine tradition of scholarship; it became renowned for this during the Renaissance, when Florentine prince Cosimo de' Medici funded the creation of a library here. The **Nuova Manica Lunga library** (Map p283; ✆041 271 02 55; ☉9am-4.30pm; ⚢San Giorgio Maggiore) is open to the public on presentation of ID.

Weekend tours allow you to stroll through the **Borges Labyrinth** and contemplate the tranquil **Chiostro dei Cipressi**, the oldest extant part of the complex, completed in 1526 by Andrea Buora. Check the website for exhibitions, events and performances in the open-air **Teatro Verde**.

DON'T MISS...
➡ Chiostro dei Cipressi
➡ Palladio's refectory
➡ Longhena's library

PRACTICALITIES
➡ Map p283, E2
➡ ✆041 220 12 15
➡ www.cini.it
➡ Isola di San Giorgio Maggiore
➡ adult/reduced incl guided tour €10/8
➡ ☉guided tours 10am-5pm Sat & Sun
➡ ⚢San Giorgio Maggiore

it hosts his photographic archive and fantastic Italian and international exhibitions of contemporary art and photography. The views of San Marco and the Punta della Dogana alone are worth the visit.

CHIESA DEL SANTISSIMO REDENTORE
CHURCH

Map p283 (Church of the Redeemer; Campo del SS Redentore 194; adult/reduced €3/1.50, or with Chorus Pass free; ☉10am-5pm Mon-Sat; ☻Redentore) Built to celebrate the city's deliverance from the Black Death, Palladio's *Il Redentore* was completed under Antonio da Ponte (of Rialto bridge fame) in 1592. Inside there are works by Tintoretto, Veronese and Vivarini, but the most striking is Paolo Piazza's 1619 *Gratitude of Venice for Liberation from the Plague*.

Survival is never taken for granted in this tidal town, and to give thanks during the **Festa del Redentore**, Venetians have been making the pilgrimage across the canal on a shaky pontoon bridge from the Zattere since 1578.

SPAZIO PUNCH
CULTURAL CENTRE

Map p283 (www.spaziopunch.com; Fondamente delle Convertite 800/o; ☉hours vary; ☻Palanca) Non-profit, Spazio Punch have transformed Giudecca's derelict beer factory into a super cool venue for temporary art, design and fashion events, which take place several times a year. Shows include collaborations with the likes of the London College of Fashion and seek to reinterpret the industrial history of the building for contemporary audiences.

◉ Isola di San Servolo

Step off *vaporetto* 20 from San Zaccaria amid the students of Venice International University and you'll be struck by the island's balmy beauty. But despite the exotic palms, San Servolo has long sent a chill down Venetian spines, serving as it did as the city's main insane asylum from the 18th century until 1978.

Home to Benedictine monks since the 7th century, the island's medicinal flora saw it granted an apothecary's license in 1719 so the monks could better supply the Republic's on-site military hospital. Not long afterwards, in October 1725, San Servolo's first 'insane' patient, Lorenzo Stefani, arrived, starting a trend among

aristocratic families to have their afflicted relatives committed. At its peak, the asylum held hundreds of inmates, a large portion of them ex-ship's hands and Italian and Austrian servicemen, many of whom were simply suffering trauma or were afflicted by conditions caused by poverty and poor nutrition. A dedicated museum now documents their stories and some of the nightmarish 'treatments' practised on them.

MUSEO DELLA FOLLIA
MUSEUM

Map p284 (Museum of Madness; ☎041 524 011 914; www.fondazionesanservolo.it; Isola di San Servolo; adult/reduced €3/2; ☉by prior reservation; ☻San Servolo) As well as a poignant photographic collection displaying portraits of patients, San Servolo's Museum of Madness contains the full paraphernalia of psychiatric treatment of the day, including chains, handcuffs, cages for ice showers, early electro-therapy machines and a rare plethysmograph (the precursor of the lie detector). The tour (which must be pre-booked at least 5 days in advance) also takes in the reconstructed **anatomy theatre** beside the church and the ancient **pharmacy**.

◉ Isola di San Lazzaro degli Armeni

Once the site of a Benedictine hospice for pilgrims and then a leper colony, this island was given to Armenian monks fleeing Ottoman persecution in 1717. The entire island is still a working monastery, so access is by tour only. Take the 3.10pm *vaporetto* 20 from San Zaccaria.

★MONASTERO DI SAN LAZZARO DEGLI ARMENI
MONASTERY

Map p284 (☎041 526 01 04; Isola di San Lazzaro degli Armeni; adult/student & child €6/4.50; ☉tours 3.25-5pm; ☻; ☻San Lazzaro degli Armeni) Tours start in the glittering **church** and are conducted by multilingual monks, who amply demonstrate the Benedictine order's reputation for scholarship. After passing through the 18th-century **refectory**, you'll head upstairs to the **library**. In 1789 the monks set up a polyglot printing press here and translated many scientific and literary works into Armenian. Those works are still housed in the 150,000-strong collection alongside curios from Ancient Egypt, Sumeria and India.

An Egyptian mummy and a 15th-century Indian throne are the rather quirky main features of the room dedicated to the memory of Lord Byron, who spent six months here in 1816 helping the monks to prepare an English–Armenian dictionary. True to his eccentric nature, he could often be seen swimming from the island to the Grand Canal.

Before you leave, stop in at the **shop** to purchase some Vartanush jam made from rose petals plucked in the monastery's exotic **gardens**.

◉ Lido di Venezia

There's no doubt that the Lido is no longer the glamorous summer bolt-hole of Hollywood starlets and European aristocracy, but neither is it the unremarkable tourist resort that many detractors would have us believe. In fact, with its groomed shellac beaches, candy-coloured art deco architecture and summering Venetians sipping *prosecco* beneath candy-striped awnings, the Lido is a rather pretty and diverting seaside escape.

ANTICO CIMITERO ISRAELITICO   CEMETERY
Map p284 (☏041 71 53 59; www.museoebraico.it; Riviera San Nicolò; group tours adult/student €10/8, individual tours €80; ⊙by reservation in summer; 🚊Lido, San Nicoló) This overgrown garden was Venice's main Jewish cemetery from 1386 until the 18th century. It fell into disuse after the establishment of a new cemetery on Via Cipro and the tombstones were only rediscovered by construction workers in the 1920s. Tombstones range in design from Venetian Gothic to distinctly Ottoman. Some bear the image of a lion, not of St Mark, but of Castile and León, brought to Venice on the armorials of Sephardic Jews expelled from Spain in 1492.

Tours must be pre-booked with the **Museo Ebraico** (☏041 715 359; www.museoebraico.it; Campo del Ghetto Nuovo 2902b; adult/reduced €4/3; ⊙10am-7pm Sun-Fri except Jewish holidays Jun-Sep, 10am-5.30pm Sun-Fri Oct-May; 🚊Guglie).

MALAMOCCO   TOWN
Map p284 (🚊Lido) Pass over Ponte di Borgo to explore the canals and *calli* (lanes) of a less overwhelming lagoon town, with just a few churches and a Gothic *palazzo* (mansion). A miniature version of Venice right down to the lions of St Mark on medieval facades, Malamocco was actually the lagoon capital from 742 to 811.

PINETA DEGLI ALBERONI   BEACH
Map p284 (🚲; 🚊Lido) Right at the southern tip of the island, the Alberoni pine forest slopes down to the Lido's wildest, most scenic beach. These WWF-protected dunefields and walking trails are the stuff of Shelley's poems and Byron's early-morning rides. The majority of the beach is open to the public. To reach Alberoni, take bus A from the *vaporetto* stop.

◉ Pellestrina

Stretching south of Lido and repeating its long, sinuous shape, Pellestrina reminds you what the lagoon might have been like if Venice had never been dreamed of. The

---

LIDO STYLE

Between 1850 and WWI, the Lido became the world's most exclusive seaside resort and is still defined by the *stile liberty* (art nouveau) of the period. Walking itineraries around the most extravagant villas are available to download at www2.comune.venezia.it/lidoliberty.

Sensing an opportunity, canny business tycoon Nicolò Spada (founder of the Italian hotel group CIGA) started buying up Lido land, opening the island's two grandest hotels, the **Grand Hotel Excelsior** and the **Grand Hotel des Bains** (not open to the public), in 1908 and 1909 respectively. Giovanni Sardi's Excelsior, which sits decorated on the beach, is a Veneto-Moorish fantasy palace with interiors decorated by Mariano Fortuny, while the more conservative Hotel des Bains, designed by Francesco Marsich, is an art-nouveau monolith, recalling the great luxury spas of Baden Baden. The latter was immortalised in Thomas Mann's best-selling novella *Death in Venice*, adapted for the screen by Luchino Visconti in 1971 and filmed in the hotel.

LIDO BEACHES

All Lido beaches are to be found on the seaward side of the island, easily accessed from the *vaporetto* along the Gran Viale. In May 2012 they were awarded Blue Flag eco-accreditation (www.blueflag.org), and their shallow gradient makes them ideal for young children and even toddlers.

There are only three 'free' beaches open to the public: the **spiaggia comunale** accessed through the **Blue Moon** (Map p284; Piazzale Bucintoro 1; ⊙10am-6.30pm summer; ☻; ☻Lido) complex, the **San Nicolò beach** to the north and the **Alberoni beach** (p141) at the southern end of the island. The rest of the shoreline is occupied by *stabilimenti*: privately managed areas lined with wooden *capannas* (cabins), a relic of the Lido's 1850s bathing scene. Many of them are rented by the same families year in, year out or reserved for guests of seafront hotels. The *stabilimenti* also offer showers, sun loungers and umbrellas (€13 to €18) and small lockers (€30 to €75). Rates drop after 2pm.

11km-island is home to three tight-knit fishing communities – San Pietro in Volta, Porto Secco and Pellestrina – strung out along the water's edge. There are no hotels here, or sun loungers, just elderly women sitting on their porches and fishermen mending their nets.

Much of Pellestrina's seafront is lined by a remarkable feat of 18th-century engineering known as the **murazzi**. Although not immediately impressive to modern eyes, these massive sea walls represent Herculean handiwork from a preindustrial age. Designed to keep high seas from crashing into the lagoon, they remain an effective breakwater even today. The island is also blissfully flat, making it ideal biking country. The scenic side faces the lagoon and is lined with fishermen's shacks built over beds of mussels.

Bus 11 travels from the Lido *vaporetto* stop to Pellestrina.

EATING

✕ Giudecca

FOOD + ART
VENETIAN €

Map p283 (☎393 559 76 26; Campo Junghans 487; meals €8-15; ⊙11am-3pm Mon-Fri) This popular, self-service *mensa* (canteen) was previously located in Giudecca's boatyards. Now it's moved to the more upmarket *campo* near Teatro Junghens, but the formula is still the same – self-service food at reasonable prices in a creative environment. Students can get a three-course meal for €8, otherwise you'll pay the princely sum of €12 to €15.

LA PALANCA
VENETIAN €€

Map p283 (☎041 528 77 19; Fondamenta al Ponte Piccolo 448; meals €20-30; ⊙8am-8.30pm Mon-Sat; ☻Palanca) Lunchtime competition for canalside tables is stiff, but the views of the Zattere make *tagliolini ai calamaretti* (narrow ribbon pasta with tiny calamari) and swordfish carpaccio with orange zest. At €7 to €9 for plates of pasta, you'll be forking over half what diners pay along the waterfront in San Marco. Dinner is not served, but you can get *cicheti* (bar snacks) right up to closing time.

TRATTORIA AI CACCIATORI
VENETIAN €€

Map p283 (☎328 736 33 46; www.aicacciatori.it; Giudecca 320; ⊙11am-11pm Tue-Sun; ☻Palanca) 'The Hunter' is the oldest inn on Giudecca, so called after the hunters who bagged lagoon waterfowl for the tasty duck *ragù*. Other hail and hearty dishes includes grilled cheese with chestnut honey and walnuts, baked wild rabbit, and monkfish with creamed chickpeas and rosemary.

★TRATTORIA ALTANELLA
VENETIAN €€€

Map p283 (☎041 522 77 80; Calle delle Erbe 268; meals €35-45; ⊙noon-2.30pm & 7-10.30pm Tue-Sat; ☻Palanca) In 1920, fisherman Nane Stradella and his wife, Irma, opened a trattoria overlooking the Rio di Ponte Longo. Their fine Venetian cooking was so successful he soon gave up fishing and the restaurant now sustains a fourth generation of family cooks. Inside, the vintage interior is hung with artworks, reflecting the restaurant's popularity with artists, poets and writers, while outside a flower-fringed balcony hangs over the canal. Eat Irma's potato gnocchi with cuttlefish or Nane's enduringly good John Dory fillet.

★**HARRY'S DOLCI**   MODERN VENETIAN **€€€**

Map p283 (☑041 522 48 44; www.cipriani.com; Fondamenta San Biagio 773; meals €80-120; ☺11am-4pm Mon & 11am-11pm Wed-Sun summer; ⬛Palanca) The sun-washed Tiffany-blue canopy along the waterfront marks out this home away from home for the designer-sunglasses set. The service is low-key and the decor retro (think bistro chairs and subway tile), though the prices have more than kept up with inflation. In the early evening, the pontoon seating is the perfect spot for an early evening peach bellini, with rosy views across the water to the Zattere.

✗ Lido di Venezia

AL MERCÀ   CICHETI, SEAFOOD **€**

Map p284 (☑041 526 45 49; Via Enrico Dandolo 17a; cicheti €1.50-3.50, meals €15-20; ☺10.30am-3pm & 6.30-midnight Tue-Sun; ⬛Lido) Located in the old Lido fish market, al Mercà is popular with students who come for the abundant *cicheti*, outdoor seating and well-priced wine by the glass. Take a pew at one of the marble counters and order up a seafood snack of *folpetti* (mini octopus), fried shrimps and creamy salt cod.

MAGICHE VOGLIE   GELATERIA **€**

Map p284 (☑041 526 13 85; Gran Viale 47g; cones €2.50-4.50; ⬛Lido) The best ice cream in Lido is made every morning on the premises at this family-owned gelateria. Mull over the soft peaks of new-world flavours such as açaí berry and caja fruit, or plump for the classic purplish-black cherry or Sicilian pistachio.

★**LA FAVORITA**   SEAFOOD **€€**

Map p284 (☑041 526 16 26; Via Francesco Duodo 33; meals €35-45; ☺12.30-2.30pm & 7-10.30pm Fri-Sun, 7-10.30pm Tue-Thu; ⬛Lido) For long, lazy lunches, bottles of fine wine and impeccable service, look no further than La Favorita. The menu is as elegant as the surroundings, giant *rhombo* (turbot) simmered with capers and olives, spider-crab *gnochetti* (mini-gnocchi) and classic fish risotto. Book ahead for the wisteria-filled garden and well ahead during the film festival, when songbirds are practically outsung by the ringtones of movie moguls.

★**AL PONTE DI BORGO**   VENETIAN **€€**

Map p284 (☑041 77 00 90; Calle delle Mercerie 27, Malamocco; meals €25-35; ☺12.30-2.30pm & 7-10pm Apr-Oct; ⬛Lido) If you make it this far, you deserve to be rewarded with Mauretto's slap-up plates of sweet, briny crab served in its shell, garlicky bowls of *vongole* (clams) and pasta *alla malamocchina* (with mussels, tomatoes, oregano and smoked cheese). At weekends the shaded patio is crammed with locals and in the evening the bar serves typical *cicheti* with slugs of *prosecco*. Check lunch hours in low season, as it isn't always open.

★**LE GARZETTE**   VENETIAN **€€€**

Map p284 (☑041 712 16 53; www.legarzette. it; Lungomare Alberoni 32, Lido; meals €40-50; ☺12.30-2.30pm & 7-10.30pm mid-Jan–mid-Dec; ⬛; ⬛Lido) ✔ Nestled amid gardens overflowing with red radicchio, astringent fennel, handsome pumpkins and dark-green courgettes is the rust-red *agriturismo* of Renza and Salvatore. Book to stay (p197) in one of the breezy first-floor rooms with views over the vegetable patch, or come for a delicious country feast of organic dishes: crepes filled with juicy asparagus, lightly fried Malamocco artichokes and mouthwatering pear tart made with farm eggs.

If you aren't staying the night, reservations are essential for the restaurant.

ORGANIC PRISON MARKET

Mercato Settimanale de Lido (Map p284; Riviera di Corinto, Lido; ☺7am-2pm Tue) The Lido's open-air market is jam-packed with specialty food products. It is second only to the Rialto and has views across the Lagoon to boot.

Giudecca Organic Market (Map p283; www.rioteradeipensieri.org; Fondamenta delle Convertite, Giudecca; ☺9am-noon Wed; ⬛Palanca) Every Wednesday morning locals jostle for the best of the organic produce available at this unusual twist on a farmers market. In this case, the farmers happen to be prisoners of the adjacent women's correctional facility. Proceeds help pay for job retraining and post-release reintegration.

✕ Pellestrina

⭐**RISTORANTE DA CELESTE**   SEAFOOD €€€
(☑041 96 73 55; Sestier Vianelli 625; meals €60-80; ☺12.30-2.30pm & 7-9.15pm Thu-Tue; ⛴Pellestrina) At the far end of Pellestrina, this simple restaurant serves lagoon-fresh fish on its pontoon terrace. Go at sunset, when the rose-tinted sky kisses the glassy lagoon, and let Rossano guide you through the best daily offerings from polenta with tiny shrimp to a whole host of cockles, clams, scallops, spider crab and – the house special – fish pie. Reservations essential.

🍷 DRINKING & NIGHTLIFE

⭐**SKYLINE ROOFTOP BAR**   BAR
Map p283 (☑041 272 33 11; www.skylinebar venice.com; Fondamenta San Biagio 810, Giudecca; ☺5pm-1am; ⛴Palanca) From white-sneaker cruise passengers to the €300-sunglasses set, the rooftop bar at the Hilton Molino Stucky wows everyone with its vast panorama over Venice and the lagoon, with drink prices to match. From May to September, the bar offers a lunch buffet, live music and poolside parties.

⭐**VILLA LAGUNA**   BAR
Map p284 (☑041 526 13 16; http://villalaguna. hotelinvenice.com; Via Sandro Gallo 6, Lido; ⛴Lido) Sunset photo-ops don't come any better than on the terrace of Villa Laguna. This restored, Hapsburg holiday chalet is the only lagoon-facing hotel on the Lido and its west-facing terrace and lounge bar guarantees views of San Marco framed by a blushing pink sky.

LOCAL KNOWLEDGE

EL PECADOR
• •

El Pecador (Map p284; Lungomare Gabriele d'Annunzio; sandwiches €2.50-5; ☺11am-3am Apr-Oct; ⛴Lido) No, you're not suffering from heat stroke, that really is a red, double-decker bus parked up against the kerb – and what's more, it's dishing out the Lido's finest stuffed sandwiches and *spritz*, so why not take a seat on the canopied top deck?

LEPANTO   BAR
Map p284 (Piazzetta Lepanto 1/l; cocktails €3-9; ☺8am-11.30pm; ⛴Lido) With its gleaming bar lined with multicoloured booze bottles, this bustling place in Piazzetta Lepanto is a year-round favourite. Come for coffee in the morning, sandwiches and salads at lunchtime and the best mojitos and Manhattans on the Lido.

DA CRI CRI E TENDINA   CICHETI
Map p284 (☑041 526 54 28; Via Sandro Gallo 159; cicheti €1.50-3, meals €25-30; ☺11am-8pm; ⛴Lido) Leave the socialites at the Excelsior and head to this neighbourhood bar for DOC Veneto wines, beers on tap and a counter full of tasty *cicheti*. The bar is best in summer when all the tables are set outside and local card sharks sip their *spritz* and goad each other loudly in Venetian dialect. At lunch time there's a huge selection of stuffed *panini*, perfect for picnics.

LION'S BAR   BAR
Map p284 (Lungomare Marconi 31, Lido; sandwiches €2-7, salads €8-12; ☺during the festival 8am-3am; ⛴Lido) With its sexy baroque curves, stately porticos and exuberant sunburst demilune above the front door, the Lion's Bar is the Lido's most prestigious drinking den, although sadly it's only open during the Film Festival. Designed by Giovanni Sicher in the 1920s, it's a classic art-nouveau extravagance with a sweeping staircase, mullioned windows and a large terrace ideal for late-night DJ sets.

☆ ENTERTAINMENT

TEATRO JUNGHANS   THEATRE
Map p283 (☑041 241 19 74; www.accademiatea traleveneta.com; Piazza Junghans 494, Giudecca; prices vary; ♿; ⛴Redentore) The experimental theatre of Venice's acting academy, nicknamed Teatro Formaggino (Little Cheese), seats 150 around its three-sided stage. But you're not expected to just sit there: Teatro Junghans offers workshops on costume design, mask-acting, and *commedia dell'arte* (improvisational comedy). If you'd rather leave that sort of thing to professionals, check the online calendar for performances.

⭐**PACHUKA**   CLUB
(☑041 242 00 20; www.pachuka.it; Viale Umberto Klinger, Lido; ☺9am-4am Wed-Mon Oct-May,

THE PALACE OF CINEMA

Eugenio Miozzi's rigid, Rationalist **Palazzo della Mostra del Cinema** (Map p284; www.labiennale.org; Lungomare Marconi 30; Lido) seems as ill-suited to the playboy Lido as a woolly bathing suit. But its severe Fascist lines were well in keeping with the ambitious modernism of the era, when business tycoon and Fascist minister Count Giuseppe di Volpi conceived of the film festival as a means of fostering the Lido's up-market tourism industry.

Inaugurated in August 1932 on the terrace of the Excelsior, the festival was the first of its kind (Cannes was a relative latecomer in 1946) and capitalised on the boom in the film-making industry. So great was its success, in fact, that Miozzi's *palazzo* (mansion) was commissioned within three years and remains the main festival venue – at least until the much-delayed new cinema is completed.

9am-4am daily Jun-Sep; Lido, San Nicolò) The most reliable of the Lido's summertime dance spots, this place right on the beach works year-round as a snack bar and pizzeria, but summer weekend nights it cranks up as a beachside dance club, too. Live music starts at 10pm on the weekend, while disco hits the beach with DJ sets on Saturdays and Sundays.

🛍 SHOPPING

★**FORTUNY TESSUTI ARTISTICI** FACTORY OUTLET
Map p283 (041 528 76 97; www.fortuny.com; Fondamenta San Biagio 805; 10am-1pm & 2-6pm Mon-Sat; Palanca) Marcel Proust waxed rhapsodic over Fortuny's silken cottons printed with boho-chic art-nouveau patterns. Find out why at Fortuny's version of a factory outlet. Visitors can browse 260 textile designs in the showroom, but fabrication methods have been jealously guarded in the garden studio for a century. To see more of Fortuny's original designs and his home studio, head to Museo Fortuny (p59).

★**CARTAVENEZIA** HANDICRAFTS
Map p283 (041 524 12 83; www.cartaven ezia.it; Campo di S Cosmo 621/f, Giudecca; by appt; Palanca) Paper is anything but two-dimensional here: paper maestro Fernando di Masone embosses and sculpts handmade cotton paper into seamless raw-edged lampshades, hand-bound sketchbooks, and paper versions of marble friezes that would seem equally at home in a Greek temple or a modern loft. White gloves are handy for easy, worry-free browsing; paper-sculpting courses are available by prior request.

★**LAURA MIRÈ DESIGN** FASHION
Map p283 (340 231 86 69; www.lmiredesign. com; Fondamenta de le Convertite 710/c, Giudecca; by appt; Palanca) Globe-trotting Laure Mirè studied fashion in Paris and LA, worked in film with Steven Spielberg and now fashions extraordinary, sculptural knitwear in her Giudecca studio. Pieces are created from the finest cashmere (from Tibetan goats) and then knitted into geometric patterns, giant looped gilets and ribbed and braided sweaters of extraordinary detail. Each piece takes roughly 150 hours of work; treasure it.

🏃 SPORTS & ACTIVITIES

🏄 Lido di Venezia

LIDO ON BIKE CYCLING
Map p284 (041 526 80 19; www.lidoonbike.it; Gran Viale 21b; bikes per hour/day €5/9; 9am-7pm; Lido) Bike hire near the *vaporetto* stop, with reasonable prices that include a helmet and free map with recommended routes. ID is required for rental and the leader of the group must be 18 or over.

SURF CLUB VENEZIA SURFING
Map p284 (www.surfvenezia.org; Lungomare Marconi; single session €35) Between June and mid-September ISA and IKO qualified instructors are out on the beach nurturing Venetian surfer dudes and teaching the finer points of standup paddle boarding, windsurfing and kitesurfing. Single sessions, multi-day and weekly courses are available.

STRIKE A POSE WITH VENICE YOGA

One minute you're admiring Palladio's facade on San Giorgio Maggiore and the next you're striking a pose on the *fondamente* as bemused tourists wonder whether *you're* a modern art installation. It's all in a day's yoga class for Californian Julia Curtis, who runs **Yoga Venezia** (Map p283; ☑346 795 59 84; http://yogavenezia.com; Fondament Sant'Eufemia 317; classes €15, tours €30-50; ▮; ▮Palanca) and leads urban **yoga tours** around Venice as well as presiding over **classes** at her Giudecca studio. Other classes take place at Venice's most beautiful gym, the *palestra* on San Giorgio, and at **La Serra** (p132) in Castello.

Trained in Hatha, Vinyasa and Anusara yoga styles, Julia incorporates the fundamentals of meditation into her practice, making her **weekend retreats** in the gardens of Il Redentore a perfect fit for the monastic environment. Bespoke sessions in Giudecca gardens or client hotels, kids' yoga and range of detox and de-stress massages are also on offer.

CIRCOLO DEL GOLF VENEZIA GOLF

Map p284 (☑041 73 13 39; www.circologolf venezia.it; Via Strada Vecchia 1, Alberoni; green fees weekdays/weekends €97/116; ☺8.30am-6.30pm Tue-Sun; ▮; ▮Lido) The golf club sits on a 100-hectare site protected by the World Wildlife Fund. The original nine-hole course (there are now 18) was designed by Cruikshank of Glasgow in 1928 and incorporates the walls of the old Alberoni fort as key elements in a number of holes. Photos of club regulars, such as the Duke of Windsor, still hang in the bar, although the club's most notorious guest was Adolf Hitler, who visited in 1934.

HELIAIR VENICE HELICOPTER TOUR

Map p284 (☑041 526 02 15; http://executivejet. wix.com/heliair; Aeroporto G Nicelli, Via Renato Morandi 9; tours per person €75-330) Lift off in Heliair's bumble-bee yellow copters for an aerial view of the lagoon. Tours last from six minutes to half an hour and offer stunning views over the island jigsaw puzzle. After the tour, have a drink in the airport's retro 1930s **bar**, which is often used for film shoots and fashion shows.

Isola di San Giorgio Maggiore (p138)

Murano, Burano & the Northern Islands

ISOLA DI SAN MICHELE | MURANO | BURANO & MAZZORBO | TORCELLO | ISOLA DI SAN FRANCESCO DEL DESERTO | SANT' ERASMO | LE VIGNOLE | ISOLA DELLA CERTOSA | BURANO

Neighbourhood Top Five

1 Engaging with vivid biblical tales at **Basilica di Santa Maria Assunta** (p149), where devilish imps steal all the attention away from a glittering, golden heaven.

2 Witnessing artistry in action at the glass-blowing showrooms in **Murano** (p151) and rewarding their

originality with your purchases.

3 Basking in sun and culinary glory on the vineyard patio at **Venissa** (p157) or beneath the rose pergola at **Locanda Cipriani** (p157).

4 Watching colourful houses wiggle with delight at their reflections in the canals of **Burano** (p151).

5 Exploring religious retreats, deserted islands and ruined Forte Sant'Andrea by **barge** (p150), **batèla** (p154) or **kayak** (p159).

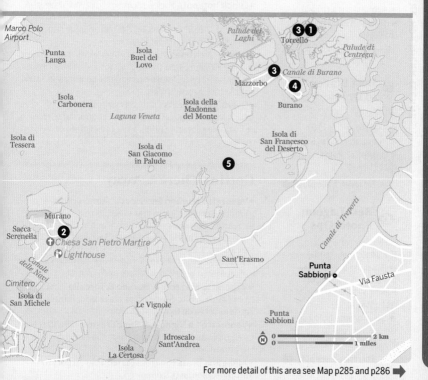

For more detail of this area see Map p285 and p286 ➡

Lonely Planet's Top Tip

Plan your trip carefully around your priorities – or it can be tricky to squeeze in Murano glass, Burano photography, Mazzorbo lunches and Torcello nature and history. Hit the outer islands first (boats to Torcello take 50 minutes) before *vaporetti* get crowded, then work your way back to Murano, aiming to hit the shops as crowds start to thin out in the early evening. Murano is only 10 minutes from Venice, so it's fast and easy to reach if you need to return for more glass.

MURANO, BURANO & THE NORTHERN ISLANDS

Best Places to Eat

➔ Venissa (p157)
➔ Locanda Cipriani (p157)
➔ Acquastanca (p156)
➔ Trattoria al Gatto Nero (p157)

For reviews, see p156. ➡

Best Places to Drink

➔ Venissa (p157)
➔ Il Certosino (p156)
➔ Acquastanca (p156)
➔ Caffè-Bar Palmisano (p157)

For reviews, see p156. ➡

Best Lagoon Photo-Ops

➔ Houses reflected in Burano canals (p151)
➔ Far-flung lagoon views from the belltower of Basilica di Santa Maria Assunta (p149)
➔ Cormorants holding their wings out to dry on Mazzorbo (p151)

For reviews, see p149. ➡

BASILICA DI SANTA MARIA ASSUNTA

Life choices are presented in no uncertain terms in Santa Maria Assunta's vivid cautionary tale: look ahead to a golden afterlife amid saints and a beatific Madonna, or turn your back on her to face the wrath of a devil gloating over lost souls. In existence for more than a millennium, the cathedral is the lagoon's oldest Byzantine-Romanesque monument.

Madonna & Last Judgment Mosaics

The restrained brick exterior (c 824) betrays no hint of the colourful scene that unfolds as you enter. The Madonna rises in the east like the sun above a field of corn poppies in the 12th-century apse mosaic, while the back wall vividly depicts the dire consequences of dodging biblical commandments. This extraordinary *Last Judgment* mosaic shows the Adriatic as a sea nymph ushering souls lost at sea towards St Peter, while a sneaky devil tips the scales of justice, and the Antichrist's minions drag sinners into hell.

Chapel Mosaics & Other Key Works

The right-hand chapel is capped with another 12th-century mosaic showing Sts Augustine, Ambrose, Martin and Gregory amid splendid, symbolic plants: lilies (representing purity), grapes and wheat (representing the wine and host of the holy sacrament), and corn-poppy buds (evoking Torcello's island setting).

Polychrome marble floors are another medieval masterpiece, with swirling designs and interlocking wheels symbolising eternal life. Saints line up atop the gilded iconostasis, their gravity foiled by a Byzantine screen teeming with peacocks, rabbits and other fanciful beasts.

DON'T MISS...

➡ *Last Judgment* mosaic

➡ *Madonna apse* mosaic

➡ Chapel saints mosaic

➡ Iconostasis

➡ Views from the *campanile*

PRACTICALITIES

➡ Map p286, C4

➡ ☏041 73 01 19

➡ Piazza Torcello

➡ adult/reduced €5/4, incl museum €8/6, incl campanile €9

➡ ⊙10.30am-6pm summer, 10am-5pm winter

➡ ⊠Torcello

⊙ SIGHTS

⊙ Isola di San Michele

Shuttling between Murano from the Fonda-mente Nuove, *vaporetti* 4.1 and 4.2 stop at Venice's **city cemetery**.

CIMITERO HISTORIC SITE

(⊙7.30am-6pm summer, to 4pm winter; ⊞Cimit-ero) FREE Until Napoleon established a city cemetery on Isola di San Michele, Venetians had been buried in parish plots across town – not the most salubrious solution, as Napoleon's inspectors realised. Today, goths, incorrigible romantics and music-lovers pause here to pay respects to Ezra Pound, Joseph Brodsky, Sergei Diaghilev and Igor Stravinsky. Architecture buffs stop by to see the Renaissance **Chiesa di San Michele in Isola**, begun by Codussi in 1469, and the ongoing **cemetery extension** by David Chipperfield Architects (scheduled for completion in 2016), including the recently completed **Courtyard of the Four Evangelists** – a sunken bunker, with a concrete colonnade and basalt-clad walls engraved with the Gospels.

⊙ Murano

Venetians have been working in crystal and glass since the 10th century, but due to the fire hazards of glass-blowing, the industry was moved to the island of Murano in the 13th century. Woe betide the glass-blower with wanderlust: trade secrets were so jealously guarded that any glass worker who left the city was guilty of treason and subject to assassination. Today, glass artisans ply their trade at workshops along Murano's **Fondamenta dei Vetrai**.

Vaporetto services 4.1 and 4.2 run here every 10 minutes throughout the day.

★**MUSEO DEL VETRO** MUSEUM

Map p285 (Glass Museum; ☑041 527 47 18; www.museovetro.visitmuve.it; Fondamenta Giustinian 8; adult/reduced €10.50/8; ⊙10am-6pm summer, to 5pm winter; ⊞Museo) Since 1861, Murano's glass-making prowess has been celebrated in Palazzo Giustinian (the seat of the Torcello bishopric from 1659 until its dissolution) and recent renovations finally do justice to the fabulous collection. On entry a video geeks out on the technical processes innovated on Murano, while upstairs eight rooms take you through a beautifully

---

◉ TOP SIGHT
A NORTHERN LAGOON BOAT TRIP

Whereas other cities sank their history in foundations, Venice cast out across the lagoon's patchwork of shifting mudflats, so seeing and understanding something of the lagoon is integral to understanding Venice. Unesco recognised this by specifically including the 550-sq-km (212-sq-mile) lagoon – the largest coastal wetland in Europe – in its designation of Venice as a World Heritage Site in 1987.

Rich in unique floral and fauna, the tidal *barene* (shoals) and salt marshes are part of the city's psyche. Between September and January over 130,000 migrating birds nest, dive and dabble in the shallows; while year-round fishermen tend their nets and traps, and city-council workers dredge canals and reinforce the shifting islands of cord-grass and saltwort so essential to the lagoon's survival.

Take a boat tour with **Terra e Acqua** (p150) and explore the tranquil **Monastero di San Francesco del Deserto** (p155), the quarantine island of Lazzaretto Nuovo and Sant'Andrea, the finest fort in the lagoon. Then return to Venice as a rosy-tinted sunset frames the city's *campaniles*.

DON'T MISS

➡ Tour of Monastero di San Francesco del Deserto

➡ Fisherman's lunch on board

➡ Migrating birds in November

➡ Forte Sant'Andrea

PRACTICALITIES

➡ ☑347 4205004

➡ www.veneziainbarca.it

➡ ⊙day trips incl lunch for 9-12 people €380-460

➡ ⊞

curated collection dating back to the 5th century AD.

From the glowing, backlit cabinets of precious Roman glassware in the Origins room, step into the **Salone Maggiore** (Grand Salon) where three enormous chandeliers appear to float beneath the frescoed ceiling that's above an exhibit showcasing the Golden Age of glassmaking between the 14th and 17th century. Beyond, colourthemed rooms diverge into glassmaking fashions – etchings, mirrors, table pieces and imitation porcelain made from opaque glass – and the vast and profitable industry of Venetian beads, which were traded worldwide for goods and slaves.

Back downstairs, rotating contemporary glass exhibits are on show in the **Spazio Coterie** just beyond the museum shop, which now stocks top quality Murano glass gifts, jewellery and art books. On Tuesday and Thursday it's possible to take an Italian (noon) or English (2.30pm) guided tour of the museum, followed by a glassworking demonstration at the **Scuola del Vetro Abate Zanetti** (Map p285; ☑041 273 77 11; www.abatezanetti.it; Calle Briati 8b; demonstration incl museum tour €15; ⛴Faro).

BASILICA DEI SS MARIA E DONATO   CHURCH
Map p285 (Campo San Donato; ⊙9am-noon & 3.30-7pm Mon-Sat, 3.30-7pm Sun; ⛴Museo) FREE Fire-breathing is the unifying theme of Murano's medieval church, with its 12th-century gilded glass **Madonna apse mosaic** made in Murano's *fornaci* (furnaces) and the bones of a dragon hanging behind the altar. According to legend, these are the bones of a beast slayed by San Donato, whose mortal remains also rest here. The other masterpiece here is underfoot: a Byzantine-style 12th-century mosaic pavement of waving geometric patterns and peacocks rendered in porphyry, serpentine and other precious stones.

☉ Burano & Mazzorbo

Once Venice's lofty Gothic architecture leaves you feeling slightly loopy, Burano brings you back to your senses with a reviving shock of colour. The 50-minute ferry ride on Line 12 from the Fondamente Nuove is packed with photographers bounding into Burano's backstreets, snapping away at pea-green stockings hung to dry between hot-pink and royal-blue houses.

A GLIMPSE INSIDE MURANO'S GLASS FURNACES

For a unique glimpse into the world of the Murano glass furnace, consider staying at Villa Ines, the Seguso family home on the Lido. As their guest, you'll have access to an exclusive tour of the prestigious **Seguso furnace**, which is normally off-limits to the public.

Alternatively, consider gathering a group of friends for a unique **furnace-lit dining experience**, where foraged Lagoon seafood is cooked on the radiantly hot stone 'door' of one of Murano's *fornace* (furnace). These exceptional evenings are arranged by contemporary-glass gallery **Venice in a Bottle** (p129), which works with designers and scientists on cutting-edge, experimental glass projects that continue to push the boundaries of Murano's glass masters. Dinners from two to 16 people are possible and, if you're interested to learn more, you'll be joined by the designers and art directors working on their latest project. To find out more, see www.fornasa experience.org.

Burano is famed for its handmade lace, which once graced the decolletage and ruffs of European aristocracy. Unfortunately the ornate styles and expensive tablewear fell out of vogue in lean post-WWII times and the industry has since suffered a terminal decline. Some women still maintain the traditions, but few production houses remain – most of the lace for sale in local shops is of the imported, machine-made variety.

If you fancy a stroll, hop across the 60m bridge to Burano's even quieter sister island, Mazzorbo. Little more than a broad grassy knoll, Mazzorbo is a great place for a picnic or a long, lazy lunch. Line 12 also stops at Mazzorbo, and Line 9 runs a shuttle between Burano and Torcello.

MUSEO DEL MERLETTO   MUSEUM
Map p286 (Lace Museum; ☑041 73 00 34; http://museomerletto.visitmuve.it; Piazza Galuppi 187; adult/reduced €5.50/4; ⊙10am-6pm Tue-Sun summer, to 5pm winter; ⛴Burano) Burano's Lace Museum tells the story of a craft that cut across social boundaries, endured for centuries and evoked the epitome of

Venetian Artistry

Glass

Venetians have been working in crystal and glass since the 10th century, though fire hazards prompted the move of the city's furnaces to Murano in the 13th century. Trade secrets were so closely guarded that any glass-worker who left the city was considered guilty of treason. By the 15th century Murano glass-makers were setting standards that couldn't be equalled anywhere in the world. They monopolised the manufacture of mirrors for centuries, and in the 17th century their skill at producing jewel-bright crystal led to a ban on the production of false gems out of glass. For a short course in Murano's masterly skill, head to the **Museo del Vetro** (p150).

Today, along Murano's Fondamenta dei Vetrai, centuries of tradition are upheld in Cesare Toffolo's winged goblets and Davide Penso's lampworked glass beads, while striking modern glass designs by Nason Moretti at ElleElle, Marina e Susanna Sent and Venini keep the tradition moving forward.

Paper

Embossing and marbling began in the 14th century as part of Venice's burgeoning publishing industry, but these bookbinding techniques and *ebru* (Turkish marbled paper) endpapers have taken on lives of their own. Artisan Rosanna Corrò of Cárte uses bookbinding techniques to create marbled, book-bound handbags and even furniture, while Cartavenezia turns hand-pulped paper into embossed friezes and free-form lamps. Gianni Basso uses 18th-century book symbols to make letter-pressed business cards with old-world flair, and

1. Glass-shop window display 2. Lace-making 3. Paper in a bookbinder's shop

you can watch a Heidelberg press in action at Veneziastampa, churning out menus and ex-libris (bookplates).

Textiles

Anything that stands still long enough in this city is liable to end up swagged, tasselled and upholstered. Venetian lace was a fashion must for centuries as Burano's **Lace Museum** (p151) attests, and Bevilacqua still weaves luxe tapestries (and donates scraps to nonprofit Banco Lotto 10 to turn into La Fenice costumes and handbags).

But the modern master of Venetian bohemian textiles is Fortuny, whose showroom on Giudecca features hand-stamped wall coverings created in strict accordance with top-secret techniques. But though the methods are secret, Fortuny's inspiration isn't: it covers the

walls of his home studio, from Persian armour to portraits of socialites who tossed aside their corsets for Fortuny's Delphi gowns – now available for modern boho goddesses at Venetia Studium.

TOP FIVE NON-TOURISTY SOUVENIRS

➡ Customised business cards at **Gianni Basso** (p114).

➡ Lilac smoking jacket with handprinted scarlet skulls from **Fiorella Gallery** (p68).

➡ Blown-glass soap-bubble necklaces from **Marina e Susanna Sent** (p82).

➡ Lux, hand-stamped velvet evening bags in gold and mulberry from **Venetia Studium** (p69).

➡ Bold, funky, cardboard-and-paper handbags from **Cárte** (p100).

LOCAL KNOWLEDGE

REGATTA REVELRY

The biggest event in the northern lagoon calendar is the 32km **Vogalonga long row** (www.vogalonga.com) from Venice to Murano and Burano and back each May. It's a fabulously festive occasion when hundreds of enthusiasts take to the waters in their wooden *batèla* (flat-bottomed boat) and motorised boats are banned from the lagoon for the day.

Plan in advance and find a grassy picnic spot on Mazzorbo. If you'd like to have a go yourself get in touch with Jane Caporal of **Row Venice** (Map p278; ☑347 7250637; www.rowvenice.org; 90min lessons 1-2 people €80, 4 people €120), who'll soon show you how to wield an oar like a *gondolieri*.

civilisation reached during the Republic's heyday. From the triple-petalled corollas on the fringes of the Madonna's mantle in Torcello's 12th-century mosaics, to Queen Margherita's spider web–fine 20th-century mittens, lace-making was both the creative expression of female sensitivity and a highly lucrative craft.

Enter the exhibition downstairs with a video detailing the early origins of lacemaking and its geographical spread from Northern France to Bohemia, Malta and Turkey. Upstairs, four rooms cover the major developments from the 16th to the 20th century. Pattern books, journals, paintings, furniture and costumery place the evolving art in its historical context, starting with ecclesiastical garments and delicate *trinette* (accessories), and branching out into naughty, fringed underwear and sumptuously embroidered bodices shot through with silver thread.

In the final room, a group of local lacemakers sit tatting and gossiping beneath pictures of the Lace School (where many of them learnt their craft), which was located here from 1872 to 1970. Don't be shy to ask questions about their work.

CHIESA DI SAN MARTINO CHURCH

Map p286 (☑041 73 00 96; Piazza Galuppi; ⊙8am-noon & 3-7pm; 🚢Burano) **FREE** This 16th-century church is worth a peek for Giambattista Tiepolo's 1725 *Crocifissione*, showing Mary gone grey with grief, and

Giovanni di Niccolo Mansueti's fanciful *Flight from Egypt* (c 1492), which looks suspiciously like Torcello. The Russian icon near the altar is the *Madonna di Kazan*, a masterpiece of enamelwork with astonishingly bright, lifelike eyes.

◉ Torcello

On the pastoral island of Torcello, sheep outnumber the 14 or so human residents. This bucolic backwater was once a Byzantine metropolis of 20,000, but rivalry with Venice and a succession of malaria epidemics systematically reduced its population. Of its original nine churches and two abbeys, all that remain are the Basilica di Santa Maria Assunta (p149) and the 11th-century **Chiesa di Santa Fosca** (Map p286; ⊙10am-4.30pm; 🚢Torcello). On leisurely walks around the island you'll spot a few relics, including a worn stone **throne** (Attila the Hun's Throne; Map p286; 🚢Torcello) Attila the Hun is said to have occupied when he passed through the area in the 5th century.

From Fondamente Nuove, Line 12 runs every 15 minutes until midnight. Line 9 connects Torcello with Burano. Follow the path along the canal, Fondamenta Borgognoni, which leads you from the ferry stop to the cathedral.

MUSEO ARCHEOLOGICO DI TORCELLO MUSEUM

Map p286 (Piazza Torcello; adult/reduced €3/1.50, incl basilica €8/6; ⊙10.30am-5pm Tue-Sun summer, 10am-5pm winter; 🚢Torcello) Across the square from the cathedral in the 13th-century **Palazzo del Consiglio** is this museum dedicated to Torcello's bygone splendours. Downstairs are early Byzantine mosaics; while upstairs you'll find Roman items unearthed at the now-vanished Altinum. The show-stopper is a lively 1st-century Greek marble bust of a baby, lips parted as though about to utter his first word.

◉ Isola di San Francesco del Deserto

Given that the Venetian lagoon is situated on one of the most important bird migration routes in Europe, it only seems right that Francis of Assisi, the saint so famous for talking to birds, should have sought shelter here after his journey to Palestine in 1220. He built a chapel and a humble cell, and after his death, Jacopo Michiel, the owner of the island, decided to give it to the Franciscans in perpetuity. In 1420 the friars were forced to desert the island (hence the name) due to rampant malaria, but in 1856 Monsignor Portogruaro brought them back and here they have remained as caretakers ever since.

Today, visits are only possible by prior arrangement with the **monastery** (☑041 528 68 63; www.sanfrancescodeldeserto.it; donations appreciated; ☺9-11am & 3-5pm Tue-Sun) FREE, and are led by a Franciscan brother. As this is a place of prayer, visitors are kindly asked to speak in hushed tones as they are led around the two cloisters and into the serene chapel where St Francis himself is said to have prayed. Best of all are the peaceful, cypress-scented **gardens** with their dreamlike views of Burano.

To get here you'll need to hire a private boat or water taxi (approx €80 to €100 return for up to four people, including the 40- to 60-minute wait time) or book a seat aboard one of **LagunaFla's** (☑339 7781132; www.lagunafla.it) shuttles from Burano, which costs €10 per person for a group of five to six people.

◉ Sant'Erasmo

Sant'Erasmo is known as the *orto di Venezia* (Venice's garden), and if you're visiting in April and early May, don't miss the **Sagra di Violetti** (Festival of Sant'Erasmo purple artichokes; www.carciofosanterasmo.it), when the island celebrates the first crop of its purple-hued artichokes. At 4.5km (2.8 miles) long, Sant'Erasmo is as long as Venice, although it's just 1km (0.6 miles) wide at its widest point. Seven hundred and fifty farmers still plough its fields, supplying not only artichokes but also asparagus, squash, tomatoes and cardoons to the Rialto market and Venice's restaurants.

Once a rural retreat for aristocrats, the island now provides a largely tourist-free refuge for Venetian families who moor their boats along its mudbanks and picnic on its narrow 'beaches'. Essential shots of coffee and pizza lunches are provided by the seasonal bar behind the beach, while bikes (€5 for two hours, €1 every hour thereafter) can be rented at the island's only accommodation, Il Lato Azzurro (p198).

Vaporetto 13 docks at Chiesa, from where it's a half-hour walk to the southern Capannone stop, and another 15 minutes east to the beach near the partly ruined **Torre Massimiliana** (☑041 244 41 42; Via dei Forti, Isola di Sant'Erasmo; ☺3-7pm Wed-Fri, 11am-7pm Sat & Sun; ☒Capannone), a 19th-century Austrian fort sometimes used for art exhibitions. In summer only, line 18 departs from the Lido and stops at Torre Massimiliana.

◉ Le Vignole

Welcome to the Venetian countryside! Together the two islands of Vignole Vecchie and Vignole Nuove have long produced the doges' wine, and their 50 inhabitants still live mainly from agriculture. Like that of nearby Sant'Erasmo, the landscape is covered in fields, groves and vineyards, and people are few and far between. *Vaporetto* 13 runs to Le Vignole from Fondamente Nuove via Murano (Faro stop).

A couple of rustic restaurants – **Trattoria alla Vignole** (☑041 528 97 07; Isola Vignole 12; meals €25-30; ☺10am-10pm Tue-Sun summer; ☒Vignole) and **Agriturismo da Zangrando** (☑041 528 40 20; Via delle Vignole 26; meals €25-35; ☺noon-2.30pm & 6.30-11pm Sat-Mon summer; ☒; ☒Vignole) – on the southwestern shore open in summer to accommodate weekending Venetians and intrepid lagoon explorers. At the southeastern tip a promontory ends in the Isola di Sant'Andrea, the location of the best-preserved fort on the lagoon: 16th-century **Forte Sant'Andrea**.

◉ Isola della Certosa

Once home to Carthusian monks (hence the island's name), La Certosa was the site of a grand monastery, its church graced with ducal tombs and rich artworks. All of that was lost, however, when the island was taken over by the military in the 19th century. Even its cloister was purchased by Prince Charles of Prussia and rebuilt in his summer castle in Berlin in 1850.

Today, thanks to EU funding and a successful public–private partnership, La Certosa has been revived as a marina complex and lush public park under the Vento di Venezia (p25) umbrella headed by former Italian sailing champion Alberto Sonino. Years of hard work have seen the rehabilitation of the historic parkland, as well as the

ARCHAEOLOGICAL SUMMER CAMPS

Every summer since 1988, amateur archaeologists, university graduates and school-children have made the journey out to the island of **Lazzaretto Nuovo** (☑041 244 40 11; www.lazzarettonuovo.com; ⊙9.45am-4.30pm Sat & Sun summer) to work on one of the most fascinating historic sites in the lagoon, the **Tezon Grande**.

The quarantine depot for the Republic between 1468 and the 1700s, the Tezon is the largest public building in the lagoon after the Corderie at the Arsenale. Around its perimeter, excavations have revealed one-room cottages where travelling merchants waited out their 40-day exile, trying to avoid the plague while city officials fumigated their cargoes. Archaeological groups have catalogued hundreds of artefacts and uncovered extensive graffiti describing harrowing voyages from Cyprus and Constantinople.

Budding Indiana Jones wannabes can enjoy an active role in the Lazzaretto's rehabilitation during the archaeological **summer camps** (€350 per week including food and lodging). Between April and October it's also possible to visit the island on Saturday and Sunday. Take *vaporetto* 13 from the Fondamente Nuove and request the stop.

creation of a contemporary marina complex incorporating a fully fledged sustainable-tourism project, with a sailing school, a yoga centre and the restored 15th-century charterhouse, providing a venue for educational programs.

To accompany it all, an 18-room hotel offers a range of sailing, kayaking and cycling packages and an alfresco restaurant-bar. It's a great place to escape the crowds on a hot summer day, and share a drink with the sailing fraternity on the patio of **Il Certosino** (☑041 520 00 35; www.ristoranteilcertosino.com; Isola di Certosa; meals €30-40; ⊙noon-2.30pm & 7-10pm Thu-Tue summer, noon-2.30pm Thu-Tue winter; ⛴Certosa).

Between 6am and 9pm *vaporetti* 4.1 and 4.2 connect Venice with Certosa, but you must request the stop. At night, take Line N or 5.1 to Sant'Elena from where you can get the hotel shuttle.

✕ EATING & DRINKING

✕ Murano

GELATERIA
AL PONTE
GELATERIA, SANDWICHES €

Map p285 (☑041 73 62 78; Fondamenta Riva Longa 1c; snacks €2-5; ⊙9am-5pm Mon-Sat; ♿; ⛴Museo) Toasted prosciutto-and-cheese *panini* and gelato give shoppers a second wind, without cutting into Murano glass-buying budgets – sandwiches run at €3 to €5 and ice creams €2.

OSTERIA AL DUOMO
OSTERIA €

Map p285 (☑041 527 43 03; www.osteriadelduomo.com; Fondamenta Maschio 20-21; meals €15-25; ♿; ⛴Museo) Originally opened by the parish priest in 1908 as a co-op grocery shop, this *osteria* is still collectively owned by 50 Muranese families. Don't be surprised then by the honest bowls of pasta and hands-down the best pizza in Venice – as you'd expect, considering the furnace they have to cook them in! In summer, sit out in the secluded walled garden.

OSTERIA LA PERLA – AI BISATEI
OSTERIA €

Map p285 (☑041 73 95 28; Campo San Bernardo 1; meals €15-20; ⊙noon-3pm Thu-Tue; ♿; ⛴Museo) Seek out this vintage *osteria* where glassblowers head for plates of *frittura mista* (mixed fried fish), seafood risotto, spaghetti *vongole* (spaghetti with clams) and *bigoli* (whole-wheat pasta) with onions and anchovies. Try to nab a seat in the front room, a throwback to the 1950s with a wood-panelled bar and photos of raucous-looking lock-ins. The alternative is a featureless 'garden room' out back. Still, no one's looking at the decor.

The only dessert is S-shaped *buranelli* biscuits, which should be shamelessly dipped in glasses of sweet *vin santo*.

★ACQUASTANCA
OSTERIA €€

Map p285 (☑041 319 51 25; www.acquastanca.it; Fondamenta Manin 48; meals €30-40; ⊙9am-8pm Tue-Thu & Sat, to 11pm Mon & Fri; ⛴Faro) Caterina and Giovanna's old bakery has been transformed into a warm, modern space with nary a garish Murano trinket in sight.

Sit down amid a symphony of marble, concrete and brushed steel, and order plump prawns in a web of filo pastry or exquisitely sweet tuna tartare and homemade gnocchi with scallops.

There's also a great **bar**, where you can grab a good coffee in the morning or an *aperitivo* with locals come evening.

✕ Burano & Mazzorbo

★CAFFÈ-BAR PALMISANO   CAFE €
Map p286 (Via San Martino 351, Burano; snacks €2-5; ⊙7am-8pm; 🛥Burano) Refuel with espresso and a sandwich at this cafe on the sunny side of the street, and return later to celebrate photo-safari triumphs over *spritz* or DOC wine with regular crowds of fishermen and university students.

TRATTORIA DA PRIMO   VENETIAN €€
Map p286 (⏰041 73 55 50; www.trattoria-pri moepaolo.it; Piazza Galuppi 285, Burano; meals €30-35; ⊙noon-4pm Tue-Sun; 🛥Burano) Hiding in plain sight is unassuming looking da Primo. Don't be fooled. On entering you'll find a large canteen-style dining room panelled like the hull of a ship and filled with locals ordering plates of raw-fish antipasti and the speciality Gò fish risotto.

★TRATTORIA AL GATTO NERO   SEAFOOD €€
Map p286 (⏰041 73 01 20; www.gattonero.com; Fondamenta della Giudecca 88, Burano; meals €30-40; ⊙noon-3.30pm & 7.30-10pm Tue-Sun; 🛥Burano) Once you've tried the homemade *tagliolini* with spider crab, whole grilled fish, and perfect house-baked Burano biscuits, the ferry ride to Burano seems a minor inconvenience – a swim back here from Venice would be worth it for that decadent langoustine risotto alone. Call ahead and plead for canalside seating.

ALLA MADDALENA   SEAFOOD €€
Map p286 (⏰041 73 01 51; www.trattoriamad dalena.com; Fondamenta di Santa Caterina 7b, Mazzorbo; meals €30-40; ⊙8am-8pm Fri-Wed; 🛥Mazzorbo) 🖉 Just a footbridge away from Burano's frantic, photo-snapping crowds are lazy seafood lunches on the island of Mazzorbo. Relax by the canal or in the garden out the back with fresh fish dishes and, during autumn hunting season, the signature pasta with wild-duck *ragù*. Bookings recommended, particularly for dinner.

✕ Torcello

★LOCANDA CIPRIANI   ITALIAN €€€
Map p286 (⏰041 73 01 50; www.locandacipriani. com; Piazza Santa Fosca 29; meals €40-55; ⊙by

---

GASTRO-RETREAT VENISSA

During the Renaissance, most of the wine served at Venice's high tables came from vineyards on the lagoon islands. It was fermented from hardy, ancient varieties like Dorona and was golden hued in colour and bone dry to taste. But as the empire expanded, the Venetians abandoned their unyielding island vineyards for more productive possessions around Soave and Valpolicella. That is, until Gianluca Bisol, a *prosecco* producer from Valdobbiadene, heard of an ancient vineyard for sale on Mazzorbo in 1999. Since then, Bisol has worked magic rehabilitating the orchard and vegetable patches, restocking the brick-lined *peschiera* (cultivated fish pond) with eels, mullet and crab, and reintroducing the rare Dorona grape from just eight vines, which survived the devastating 1966 *acqua alta* (high tide).

Once he'd reclaimed Venissa's garden and left it in the care of a team of Burano pensioners, he turned his attention to the farm buildings, which he converted into a contemporary, six room guesthouse and **osteria** (meals €50; ⊙11am-8pm). Since then a gourmet **restaurant** (Map p286; ⏰041 527 22 81; www.venissa.it; Fondamenta Santa Caterina 3, Mazzorbo; 4-/5-course tasting menu €100-120; ⊙summer, by reservation only; 🛥Mazzorbo) 🖉 has been added in the garden, staffed each year by a team of four culinary talents whose brief is to interpret afresh the garden's produce and the bounty of the Lagoon. More is still to come with the opening of an *albergo diffuso* (community hotel) in 2016 in several fishermen's cottages on Burano. It's an idyllic escape from the stony pleasures of the Rialto, where guests can indulge in days of cooking by world-renowned chefs and fishing or photography with local Burano fishermen and artists.

LIDO DI JESOLO

This strand of sand a couple of kilometres away from Jesolo is far and away Venetians' preferred beach, with fine, clean sand, warm, calm waters and beach nightclubs. The most memorable entertainment options are often spontaneous – so in July and August keep an eye out for flyers offering free admission to clubs (at €5 to €20 value) and announcements of free beach concerts, often featuring international acts.

Getting to Jesolo takes about an hour by car, and can be reached by public transport: take ATVO bus 10a (€3.80, 70 minutes) from Piazzale Roma. The problem is getting back – the last bus usually leaves at 11.20pm in summer, and taxis cost upwards of €80. If you can make it to Punta Sabbioni at the tip of the peninsula, you might be able to catch Line 12 or 14 back to Venice or the Lido. For more information, try the **Palazzo del Turismo** (☑041 37 06 01; www.jesolo.it) in Jesolo.

reservation Wed-Mon summer; ⊠Torcello) A rustic retreat run by the Cipriani family since 1934, the Locanda is Harry's Bar gone wild. Go with seasonal specialities like *bigoli* (fat wholewheat spaghetti) with rabbit, lamb with wild herbs, or plan a lazy afternoon around the €45 Torcello menu fit for a famished Hemingway. Lunches and dinners are served by the fireplace or in the garden under the rose pergola.

SHOPPING

Watch red-hot home decor emerge from the fiery *fornaci* of Murano, hidden behind the showrooms along Fondamenta Vetrai and Ramo di Mula. Showroom staff let you handle pieces if you ask first, but wield parcels and handbags with care – what you break, you buy. On sunny Burano, Via Galuppi, is lined with lace shops. Look for '*fatto a Burano*' (made in Burano) and 'Vero Artistico Murano' guarantees, since almost all of the less-expensive stock is imported.

Murano

⭐ELLEELLE   CRAFTS
Map p285 (☑041 527 48 66; www.elleellemurano. com; Fondamenta Manin 52; ⊙10.30am-1pm & 2-6pm; ⊠Colonna) Burlesque dancers inspire curvy, red-hot wineglasses, crystal icebergs become champagne flutes and lagoon waters seem to swirl inside free-form, two-tone green-and-blue vases. Nason Moretti have been making modernist magic happen in glass since the 1950s, and the third-generation glass designers are in rare form

in this showroom. Prices start at €30 for signed, hand-blown drinking glasses.

DAVIDE PENSO   CRAFTS
Map p285 (☑041 527 56 59; www.davidepenso. com; Fondamenta Rivalonga 48; ⊙10am-5.30pm Mon-Sat; ⊠Museo) Davide Penso has taken the art of bead making to dizzying heights with exhibits at the Museo Correr, Boston's Fine Arts Museum and the San Marco Museum of Japan. Made using the lampworking process, each bead is worked into striking geometric forms and individually painted in matte modern colours.

A tutor at the Abate Zanetti school, Davide also offers private lamp blowing courses in his atelier (€250 per person for two days).

VENINI   CRAFTS
Map p285 (☑041 273 72 04; www.venini.it; Fondamenta Vetrai 47; ⊙9.30am-6pm Mon-Sat; ⊠Colonna) Even if you don't have the cash to buy a Venini, pop into this gallery to see how it's done by the glass experts. Of the big houses – Seguso, Salviati, Barovier & Toso and C.A.M – Venini remains the most relevant, having embraced modernist trends since the 1930s, and its enviable range of is bolstered by collaborations with design greats such as Carlo Scarpa and Gae Aulenti.

⭐MARINA E SUSANNA
SENT STUDIO   CRAFTS
Map p285 (☑041 527 46 65; www.marinaesusanna sent.com; Fondamenta Serenella 20; ⊙10am-1pm & 2-5pm Mon-Fri; ⊠Colonna) This minimalist space dedicated to the work of the pioneering Sent sisters is as sleek as their jewellery: exposed-concrete walls, a double-height ceiling and huge picture windows flood the room with light, setting their signature bubble necklaces ablaze. The collection

is displayed in colour groups and neatly stashed in drawers – don't be too shy to ask for assistance; there's a lot to see.

Another shop, with a more highly curated selection, is in Dorsoduro (p82).

CAMPAGNOL & SALVADORE CRAFTS
Map p285 (☑041 73 67 72; Fondamenta Vetrai 128a; ☾10.30am-6pm Mon-Sat; ☀Colonna) The Japanese-Murano couple behind Campagnol & Salvadore specialise in light-hearted creations: their aqua and sunshine-yellow bead necklaces look like strands of tiny beach balls. Psychedelic, Tim Burton–esque colour schemes make these baubles runway-ready, and aspiring designers are encouraged to create their own looks from individual blown-glass beads (€3 to €15 per bead).

TOFFOLO GALLERY CRAFTS
Map p285 (☑041 73 64 60; www.toffolo.com; Fondamenta Vetrai 37; ☾10am-6pm; ☀Colonna) Classic gold-leafed winged goblets and mind-boggling miniatures are the trademarks of this Murano glass-blower, but you'll also find some dramatic departures: chiselled cobalt-blue vases, glossy black candlesticks that look like Dubai minarets, and extraordinary, anatomically accurate beetles.

🔒 Burano

EMILIA CRAFTS
Map p286 (☑041 73 52 99; www.emiliaburano.it; Piazza Galuppi 205; ☀Burano) Doyenne Emilia di Ammendola is a third-generation lace-maker and has passed on her skills to her son and daughter. You'll often find her son, Lorenzo, at the drawing board designing elaborate floral schemes, which are then brought to life by a team of local lacemakers. Prices for off-the-shelf tablewear start at €60 and rise rapidly into the hundreds for tablecloths, lace-fringed towels, cut-work and embroidered linens hand-loomed in Venice.

🏃 SPORTS & ACTIVITIES

★VENICE KAYAK KAYAKING
(☑346 4771327; www.venicekayak.com; Isola di Certosa; half-/full-day tours for 2-6 people €90/120) Of all Venice's watery pursuits, kayaking with René Seindal is probably the best, most affordable fun you can have without a license or the pirouetting skill of a gondolier. His well-planned half- or full-day tours take you into the warren of Venice's canals alongside police boats, fire boats and floating funeral hearses, or out into the broad garden of the lagoon to Burano, Torcello and Sant'Erasmo. Why not do both and you'll come to appreciate how the Lagoon is as much a part of the city's history as the basilica.

Private tours and multi-day lagoon safaris are also possible. All tours begin and end at Vento di Venezia. All paddling equipment is provided.

A row of houses in Burano (p151)

n

their summers

co cycles from its

classical re-
villas.

ne of the Veneto's

ory lives on its
e gardens.

, while Soave

Riviera Brenta

Explore

For centuries, summer officially started on 13 June as a flotilla of fashionable Venetians headed for their summer residences along the banks of the Brenta. There were once over 3000 villas in the Venetian hinterland, built between the 15th and the 18th century; now fewer than 80 survive and of those four are open as museums, including Palladio's exquisite Villa Foscari and the grand Villa Pisani Nazionale. They can be seen in a day, especially on a river cruise aboard the traditional *burchiello* (barge). If on your own, note that sites are scattered, so cars are a better option than trains. Or better still, hop on a bike, this is very flat country that begs to be cycled. If you decide to linger, spend the night in nearby Padua, where the cruise ends.

The Best...

➡**Sight** Villa Foscari
➡**Place to Eat** Osteria Da Conte (p163)
➡**Place to Drink** I Molini del Dolo (p163)

Top Tip

The Riviera Brenta is best seen from the decks of flat-bottomed riverboats – the same way Venetians did, at least until Napoleon's troops shut down the centuries-long party in 1797.

Getting There & Away

➡**Boat** Organised boat tours leave from both Venice and Padua.

➡**Train** Regional trains between Venice and Padua stop at Dolo (€3.30, 25 minutes, one to three per hour) en route to Padua.

➡**Bus** ACTV's Venezia–Padova Extraurbane bus 53 leaves from Venice's Piazzale Roma about every half-hour, stopping at key Brenta villages en route to Padua.

➡**Car** Take SS11 from Mestre-Venezia towards Padova (Padua), and take the Autostrada A4 towards Dolo/Padova.

Need to Know

➡**Area Code** ☑041
➡**Location** 15km to 30km west of Venice

⊙ SIGHTS

The Brenta River had long acted as a commercial waterway between inland farms and Venice, transporting meat, fruit, vegetables, flour and even fresh water to the city, and exporting its spices, cloth, soap, glass and fish inland. But the river's regular and ferocious torrents, coupled with a pre-1345 decree forbidding Venetians to own mainland property, meant the area remained largely undeveloped until the 15th century.

That all changed in 1407, when Padua came under Venetian control and the Brenta's flow was finally tamed by hydraulic intervention. Almost immediately life on the river began to change as aristocratic families set up fabulous country estates, enhancing their incomes with farming and indulging in wild parties. Famous artists and architects were brought in to design and decorate their homes, and soon the river was traffic-logged with nobles who spent the days cruising between villas, engaging in what became known as *villeggiatura*.

VILLA FOSCARI   HISTORIC BUILDING
(☑041 520 39 66; www.lamalcontenta.com; Via dei Turisti 9, Malcontenta; admission €10; ⊗9am-noon Tue & Sat May-Oct) The most romantic Brenta villa, the Palladio-designed 1555–60 Villa Foscari got its nickname La Malcontenta from a grand dame of the Foscari clan who was reputedly exiled here for cheating on her husband – though these bright, highly sociable salons hardly constitute a punishment. The villa was abandoned for years, but Giovanni Zelotti's frescoes have now been restored to daydream-inducing splendour.

ⓘ BRENTA BY BIKE

Speed past tour boats along 150km of cycling routes along the Brenta Riviera. **Veloce** (☑346 8471141; www. rentalbikeitaly.com; Via Gramsci 85, Mira; touring/mountain/racing bicycle per day €20/25/35; ⊗8am-8pm) offers a handy pick-up and drop-off service at railway stations and hotels in many Veneto towns, including Padua, Venice and Mira. City and mountain bikes are available, along with GPS units pre-loaded with multilingual Brenta itineraries (€10).

RIVER CRUISES

When Venetians set out from Piazza San Marco for the Brenta, many of them would step aboard the commodious barge *Il Burchiello*, which was drawn along the tow-path by a team of horses. Goethe arrived on the lagoon in this fashion in 1786, and today a small fleet of modern *burchielli* ply the river between Venice and Padua.

There's no doubt that seeing the Brenta from the perspective of a boat (rather than through the snarl of Venetian and Padovan suburbs) is the best way to experience the river and its villas, most of which were designed to show their best face to the water. As you pass through the five locks and nine swing bridges, you'll appreciate the 15th-century hydraulic locks system, which diverted the main floodwaters of the river to Chioggia, putting a stop to the accumulation of silt in the lagoon.

Il Burchiello (p26) is a modern luxury barge offering full-day cruises between Venice and Padua, stopping at Foscari, Widmann (or Barchessa Valmarana), and Pisani villas. From Venice, cruises depart from Pontile della Pietà pier on Riva degli Schiavoni (Tuesday, Thursday and Saturday). From Padua, cruises depart from Pontile del Portello pier (Wednesday, Friday and Sunday). Half-day tours, which stop at one or two villas and run from Venice or Padua to/from Oriago, are also available. See the website for details.

VILLA WIDMANN REZZONICO FOSCARI   HISTORIC BUILDING

(☑041 547 00 12; www.lamalcontenta.com; Via Nazionale 420, Mira; admission €10; ⊘9am-noon Tue & Sat May-Oct) To appreciate both gardening and Venetian-style social engineering, stop just west of Oriago at Villa Widmann Rezzonico Foscari. Originally owned by Persian-Venetian nobility, the 18th-century villa captures the Brenta's last days of rococo decadence, with Murano sea-monster chandeliers and a frescoed grand ballroom with upper viewing gallery. Head to the gallery to reach the upstairs ladies' gambling parlour where, according to local lore, villas were once gambled away in high-stakes games.

VILLA BARCHESSA VALMARANA   HISTORIC BUILDING

(☑041 426 63 87; www.villavalmarana.net; Via Valmarana 11, Mira; adult/reduced €6/5; ⊘10am-6pm Tue-Sun summer, by appointment winter) Debuting on the riviera in the 17th century, Villa Barchessa Valmarana was commissioned by Vicenza's aristocratic Valmarana family. You'll find them enjoying *la dolce vita* (the sweet life) in the villa's fanciful frescoes, painstakingly restored in 1964. These days, the elegant building is mainly used as a function centre.

VILLA PISANI NAZIONALE   HISTORIC BUILDING

(☑049 50 20 74; www.villapisani.beniculturali. it; Via Doge Pisani 7, 8Stra; adult/reduced €7.50/3.75, park only €4.50/2.25; ⊘9am-7pm Tue-Sun Apr-Sep, to 5pm Oct, to 4pm Nov-Mar) To keep hard-partying Venetian nobles in line, Doge Alvise Pisani provided a Versailles-like reminder of who was in charge. The 1774, 114-room Villa Pisani Nazionale is surrounded by huge gardens, a labyrinthine hedge-maze and pools to reflect the doge's glory. Here you'll find the bathroom with a tiny wooden throne used by Napoleon; the sagging bed where new king Vittorio Emanuele II slept; and, ironically, the reception hall where Mussolini and Hitler met in 1934 under Tiepolo's ceiling depicting the *Genius of Peace*.

On our last visit, the poorly funded property was badly lit, so consider visiting during full daylight hours to avoid staring into darkened rooms. Temporary exhibitions are also held at the villa throughout the year, generally between March and October.

VILLA FOSCARINI ROSSI   HISTORIC BUILDING

(☑049 980 10 91; www.villafoscarini.it; Via Pisani 1/2, Stra; adult/reduced €7/5; ⊘9am-1pm & 2-6pm Mon-Fri, 2.30-6pm Sat & Sun Apr-Oct, 9am-1pm Mon-Fri Nov-Mar) Well-heeled Venetians wouldn't have dreamt of decamping to the Brenta without their favourite cobblers, sparking a local tradition of shoemaking. Today, 538 companies produce about 19 million pairs of shoes annually. Their lasting contribution is commemorated with a **Shoemakers' Museum** at this 18th-century villa, its collection including 18th-century slippers and kicks created for trendsetter Marlene Dietrich. Admission includes access to the villa's 17th-century *foresteria* (guesthouse), which wows with allegorical frescoes by Pietro Liberi and trompe-l'œil effects by Domenico de Bruni.

⚔ EATING & DRINKING

OSTERIA DA CONTE MODERN VENETIAN €€

(☑049 47 95 71; www.osteriadaconte.it; Via Caltana 133, Mira; meals €25-35; ⏰noon-2.30pm & 8-10.30pm Tue-Sat, noon-2.30pm Sun) An unlikely bastion of culinary sophistication lodged practically underneath an overpass, Da Conte has one of the most interesting wine lists in the region, plus creative takes on regional cuisine, from shrimps with black sesame and pumpkin purée to gnocchi in veal-cheek *ragù*. If it's on the menu, end your meal with the faultless *zabaglione* (egg and Marsala custard).

I MOLINI DEL DOLO WINE BAR

(www.molinidolo.com; Via Garibaldi 3, Dolo; ⏰10am-2am Tue-Sun) Adorned with hulking wooden machinery, this atmospheric, canal-side wine bar occupies a restored 16th-century mill. Swill a coffee, or settle in with a regional *vino* and an interesting selection of cheeses and cured meats, from local *porchetta* (pork) to rustic *ventricina* (salami) from Italy's south. If the weather's warm, sit on the alfresco patio.

Padua (Padova)

Explore

Though under an hour from Venice, Padua (population 209,700) seems a world away with its medieval marketplaces, Fascist-era facades and hip student population. As a medieval city-state and home to Italy's second-oldest university, Padua challenged both Venice and Verona for regional hegemony. A series of extraordinary fresco cycles recalls this golden age – including Giotto's remarkable Cappella degli Scrovegni, Menabuoi's heavenly gathering in the Duomo's bapistry and Titian's *St Anthony* in the Scoletta del Santo. With convenient train connections and a dense historic centre, Padua is an easy day trip from Venice, although its many and varied sites could fill a number of days. If you stay overnight, be sure to

watch the *piazze* come alive as the highly social Padovans gather for their evening *aperitivo*.

The Best...
➡**Sight** Cappella degli Scrovegni (p164)
➡**Place to Eat** Belle Parti (p170)
➡**Place to Drink** Enoteca Il Tira Bouchon (p170)

Top Tip
Reservations are required to see Giotto's extraordinary Cappella degli Scrovegni – sometimes as many as a few weeks ahead for summer weekends and during holidays.

Getting There & Away
➡**Car** The A4 (Turin–Milan–Venice–Trieste) passes to the north of town, while the A13 to Bologna starts south of town.
➡**Bus** Services from Venice's Piazzale Roma (€4.60, 45 minutes, one to two hourly) on **Busitalia – SITA Nord** (☑049 820 68 34; www.fsbusitalia.it) arrive at Padova Autostazione, outside the train station. Check online for buses to Colli Euganei towns.
➡**Train** Rail is the easiest way to reach Padua from Venice (€4 to €15, 25 to 50 minutes, one to nine per hour).

Need to Know
➡**Area Code** ☑049
➡**Location** 37km west of Venice
➡**Train Station** (☑049 201 00 80; Piazza di Stazione; ⏰9am-7pm Mon-Sat, 10am-4pm Sun)
Galleria Pedrocchi (☑049 201 00 80; www.turismopadova.it; Vicolo Pedrocchi; ⏰9am-7pm Mon-Sat)

ⓘ MAKING THE MOST OF YOUR EURO
A **PadovaCard** (per 48/72hr €16/21) gives one adult and one child under 14 free use of city public transport and access to almost all of Padua's major attractions, including the Cappella degli Scrovegni (plus €1 booking fee). PadovaCards are available at Padua tourist offices, Musei Civici agli Eremitani (Cappella degli Scrovegni) and at a number of hotels. See www.padovacard.it for details.

Padua

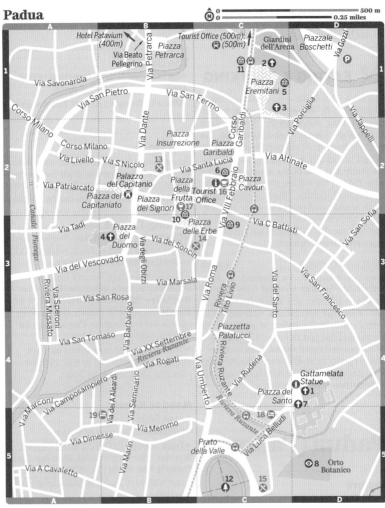

◉ SIGHTS

★ CAPPELLA DEGLI SCROVEGNI   CHURCH
(Scrovegni Chapel; ☑049 201 00 20; www.cappel
ladegliscrovegni.it; Piazza Eremitani 8; adult/
reduced €13/6, night ticket €8/6; ⊙9am-7pm,
also 7-10pm various periods through year) Padua's version of the Sistine Chapel, the Cappella degli Scrovegni houses one of Italy's
great Renaissance masterpieces – a striking
cycle of Giotto frescoes. Dante, da Vinci and
Vasari all honour Giotto as the artist who
ended the Dark Ages with these 1303–05
paintings, whose humanistic depiction of
biblical figures was especially well suited to

the chapel Enrico Scrovegni commissioned
in memory of his father, who as a money-
lender was denied a Christian burial.

Giotto's moving, modern approach
helped change how people saw themselves:
no longer as lowly vassals, but as vessels for
the divine, however flawed. And where before medieval churchgoers had been accustomed to blank stares from saints perched
on high thrones, Giotto introduced biblical figures as characters in recognisable
settings. Onlookers gossip as middle-aged
Anne tenderly kisses Joachim, and Jesus
stares down Judas as the traitor puckers up
for the fateful kiss. A 10-minute introduc-

Padua

tory video provides some helpful insights before you enter the church itself.

Pick up prebooked tickets at the Musei Civici agli Eremitani, where you access the chapel. Chapel visits last 15 to 20 minutes (depending on the time of year), plus another 20 minutes for the video. The 'double-turn' night-session ticket (€12) allows a 40-minute stay in the chapel and must be prebooked by phone.

MUSEI CIVICI AGLI EREMITANI   MUSEUM
(☑049 820 45 51; Piazza Eremitani 8; adult/reduced €10/8; ⊙9am-7pm Tue-Sun) The ground floor of this monastery houses artefacts dating from Padua's Roman and pre-Roman past. Upstairs, a rambling but interesting collection boasts a few notable 14th- to 18th-century works by Bellini, Giorgione, Tintoretto and Veronese. Among the show-stoppers is a crucifix by Giotto, showing a heartbroken Mary wringing her hands as Jesus' blood drips into the empty eye sockets of a human skull.

PALAZZO ZUCKERMANN   GALLERY
(☑049 820 56 64; Corso di Garibaldi 33; adult/reduced €10/8; ⊙10am-7pm Tue-Sun) The ground and 1st floors of the early-20th-century Palazzo Zuckermann are home to the **Museo d'Arti Applicate e Decorative**, whose eclectic assortment of decorative and applied arts spans several centuries of flatware, furniture, fashion and jewellery. On the 2nd floor is the **Museo Bottacin**, a treasury of finely worked historic coins and medals, kept company by a modest collection of 19th-century paintings and sculpture.

CHIESA DEGLI EREMITANI   CHURCH
(☑049 875 64 10; Piazza Eremitani; ⊙7.30am-12.30pm & 3.30-7pm Mon-Fri, 9am-12.30pm & 4-7pm Sat & Sun) When a 1944 bombing raid demolished the extraordinary 1448–57 frescoes by Andrea Mantegna in the Capella Overtari in the Chiesa degli Eremitani, the loss to art history was incalculable. After half a century of painstaking reconstruction, the shattered, humidity-damaged stories of Saints James and Christopher have been puzzled together, revealing action-packed compositions and extreme perspectives that make Mantegna's saints look like superheroes.

PALAZZO DEL BÒ   HISTORIC BUILDING
(☑049 827 30 47; www.unipd.it/en/guidedtours; Via VIII Febbraio; adult/reduced €5/2; ⊙see website for tour times) This Renaissance *palazzo* is the seat of Padua's history-making university. Founded by renegade scholars from Bologna seeking greater intellectual freedom, the university has employed some of Italy's greatest and most controversial thinkers, including Copernicus, Galileo, Casanova and the world's first female doctor of philosophy, Eleonora Lucrezia Cornaro Piscopia (her statue graces the stairs). The 45-minute guided tours include the world's first **anatomy theatre**.

PALAZZO DELLA RAGIONE   HISTORIC BUILDING
(☑049 820 50 06; Piazza delle Erbe; adult/reduced €4/2; ⊙9am-7pm Tue-Sun, to 6pm Nov-Jan) Ancient Padua can be glimpsed in elegant twin squares separated by the triple-decker Gothic Palazzo della Ragione, the city's tribunal dating from 1218. Inside Il Salone (the Great Hall), frescoes by Giusto de' Menabuoi and Nicolò Miretto depict the astrological theories of Padovan professor Pietro d'Abano, with images representing the months, seasons,

PIERO M BIANCHI / GETTY IMAGES ©

Prato della Valle

saints, animals and noteworthy Paduans (not necessarily in that order).

The enormous 15th-century wooden horse at the western end of the hall was modelled on Donatello's majestic bronze *Gattamelata*, which still stands in Piazza del Santo. At the other end of the hall is a modern version of Foucault's *Pendulum*.

DUOMO — CATHEDRAL

(☑049 65 69 14; Piazza del Duomo; baptistry €3; ⊙7.30am-noon & 4-7.30pm Mon-Sat, 8am-1pm & 4-8.45pm Sun & holidays, baptistry 10am-6pm) Built from a much-altered design of Michelangelo's, the whitewashed symmetry of Padua's cathedral is a far cry from its rival in Piazza San Marco. Pop in quickly for Giuliano Vangi's contemporary chancel crucifix and sculptures before taking in the adjoining 13th-century **baptistry**, a Romanesque gem frescoed with luminous biblical scenes by Giusto de' Menabuoi. Hundreds of male and female saints congregate in the cupola, posed as though for a school graduation photo, exchanging glances and stealing looks at the Madonna.

BASILICA DI SANT'ANTONIO — CHURCH

(Il Santo; ☑049 822 56 52; www.basilicadelsanto. org; Piazza del Santo; ⊙6.20am-7.45pm Apr-Oct, to 6.45pm Nov-Mar) **FREE** Il Santo is the soul of Padua, a key pilgrimage site and the buri-al place of patron saint St Anthony of Padua (1193–1231). Begun in 1232, its polyglot style incorporates rising eastern domes atop a Gothic brick structure crammed with Renaissance treasures. Behind the high altar, nine radiating chapels punctuate a broad ambulatory homing in on the **Cappella del Tesoro** (Treasury Chapel), where the relics of St Anthony reside.

You'll also notice dozens of people clustering along the left transept waiting their turn to enter the **Cappella del Santo**, where Anthony's tomb is covered with requests and thanks for the saint's intercession in curing illness and recovering lost objects. The chapel itself is a light-filled Renaissance confection lined with nine panels vividly depicting the story of Anthony's life in extraordinary relief sculptures. The panels are attributed to the Padua-born Lombardo brothers and were completed around 1510.

Other notable works include the lifelike 1360s crucifix by Veronese master Altichiero da Zevio in the frescoed **Cappella di San Giacomo**; the wonderful 1528 sacristy fresco of St Anthony preaching to spellbound fish by a follower of Girolamo Tessari; and high altar reliefs (1444–50) by Florentine Renaissance master Donatello (ask guards for access). Through the south door of the basilica you reach the attached monastery with its five cloisters. The oldest (13th century) is the **Chiostro della Magnolia**, so called because of the magnificent tree in its centre.

ORATORIO DI SAN GIORGIO & SCOLETTA DEL SANTO
CHURCH

(☑049 822 56 52; Piazza del Santo; adult/reduced €5/4; ☺9am-12.30pm & 2.30-7pm Apr-Sep, to 5pm Oct-Mar) Anywhere else the fresco cycle of the Oratorio di San Giorgio and the paintings in the Scoletta del Santo would be considered highlights, but in Padua they must contend with Giotto's Scrovegni brilliance. This means you'll have Altichiero da Zevio and Jacopo Avanzi's jewel-like, 14th-century frescoes of St George, St Lucy and St Catherine all to yourself, while upstairs in the *scoletta* (confraternity house), Titian paintings are seldom viewed in such tranquillity.

ORTO BOTANICO
GARDENS

(☑049 201 02 22; www.ortobotanicopd.it; Via dell'Orto Botanico 15; adult/reduced €10/8; ☺9am-7pm daily Apr & May, 9am-7pm Tue-Sun Jun-Sep, to 6pm Tue-Sun Oct, to 5pm Tue-Sun Nov-Mar; 🚇♿) Planted in 1545 by Padua University's medical faculty to study the medicinal properties of rare plants, Padua's World Heritage–listed Orto Botanico served as a clandestine Resistance meeting headquarters in WWII. The oldest tree is nicknamed 'Goethe's palm'; planted in 1585, it was mentioned by the great German writer in his *Voyage in Italy*. A much more recent addition is the high-tech **Garden of Biodiversity**, five interconnected greenhouses that recreate different climate zones and explore botanical and environmental themes via multimedia displays.

PRATO DELLA VALLE
PARK

At the southern edge of the historical centre this odd, elliptical garden was long used for public markets. Today it's a popular spot for locals wanting to soak up some summer rays. Framing the space is a slim canal lined by 78 statues of sundry great and good of Paduan history, plus 10 empty pedestals. Ten Venetian dogi once once occupied them, but Napoleon had them removed after he took Venice in 1797.

✕ EATING

ZAIRO
ITALIAN €

(☑049 66 38 03; http://zairo.net; Prato della Valle 51; pizzas €4-9.40, meals €25; ☺noon-2pm & 7pm-midnight Tue-Sun) The fresco above the kitchen door at this sweeping, chintzy restaurant-pizzeria dates back to 1673. But you're here for Zairo's cult hit *gnocchi verdi con gorgonzola* (spinach and potato gnocchi drizzled in a decadent gorgonzola sauce), or one of its decent, spot-hitting pizzas.

DAY TRIPS FROM VENICE PADUA (PADOVA)

SLEEPING IN PADUA

The tourist office publishes accommodation brochures and lists dozens of B&Bs, apartments and hotels online.

Ostello Città di Padova (☑049 875 22 19; www.ostellopadova.it; Via dei Aleardi 30; dm €19-23, d €46, without bathroom €40; ☺reception 7.15-9.30am & 3.30-11.30pm; 🚇) A central hostel with decent four- and six-bed dorm rooms on a quiet side street. Sheets and wi-fi are free. Breakfast is served between 7.30am and 8.30am, though there is no open kitchen. There's an 11.30pm curfew, except when there are special events, and guests must check out by 9.30am. Take bus 12 or 18, or the tram from the train station.

Belludi37 (☑049 66 56 33; www.belludi37.it; Via Luca Belludi 37; s €80, d €140-180; 🅿🚇) Graced with Flos bedside lamps and replica Danish chairs, the neutrally toned rooms at Belludi37 feature high ceilings, queen-sized beds and free minibar. Six newly opened rooms also deliver svelte bathrooms. Extra perks include a central location and helpful staff always on hand with suggestions for biking itineraries and walking tours.

Hotel Patavium (☑049 72 36 98; www.hotelpatavium.it; Via B Pellegrino 106; s €60-120, d €75-140; 🅿🚇) Smart, carpeted rooms with wide beds, flat-screen TVs and modern bathrooms define Patavium, a quick walk northwest of the city centre. Suites come with jacuzzis, while the breakfast room is a middle-class affair of candlesticks, chandeliers and corner lounge with communal TV.

Magnificent Palladio

When it comes to coffee-table architecture, no one beats Andrea Palladio. As you flip past photos of his villas, your own problematic living space begins to dissolve, and you find yourself strolling through more harmonious country. Nature is governed by pleasing symmetries. Roman rigour is soothed by rustic charms. He managed to synthesise the classical past without doggedly copying it, creating buildings that were at once inviting, useful and incomparably elegant. From London to St Petersburg, his work – cleverly disseminated by his own 'Quattro Libri', a how-to guide for other architects – shaped the way Europe thought about architecture.

And yet when Palladio turned 30 in 1538, he was little more than a glorified stonecutter in Vicenza. His big break came when nobleman and amateur architect Giangiorgio Trissino recognised his potential and noticed his inclination towards mathematics. He introduced Palladio to the work of Roman architectural theorist Vitruvius, and sent him to Rome (1545–47) to sketch both crumbling antiquities and new works such as Michelangelo's dome for St Peter's.

Something mysterious happened on those trips, because when Palladio returned to Vicenza he was forging a new way of thinking about architecture – one that focused on the relationship between ratios to create spatial harmony. So a room in which the shorter wall was one-half (1:2), two-thirds (2:3) or three-quarters (3:4) the length of the longer would inevitably *feel* more satisfying because it was rationally harmonious. Like Pallas Athena, the goddess of wisdom, from whom he took his name,

1. Teatro Olimpico (p173), Vicenza 2. Basilica Palladiana (p171), Vicenza

Palladio's ideas seemed to spring fully formed from his head.

This search for perfection was never at odds with practicality. In his villas, he squeezed stables beneath elegant drawing rooms. Lacking funds to line San Giorgio Maggiore with marble, he came up with a superior solution: humble stucco walls that fill the church with an ethereal softness. Constraint provided the path to innovation.

A Palladian villa never masters its landscape like, say, Versailles. Palladio makes his mark tactfully, as if he has merely gathered the natural forces of the land and translated them into an ideal, and distinctly human, response. His Rotonda, for example, crowns a rise in the terrain, and looks out on it from four identical facades. Nothing like it had been built before. Yet when you see it *in situ*, it seems to be the inevitable outcome of the site itself.

PALLADIAN HIGHLIGHTS

➡ **Basilica Palladiana** Restored to its former glory after a six-year, €20-million refurbishment.

➡ **La Rotonda** (p173) Palladio's most inspired design, copied the world over.

➡ **Villa di Masèr** (p176) Butter-yellow villa set against a green hillside; Palladio's prettiest composition.

➡ **Villa Foscari** (p161) River-facing facade with soaring Ionic columns that draw the eye and spirits upwards.

➡ **Palladio Museum** (Map p194; ☑0444 32 30 14; www.palladiomuseum.org; Contrà Porti 11, Vicenza; adult/reduced €6/4; ⊙10am-6pm Tue-Sun) Created by Howard Burns, the world authority on Palladio.

➡ **Teatro Olimpico** (p173) Palladio's visionary elliptical theatre.

TO MARKET, TO MARKET

One of the most enjoyable activities in Padua is browsing the markets in **Piazza delle Erbe** and **Piazza della Frutta**, which operate very much as they've done since the Middle Ages. Dividing them is the Gothic **Palazzo della Ragione** (p165), whose arcades – known locally as **Sotto il Salone** (www.sottoilsalone.it) – rumble with specialist butchers, cheesemakers, fishmongers, *salumerie* (delicatessens) and fresh pasta producers. The markets are open all day, every day except Sunday, although the best time to visit is before midday.

OSTERIA DEI FABBRI   OSTERIA €€

(☑049 65 03 36; Via dei Fabbri 13; meals €30; ☺noon-2.30pm & 7-10.30pm Mon-Sat, noon-3pm Sun) Communal tables, wine-filled tumblers and a single-sheet menu packed with hearty dishes keep things real at dei Fabbri. Slurp on superlative *zuppe* (soups) like sweet red-onion soup, or tuck into comforting meat dishes such as oven-roasted pork shank with Marsala, sultanas and polenta.

★BELLE PARTI   ITALIAN €€€

(☑049 875 18 22; www.ristorantebelleparti.it; Via Belle Parti 11; meals €50; ☺12.30-2.30pm & 7.30-10.30pm Mon-Sat) Prime seasonal produce, impeccable wines and near-faultless service meld into one unforgettable whole at this stellar fine-dining restaurant, resplendent with 18th-century antiques and 19th-century oil paintings. Seafood is the forte; standout dishes include an arresting *gran piatto di crudità di mare* (raw seafood platter). Dress to impress and book ahead.

🍷 DRINKING

Sundown isn't official until you've had your *spritz* in Piazza delle Erbe or Piazza dei Signori. Also note that Padua is the region's unofficial capital of gay and lesbian life.

CAFFÈ PEDROCCHI   CAFE

(☑049 878 12 31; www.caffepedrocchi.it; Via VIII Febbraio 15; ☺8.45am-midnight Apr-Oct, to 11pm Nov-Mar) Divided into three rooms – red, white and green – the neoclassical Pedrocchi has long been a seat of intrigue and revolution, as well as a favourite of Stendhal. Soak up its esteemed history over coffee or head in for a sprightly *spritz* and decent *aperitivo* snacks.

Decorated in styles ranging from ancient Egyptian to Imperial, the building's 1st floor is home to the **Museo del Risorgimento e dell'Età Contemporanea** (☑049 878 12 31; Galleria Pedrocchi 11; adult/child

€4/2.50; ☺9.30am-12.30pm & 3.30-6pm Tue-Sun), which recounts local and national history from the fall of Venice in 1797 until the republican constitution of 1848.

ENOTECA IL TIRA BOUCHON   WINE BAR

(☑049 875 21 38; www.enotecapadova.it; Sotto il Salone 23/24; ☺10am-2.30pm & 5-9pm Mon-Sat) With a guiding French hand behind the bar you can be sure of an excellent *prosecco*, Franciacorta or sauvignon at this traditional wine bar beneath Palazzo Ragione's arcades. Locals crowd in for *spunci* (bread-based snacks), *panini* and a rotating selection of 12 wines by the glass. You'll find about 300 wines on the shelves, including drops from emerging winemakers.

Vicenza

Explore

When Palladio escaped an oppressive employer in his native Padua in the 1520s, few could have guessed that the humble stonecutter would transform not only Vicenza (population 113,700) but also the history of European architecture. Today, Vicenza's historic centre, thick with Palladio's work, has been recognised as a Unesco World Heritage Site. Beyond the elegant balustrades and porticoes is an upbeat mix of museums, bars and eateries that guarantee an easy, satisfying side trip.

The Best...

➡**Sight** La Rotonda (p173)

➡**Place to Eat** Sòtobotega (p173)

➡**Place to Drink** Bar Borsa (p174)

Top Tip

Palladio's Teatro Olimpico (p173) was built for live performances, and that is still the best way to absorb the complex harmonies of this extraordinary space.

Getting There & Away

➡ **Train** Trains are the easiest way to reach Vicenza from Venice (€6 to €16, 45 to 80 minutes, one to five per hour).

➡ **Car** Vicenza lies just off the A4 connecting Milan with Venice, while the SR11 connects Vicenza with Verona and Padua. Several larger car parks skirt the historic centre, including the underground Park Verdi just north of the train station (enter from Viale dell'Ippodromo).

Need to Know

➡ **Area Code** 🖉0444
➡ **Location** 62km west of Venice
➡ **Tourist Office** (🖉0444 32 08 54; www. vicenzae.org; Piazza Matteotti 12; ☺9am-1.30pm & 2-5.30pm)

◉ SIGHTS

The heart of Vicenza is **Piazza dei Signori**, where Palladio lightens the mood of government buildings with his trademark play of light and shadow. Dazzling white Piovene stone arches frame shady double arcades in the Basilica Palladiana, while across the piazza, white stone and stucco grace the exposed red-brick colonnade of the 1571-designed Loggia del Capitaniato. Palladio's most iconic building, La Rotonda, lies 2.2 km southeast of Piazza dei Signori and the Basilica Palladiana.

BASILICA PALLADIANA   GALLERY

(🖉0444 22 21 22; www.museicivicivicenza.it; Piazza dei Signori; temporary exhibitions €10-13; ☺hours vary) Now a venue for world-class temporary exhibitions, the Palladian Basilica is capped with an enormous copper dome reminiscent of the hull of an upturned ship. The building, modelled on a Roman basilica, once housed the law courts and Council of Four Hundred. Palladio was lucky to secure the commission in 1549 (it took his

---

WORTH A DETOUR

COLLI EUGANEI (EUGANEAN HILLS)

Southwest of Padua, the **Euganean Hills** (www.parcocollieuganei.com) feel a world away from the urban sophistication of Venice and the surrounding plains. To help you explore the walled hilltop towns, misty vineyards and bubbling hot springs, click onto www.turismopadova.it or grab information at the tourist offices in Padova. Trains serve all towns except Arqua Petrarca.

Just south of Padua lie the natural-hot-spring resorts of **Abano Terme** and **Montegrotto Terme**. They have been active since Roman times, when the Patavini built their villas on Mt Montirone. The towns are uninspired, but the waters do cure aches and pains. Nearby, in **Galzignano Terme**, **Villa Barbarigo Pizzoni Ardemani** (🖉340 0825844; www.valsanzibiogiardino.it; adult/reduced €10/6; ☺10am-1pm & 2pm-sunset summer) is the location of one of the finest historical gardens in Europe, shot through with streams, fishponds and Bernini fountains.

In the medieval village of **Arquà Petrarca**, look for the elegant little **house** (🖉0429 71 82 94; www.arquapetrarca.com; Via Valleselle 4; adult/reduced €4/2; ☺9am-12.30pm & 3-7pm Tue-Sun Mar-Oct, 9am-12.30pm & 2.30-5.30pm Tue-Sun Nov-Feb) where great Italian poet Petrarch spent his final years in the 1370s.

At the southern reaches of the Euganei, you'll find **Monselice**, with its remarkable **medieval castle** (🖉0429 7 29 31; www.castellodimonselice.it; Via del Santuario 11, Monselice; adult/reduced €6/5; ☺1hr guided tours 9am, 10am, 11am, 3pm & 4pm Tue-Sun Apr-Nov); **Montagnana**, with its magnificent 2km defensive perimeter; and **Este**, with its rich architectural heritage and important **archaeological museum** (🖉0429 20 85; www.atestino.beniculturali.it; Via Guido Negri 9c; adult/reduced €4/2; ☺8.30am-7.30pm). Este is also home to **Este Ceramiche Porcellane** (🖉0429 22 70; www.esteceramiche. com; Via Zanchi 22a; ☺8am-noon & 2-6pm Mon, to 5.30pm Tue-Fri, by appointment Sat), one of the oldest ceramics factories in Europe.

If you want to stay overnight, consider slumbering in one of the two apartments at **Villa Vescovi** (🖉049 993 04 73; www.villadeivescovi.it; Luvigliano; 3-night weekend €620-775; 🕿👫), one of the best preserved pre-Palladio Renaissance villas in the Veneto.

Vicenza

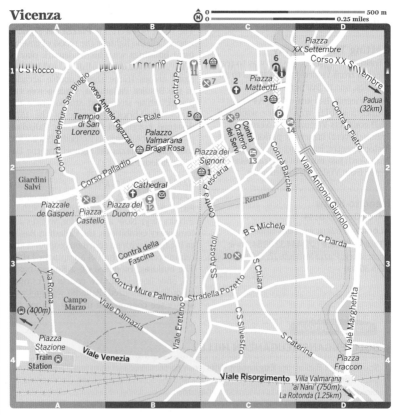

patron 50 years of lobbying the council), which involved radically restructuring the original, 15th-century *palazzo* and adding an ambitious double order of loggias (balconies), supported by Tuscan and Ionic columns topped by soaring statuary.

The building is also home to the elegant **Museo del Gioiello** (www.lineadombra.it; adult/reduced €6/4; ☉10am-6pm Mon-Fri, 9am-7pm Sat & Sun) and its dazzling collection of historic and contemporary jewellery.

★PALAZZO LEONI MONTANARI   MUSEUM
(☑800 578875; www.gallerieditalia.com; Contrà di Santa Corona 25; adult/reduced €5/3, or with MuseumCard; ☉10am-6pm Tue-Sun) An extraordinary collection of treasures await inside Palazzo Leoni Montanari, among them ancient pottery from Magna Graecia and grand salons filled with Canaletto's misty lagoon landscapes and Pietro Longhi's 18th-century satires. A recent addition

is Agostino Fasolato's astounding *The Fall of the Rebel Angels*, carved from a single block of Carrara marble and featuring no less than 60 angels and demons in nail-biting battle. Topping it all off is a superb collection of 400 Russian icons.

CHIESA DI SANTA CORONA   CHURCH
(☑0444 22 28 11; Contrà di Santa Corona; adult/reduced €3/2, or with MuseumCard; ☉9am-noon & 3-6pm Tue-Sun) Built by the Dominicans in 1261 to house a relic from Christ's crown of thorns donated to the bishop of Vicenza by Louis IX of France, this Romanesque church also houses three light-filled masterpieces: Palladio's 1576 **Valmarana Chapel** in the crypt; Paolo Veronese's *Adoration of the Magi*, much praised by Goethe; and Giovanni Bellini's radiant *Baptism of Christ*, where the holy event is witnessed by a trio of Veneto beauties and a curious red bird.

Vicenza

◎ Sights

1 Basilica Palladiana	C2
2 Chiesa di Santa Corona	C1
Museo del Gioiello	(see 1)
3 Palazzo Chiericati	C1
4 Palazzo Leoni Montanari	C1
5 Palazzo Thiene	B1
6 Teatro Olimpico	C1

⊗ Eating

7 Al Pestello	C1
8 Antico Ristorante agli Schioppi	A2
9 Gastronomia Il Ceppo	C1
10 Osteria Il Cursore	C3
Sòtobotega	(see 9)

◎ Drinking

Bar Borsa	(see 1)
11 Helmut	B1
12 Osteria al Campanile	B2

◎ Sleeping

13 Hotel Palladio	C2
14 Ostello Olimpico	C2

★**TEATRO OLIMPICO** THEATRE

(☑0444 22 28 00; www.olimpicovicenza.it; Piazza Matteotti 11; adult/reduced €11/8, or with MuseumCard; ⊙9am-5pm Tue-Sun, to 6pm early Jul-early Sep) Behind a walled garden lies a Renaissance marvel: the Teatro Olimpico, which Palladio began in 1580 with inspiration from Roman amphitheatres. Vincenzo Scamozzi finished the elliptical theatre after Palladio's death, adding a stage set modelled on the ancient Greek city of Thebes, with streets built in steep perspective to give the illusion of a city sprawling towards a distant horizon.

Today, Italian performers vie to make an entrance on this extraordinary stage; check the website for opera, classical and jazz performances.

PALAZZO CHIERICATI MUSEUM

(☑0444 22 28 11; www.museicivicivicenza.it; Piazza Matteotti 37/39; adult/reduced €5/3; ⊙10am-6pm Tue-Sun early Jul-early Sep, 9am-5pm Tue-Sun rest of year) Vicenza's civic art museum occupies one of Palladio's finest buildings, designed in 1550. The ground floor, used for temporary exhibitions, is where you'll find the **Sala dal Firmamento** (Salon of the Skies) and its blush-inducing ceiling fresco of Diana and an up-skirted

Helios by Domenico Brusasorci. Highlights in the upstairs galleries include Anthony Van Dyke's allegorical *The Four Ages* and Alessandro Maganza's remarkably contemporary *Portrait of Maddalena Campiglia*. Another floor up is the private collection of the late marquis Giuseppe Roi, including drawings by Tiepolo and Picasso.

★**LA ROTONDA** HISTORIC BUILDING

(☑049 879 13 80; www.villalarotonda.it; Via della Rotonda 45; villa/gardens €10/5; ⊙villa 10am-noon & 3-6pm Wed & Sat mid-Mar–Oct, 10am-noon & 2.30-5pm Wed & Sat Nov–mid-Mar, gardens 10am-noon & 3-6pm Tue-Sun mid-Mar–Oct, 10am-noon & 2.30-5pm Tue-Sun Nov–mid-Mar) No matter how you look at it, this villa is a show-stopper: the namesake dome caps a square base, with identical colonnaded facades on all four sides. This is one of Palladio's most admired creations, inspiring variations across Europe and the USA, including Thomas Jefferson's Monticello. Inside, the circular central hall is covered from the walls to the soaring cupola with trompe-l'œil frescoes. Catch bus 8 (€1.30, €2 on board) from in front of Vicenza's train station, or simply walk (about 25 minutes).

VILLA VALMARANA 'AI NANI' HISTORIC BUILDING

(☑0444 32 18 03; www.villavalmarana.com; Stradella dei Nani 8; adult/reduced €10/7; ⊙10am-12.30pm & 3-6pm Tue-Fri, 10am-6pm Sat & Sun early Mar-early Nov, by appointment rest of year) From La Rotonda, a charming footpath leads about 500m to the neoclassical elegance of Villa Valmarana 'ai Nani', nicknamed after the 17 statues of gnomes (ai Nani) around the perimeter walls. Step inside for 1757 frescoes by Giambattista Tiepolo and his son Giandomenico. Giambattista painted the Palazzina wing with his signature mythological epics, while his offspring executed the rural, carnival and Chinese themes adorning the *foresteria*.

 EATING

★**SÒTOBOTEGA** VENETIAN €

(☑0444 54 44 14; www.gastronomiailceppo.com; Corso Palladio 196; meals €25, set tasting menus €19.50-22; ⊙11.30am-3pm) Drop into cult-status deli **Gastronomia Il Ceppo** (☑0444 54 44 14; www.gastronomiailceppo.com; Corso Palladio 196; prepared dishes per 100g from around €2; ⊘8am-7.45pm Mon-Sat, 9am-2pm Sun) for picnic provisions, or head down into its cellar for sensational sit-down dishes like perfect house-made *bigoli* (a type of pasta) with duck *ragù*. Expect no less than 500 mostly Italian wines, including local Durella grape options, and about 25 drops by the glass. Transparent floor panels reveal an ancient Roman footpath and the foundations of an 11th-century abode.

Book ahead or head in early.

OSTERIA IL CURSORE
OSTERIA €

(☑0444 32 35 04; www.osteriacursore.it; Stradella Pozzetto 10; meals €23; ⊘11am-2pm & 6-10pm Mon & Wed-Fri, to 10.30pm Sat, 11am-2.30pm & 6-10pm Sun) A short walk from the city centre, behind a stained-glass door, Il Cursore serves up a thoroughly local scene where walls are hung with family photos and bawdy jigsaws, and where local diners keep one eye on the televised football match. Join the neighbourhood for simple, tasty, wallet-friendly grub like pork sausage and beans and sweet epilogues like ricotta, almond and Amaretto cake.

★AL PESTELLO
VENETIAN €€

(☑0444 32 37 21; www.ristorantealpestello.it; Contrà San Stefano 3; meals €32; ⊘7.30-10pm Mon, Wed & Thu, noon-2pm & 7.30-10pm Fri-Sun; ☜) ✿ Homely, brightly lit Al Pestello dishes out intriguing, lesser-known regional dishes like *la panà* (bread soup), red-wine braised donkey and *bresaola* (air-cured beef) 'lollies' filled with grappa-flavoured Grana Padano and mascarpone. The kitchen is obsessed with local ingredients, right down to the Colli Berici truffles, while the collection of harder-to-find *digestivi* makes for an enlightening epilogue. Book ahead.

ANTICO RISTORANTE AGLI SCHIOPPI
OSTERIA €€

(☑0444 54 37 01; www.ristoranteaglischioppi. com; Contrà Piazza del Castello 26; meals €30; ⊘noon-2pm & 7-10pm Tue-Sat; ☜) Tucked under an arcade just off Piazza del Castello lies one of the city's simplest and best restaurants. Owners Cinzia and Orlando are devotees of locally sourced products, from wild forest greens to baby river trout, but without any pretensions about it; it's just what they know best.

🍷 DRINKING

BAR BORSA
BAR

(☑0444 54 45 83; www.barborsa.com; Basilica Palladiana, Piazza dei Signori; ⊘5pm-midnight Mon, 10am-2am Tue-Sun; ☜) Decked out in black subway tiles and flickering candlelight, hip Borsa covers all bases, from coffee and juices, to *aperitivo* and cocktail sessions. Fresh, flavoursome food options span breakfast, brunch, lunch, snacks and dinner, with DJs spinning non-commercial tunes on Fridays and Saturdays. Note: only bar service is available on Mondays.

OSTERIA AL CAMPANILE
BAR

(☑0444 54 40 36; Piazza della Posta; ⊘9am-2pm & 5-9pm Tue-Sun) You'll find one of Vicenza's most historic watering holes tucked beneath the Roman belltower by the cathe-

'BIRDS' OF THE BANCA POPOLARE

Just off Corso Palladio, you'll find the headquarters of the Banca Popolare di Vicenza (the People's Bank of Vicenza), housed rather ironically in Palladio's **Palazzo Thiene** (☑0444 33 99 89; www.palazzothiene.it; Contrà San Gaetano Thiene; ⊘ by appointment only 9am-5pm Wed-Fri, closed Jul & Aug) **FREE**, fashioned for the aristocratic Thiene family in 1556. Purchased by the bank in 1872, the palace is now home to a variety of cultural treasures.

Most interesting of these is the unique collection of *oselle* (silver and gold coins minted by the doge each year and presented as a Christmas gift to all the noble families of the Great Council of Venice). Originally, the gift was five mallards per family, but given the growing number of nobles and the declining number of mallards, in 1521 the Council decreed that the doge should mint a silver coin instead, hence the name, *oselle*, which is Venetian for bird.

The bank owns the most complete collection in the world – 275, to be precise – and you can book (by email or phone, at least a week in advance) to see them, along with the bank's frescoed salons, fine artworks and sculpture.

dral. Eavesdrop on local gossip, nibble on scrumptious bite-sized *panini*, and swill unusual vintages such as the sparkling Durello, usually overshadowed by its more famous cousin, *prosecco*.

HELMUT
BEER HALL

(www.facebook.com/HelmutpubVicenza; Contrà Zanella 8; ☺6.30pm-2am Tue-Sun) Industrial lighting, blackboard-hued walls and an antique pharmacy cabinet set the scene at new-school Helmut. Beer is the star attraction, with no less than 18 mostly European craft beers on tap, served to a smart, friendly, 30- and 40-something crowd. Sud-soaking edibles include creative burgers (€10 to €12) made with beef from lauded local butcher Damini & Affini.

Prosecco Road Trip

Explore

A road trip north of Venice takes you through one of Italy's most sophisticated, and least visited, stretches of countryside. Some of the Veneto's finest country villas and frescoes are to be found here, while a little further north in the foothills of the Dolomites, *prosecco* vines dip and crest across an undulating landscape framed by snowy peaks. To explore it properly you'll need a car of your own; and you'll certainly want one so you can load up with the Veneto's finest fizz and firewater.

The Best...
➡**Sight** Villa di Masèr (p176)
➡**Place to Eat** Agriturismo Da Ottavio (p177)
➡**Place to Drink** Azienda Agricola Frozza (p176)

Top Tip

From mid-March to mid-June, the Veneto's DOCG-denominated hills play host to the annual **Primavera del Prosecco Superiore** (www.primaveradelprosecco.it), a series of 16 food and wine events showcasing the area's prized *prosecco* and culinary delicacies. Activities range from wine-tasting and bike tours, to guided walks and concerts. Check the website for a comprehensive listing of what's on and where. *Cin cin.*

Getting There & Away
➡**Train** Head from Venice to Mestre station, from where trains run one to four times hourly to Conegliano (€5.40, one hour).
➡**Car** Your own wheels are your best option for getting around the region at a reasonable pace and visiting wineries and farmstays. The A27 heads directly north from Mestre to Conegliano.

Need to Know
➡**Area Code** ☑0423
➡**Location** Conegliano 53km north of Venice; Castelfranco Veneto 37km northwest of Venice; Bassano del Grappa 58km northwest of Venice
➡**Tourist Office** (☑0438 2 12 30; Via XX Settembre 61, Conegliano; ☺9am-1pm Tue & Wed, 9am-1pm & 2-6pm Thu-Sun)

SIGHTS & ACTIVITIES

⊙ Valdobbiadene & Surrounds

Nestled among steep hills and lauded vineyards, the humble town of Valdobbiadene is one bookend to the Prosecco Superiore DOCG zone, a 20,000-hectare area stretching east to the town of Conegliano and home to over 170 *prosecco* producers. You can find a list of them, as well as more information on the area and its world-famous bubbles, at www.prosecco.it.

If you want to sleep among the vineyards, **Azienda Agricola Campion** (☑0423 98 04 32; www.campionspumanti.it; Via Campion 2, San Giovanni di Valdobbiadene; s €40-45, d €65-75; ☺tasting room 9am-noon & 2-6pm; P ✲ 🛜 🖳) is a farmstay set amid 14 hectares of vines in the heart of Valdobbiadene. The four rooms occupy converted farm buildings, with warm, rustic styling and the added perk of a kitchenette in each.

WORTH A DETOUR

VILLA DI MASÈR

A World Heritage Site, the 16th-century **Villa di Masèr** (Villa Barbaro; ☑0423 92 30 04; www.villadimaser. it; Via Barbaro 4; adult/reduced €9/7; ☺10.30am-6pm Tue, Thu & Sat, 11am-6pm Sun Mar, 10am-6pm Tue-Sat, 11am-6pm Sun Apr-Oct, 11am-5pm Sat & Sun Nov-Feb; P) is a spectacular monument to the Venetian *bea vita* (good life). Designed by the inimitable Andrea Palladio, its sublimely elegant exterior is matched by Paolo Veronese's wildly imaginative trompe l'œil architecture inside. Vines crawl up the Stanza di Baccho; a watchdog keeps an eye on the painted door of the Stanza di Canuccio (Little Dog Room); and in a corner of the frescoed grand salon, the painter has apparently forgotten his spattered shoes and broom. Located 7km northeast of Asolo, the villa is usually closed from early December to Christmas and from early to late January.

AZIENDA AGRICOLA BARICHEL   WINERY

(☑0423 97 57 43; www.barichel.net; Via Zanzago 9, Valdobbiadene) ⏱ Like the prodigal son, ultra-marathon runner and vintner, Ivan Geronazzo, returned to his grandfather's vineyard in Valdobbiadene after years of working at larger, high capacity wineries. Here he tends his 7 hectares by hand producing up to 60,000 bottles of natural, *frizzante*, Extra Dry and Brut *prosecco* with a pale, straw-yellow colour and apple-and-pear fragrances. Prices range from €4 to €7 per bottle.

AZIENDA AGRICOLA FROZZA   WINERY

(☑0423 98 70 69; www.frozza.it; Via Martiri 31, Colbertaldo di Vidor) Galera vines have grown on this sunny Colbertaldo hillside for hundreds of years and six generations of the Frozza family have tended them since 1870. The result: *prosecco* with a remarkable fragrance and complexity. The 2011 Brut is a particularly good vintage due to the dry summer. Expect fruity fragrances supported by a well-structured, mineral-rich body. Prices range from €4 to €7 per bottle.

⊙ Asolo

Known as the 'town of 100 vistas' for its panoramic hillside location, the medieval walled town of Asolo has long been a favourite of literary types. Robert Browning bought a house here, but the ultimate local celebrity is Caterina Corner, the 15th-century queen of Cyprus, who was given the town, its castle and the surrounding county in exchange for her abdication. She promptly became queen of the literary set, holding salons that featured writer Pietro Bembo. Asolo's penchant for finery extends to its monthly **Mercatino dell'Antiquariato** (Antiques Market; ☑0423 52 46 75; www.asolo.it; Piazza Garibaldi; ☺2nd Sun of month Sep-Jun), one of the region's finest antiques flea markets.

MUSEO CIVICO DI ASOLO   MUSEUM

(☑0423 95 23 13; www.asolo.it/en/museo; Via Regina Cornaro 74; adult/reduced €5/4; ☺10am-noon & 3-7pm Sat & Sun) In the Museo Civico you can explore Asolo's Roman past and wander through a small collection of paintings, including a pair of Tintoretto portraits. The museum also includes rooms devoted to Eleanora Duse (1858–1924) and British traveller and writer Freya Stark

(1893–1993), who retreated to Asolo between Middle Eastern forays.

ROCCA   RUIN
(☑329 8508512; admission €2; ⊙10am-7pm Sat & Sun Apr-Jun, Sep & Oct, 10am-noon & 3-7pm Sat & Sun Jul & Aug, 10am-5pm Sat & Sun Nov-Mar) Perched on the summit of Monte Ricco and looking down on central Asolo are the hulking ruins of a fortress dating back to the 12th- to early 13th-centuries. The still-visible cistern well was constructed between the 13th and 14th centuries, while the heavily restored buttresses offer a breathtaking panorama that takes in soft green hills, snow-capped mountains and the industrious Po Valley.

◎ Bassano del Grappa

Bassano del Grappa sits with charming simplicity on the banks of the River Brenta as it winds its way free from Alpine foothills.

Spanning the river is Palladio's photogenic **Ponte degli Alpini**, dating back to 1569. The covered wooden bridge has always been critical in times of war: Napoleon bivouacked here for many months and, in the Great War, the Alpine brigades adopted the bridge as their emblem. Hundreds of them died on the slopes of **Monte Grappa** (1775m), where Ernest Hemingway drove his ambulance and an enormous tiered memorial now commemorates the sacrifice of over 12,000 Italian and 10,000 Austro-Hungarian soldiers.

The town's most famous export is its namesake spirit, grappa – a fiery distillation made from the discarded skins, pulp, seeds and stems from wine-making.

POLI MUSEO DELLA GRAPPA   MUSEUM
(☑0424 52 44 26; www.poligrappa.com; Via Gamba 6; admission free, distillery guided tour €3; ⊙museum 9am-7.30pm daily, distillery guided tours 8.30am-1pm & 2-6pm Mon-Fri) Explore four centuries of Bassano's high-octane libation at this interactive museum, which includes tastings and the chance to tour the distillery of esteemed producer Poli (book distillery tours online). Although grappa is made all over Italy, and indeed inferior versions are distilled well beyond the peninsula, the people of the Veneto have been doing it since at least the 16th century. In fact, an institute of grappa distillers was even created in Venice in 1601!

ⓘ LA STRADA DEL PROSECCO

Running through a landscape of lush, verdant vineyards, **La Strada del Prosecco** (Prosecco Road; www.coneglianovaldobbiadene.it) is a driving route that takes you from Conegliano to Valdobbiadene via some of the region's best wineries. The website provides an itinerary, background information on *prosecco*, and details about stops along the way.

MUSEO CIVICO   MUSEUM
(☑0424 51 99 01; www.museibassano.it; Piazza Garibaldi 34; adult/reduced €5/3.50; ⊙9am-7pm Tue-Sat, 10.30am-1pm & 3-6pm Sun) Bassano del Grappa's Museo Civico is beautifully housed around the cloisters of the Convento di San Francesco. Endowed in 1828 by the naturalist Giambattista Brocchi, the museum houses an extensive archaeological collection alongside 500 paintings, including masterpieces such as the 1545 *Flight into Egypt* by local son Jacopo Bassano.

✖ EATING & DRINKING

★AGRITURISMO DA OTTAVIO   VENETIAN €
(☑0423 98 11 13; Via Campion 2, San Giovanni di Valdobbiadene; meals €15-20; ⊙noon-3pm Sat, Sun & holidays, closed Sep; ⊕) *Prosecco* is typically drunk with *sopressa*, a fresh local salami, as the sparkling *spumante* cleans the palate and refreshes the mouth. There's no better way to test this than at Da Ottavio, where everything on the table, *sopressa* and *prosecco* included, is homemade by the Spada family.

OSTERIA ALLA CANEVA   VENETIAN €
(☑335 5423560; Via G Matteotti 34; dishes €7-15; ⊙9am-3pm & 5.30-9.30pm Wed-Mon) Behind yellow-tinted glass lies this old-school favourite, with its hung pots, worn wooden tables and inter-generational regulars washing down rustic regional grub with a glass or three of *vino* from local wineries like Vigneto Due Santi di Zonta. Food options lean towards cured meats and pasta dishes like fettucine with artichokes. For a light bite, don't miss the moreish *baccala cicchetti* (salted cod tapas).

PROSECCO: A LOCAL'S GUIDE

Sommelier and tour guide **Mario Piccinin** (✆049 60 06 72; www.venicedaytrips.com; Via Saetta 18, Padua; semi-private/private tours per person from €165/275) gives the low-down on the Veneto's favourite *aperitivo*.

The origins of prosecco... *Prosecco* can be traced back to the Romans. It was then known as 'pucino' and was shipped direct to the court of Empress Livia from Aquileia, where it was produced with grapes from the Carso. During the Venetian Republic the vines were transferred to the Prosecco DOCG (*denominazione d'origine controllata e garantita*; quality-controlled) area, a small triangle of land between the towns of Valdobbiadene, Conegliano and Vittorio Veneto.

The social scene... Here in the Veneto we drink *prosecco* like water – sometimes it's even cheaper than water!

Describe the character of a good prosecco... Straw yellow in colour with sparkling greenish reflections. The naturally formed bubbles are tiny, numerous and long-lasting in your glass. It's fragrant with fresh notes of white fruits and fresh grass. It pleases your mouth with its crispness and aromaticity. Keep in mind that these characteristics are not long-lasting – *prosecco* is meant to be drunk young.

Pairings? *Sopressa* (a fresh local salami), buttery Asiago cheese and roasted chestnuts in season. But it really is a match for many simple dishes such as those served at **Agriturismo Da Ottavio** (p177).

VILLA CIPRIANI   MODERN ITALIAN €€€

(✆0423 52 34 11; www.villaciprianiasolo.com; Via Canova 298, Asolo; meals €60; ☺12.30-2.30pm & 8-10.30pm) The Ciprianis behind this Renaissance villa are the same as those in Venice, and they are just the latest in a long line of illustrious owners including the Guinnesses, Galantis and poet Robert Browning. Now you, too, can enjoy the perfumed rose garden, not to mention the kitchen's seasonal, market-driven menus; the pasta dishes are particularly seductive.

NARDINI   BAR

(☺8.30am-9.30pm) Flanking Bassano del Grappa's 16th-century Ponte degli Alpini (Ponte Vecchio), this historic distillery is a great place to grab a few bottles of Nardini's famous grappa, or to simply kick back with a glass of bitter-sweet *mezzo e mezzo*, a unique apertif made with Rabarbaro Nardini, Rosso Nardini, Cynar and soda water.

Verona

Explore

Shakespeare placed star-crossed lovers Romeo Montague and Juliet Capulet in Verona for good reason: romance, drama and fatal family feuding have been the city's hallmark for centuries. From the 3rd century BC, Verona (population 264,000) was a Roman trade centre with ancient gates, a forum (now Piazza delle Erbe) and a grand Roman arena, which still serves as one of the world's great opera venues. In the Middle Ages, the city flourished under the wrathful Scaligeri clan, who were as much energetic patrons of the arts as they were murderous tyrants. Their elaborate Gothic tombs, the **Arche Scaligere**, are just off **Piazza dei Signori**. To get around all the main sights in a day you'll need an early start and careful planning. Consider spending the night if you want to delve deeper – or explore Verona's remarkable wine country.

The Best...
→**Sight** Museo di Castelvecchio
→**Place to Eat** Locanda 4 Cuochi (p182)
→**Place to Drink** Osteria del Bugiardo (p182)

Top Tip
VeronaCard (24/72 hours €15/20), available at tourist sights as well as tobacconists and many hotels, grants access to most major monuments and churches, unlimited use of town buses, plus discounted tickets to selected concerts, and opera and theatre productions.

Getting There & Away

➡**Train** There are one to four trains hourly to Venice (€8.60 to €23, 70 minutes to 2¼ hours). The station is about a 20-minute walk south of the historic centre. There is a taxi rank just in front of the station, and there are also frequent local bus connections to the centre.

➡**Car** Verona is at the intersection of the A4 (Turin–Trieste) and A22 motorways.

Need to Know

➡**Area Code** 045

➡**Location** 120km west of Venice

➡**Tourist Office** (045 806 86 80; www.tourism.verona.it; Via degli Alpini 9; 9am-7pm Mon-Sat, 10am-4pm Sun)

SIGHTS

ROMAN ARENA
RUIN

(045 800 32 04; www.arena.it; Piazza Brà; adult/reduced €10/7.50, 1st Sun of month Oct-May €1; 1.30-7.30pm Mon, 8.30am-7.30pm Tue-Sun) Built of pink-tinged marble in the 1st century AD, Verona's Roman amphitheatre survived a 12th-century earthquake to become the city's legendary open-air opera house, with seating for 30,000 people. You can visit the arena year-round, though it's at its best during the summer opera festival. In winter months, concerts are held at the **Teatro Filarmonico** (045 800 51 51; www.arena.it; Via dei Mutilati 4; box office noon-5.45pm Mon-Fri, 10am-12.45pm Sat, extended hours on show days).

MUSEO DI CASTELVECCHIO
MUSEUM

(045 806 26 11; Corso Castelvecchio 2; adult/reduced €6/4.50; 1.30-7.30pm Mon, 8.30am-7.30pm Tue-Sun;) Bristling with battlements along the River Adige, Castelvecchio was built in the 1350s by Cangrande II. Severely damaged by Napoleon and WWII bombings, the fortress was reinvented by architect Carlo Scarpa, who constructed bridges over exposed foundations, filled gaping holes with glass panels, and balanced a statue of Cangrande I above the courtyard on a concrete gangplank. The complex is now home to a diverse collection of statuary, frescoes, jewellery, medieval artefacts and paintings by Pisanello, Giovanni Bellini, Tiepolo and Veronese.

BASILICA DI SAN ZENO MAGGIORE
BASILICA

(www.chieseverona.it; Piazza San Zeno; admission €2.50; 8.30am-6pm Mon-Sat, 12.30-6pm Sun Mar-Oct, 10am-1pm & 1.30-5pm Mon-Sat, 12.30-5pm Sun Nov-Feb) A masterpiece of Romanesque architecture, the striped brick and stone basilica was built in honour of the city's patron saint. Enter through the flower-filled cloister into the nave – a vast space lined with 12th- to 15th-century frescoes. Painstaking restoration has revived Mantegna's 1457–59 *Majesty of the Virgin* altarpiece, painted with such astonishing perspective that you actually believe there are garlands of fresh fruit hanging behind the Madonna's throne.

Under the rose window depicting the Wheel of Fortune you'll find meticulously detailed 12th-century bronze doors, which include a scene of an exorcism with a demon being yanked from a woman's mouth. Beneath the main altar lies a brooding crypt, with faces carved into medieval capitals and St Zeno's corpse glowing in a transparent sarcophagus.

PIAZZA DELLE ERBE
SQUARE

Originally a Roman forum, Piazza delle Erbe is ringed with buzzing cafes and some of Verona's most sumptuous buildings, including the elegantly baroque **Palazzo Maffei**, which now houses several shops at its northern end.

Just off the piazza, the monumental arch known as the **Arco della Costa** is hung with a whale's rib. Legend holds that the rib will fall on the first just person to walk beneath it. So far, it remains intact, despite visits by popes and kings.

LOCAL KNOWLEDGE

PONTE PIETRA

At the northern edge of the city centre, this **bridge** is a quiet but remarkable testament to the Italians' love of their artistic heritage. Two of the bridge's arches date from the Roman Republican era in the 1st century BC, while the other three were replaced in the 13th century. The ancient bridge remained largely intact until 1945, when retreating German troops blew it up. But locals fished the fragments out of the river, and painstakingly rebuilt the bridge stone by stone in the 1950s.

Verona

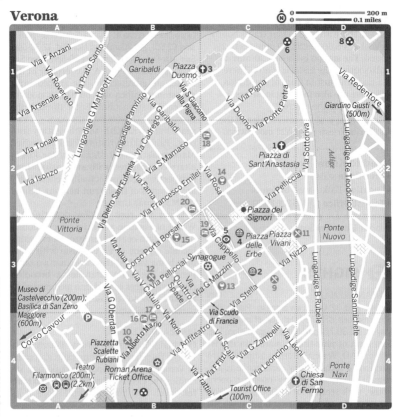

TORRE DEI LAMBERTI   TOWER

(☑045 927 30 27; Via della Costa 2; adult/reduced incl Galleria d'Arte Moderna Achille Forti €8/5; ⊙10am-6pm Mon-Fri, last entry 5.15pm, 10am-7pm Sat & Sun, last entry 6.15pm) For panoramic views of Verona and nearby mountains, head up this 84m-high watchtower. Begun in the 12th century and finished in 1463 – too late to notice invading Venetians – it sports an octagonal bell tower whose two bells retain their ancient names: Rengo once called meetings of the city council, while Marangona warned citizens of fire. A lift whisks you up two-thirds of the way but you have to walk the last few storeys.

Full-price admission to the tower is reduced to €5 on Mondays as the adjoining Galleria d'Arte Moderna Achille Forti is closed.

★GALLERIA D'ARTE
MODERNA ACHILLE FORTI   MUSEUM

(Palazzo della Ragione; ☑045 800 19 03; www.palazzodellaragioneverona.it; Cortile Mercato Vecchio; adult/reduced €4/2.50, incl Torre dei Lamberti €8/5; ⊙11am-7pm Tue-Sun Jun-Aug, 10am-6pm Tue-Fri, 11am-7pm Sat & Sun Sep-May) In the shadow of the Torre dei Lamberti, the Romanesque Palazzo della Ragione is home to Verona's jewel-box Gallery of Modern Art. Reached via the Gothic **Scala della Ragione** (Stairs of Reason), the collection of paintings and sculpture spans 1840 to 1940 and includes influential Italian artists such as Giorgio Morandi and Umberto Boccioni. Among the numerous highlights are Francesco Hayez' arresting portrait *Meditazione* (Meditation), Angelo Dall'Oca's haunting *Foglie cadenti* (Falling Leaves) and Ettore Berladini's darkly humourous *I vecchi* (Old Men).

Verona

CASA DI GIULIETTA   MUSEUM
(Juliet's House; ☑045 803 43 03; Via Cappello 23; adult/reduced €6/4.50, or with VeronaCard; ☺1.30-7.30pm Mon, 8.30am-7.30pm Tue-Sun) Never mind that Romeo and Juliet were completely fictional characters, and that there's hardly room for two on the narrow stone balcony, romantics flock to this 14th-century house to add their lovelorn pleas to the sea of Post-it notes lining the courtyard gateway. In truth, Juliet's House is altogether underwhelming, so consider a free glance from the courtyard and search for your Romeo elsewhere.

★**BASILICA DI
SANT'ANASTASIA**   BASILICA
(www.chieseverona.it; Piazza di Sant'Anastasia; admission €2.50; ☺9am-6pm Mon-Sat, 1-6pm Sun Mar-Oct, 10am-1pm & 1.30-5pm Mon-Sat, 1-5pm Sun Nov-Feb) Dating from the 13th to 15th centuries and featuring an elegantly decorated vaulted ceiling, the Gothic Basilica di Sant'Anastasia is Verona's largest church and a showcase for local art. The multitude of frescoes is overwhelming, but don't overlook Pisanello's story-book-quality fresco *St George and the Princess* that's above the entrance to the **Pellegrini Chapel**, or the 1495 holy water font featuring a hunchback carved by Paolo Veronese's father, Gabriele Caliari.

DUOMO   CATHEDRAL
(☑045 59 28 13; www.chieseverona.it; Piazza Duomo; admission €2.50; ☺10am-5.30pm Mon-Sat, 1.30-5.30pm Sun Mar-Oct, 10am-1pm & 1.30-5pm Mon-Fri, to 4pm Sat, 1.30-5pm Sun Nov-Feb) Verona's 12th-century cathedral is a striking Romanesque creation, with bug-eyed statues of Charlemagne's paladins Roland and Oliver, crafted by medieval master Nicolò, on the west porch. Nothing about this sober facade hints at the extravagant 16th- to 17th-century frescoed interior with angels aloft amid trompe l'œil architecture. At the left end of the nave is the **Cartolari-Nichesola Chapel**, designed by Renaissance master Jacopo Sansovino and featuring a vibrant Titian *Assumption*.

**TEATRO ROMANO E MUSEO
ARCHEOLOGICO**   ARCHAEOLOGICAL SITE
(☑045 800 03 60; Regaste Redentore 2; adult/reduced €6/4.50, or with VeronaCard; ☺8.30am-7.30pm Tue-Sun, 1.30-7.30pm Mon) Just north of the historic centre you'll find a **Roman theatre**. Built in the 1st century BC, it is cunningly carved into the hillside at a strategic spot overlooking a bend in the river. Take the lift at the back of the theatre to the former convent above, which houses an interesting collection of Greek and Roman pieces.

★**GIARDINO GIUSTI**   GARDENS
(☑045 803 40 29; Via Giardino Giusti 2; adult/reduced €7/5; ☺9am-8pm Apr-Sep, to 7pm Oct-Mar; ▣) Across the river from the historic centre, these sculpted gardens are considered a masterpiece of Renaissance landscaping, and named after the noble family that has tended them since opening them to the public in 1591. The vegetation is an Italianate mix of the manicured and natural, graced by soaring cypresses, one of which the German poet Goethe immortalised in his travel writings.

According to local legend, lovers who manage to find each other in the gardens' petite labyrinth are destined to stay together. If you do, whisper sweet nothings while gazing out at the city from the *belvedere* (lookout), accessed from the back of the gardens.

EATING

PIZZERIA DU DE COPE — PIZZA €

(☎045 59 55 62; www.pizzeriadudecope.it; Galleria Pelicciai 10; pizzas €5.50-13.50, salads €7-12; ⊗noon-2.30pm & 7-11pm) Pimped with colourful wall tiles, chairs and placemats, Du de Cope is a thoroughly modern, convivial pizzeria. Peek over the counter and watch your pizza bubbling in the wood-fired oven, or ease up on the carbs with one of the high-quality salads.

PASTICCERIA MIOZZI — PASTRIES €

(☎045 927 50 18; Via A Diaz 7a; brioche €1.10; ⊗7am-8pm Mon-Sat, 7am-1.30pm & 3.30-7pm Sun) Not only home to Verona's plumpest brioche, sassy Miozzi peddles finger-licking pastries (including mini versions), *biscotti* and chocolates. The coffee is rich and aromatic, and there's a handful of tables for a leisurely pit-stop.

★LOCANDA 4 CUOCHI — MODERN ITALIAN €€

(☎045 803 03 11; www.locanda4cuochi.it; Via Alberto Mario 12; meals €35, 3-course set menu €24; ⊗7.30-10.30pm Tue, 12.30-2.30pm & 7.30-10.30pm Wed-Sun; 🎤) With its open kitchen, urbane vibe and hot-shot chefs, you're right to expect great things from the Locanda. Culinary acrobatics play second fiddle to prime produce cooked with skill and subtle twists. Whether it's perfectly crisp suckling pig with lemon and sage, or an epilogue of whipped ricotta cut with raspberry salsa and pistachio crumble, expect to swoon.

LA TAVERNA DI VIA STELLA — VERONESE €€

(☎045 800 80 08; www.tavernadiviastella.com; Via Stella 5c; meals €30; ⊗7.15-11pm Mon, 12.15-2.15pm & 7.15-11pm Wed-Sun) Brush past the haunches of prosciutto dangling over the deli bar and make your way into the dining room, decorated Tiepolo-style with rustic murals of chivalric knights and maidens. This is the place you'll want to sample traditional Veronese dishes such as *pastissada* (horse stew), *bigoli* (extruded pasta) with duck *ragù* and DOP Lessinia cheeses from Monte Veronese. Cash only for bills under €30.

★PESCHERIA I MASENINI — SEAFOOD €€€

(☎045 929 80 15; www.imasenini.com; Piazzetta Pescheria 9; meals €50; ⊗7.30-10pm Tue, 12.30-2pm & 7.30-10pm Wed-Sun; 🎤) Located on the piazza where Verona's Roman fish market once held sway, softly lit Masenini quietly serves up Verona's most imaginative, modern fish dishes. Inspired flavour combinations might see fresh sea bass carpaccio paired with zesty green apple and pink pepper, black-ink gnocchi schmoozing with lobster *ragù*, or sliced amberjack delightfully matched with crumbed almonds, honey, spinach and raspberries.

🍷 DRINKING

★OSTERIA DEL BUGIARDO — WINE BAR

(☎045 59 18 69; Corso Porta Borsari 17a; ⊗11am-midnight, to 1am Fri & Sat) Crowds converge at friendly Bugiardo for glasses of upstanding Valpolicella bottled specifically for the *osteria*. Feeling peckish? Order the yellow polenta with creamy gorgonzola and salami. On weekdays from November to January, pair a powerhouse Amarone with the very local *lesso e pearà* (boiled meat stew with a peppery beef, hen, bone marrow and breadcrumb sauce).

ANTICA BOTTEGA DEL VINO — WINE BAR

(☎045 800 45 35; www.bottegavini.it; Vicolo Scudo di Francia 3; cicheti €2, meals €40; ⊗noon-11pm; 🎤) While *vino* is the primary consideration at this historic, baronial-style wine bar (the cellar holds around 18,000 bottles), the linen-lined tables promise a satisfying feed. Ask the sommelier to recommend a worthy vintage for your Amarone risotto, sugar and cinnamon gnocchi, or suckling pig – some of the best wines here are bottled specifically for the *bottega*. Note it sometimes closes in November and February.

CAFFÉ MONTE BALDO — WINE BAR

(☎045 803 05 79; Via Rosa 12; tartine €1.20; ⊗10am-11pm Tue-Thu, to 1am Fri, 11am-1am Sat, 11am-11pm Sun) Packed to bursting come *aperitivo* hour, wood-panelled, marble-topped Monte Baldo lures with its generous *aperitivo* bar and around 120 mostly regional wines, over 30 available by the glass. Graze on meatballs or *tartine*, tapas-sized bread artfully topped with ingredients like local *sopressa*, or cream cheese with hazelnuts and radicchio.

SLEEPING IN VERONA

Try to book well ahead if you plan to be here during the summer opera season.

Anfiteatro B&B (✆347 2488462; www.anfiteatro-bedandbreakfast.com; Via Alberto Mario 5; s €60-90, d €80-130, tr €100-150) Opera divas rest up steps from the action in this 19th-century townhouse, one block from the Roman Arena and just off boutique-lined Via Mazzini. Spacious guestrooms have high wood-beamed ceilings, antique armoires for stashing purchases and divans for swooning after shows.

The charming owners also run nearby **Alla Galleria B&B** (✆347 2488462; www. bedandbreakfastallagalleria.com; Via A Cantore 4; s €65-90, d €85-130; 🖤), a tranquil, three-bedroom place with pastel hues, antique rugs and balconies.

Corte delle Pigne (✆333 7584141; www.cortedellepigne.it; Via Pigna 6a; s €60-90, d €90-130, tr & q €110-150; P🖤🖤) In the heart of the historic centre, this three-room B&B is set around a quiet internal courtyard. It offers tasteful rooms and plenty of personal touches: sweet jars, luxury toiletries and even a Jacuzzi for one lucky couple.

Hotel Aurora (✆045 59 47 17; www.hotelaurora.biz; Piazzetta XIV Novembre 2; d €100-250, tr €130-280; 🖤🖤) Overlooking Piazza delle Erbe, friendly Aurora offers recently renovated rooms, some with piazza views and all with classic wooden furniture and fresh, modern bathrooms. The open-air terrace makes for a perfect spot to enjoy breakfast or a lazy sundowner.

Hotel Gabbia d'Oro (✆045 59 02 93; www.hotelgabbiadoro.it; Corso Porta Borsari 4; d from €200; 🖤🖤) One of the city's top addresses and also one of its most romantic, the Gabbia d'Oro features luxe rooms inside an 18th-century *palazzo* that manage to be both elegant and cosy. The rooftop terrace and central location are the icing on the proverbial cake.

Verona's Wine Country

Explore

Approximately 73 sq km of the Veneto are planted with vines, with the most productive vineyards – Soave and Valpolicella – within easy reach of Verona. Northwest of Verona, Valpolicella is celebrated for Amarone – an intense red wine made from partially dried grapes – while Soave delivers its crisp namesake whites amid storybook medieval walls between Vicenza and Verona. You'll need wheels to visit far-flung vineyards. Most growing areas are also bike-friendly. Since vineyards are spread out, each region requires a full day for relaxed appreciation, including a long, vinous lunch.

Open only to food and wine professionals, Italy's largest national wine fair, **Vinitaly** (www.vinitaly.com) is held in Verona in March or April, with infinite sampling opportunities.

The Best...

➡ **Sight** Castello di Soave (p184)
➡ **Place to Eat** Trattoria Caprini (p185)
➡ **Place to Drink** Enoteca della Valpolicella (p185)

Top Tip

If you don't want to bother renting a car, **Pagus** (✆340 0830720, 349 1579090; www.pagusvalpolicella.net; 3½hr group tour adult/under 14yr from €60/50) offers half- and full-day tours of Valpolicella and Soave, leaving regularly from Verona. Tours include unusual sites, impromptu country rambles, lunches in local restaurants and, of course, wine tastings. Tours can also be customised.

Getting There & Away

➡ **Train** To get to Soave from Venice, take the train to San Bonifacio (90 minutes, €7.35, hourly), walk south along Corso Venezia for 200m to Via Trento and catch a westbound local ATV bus 130 (€2.10, 10 minutes, about twice hourly). Buy your ticket on board. Trains do not serve Valpolicella.

DAY TRIPS FROM VENICE VERONA'S WINE COUNTRY

Car Your own wheels are your best option for visiting individual wineries. Valpolicella lies just past Verona's northwest suburbs, just off the E45. Soave lies just off the A4, which connects Verona and Mestre.

Need to Know
Area Code 041
Location Valpolicella (140km west of Venice); Soave (85km west of Venice)
Tourist Offices Soave (045 619 07 73; Piazza Foro Boario I, Soave; 10am-5pm Mon, 9am-6pm Tue-Fri, 9am-3pm Sat & Sun Apr-Oct, 9am-5pm Tue-Fri, to 2pm Sat & Sun Nov-Mar); **Valpolicella** (045 770 19 20; www.valpolicellaweb.it; Via Ingelheim 7; 9am-1pm Mon-Fri)

◉ SIGHTS & ACTIVITIES

◉ Soave

Barely 20km from Verona, Soave is nestled in a landscape of gentle green hills and vineyards. The DOC quality-controlled zone includes the parishes of Soave, Castelcerino, Fittà, Castelletto and Costeggiola. Head up to Fittà on a sunny day and you'll have a splendid view of the Val d'Alpone that channels the mountain meltwaters down to Soave and, in the process, feeds its abundant crop of cherries.

Soave itself is a charming medieval town, mapped out along the Roman axis of Via Roma and Via Camuzzoni. Notable buildings line the route, culminating in the Venetian Gothic Palazzo Scaligeri, now the Town Hall. May, June and September are the liveliest times to visit, when the wine festival, cherry season and harvest are in full swing.

CASTELLO DI SOAVE   HISTORIC BUILDING
(045 768 00 36; www.castellodisoave.it; adult/reduced €7/4; 9am-noon & 3-6.30pm Tue-Sun Apr-Oct, 9am-noon & 2-4pm Nov-Mar) Built on a medieval base by Verona's fratricidal Scaligeri family, the Castello complex encompasses an early-Renaissance villa, grassy courtyards, the remnants of a Romanesque

church and the Mastio (the defensive tower apparently used as a dungeon): during restoration, a mound of human bones was unearthed here. Be sure to make your way to the upper ramparts for fine views of the town and surrounding countryside.

AZIENDA AGRICOLA COFFELE   WINERY
(045 768 00 07; www.coffele.it; Via Roma 5; wine tasting €9-12; 9am-1pm & 2.30-6.30pm Mon-Sat & by appointment) Across from the old-town church, this family-run winery offers tastings of lemon-zesty DOC Soave Classico and an elegant, creamy DOC Coffele Ca' Visco Classico. The family also rents out rooms among vineyards a few kilometres from town. Book wine tastings in advance: two days ahead in winter and about a week ahead in summer.

★SUAVIA   WINERY
(045 767 50 89; www.suavia.it; Via Centro 14, Fittà; 9am-1pm & 2.30-6.30pm Mon-Fri, 9am-1pm Sat & by appointment; P) Soave is not known as a complex white, but this trailblazing winery, located 8km outside Soave via SP39, is changing the equation. Don't miss DOC Monte Carbonare Soave Classico, with its mineral, ocean-breeze finish.

◉ Valpolicella

The 'valley of many cellars', from which Valpolicella gets its name, has been in the business of wine production since the ancient Greeks introduced their *passito* technique (the use of partially dried grapes) to create the blockbuster flavours we still enjoy in the region's Amarone and Recioto wines.

Situated in the foothills of Monti Lessini, the valleys benefit from a happy microclimate created by the enormous body of Lake Garda to the west and cooling breezes from the Alps to the north. No wonder Veronese nobility got busy building showy weekend retreats here. Many of them, like the extraordinary **Villa della Torre** (045 683 20 60; www.villadellatorre.it; Via della Torre 25, Fumane; guided tour €10, with wine tasting & snack €30-40; villa tours 11am & 4pm Mon-Sat by appointment; P), still house noble wineries, while others, like **Villa Spinosa** (045 750 00 93; www.villaspinosa.it; Via Colle Masua 12, Negrar; apt per 2 people €90-130, per 4 people €180-210, minimum 2-night stay; wine shop 10am-noon & 3-6pm Mon-Fri year-round, also

10am-noon Sat mid-Apr–mid-Oct, wine tastings by appointment; [P]), provide very comfortable accommodation.

Five *comuni* (local councils) compose the DOC quality-controlled area: Fumane, Negrar, San Pietro in Cariano, Sant'Ambrogio di Valpolicella and Marano di Valpolicella.

ALLEGRINI   WINERY

([☎]045 683 20 11; http://allegrini.it; Via Giare 9/11, Fumane; wine tasting & cellar tour €20, tour of villa €10, tour of villa with wine tasting & snack €30-40; ⊙cellar tour & wine tasting 10.30am & 3.30pm Mon-Fri by appointment, villa tours 11am & 4pm Mon-Sat by appointment; [P]) One of the leading wineries of the Valpolicella region, the Allegrini family have been tending vines in Fumane, Sant'Ambrogio and San Pietro since the 16th century. Pride of place goes to the *cru* wines produced from Corvinia and Rondinella grapes grown on the La Grola hillside (La Poja, La Grola and Palazzo della Torre). Wine-tastings in the historic 16th-century **Villa della Torre** are a fabulous experience.

ZÝMĒ   WINERY

([☎]045 770 11 08; www.zyme.it; Via Cà del Pipa 1, San Pietro in Cariano; wine tastings €15; ⊙shop 9am-5pm Mon-Sat, tastings by appointment 9am-noon & 2-6pm Mon-Sat) An award-winning winery with striking contemporary architecture by Moreno Zurlo, an ancient quarry-turned-cellar, and a reputation for bold, big-blend wines. The most famous of these is Zýmē's signature Harlequin, a thrilling, opulent IGP wine made using 15 local grape varieties (11 red, four white). Book wine tastings in advance; around three weeks for Saturday tastings, and around 10 days for weekday tastings.

PIEVE DI SAN GIORGIO   CHURCH

(San Giorgio, Valpolicella; ⊙7am-6pm) [FREE] In the tiny hilltop village of San Giorgio a few kilometres northwest of San Pietro in Cariano, you'll find this fresco-filled, cloistered 8th-century Romanesque church. Not old enough for you? In the little garden to its left you can also see a few fragments of an ancient Roman temple.

✖ EATING & DRINKING

★ TRATTORIA CAPRINI   TRATTORIA €€

([☎]045 750 05 11; www.trattoriacaprini.it; Via Zanotti 9, Negrar; meals €30; ⊙noon-2.30pm & 7-10pm Thu-Tue) In the centre of Negrar, family-run Caprini serves heart-warming grub you wish your mama could make. Many items on the menu are homemade, including the delicious *lasagnetta* with hand-rolled pasta, and a *ragù* of beef, tomato, porcini and finferli mushrooms. Downstairs, beside the fire of the old *pistoria* (bakery), you can sample some 200 Valpolicella labels.

★ ENOTECA DELLA VALPOLICELLA   VENETIAN €€

([☎]045 683 91 46; www.enotecadellavalpolicella. it; Via Osan 47, Fumane; meals €25; ⊙noon-2.30pm Sun, noon-2.30pm & 7.30-10pm Tue-Sat) Gastronomes flock to the town of Fumane, just a few kilometres north of San Pietro in Cariano, where an ancient farmhouse has found renewed vigor as a rustically elegant restaurant. Put your trust in gracious owners Ada and Carlotta, who will eagerly guide you through the day's menu, a showcase for fresh, local produce.

LOCANDA LO SCUDO   MODERN ITALIAN €€

([☎]045 768 07 66; www.loscudo.vr.it; Via Covergnino 9, Soave; meals €35, s/d €65/80; ⊙noon-2.30pm & 7.30-10.30pm Tue-Sat, noon-2.30pm Sun; [☎]) Just outside the medieval walls of Soave, Lo Scudo is half country inn and half high-powered gastronomy. Cult classics include a risotto of scallops and porcini mushrooms, though – if it's on the menu – only a fool would resist the extraordinary dish of tortelloni stuffed with local pumpkin, Grana Padano, cinnamon, mustard and Amaretto, and topped with crispy fried sage.

DAY TRIPS FROM VENICE VERONA'S WINE COUNTRY

...he sound of lagoon waters
...'s an unforgettable experience –
...nd hotels are no longer your only
...homes as locande (guesthouses),
...iday rental apartments.

...nd August also bring bargains, though
...ly not as substantial. Even in high sea-
...midweek rates tend to be lower than
...end ones. By contrast, expect to pay a
...premium during Carnevale, New Year's
...Easter.

...tes cited here should be considered a
...e, since hotels often make constant ad-
...ents according to season, day of week
...olidays of varying importance.

...nities

...neral, rooms tend to be small in Venice –
...ometimes dark or awkwardly shaped as
...he quirks of ancient *palazzi*. Unless oth-
...e stated, guestrooms come with private
...room, often with a shower rather than
...htub. Business centres are rarely well
...ped, even in swanky hotels. Only a few
...hotels have a pool – mostly on the Lido.
...e increasingly available, wi-fi doesn't
...ys penetrate thick stone walls and may
...be available in common areas.

...er Beware

...ll hotels in Venice are grand: some are
...ped, frayed and draughty, with lacka-
...al service. Budget and midrange places
...d the train station tend to be especially
...y – sometimes despite glowing internet
...ws'. Note also that many hotels boast of
...tian-style' rooms. Sometimes this im-
...real antiques and Murano chandeliers,
...can mean a kitsch version of baroque
...oms whose former charms have been re-
...lled out of existence.

Lonely Planet's Top Choices

Novecento (p190) Plush, bohemian-chic getaway ideal for modern Marco Polos.

Al Ponte Antico (p195) A silk-swathed *palazzo* with dreamy views of the Rialto bridge.

Oltre Il Giardino (p193) Stylish secret-garden hideaway in the heart of Venice.

Hotel Palazzo Barbarigo (p194) Dark, plush elegance right on the Grand Canal.

Corte di Gabriela (p191) Cool, contemporary interiors framed by 19th-century elegance.

Best by Budget

€

Albergo San Samuele (p189) Rock-bottom prices right by Palazzo Grassi.

B&B Corte Vecchia (p191) A simple, stylish bargain close to major masterpieces.

Gen Venice (p197) Contemporary hostel cool with canal views.

Allo Squero (p194) Cannaregio home comforts.

€€

Hotel Flora (p189) A classy, ivy-covered retreat that outdoes grander neighbours.

Al Ponte Mocenigo (p193) Courtyard tranquility and period details across a petite bridge.

Hotel Sant'Antonin (p196) A grand merchant home in a flower-filled garden.

Venissa (p198) Farmhouse chic and gourmet treats.

€€€

Gritti Palace (p190) Grand Canal rooms in a doge's palace.

Oltre Il Giardino (p193) A

romantic garden retreat once home to Alma Mahler's widow.

Al Ponte Antico (p195) Old world glamour accompanied by gracious service.

Novecento (p190) Spice route style enjoyed by the international set.

Best Design or Boutique Hotel

Corte di Gabriela (p191) Design greats bring palace living into the 21st century.

Hotel Palazzo Barbarigo (p194) A decadent concoction of smoky mirrors and curvaceous deco accents.

iQS (p196) A moody colour palette, uplifted textural details and canal reflections.

Domus Orsoni (p194) Bedrooms full of glittering mosaic details.

Most Romantic

Al Ponte Antico (p195) A Grand Canal hideaway worthy of Casanova.

Locanda Cipriani (p198) Rustic style and a rose garden.

Oltre Il Giardino (p193) Effortless elegance with a whimsical, artistic soul.

Bloom & 7 Cielo (p190) Extravagant decor for passionate hearts.

Best Heritage

Gritti Palace (p190) Prestigious hotel full of opulent details.

Hotel Danieli (p196) As eccentric and long-lasting as Venice itself.

Palazzo Abadessa (p195) A frescoed palace ready for romance since 1540.

Oltre il Giardino (p193) A 1920s garden villa with historic touches.

NEED TO KNOW

Price Ranges

Price ranges are for standard double rooms with private bathroom and breakfast included.

€ less than €110

€€ €110–200

€€€ over €200

Reservations

➡ Book ahead at weekends and any time during high season.

➡ The best, and best-value, hotels are always in high demand; book well ahead.

➡ Check individual hotel websites for increasingly common online deals.

➡ Confirm arrival at least 72 hours in advance, especially during high season.

Getting to Your Hotel

➡ Pack light to better negotiate twisting alleys, footbridges and narrow staircases.

➡ Try to arrive during daylight to avoid getting lost in night-time Venice.

➡ Get directions from your hotel, plus a detailed map.

➡ Though expensive, water-taxis can be worth the price for night arrivals or if you're heavily laden.

Breakfast

Except in higher-end places, breakfast tends to be utilitarian. *Affittacamere* (rooms for rent) generally don't offer breakfast because of strict dining codes. However, you're never far from a great local cafe.

Where to Stay

NEIGHBOURHOOD	FOR	AGAINST
San Marco	Historic and design hotels in central location, optimal for sightseeing and shopping.	Rooms often small with little natural light; streets crowded and noisy in the morning; fewer good restaurant options.
Dorsoduro	Lively art and student scenes, with design hotels near museums and seaside getaways along Zattere.	Lively student scene can mean noise echoing from Campo Santa Margherita until 2am, especially on weekends.
San Polo & Santa Croce	Top value on spacious B&Bs and opulent boutique hotels with prime local dining, Rialto markets, drinking and shopping; convenient to train and bus.	Easy to get lost in maze of streets, and it may be a long walk to major sights and a *vaporetto* stop.
Cannaregio	Venice's best deals on B&Bs with character and hotels convenient to the train and bus stop, with canal-bank happy hours and restaurants frequented by locals.	Long walk or *vaporetto* ride to San Marco sightseeing; pedestrian traffic between train station and Rialto.
Castello	Calmer and fewer tourists as you move away from San Marco; good budget options close to San Marco and the park.	The eastern fringes near Sant'Elena are far away from key sights and devoid of services.
Giudecca, Lido & the Southern Islands	Good value for money; beaches within walking distance in summer; fewer tourists.	Far from the action, especially at night; must rely on expensive *vaporetti* and less-frequent services at night.
Murano, Burano & the Northern Islands	Murano is a crowd-free, good value alternative base within 10 minutes of Cannaregio. Outer islands are remote, but great for gourmet weekend retreats.	Limited eating and drinking options; outer islands are far from Venice; very quiet in low season.

📖 San Marco

GIÒ & GIÒ
B&B €

Map p268 (📞347 3665016; www.giogiovenice. com; Calle delle Ostreghe 2439; d €90-155; ✸🛜; 🚤Santa Maria del Giglio) Restrained baroque sounds like an oxymoron, but here you have it: burl-wood bedsteads, pearl-grey silk draperies, polished parquet floors and spotlit art. Packaged breakfasts are available in the shared kitchen. Ideally located near Piazza San Marco, along a side canal; angle for rooms overlooking the gondola stop, and wake to choruses of '*Volare, oh-oh-oooooh!*'

LOCANDA CASA PETRARCA
B&B €

Map p268 (📞041 520 04 30; www.casapetrarca. com; Calle Schiavine 4386; d €105-155, without bathroom €80-125; ✸; 🚤Rialto) A budget option with heart and character, this family-run place offers seven unfussy, sparkling rooms in a historic brick apartment building, with breakfast serenades from passing gondolas. Five rooms have air-con and en suite bathrooms; rooms facing the side canal are brighter and slightly bigger. Fair warning: the route to nearby Piazza San Marco is lined with tempting boutiques.

ALBERGO SAN SAMUELE
HOTEL €

Map p268 (📞041 852 14 15; www.hotelsansamu ele.com; Salizzada San Samuele 3358; s €30-50, d €35-80; 🚤San Samuele) The one star San Samuele is one of San Marco's most affordable accommodation options. These neat digs, wrapped around a central courtyard, offer 10 simple, en suite rooms furnished with firm beds and brightened up with graphic posters from the 1930s. There's no air-con and breakfast isn't served, but you're steps away from café-fringed Campo San Stefano. Book at least a month in advance.

HOTEL AI DO MORI
HOTEL €

Map p268 (📞041 520 48 17; www.hotelaido mori.com; Calle Larga San Marco 658; d €50-150; ✸🛜; 🚤San Zaccaria) Artist's garrets just off Piazza San Marco, each as snug as an Arsenale ship's cabin. Book ahead to score upper-floor rooms with sloped wood-beamed ceilings, parquet floors, wall tapestries and close-up views of basilica domes and the clock tower's Do Mori (bell ringers) in action. Ask for No 11, with a private terrace – but pack light, because there's no lift.

LOCANDA ART DECO
B&B €

Map p268 (📞041 277 05 58; www.locandaart deco.com; Calle delle Botteghe 2966; d €50-120; ✸🛜; 🚤Accademia) Rakishly handsome, cream-coloured guestrooms with terrazzo marble floors, antique tables and comfy beds in wrought-iron bed frames. Wood-beamed lofts are romantic hideaways, if you don't mind low ceilings and stairs. Honeymooners may prefer the Locanda's apartments with hotel perks (kitchenettes, in-room breakfast, maid service). The B&B annexe is less charming, but cheaper.

★HOTEL FLORA
HOTEL €€

Map p268 (📞041 520 58 44; www.hotelflora. it; Calle Bergamaschi 2283a; d €105-365; ✸🛜; 🚤Santa Maria del Giglio) Down a lane from glitzy Calle Larga XXII Marzo, this ivy-covered retreat quietly outclasses brash designer neighbours with its delightful tearoom, breakfasts around the garden fountain and gym offering shiatsu massage. Guestrooms feature antique mirrors, fluffy duvets atop hand-carved beds, and tiled en suite baths with apothecary-style amenities. Damask-clad superior rooms overlook the garden. Strollers and kids' teatime complimentary; babysitting available.

PALAZZO PARUTA
HOTEL €€

Map p268 (📞041 241 08 35; www.palazzo paruta.com; Campo Sant'Angelo 3824; d €120-350; ✸🛜; 🚤Sant'Angelo) Kissing frogs won't get you princely palace getaways like this: lantern-lit courtyard staircases beckon to silken boudoir bedrooms with mirrored bedsteads and Carrara marble en suite baths. Museum-worthy suites feature velvet-draped beds, stuccoed ceilings and parquet floors; ask for marble fireplaces and canal views. Breakfasts seduce gourmets with freshly squeezed juices, award-winning local cheeses and cured meats, fresh pastries, pancakes and eggs.

B&B AL TEATRO
B&B €€

Map p268 (📞333 9182494; www.bedandbreak fastalteatro.com; Fondamenta de la Fenice 2554; d €90-210; 🛜; 🚤Santa Maria del Giglio) With La Fenice for your neighbour and a chorus of singing *gondolieri* passing beneath your windows, you'll need to book early to nab one of the three rooms in Eleanora's 15th century family home. Inside, old world elegance meets a minimalist style with wrought iron beds dressed in white linens, shapely walnut wardrobes and Murano chandeliers. Eleanora hosts breakfast every morning tossing out recommendations over freshly brewed coffee.

BLOOM & 7 CIELO
B&B €€

Map p268 (✆340 1498872; www.bloom-venice. com; Campiello Santo Stefano 3470; d €168-290; ❋; ⬤Accademia) Fraternal-twin B&Bs occupy two upper floors of a historic home overlooking Santo Stefano right across the *calle* (alleyway). Bloom offers glam-rock rooms in shocking scarlet, fuchsia and gold damask with leather bedsteads and full-frontal cathedral views. Downstairs, 7 Cielo (Seventh Heaven) is artfully romantic, with exposed-brick walls and Murano glass mosaic bathrooms. Take breakfast on the sunny top-floor terrace.

LOCANDA ORSEOLO
B&B €€

Map p268 (✆041 520 48 27; www.locandaorse olo.com; Corte Zorzi 1083; d €150-290; ❋@🛜; ⬤Vallaresso) Hide out behind Piazza San Marco: no one will know but the *gondolieri*, who regularly row past the lobby. Consistently warm greetings and cosy wood-trimmed rooms – some with vintage-kitsch Carnevale murals – make this the ideal launch pad. Upgrade to canal views, and don't try to resist owner Barbara's home-made crêpes at breakfast. Babysitting, restaurant and concert bookings available.

CA' DEL NOBILE
HOTEL €€

Map p268 (✆041 528 34 73; www.cadelnobile. com; Rio Terà delle Colonne 987; d €80-270; ❋🛜; ⬤San Marco) Move over, Casanova – Casa del Nobile makes romantic getaways behind Piazza San Marco easy. The exposed-brick Casanova room has a canopied bed; cosy standards have wood-beamed ceilings and sleigh beds; deluxe rooms have room for daybeds and cribs. Mention you're celebrating your anniversary or wedding when booking, and strewn rose petals may await your arrival. Fresh breakfast pastries, but no views.

HOTEL AL CODEGA
HOTEL €€

Map p268 (✆041 241 46 21; www.hotelalcodega. com; Corte del Forno Vecchio 4435; d €102-315; ❋🛜; ⬤Rialto) Unicorns are easier to find in Venice than a quiet, affordable, well-lit, family-run hotel five minutes' walk to Piazza San Marco – yet here you have it. Veer off boutique-lined Calle Goldoni, duck under the *sotoportego* (archway), and this flower-trimmed yellow inn greets you in the courtyard. Request sunny courtyard-facing rooms or the easy-access ground-floor Casanova room (there's no lift).

★GRITTI PALACE
HOTEL €€€

Map p268 (✆041 79 46 11; www.thegrittipal ace.com; Campo di Santa Maria del Giglio 2467; d €395-700, ste from €1200; ❋🛜; ⬤Santa Maria del Giglio) Guests at the Gritti Palace on the Grand Canal don't have to leave their balconies to go sightseeing: this landmark 1525 doge's palace sports Landmark Grand Canal rooms with Rubelli silk damask lining, antique fainting couches, stucco ceilings, hand-painted vanities and bathrooms sheathed in rare marble. Luxury hotel specialist Starwood manages operations to international standards, and chef Daniele Turco creates inspired Venetian trade-route cuisine for fabulous dockside meals.

★NOVECENTO
BOUTIQUE HOTEL €€€

Map p268 (✆041 241 37 65; www.novecento. biz; Calle del Dose 2683/84; d €160-340; ❋🛜; ⬤Santa Maria del Giglio) Sporting a boho-chic look, the Novocento is a real charmer. Its

LONGER-TERM RENTALS

For longer stays and groups of three or more, renting an apartment is an economical option that gives you the freedom to cook your own meals. To rent a studio for yourself, expect to pay €800 to €1200 per month. Aside from **Airbnb** (www.airbnb.co.uk) there are also several Venice-only dedicated websites:

Venetian Apartments (www.venice-rentals.com) Arranges accommodation in flats, often of a luxurious nature. Two- to four-person apartments start at around €895 per week.

Views on Venice (www.viewsonvenice.com) A collection of 70 apartments picked for their personality, character and view, of course. Rentals start around €1000 per week.

Luxrest-Venice (www.luxrest-venice.com) A carefully curated, handpicked selection of apartments starting at €950 per week.

nine individually designed rooms ooze style with Turkish kilim pillows, Fortuny draperies and 19th-century carved bedsteads. Outside, its garden is a lovely spot to linger over breakfast. Want more? You can go for a massage at sister property Hotel Flora, take a hotel-organised course in landscape drawing, or mingle with creative fellow travellers around the honesty bar.

CORTE DI GABRIELA   DESIGN HOTEL €€€

Map p268 (☑041 523 50 77; www.cortedigabriela.com; Calle degli Avvocati 3836; d €300-470; ❇❡; ⬆Sant'Angelo) Yes, Corte di Gabriela is a 19th century *palazzo*, but there's nothing old or traditional about its 11 rooms, which inventively play with the palace's historic features, combining frescoed ceilings and terrazzo floors with contemporary design pieces, high-spec finishes and a modern colour palette of mauve, ochre, chocolate and pea green. The views are undeniably romantic, and the atmosphere sophisticated. No children under 16 years of age.

🛏 Dorsoduro

★B&B CORTE VECCHIA   B&B €

Map p272 (☑041 822 12 33; www.cortevecchia.net; Rio Terà San Vio 462; s €60-100, d €100-130; ❇❡; ⬆Accademia) Corte Vecchia is a stylish steal, run by young architects Antonella and Mauro and a stone's throw from Peggy Guggenheim, Accademia and Punta della Dogana. Choose from a snug single with en suite, or two good-sized doubles: one with en suite, the other with an external private bathroom. All are simple yet understatedly cool, with contemporary and vintage objects, and a tranquil, shared lounge.

HOTEL GALLERIA   INN €

Map p272 (☑041 523 24 89; www.hotelgalleria.it; Campo della Carità 878a; d €140-240; ❡; ⬆Accademia) Smack on the Grand Canal alongside the Ponte dell'Accademia is this classic hotel in a converted 18th-century mansion. Book ahead, especially for rooms 7 and 9, small doubles overlooking the Grand Canal. Room 10 sleeps six and comes with an original ceiling fresco. Renovations were underway at the time of research to give all rooms their own private bathroom.

B&B DORSODURO 461   B&B €

Map p272 (☑041 582 61 72; www.dorsoduro461.com; Rio Terà San Vio 461; d €80-130; ❇❡;

⬆Accademia) Get to know Venice from the inside out at Sylvia and Francesco's homestyle B&B, around the corner from Peggy Guggenheim's place. Your hosts' shared love of books, antique restoration and design is obvious in the bookshelf-lined breakfast room and three well-curated guestrooms, with Kartell lamps perched atop 19th-century poker tables. Aside from cooking tasty bacon and eggs, English-speaking violin-maker Francesco dishes up excellent Venice tips.

LOCANDA CA' DEL BROCCHI   B&B €

Map p272 (☑041 522 69 89; www.cadelbrocchi.it; Rio Terà San Vio 470; d €109-199; ❒❇❡; ⬆Accademia) A colourful character inhabiting a quiet side street in Dorsoduro's museum district, Ca' del Brocchi has small yet over-the-top baroque-styled rooms – tasselled, gilt to the hilt and upholstery belaboured, with matching scrollwork wallpaper. Lower-level rooms have porthole-sized windows; better options have garden views, balconies and/or Jacuzzi tubs. Babysitting and cradles are available for families.

B&B LEONARDO   B&B €

Map p272 (☑347 6805871; www.bebleonardo.com; Calle delle Botteghe 3153; d €60-180, tr €80-250; ❇❡; ⬆Ca' Rezzonico) Take a break from baroque in this serene, simple retreat overlooking Ca' Rezzonico's formal garden. Two snug, ship-shape guestrooms await upstairs (no lift), with televisions stashed in deco dressers and compact private bathrooms. Rates rarely hit maximum and a basic breakfast is included.

SILK ROAD   HOSTEL €

Map p272 (☑388 1196816; www.silkroadhostel.com; Zattere 1420e; dm €27, d €60; ❡; ⬆San Basilio) Breathe easy along the Giudecca Canal in this clean, hassle-free hostel, complete with communal kitchen, wi-fi and, best of all, no curfew. Both of the airy, four-bed dorms (one mixed-gender, one female-only) come with water views, and there's one private room to boot. The hostel is down the block from a supermarket, canalfront cafes and *gelaterie*, plus handy *vaporetto* stops.

★PENSIONE ACCADEMIA VILLA MARAVEGE   INN €€

Map p272 (☑041 521 01 88; www.pensione accademia.it; Fondamenta Bollani 1058; d €145-340; ❇❡; ⬆Accademia) Step through the ivy-covered gate of this 17th-century garden villa just off the Grand Canal, and you'll forget you're a block from the Accademia. Although some of the 27 guestrooms are rather small, all are effortlessly elegant, with parquet floors, antique desks and shiny bathrooms – one even comes with four-poster bed, wood-beamed ceilings and glimpses of the canal.

Ask for Thelma, a superior double with its own patch of greenery, named after a regular who loved reading in the garden. Buffet breakfasts are served on the lawn in summer, sunsets are toasted with a complimentary drink at the bar, and garden swings for two promise romance under the stars. Wheelchair-accessible rooms and wheelchair use upon request; laundry service available for an additional fee.

LOCANDA SAN BARNABA   B&B €€

Map p272 (🖉041 241 12 33; www.locanda-san barnaba.com; Calle del Traghetto 2785-6; d €120-185; ❄ 🛜; 🚤Ca' Rezzonico) The stage is set for intrigue at this 16th-century *palazzo* (mansion), with its frescoed grand salon, hidden courtyard garden and cupboards concealing a secret staircase. Ask for the romantic wood-beamed Poeta Fanatico room; Campiello, with skylight views of a neighbouring bell tower; or the superior Il Cavaliere e la Dama, for 18th-century frescoed ceilings and balconies dangling over the canal.

PALAZZO GUARDI   B&B €€

Map p272 (🖉041 296 07 25; www.palazzoguardi venice.com; Calle del Pistor 995; d €114-229; ❄ @🛜; 🚤Accademia) Relive the Renaissance at 15th-century Palazzo Guardi, right around the corner from Accademia – you're never more than a minute away from a Titian masterpiece or glass of Amarone. Dashing baroque-style guestrooms with modern baths accommodate two to five guests, but only the suites and breakfast room have canal vistas worthy of a Guardi painting.

LA CHICCA   B&B €€

Map p272 (🖉041 522 55 35; www.lachicca-ven ezia.com; Calle Franchi 644; d €70-200; ❄🛜; 🚤Accademia) It's wedged among Dorsoduro's trifecta of museums – Accademia, Peggy Guggenheim and Punta della Dogana – yet all you'll hear at night in this elegant B&B is the lapping of the canal at the end of the *calle*. Hosts Sabrina and Massimo are helpful, their Venetian damask-clad, terrazzo-

floored guestrooms spacious and blessedly uncluttered after a museum binge.

LA CALCINA   INN €€

Map p272 (🖉041 520 64 66; www.lacalcina.com; Zattere 780; d €100-370; ❄ @🛜; 🚤Zattere) Upgrade from ordinary seaside resorts to La Calcina, with breezy roof-garden breakfasts, a canal-dock restaurant, and panoramas of Palladio's Redentore church across Giudecca Canal. Antique armoires and brocade bedspreads come standard with airy, parquet-floored guestrooms. Bathrooms are clean though tired and uninspiring. Book ahead for waterfront rooms – especially No 2, where John Ruskin wrote his classic (though inexplicably Palladio-bashing) 1876 *The Stones of Venice.*

CA' PISANI   DESIGN HOTEL €€€

Map p272 (🖉041 240 14 11; www.capisanihotel. it; Rio Terà Antonio Foscarini 979a; d €210-351; ❄ @🛜; 🚤Accademia) Sprawl out in style right behind the Accademia, and luxuriate in sleigh beds, Jacuzzi tubs and walk-in closets. Mood lighting and sound-proofed walls make downstairs deco-accented rooms right for romance, while families appreciate top-floor rooms with sleeping lofts. Venetian winters require in-house Turkish steam baths, while summers mean roof-terrace sunning and patio breakfasts. A hushed, elegant, antiques-laced retreat.

🛏 San Polo & Santa Croce

CA' DELLA CORTE   B&B €

Map p277 (🖉041 715 877; www.cadellacorte. com; Campo Surian 3560, Santa Croce; d €75-170; ❄🛜; 🚤Piazzale Roma) Live like a Venetian in this 16th-century family home near Campo Santa Margherita, yours with a Liberty frescoed salon, adjacent piano room, self-service bar, top-floor terrace overlooking Gothic palaces, and breakfasts delivered to your room. Stay in wood-beamed garrets, chandelier-lit superior rooms or feng-shui eco-rooms. Sporty types should ask helpful staff to organise sailing, tennis, and horse-riding on the Lido; babysitting and shiatsu massage are also available.

AL GALLION   B&B €

Map p274 (🖉380 4520466, 041 524 47 43; www. algallion.com; Calle Gallion 1126, Santa Croce; d €75-110; 🛜; 🚤San Biasio) A couple of bridges away at train-station hotels, weary tourists wait at front desks – while in this 16th-century family home, you'll be chatting and sipping espresso in the living room. The whitewashed guestroom (which can be divided in two and turned into a quad) is handsomely furnished with walnut desks, cheerful yellow bedspreads, terrazzo floors and host Daniela's family art collection. Breakfasts are homemade spreads; tasty, affordable restaurants abound nearby.

AL PONTE MOCENIGO
HOTEL €€

Map p274 (☑041 524 47 97; www.alpontemoceni go.com; Fondamenta Rimpetto Mocenigo 2063, Santa Croce; d €85-170; ❊❖; ⌖San Stae) A doge of a deal near the Grand Canal, just steps from San Stae *vaporetto* stop, with prime dining and a handful of museums nearby. Reached via a petite bridge, this little oasis offers elegant guestrooms, some with Murano chandeliers illuminating high wood-beamed ceilings, four-poster beds, gilt-edged armoires and salon seating. Ask for rooms overlooking Rio San Stae or the courtyard.

CA' ANGELI
BOUTIQUE HOTEL €€

Map p274 (☑041 523 24 80; www.caangeli. it; Calle del Traghetto de la Madoneta 1434, San Polo; d €95-225, ste from €200; ❊❖; ⌖San Silvestro) Murano glass chandeliers, a Louis XIV love-seat and namesake 16th-century angels set a refined tone at this restored, canalside *palazzo*. Guestrooms are a picture with beamed ceilings, antique carpets and big bathrooms, while the dining room looks out onto the Grand Canal. Breakfast includes organic products where possible.

DOMINA HOME CA' ZUSTO
BOUTIQUE HOTEL €€

Map p274 (☑041 524 29 91; www.dominava canze.it; Campo Rielo 1358, Santa Croce; d €195-250; ❊❖; ⌖Riva di Biasio) Gothic goes pop at this palace, whose stately Veneto-Byzantine exterior disguises a colourful wild streak. Designer Gianmarco Cavagnino serves up 22 mod-striped, harem-styled suites named after Turkish princesses. Pedestal tables flank baroque beds fit for pashas, and Jacuzzis soothe frazzled darlings in the deluxe rooms. Wi-fi only available on the 1st floor.

HOTEL AL DUCA
HOTEL €€

Map p274 (☑041 812 30 69; www.alducadiven ezia.com; Fontego dei Turchi 1739, Santa Croce; d €80-300; ❊@❖; ⌖San Stae) Bedrooms swagged with red damask and black Mu-

STUDENT STAYS

From July to mid-September, **ESU** (☑041 524 67 42; www.esuvenezia.it), the city's student administration agency, opens its residences to students and academics visiting town. Singles, doubles and triples are available. Prices run around €25 to €35 per person per night. Residence halls are located in Cannaregio, Castello, San Polo, Dorsoduro and Giudecca.

rano chandeliers are Venetian bordello-chic, honouring the courtesans that once ruled nearby Rialto backstreets – but all-bronze guestrooms are serene Serenissima retreats. Get an insider's view of Venice at family-friendly kitchenette apartments, conveniently close to Campo San Giacomo dell'Orio happy hours. Reception open 24 hours; babysitting, laundry and wheelchair-accessible guestrooms available.

CAMPIELLO ZEN
B&B €€

Map p274 (☑041 71 03 65; www.campiellozen. com; Rio Terà 1285, Santa Croce; d €160-190, ste €190-210; ❊❖; ⌖Riva de Biasio) Hotels would have you believe Venetians live a twee existence in fussy brocade-upholstered pink salons, but this B&B in a traditional family home treats guests to comfortable beds, handsome antique wardrobes, quirky wall niches and every modern convenience, especially in the bathrooms. The high-ceilinged upstairs suite accommodates a third bed (fee applies). Handy to train and *vaporetto*, but blissfully off the tourist track.

PENSIONE GUERRATO
PENSION €€

Map p274 (☑041 528 59 27; www.pensioneguer rato.it; Calle Drio la Scimia 240a, San Polo; d/tr/q €145/165/185; ❊❖; ⌖Rialto Mercato) In a 1227 tower that was once a hostel for knights headed to the Third Crusade, the smart guestrooms here haven't lost their sense of history – some have frescoes or glimpses of the Grand Canal. Sparkling modern bathrooms, a prime Rialto Market location and helpful owners add to the package. No lift.

The owners also have a couple of apartments (€180 to €240) with kitchens.

★OLTRE IL GIARDINO
BOUTIQUE HOTEL €€€

Map p274 (☑041 275 00 15; www.oltreilgiardino-venezia.com; Fondamenta Contarini, San Polo

2542; d €180-250, ste €200-500; ❄☎; ❖San Tomà) Live the dream in this garden villa, the 1920s home of Alma Mahler, the composer's widow. Hidden behind a lush walled garden, its six high-ceilinged guestrooms marry historic charm with modern comfort: marquetry composer's desks, candelabras and 19th-century poker chairs sit alongside flat-screen TVs and designer bathrooms, while outside, pomegranate trees flower in the garden.

★**HOTEL PALAZZO BARBARIGO**　　　　　　　DESIGN HOTEL €€€

Map p274 (☎041 740 172; www.palazzobarbarigo. com; Grand Canal 2765, San Polo; d €240-440; ❄☎; ❖San Tomà) Brooding, chic and seductive, Barbarigo delivers 18 plush guestrooms combining modern elegance and masquerade intrigue – think dark, contemporary furniture, sumptuous velvets, feathered lamps and the odd fainting couch. Whether you opt for junior suites overlooking the Grand Canal (get triple-windowed Room 10) or standard rooms overlooking Rio di San Polo, indulge in sleek bathrooms, positively royal breakfasts and smart, attentive service.

🛏 Cannaregio

★**ALLO SQUERO**　　　　　　　　　　　　　B&B €

Map p278 (☎041 523 69 73; www.allosquero.it; Corte dello Squero 4692; s €60-80, d €90-120; ☎; ❖Fondamenta Nuove) Dock for the night at this historic gondola *squero* (shipyard), recently converted into a garden retreat. Gondolas passing along two canals are spotted from modern, sunny upstairs guestrooms, with terrazzo marble floors and sleek mosaic-striped en suite baths, some with tubs. Hosts Andrea and Hiroko offer Venice-insider tips over cappuccino and pastry breakfasts in the fragrant, wisteria-filled garden. Cots and cribs available.

CASA BASEGGIO　　　　　　　　　　　　B&B €

Map p278 (☎041 099 40 79; www.casabaseg gio.it; Fondamenta dell'Abazia 3556; d €65-150; ☎; ❖Orto) *Venexianárse* (become Venetian) at this family home converted to a B&B in a quiet, untouristy Cannaregio corner handy to happy-hour hotspots along the Fondamenta della Misericordia. In fact, Marco and Alessandra's house is situated in a wing of the Misericordia abbey and from the 1st-floor bedroom there are views through the cypresses into the abbey garden. The highlight is breakfast in the garden, once part of the ancient cloister and now surrounded by well-tended flowers.

DOMUS ORSONI　　　　　　　　　　　　　B&B €€

Map p278 (☎041 275 95 38; www.domusor soni.it; Corte Vedei 1045; s €80-150, d €100-250; ❄@; ❖Guglie) Surprise: along a tranquil Ghetto lane and behind a rosy, historic facade is Venice's most original artist's retreat. Continental breakfasts are served in the palm-shaded garden near the Orsoni mosaic works, located here since 1885 – hence the custom mosaics glittering across walls, bathrooms and tables. Find artistic bliss in five mosaic-splashed guestrooms, or join Venetian crowds mid-toast around the corner.

CA' DOGARESSA　　　　　　　BOUTIQUE HOTEL €€

(☎041 275 9441; www.cadogaressa.com; Fondamenta di Cannaregio 1018; d €50-170; ste €125-300; ❄@☎; ❖Guglie) A splashy canalside inn with Venetian charm – princess beds, gilt mirrors, chandeliers – that won't drain your holiday budget. Roofterrace views and designer bathrooms are four star–worthy, and canalbank breakfasts beat most B&Bs. Your Antenori family hosts offer major hotel-chain perks, including 24-hour reception, laptops for in-room use and laundry service. The annexe is cheaper but smaller, with shared bathrooms.

3749 PONTE CHIODO　　　　　　　　　　B&B €€

Map p278 (☎041 241 39 35; www.pontechiodo. it; Fondamenta di San Felice 3749; d €70-180; ❄☎; ❖Ca' d'Oro) Dodge tourists taking selfies on Venice's only remaining bridge without parapets to arrive at this friendly B&B. All bridges in Venice were once like this before too many drunks took the plunge and the government decreed new safety measures. If you make it across you'll find smiling Mattia and four sweetly decorated rooms with period furnishings and views over the canal.

CA' POZZO　　　　　　　　　　　　　　　INN €€

Map p278 (☎041 524 05 04; www.capozzoinn. com; Sotoportego Ca' Pozzo 1279; d €90-230; ❄@☎; ❖Guglie) Recover from Venice's sensory onslaught at this minimalist-chic hotel near the Ghetto. Sleek, contemporary guestrooms feature platform beds, abstract artwork and cube-shaped bathroom fixtures. Some have balconies, two accommodate disabled guests, and sprawling No 208 could house a Damien Hirst entourage. Laundry, concert-booking and ticket-printing services available.

RESIDENZA CA' RICCIO   B&B €€
Map p278 (☑041 528 23 34; www.cariccio.com; Campo dei Miracoli 5394a; d €105-210; ❄@❢; ☻Fondamenta Nuove) The Riccio family's lovingly restored 14th-century residence is a hidden yet convenient getaway between the Rialto bridge and Fondamenta Nuove *vaporetto* stop. Seven rooms over two top floors overlook the courtyard, with simple wrought-iron beds, wood-beamed ceilings, Murano glass lamps, terracotta-tiled floors, and whitewashed walls. Restaurants are around the corner.

WE CROCIFERI   HOSTEL, APARTMENTS €€
Map p278 (☑041 528 61 03; www.we-crociferi.it; Campo dei Gesuiti 4878; s €96, d €109-120, 4-person apt €220-250; ❢; ☻Fondamente Nove) In contrast to the bombastic Gesuiti church next door, this convent-turned-barracks-turned-hostel provides minimalist, white rooms overlooking a serene arcaded courtyard. Used as university digs throughout the year, there's a friendly vibe to the place with an on-site cafe (breakfast isn't included), shop, laundry and mess hall. Most rooms have kitchens, but you'll need to rent cutlery (€12). A gym is planned for 2016.

★AL PONTE ANTICO   BOUTIQUE HOTEL €€€
Map p278 (☑041 241 19 44; www.alponteantico.it; Calle dell' Aseo 5768; d €240-430; ❢; ☻Rialto) Like a courtesan's boudoir, the Peruch's 16th century *palazzo* is swathed in damask wall coverings, heavy silk curtains and thick, plush carpets. A smiling host greets you at the padded, golden reception desk and whisks you up to the old-rose salon where guests gossip over coffee and *petit fours* in snug banquettes. Rooms are large and unabashedly lavish with enough gilt to satisfy Louis XIV; and in the evening romance blossoms on the terrace, framed by views of the Rialto bridge.

PALAZZO ABADESSA   BOUTIQUE HOTEL €€€
Map p278 (☑041 241 37 84; www.abadessa.com; Calle Priuli 4011; d €115-375; ❄❢; ☻Ca' d'Oro) Evenings seem enchanted in this opulent 1540 Venetian *palazzo*, with staff fluffing pillows, plying guests with *prosecco*, arranging water taxis to the opera and plotting irresistible marriage proposals. Classic

guestrooms feature kingly beds, silk damask-clad walls, Murano glass lamps and wood-beamed ceilings; go for baroque in frescoed superior rooms with 18th-century vanities and canal vistas. Breakfast is served in the tree-shaded, lily-perfumed garden.

🛏 Castello

★B&B SAN MARCO   B&B €
Map p280 (☑041 522 75 89; www.realvenice.it/smarco; Fondamente San Giorgio 3385l; d €70-135; ❄; ☻Pietà, Arsenale) One of the few genuine B&Bs in Venice. Alice and Marco welcome you warmly to their home overlooking Carpaccio's frescoed Scuola di San Giorgio Schiavoni. The 3rd-floor apartment (no elevator), with its parquet floors and large, bright windows, is furnished with family antiques and offers photogenic views over the terracotta rooftops and canals. Marco and Alice live upstairs, so they're always on hand with great recommendations.

FORESTERIA VALDESE   HOSTEL €
Map p280 (Palazzo Cavagnis; ☑041 528 67 97; www.foresteriavenezia.it; Castello 5170; dm €30-35, d €90-140, q €155-170; ☻Ospedale, San Zaccaria) Holy hostel: this rambling palace retreat owned by the Waldensian church has 1st-floor guestrooms with 18th-century frescoes by Bevilacqua, and canal views one floor up. Dorm beds are available only for families or groups; book well ahead. Rates include breakfast.

ALLOGGI BARBARIA   B&B €
Map p280 (☑041 522 27 50; www.alloggibarbaria.it; Calle delle Cappuccine 6573; s €40-80, d €50-120, q €110-170; ❄; ☻Ospedale) Located near the Fondamente Nuove, this *pensione* isn't easy to find – but that's part of its charm, and so are the intrepid fellow travellers you'll meet over breakfast on a shared balcony. All six rooms are simple but tidy, bright and airy, and rates rarely hit the quoted maximums. Giorgio and Fausto also maintain a great blog (see website for details), which is worth browsing before travelling.

LOCANDA SANT'ANNA   B&B €
Map p280 (☑041 528 64 66; www.locandasantanna.com; Corte del Bianco 269; s €35, d €45-100; ❄@; ☻Giardini) Escape the madding crowd on a quiet *campiello* (small square)

on the sleepy side of Castello. Antique vanities, marquetry bedsteads and parquet floors add character to spacious rooms, some with views of Isola San Pietro. A little terrace is ideal for sunny days, and the reading room makes a welcome retreat when lagoon mists roll in. Prices drop by 50% in low season.

★ HOTEL SANT'ANTONIN BOUTIQUE HOTEL €€
Map p280 (☏041 523 16 21; www.hotelsantan tonin.com; Fondamenta dei Furlani 3299; d €100-280; ❅ 🛜; ⛴San Zaccaria) Enjoy the patrician pleasures of a wealthy Greek merchant at this 16th century *palazzo* perched on a canal near the Greek church. Grand proportions make for light, spacious rooms with cool terrazzo floors, geranium-draped balconies, frescoed ceilings and impressive Baroque furnishings. Come breakfast and you can trip down the stone staircase and out into one of the largest private gardens in Venice, complete with a pretty stone pergola and gurgling fountain. A perfect option for families.

CA' DEI DOGI BOUTIQUE HOTEL €€
Map p280 (☏041 241 37 51; www.cadeidogi.it; Corte Santa Scolastica 4242; s €75-95, d €110-250; ❅ @; ⛴San Zaccaria) Even the nearby Bridge of Sighs can't dampen the high spirits of the sunny yellow Ca' Dei Dogi, with guestroom windows sneaking peeks into the convent cloisters next door. Streamlined, modern rooms look like ships' cabins, with tilted wood-beamed ceilings, dressers that look like steamer trunks, and compact mosaic-covered bathrooms – ask for the one with the terrace and Jacuzzi.

Friendly staff can arrange concert tickets, free trips to Murano and sunset gondola rides. Book well ahead.

RESIDENZA L'OSMARIN B&B €€
Map p280 (☏347 4501440; www.residenzadelos marin.com; Calle Rota 4960; d €109-180; ❅ 🛜; ⛴San Zaccaria) This three-bedroom B&B is extraordinarily good value considering it is barely 300m from Piazza San Marco. Rooms – one with a roof terrace and another with a courtyard-facing terrace – are quaintly decorated with quilted bedspreads, painted wardrobes and period furnishings. Hosts Elisabetta and Rodolfo make guests feel warmly welcome with slap-up breakfasts of homemade cakes, brioche and platters of ham and cheese.

HOTEL SANT'ELENA HOTEL €€
(☏041 271 78 11; www.hotelsantelena.com; Calle Buccari 10; d €105-225; ❅ 🛜; ⛴Sant'Elena) Retreat to this once holy convent that was later appropriated by the navy as a holiday resort for admirals. Clever them. It's quiet location, spacious halls, grassy cloister and ample, window-lined rooms are unusual for Venice. Inside a minimalist, modern style complements the 1930s Brutalist makeover while providing a high level of comfort and facilities. Families are particularly well catered for here with cribs, kids' menus, Nintendo and babysitting on tap. The hotel is also well located near the Parco delle Rimembranze and is a one-stop hop to the Lido.

★ IQS DESIGN HOTEL €€€
Map p280 (☏041 277 02 62; www.thecharming house.com; Campiello Querini Stampalia 4425; ste €289-€690; ❅ @ 🛜; ⛴San Zaccaria) Step out of your motor launch ahead of art-show aficionados and into the romantic lobby of iQS. These achingly cool suites designed by Mauro Mazzolini are arranged around an ancient Gothic courtyard and are hung with modern art and furnished in B&B Italia style. All four of them look out on the vivid teal waters of the Rio di Santa Maria Formosa, made even more luminous by the deliciously dark colour palate of the high-design interiors.

AQUA PALACE LUXURY HOTEL €€€
Map p280 (Palazzo Scalfarotto; ☏041 296 04 42; www.aquapalace.it; Calle de la Malvasia 5492; d €130-340, ste €160-500; ❅ @ 🛜; ⛴San Marco, San Zaccaria) With its exotic, spice-route vibe and burnished colour palate of gold, bronze and old grey, the Aqua Palace is a heady mixture of modern amenities and Eastern romance. Suites 'interpret' the distant past of Marco Polo, and with only 25 of them you can expect aristocratic proportions: acres of weighty fabric and bathrooms marbled within an inch of their lives. Complete with its own private gondola pier, this is the hotel for love birds.

HOTEL DANIELI HISTORIC HOTEL €€€
Map p280 (☏041 522 64 80; www.danielihotel venice.com; Riva degli Schiavoni 4196; d €380-700; ❅ @ 🛜; ⛴San Zaccaria) As eccentric and luxurious as Venice itself, the Danieli has attracted artistic bohemians, minor royalty and their millionaire lovers for over a century. The hotel sprawls along the lagoon in three landmark buildings: the 14th-century

casa vecchia (old house), built for Doge Enrico Dandolo, with frescoed, antique-filled rooms; the 18th-century, gilt to the hilt *casa nuova* (new house); and the Danielino, a Fascist edifice with a modern-luxe interior redesign by Jacques Garcia.

In summer weather, breakfast is served on the rooftop terrace, with its extraordinary views of San Marco and the lagoon. This is also *the* best place in Venice for summer sundowners. However, at these prices, the €15 surcharge for internet use seems churlish.

🛏 Giudecca, Lido & the Southern Islands

★ VILLA INES   B&B €€

Map p284 (☑041 526 72 26; www.villa-ines.com; Via Lazzaro Mocenigo 10, Lido; s €119-130, d €110-155, 3-bed apt €340; ❊❋🛜; 🚤Lido) Lilac hydrangeas, caution-orange violas and intensely perfumed rose bushes froth around this quintessential Liberty Lido villa. It's the home of the Seguso family so, as you'd expect, rooms come with top quality fittings: Seguso chandeliers, enormous damask-clad beds, flat-screen TVs and Jacuzzi bathtubs. Hostess Marika is a professional caterer and runs the Acquolina cookery school on-site. Ask at reception about lessons and tours of the Seguso glass factory on Murano.

AL REDENTORE DI VENEZIA APARTMENTS €€

Map p283 (☑041 522 94 02; www.alredentore divenezia.com; Fondamenta Ponte Longo 234a, Giudecca; 2-person apt €160-280; ❊🛜; 🚤Redentore) Within the shadow of Il Redentore, these fully serviced apartments offer divine views across the water to San Marco. From the travertine-marble lobby, up the ash-clad staircase to the anallergic pillows and high-end, courtesy bath products, Al Redentore has thought of it all.

LE GARZETTE   FARMSTAY €€

(☑041 712 16 53; www.legarzette.it; Lungomare Alberoni 32, Lido; s €70-80, d €90-120; ◷closed mid-Dec–mid-Jan; P❋; 🚤Lido) Nestled amid gardens overflowing with red radicchio, astringent fennel, handsome pumpkins and dark-green courgettes is the rust-red *agriturismo* of Renza and Salvatore. Book for lunch (p143), then retire to your comfortable room for a nap on your 19th-century bed as herb-scented sea breezes waft through the window. Bicycles are provided for free.

ALBERGO QUATTRO FONTANE HOTEL €€€

Map p284 (☑041 526 07 26; www.quattrofon tane.com; Via Quattro Fontane 16, Lido; s €110-210, d €155-290, apt €340-470; ◷summer; P❋@🛜; 🚤Lido) Strange but true: this alpine chalet is just a stone's throw from Lido beaches, and its shaded gardens swarm with film buffs during the festival. Celebrities are nothing new to this inn, with a chequered past as a casino frequented by

---

GIUDECCA'S BUDGET SLEEPS

With its ex-industrial buildings and cavernous monasteries, Giudecca offers some of Venice's best budget sleeps.

Ostello Jan Palach (Map p283; ☑041 522 13 21; www.ostellojanpalach.it; Fondamenta di San Giacomo 186; dm €24-30, d €50-55; ◷check-in 11.30am-noon & 4-8pm; 🛜; 🚤Redentore) Once school's out, this university halls of residence does duty as a excellent hostel offering shared and private twin rooms and a large communal kitchen. Rooms are simply and clinically furnished with a bed, study desk and the odd poster or two. The views of the Zattere and Salute, though, are superb.

Gen Venice (Map p283; ☑041 877 82 88; www.generatorhostels.com; Fondamenta delle Zitelle 86; dm €16-50, d €45-95; ◷check-in 3.30-10pm; ❋@🛜; 🚤Zitelle) Giudecca's Generator hostel rocks a sharp, contemporary interior including a fabulous bar-restaurant. Arrive promptly at 3.30pm to claim that perfect bunk by the window. Sheets, blanket, and a pillow are provided; breakfast is an additional €4.50.

Foresteria Redentore (Map p283; ☑041 522 53 96; www.campluisliving.it; Calle de le Cape 194; d €45; 🛜; 🚤Redentore) The rigorous monastic lives of the Redentore's Capuchin monks were surely eased by the view from their cells over the cypress lined garden. A recent revamp now gives access to the 48 simple, en suite rooms with kitchen and laundry facilities to boot.

royalty in the 16th century, and a tavern beloved of Robert Browning and his 19th-century bohemian crowd. Rooms are vast and unabashedly retro in the 1970s A-frame annexe; the original building offers more traditional quarters with charming wrought-iron beds.

Bicycle rental, laundry and babysitting services available.

🛏 Murano, Burano & the Northern Islands

IL LATO AZZURRO   INN €

(☎041 523 06 42; www.latoazzurro.it; Via Forti 13, Sant'Erasmo; dm €30, s €55, d €60-120, q €95-190; @☞; 🚇Capannone) 🚲 Sleep among the artichokes on Venice's garden isle of Sant'Erasmo in a red-roofed country villa, 25 minutes by boat from central Venice. Spacious guestrooms with parquet floors and wrought-iron beds open onto a wraparound verandah. Meals are largely home-grown, organic and fair trade, bicycles are available, and the lagoon laps at the end of the lane – bite-prone guests should bring mosquito repellent.

The guesthouse supports a nonprofit cultural organisation, and guests are invited to participate in nature excursions, archaeological digs, theatre performances and cultural exchange programs.

⭐ VILLA LINA   B&B €€

Map p285 (☎041 527 53 58; www.villalinavenezia.com; Calle Dietro gli Orti 12; s €80-100, d €135-185, tr €165-215; ⊘Mar-Dec; 🅰☞; 🚇Colonna) Finding Villa Lina in the grounds of the Nason Moretti furnace is like chancing upon a wonderful secret. The home of glass designer Carlo Nason and his wife, Evi, the villa has a mod 1950s vibe and is scattered with his glass designs. In the living room, large picture windows overlook the flowering garden and the Serenella canal, while bedrooms are large, comfortable and contemporary. Trust Evi's dining recommendations and then return for naps on the loungers beneath the fig tree.

VENISSA   INN €€

Map p286 (☎041 527 22 81; www.venissa.it; Fondamenta Santa Caterina 3, Mazzorbo; d €95-195; ⊘Feb-Dec; 🅰☞; 🚇Mazzorbo) Gourmet getaways are made in the shade of the vineyards at Venissa, which offers some of the lagoon's finest, freshest dining as well as six

Scandinavian-chic rooms under the farmhouse rafters. Breakfast – if that's what you can call the lavish gourmet affair – is extra, either prix fixe (€15) or à la carte. Pre-book for cookery classes with world-class chefs, crab fishing with Burano fishermen or photography and rowing outings.

In 2016, Venissa plan to add 13 more rooms in a handful of fishermen's cottages on Burano.

MURANO PALACE   BOUTIQUE HOTEL €€

Map p285 (☎041 73 96 55; www.muranopalace.com; Fondamenta Ventrai 77, Murano; d €110-180; 🅰☞; 🚇Colonna) Come here for designer fabulousness at an outlet price. Jewel-toned colour schemes and (naturally) Murano glass chandeliers illuminate high-ceilinged, parquet-floored rooms, and there are free drinks and snacks in the minibar. Expect canal views and unparalleled art-glass shopping, but eerie calm once the shops close around 6pm. Ask at the front desk about fishing excursions and Venetian rowing lessons.

VENICE CERTOSA HOTEL   HOTEL €€

(La Certosa; s €55-95, d €75-140; 🅰☞; 🚇Certosa) Nautical talk abounds at the outdoor breakfast tables at La Certosa's activity-focused hotel before guests head off on jogging trails, sailing courses or kayak tours of Cannaregio canals. Throughout the day the sailing fraternity and marina workers drop in at the bar and restaurant, although come evening you may want to head across the water for some late night life. Rooms are designed to suit the outdoor crowd and are modern, practical and unfussy.

At night, when the *vaporetto* service ends, the hotel runs a shuttle from Sant'Elena on request.

⭐ LOCANDA CIPRIANI   B&B €€€

Map p286 (☎041 73 01 50; www.locandacipriani.com; Piazza Santa Fosca 29, Torcello; s/d €140/280; ⊘closed Tue & Jan; 🅰; 🚇Torcello) Not much has changed since this rustic wine shop was transformed into a country inn in 1934 by Harry's Bar founder Giuseppe Cipriani. The six spacious rooms are more like suites, with stocked libraries and easy chairs in lieu of TVs for a true literary retreat. You're bound to find inspiration for your next novel in Hemingway's favourite room, Santa Fosca, with its balcony overlooking the garden and original creaky oak floors.

Understand Venice & the Veneto

Venice Today

It seems that everyone wants a piece of Venice, from selfie-stick-wielding tourists and foreign entrepreneurs to avaricious politicians and the rising Adriatic Sea. As La Serenissima sails further into the 21st century, new (and revisited) challenges are stirring up some rather choppy seas. How does a city reconcile its magnetism with its fragility, its longstanding individuality with an increasingly homogenised, globalised world?

Best on Film

Pane e Tulipani (Bread & Tulips) (2000) An AWOL housewife starts life anew in Venice.

Casanova (1976) Fellini's take on Venice's seducer with Donald Sutherland tops Lasse Halström's with Heath Ledger.

Don't Look Now (1973) A couple's demons follow them to Venice in Nicolas Roeg's taut thriller.

Casino Royale (2006) James Bond hits the Grand Canal (don't worry, that palace survived).

Best in Print

Watermark (1992) Nobel Laureate Joseph Brodsky's 17-year fascination with Venice spills onto every page.

Invisible Cities (1972) Italo Calvino imagines Marco Polo recounting his travels to Kublai Khan – yet every city he describes is Venice.

Stabat Mater (2009) Tiziano Scarpa won Italy's top literary prize for this tale based on the true story of Antonio Vivaldi's orphan-girl orchestra.

Shakespeare in Venice (2007) Alberto Toso Fei and Shaul Bassi unravel local legends intertwined with Shakespearean dramas.

Welcome to Veniceland

In 2015, a record-breaking number of visitors hit Venice over the Easter weekend, considered the official start of the tourist season. While a boon for the tourist sector, not everyone is popping the *prosecco* (sparkling wine). According to a 1988 benchmark study by Ca' Foscari University, the city can sustainably accommodate 7.5 million annual visitors, a far cry from today's near 30 million arrivals. The pressure is increasingly evident, from the overcrowding of *vaporetti* (commuter ferries) to accelerated damage to the very pylons and limestone foundations that keep Venice afloat.

It's also affecting the cost of living. When tourists are willing to pay €1000 a week to rent an apartment, renting to locals for a quarter of the price seems hardly enticing to many landlords. Soaring real estate prices have also hit the commercial sector, with a growing number of everyday businesses being forced to close down. Talk to any local long enough and chances are they'll lament the dwindling number of useful services – from shoe repairers to bakeries – not to mention the growing number of tatty souvenir shops taking their place. Many of these shops sell cheap, foreign-made products at prices Venetian artisans simply cannot match. Together, these pressures are fuelling the city proper's dwindling resident population, which has plummeted from 175,000 at the end of WWII to less than 60,000 today.

These challenges are propelling a number of grassroots organisations – including Venessia (venessia. com), Salviamo Venezia (salviamovenezia.wordpress. com) and We Are Here Venice (www.weareherevenice. org) – to raise greater public awareness of these issues, as well as to lobby politicians to take concrete action to protect Venice's environment and heritage. Exactly what action to take remains a hotly contested issue; the ever-growing number of proposals include stricter regulations for new retailers, resident-only ferry services to ease congestion, and the introduction of online bookings and admissions for tourists wanting to visit Piazza San Marco in high season.

Rising Tides & Scandals

It might be named for the Old Testament hero, but Venice's MoSE (Italian for Moses) is taking significantly longer to part the sea. Since construction commenced in 2003, the city's ambitious new floodgate system has missed a series of completion deadlines – the scheduled wrap-up is now June 2017. When it is finally up and running, MoSE's 78 inflatable barriers are expected to block potentially damaging tides at the lagoon's three inlets. One can only hope it has better luck at blocking the Adriatic than it has at preventing budget blowouts and scorching scandal. In 2015, the project's €5.4 billion price tag had exceeded €7 billion.

A year earlier, the project's managing consortium, Consorzio Venezia Nuova (CVN), hit world headlines for allegedly stashing away a €25 million slush fund used to bribe officials. The revelation led to the arrests of 36 politicians and business figures in June 2014, among them Venice mayor Giorgio Orsoni, accused of accepting €560,000 in donations during his 2010 electoral campaign. Although Orsoni claimed ignorance about the illegality of the gift, he swiftly resigned from office and accepted a four-month sentence in a plea agreement; a sentence so brief it may never be served.

A Reborn Republic?

In March 2014, an unofficial, online referendum conducted by Veneto pro-independence committee Plebiscito.eu proposed the question: Do you want the Veneto to become an independent and sovereign federal republic? According to the group, of the 2.3 million Venetians who voted, 2.1 million answered *sì* (yes). While the result sparked much jubilation and flag-waving among Venetians wanting secession from a debt-burdened Italy, it was quickly disputed by various news sources, who cited figures provided by internet data companies who put the number of voters at only 135,000, among them voters based abroad. In response, Plebiscito.eu appointed an independent committee of international observers to re-examine – and ultimately re-confirm – the original result.

Despite the disputed numbers, Venetian nationalism enjoys significant local support in the region. Venetian nationalist party Liga Veneta remains the Veneto's largest single political party and the desire for – at the very least – a fiscally independent Veneto has strong appeal in a highly industrialised region offered €5 back in services for every €7 paid to Rome in taxes.

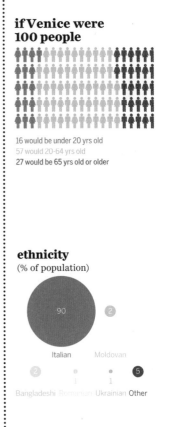

if Venice were 100 people

16 would be under 20 yrs old
57 would 20-64 yrs old
27 would be 65 yrs old or older

ethnicity
(% of population)

90 Italian
2 Moldovan
2 Bangladeshi
1 Romanian
1 Ukrainian
5 Other

population per sq km

VENICE ITALY

👤 ≈ 200 people

History

Not content with conquering the known world with its naval fleets, Venice dispatched intrepid explorers like Marco Polo to expand its trade horizons. When its maritime empire passed its high-water mark, Venice refused to concede defeat on the world stage. Instead the city itself became a stage, attracting global audiences with its vivid painting, baroque music, modern opera, independent thinkers and parties without parallel. In its audacious 1000-year history, Venice has not only risen above sea level, but repeatedly risen to the occasion.

From Swamp to Empire

A malarial swamp seems like a strange place to found an empire, unless you consider the circumstances. Celtic Veneti had lived along the Adriatic coast relatively peacefully since 1500 BC, had been Roman citizens since 49 BC, and were not in the habit of war. But between the 5th and 6th centuries, when Visigoths, Huns and Lombards started to sack Veneto towns such as Aquileia, many Veneti fled to the murky wetlands of the lagoon. They settled first on the island of Torcello; others moved to the now-submerged island of Malamocco, then Chioggia, and finally the Rivoalto (colloquially known as Rialto).

By 466, these nascent island communities had elected tribunes and formed a loose federation. When Emperor Justinian claimed Italy's northeast coast for the Holy Roman Empire in 540, Venetia (roughly today's Veneto region) sent elected representatives to the local Byzantine government in Ravenna. This council reported to central authority in Constantinople (now called Istanbul), but as Byzantine power waned in the early 8th century, Venice seized the opportunity for independence.

In 726 the people of Venice elected Orso Ipato as their *dux* (Latin for leader), or doge (duke) in the Venetian dialect, the first of 118 elected Venetian dogi that would lead the city for more than 1000 years. Like some of his successors, Orso tried to turn his appointment into a hereditary monarchy. He was assassinated for overstepping his bounds. At first, no one held the doge's hot seat for long: Orso's successor, Teodato, managed to transfer the ducal seat to Malamocco in 742 before being

In *The Wings of the Dove* (1902), a dapper con man and sickly heiress meet in Venice, with predictable consequences – but Henry James' gorgeous storytelling makes for riveting reading.

TIMELINE	c 1500 BC	7th–9th Century AD	AD 726
	Celtic Veneti tribes, possibly from Anatolia (in present-day Turkey), arrive in northeast Italy to inhabit the region now known as the Veneto.	Glass-making furnaces on Torcello get fired up, creating the cathedral's Byzantine glass-mosaic masterpieces.	Orso Ipato becomes the first Venetian doge. The Byzantines consider Ipato's election an act of rebellion, and are not devastated by Ipato's assassination in 737.

deposed. Gradually the office of the doge was understood as an elected office, kept in check by two councillors and the Arengo (a popular assembly).

When the Franks invaded the lagoon in 809, they were surprised by resistance led by Agnello Partecipazio from Rivoalto, a shallow area of the lagoon inaccessible to most seafaring vessels. Partecipazio's success led to his election as doge and the establishment of a fortress on the eventual site of the Palazzo Ducale. Thus the cluster of islets around Rivoalto became the focus of community development. Land was drained, earth was lifted above the tides with wooden pylons driven into the soft silt, and soon Venetians rose above their swampy circumstances.

War & Spoils

Once terra firma was established, Venice set about shoring up its business interests. When consummate diplomat Pietro Orseolo was elected doge in 991, he positioned Venice as a neutral party between the western Holy Roman Empire and eastern territories controlled by Constantinople, and won the medieval equivalent of most-favoured-nation status from both competing empires.

Even at the outset of the Crusades, Venice maintained its strategic neutrality, continuing to trade with Muslim leaders from Syria to Spain while its port served as the launching pad for crusaders bent on wresting the Holy Land from Muslim control. With rivals Genoa and Pisa vying for lucrative contracts to equip crusaders, Venice established the world's first assembly lines in the Arsenale, capable of turning out a warship a day. Officially, La Serenissima ('The Most Serene'; the Venetian Republic) remained above the fray, joining crusading naval operations only sporadically – and almost always in return for trade concessions.

Constantinople knew who was supplying the crusaders' ships, and in the wake of the First Crusade in 1095, Venice's relations with Byzantium were strained. Byzantine emperor Manuele Comnenus played on Venetian–Genoese rivalries, staging an 1171 assault on Constantinople's Genoese colony and blaming it on Constantinople's Venetian residents, who were promptly clapped into irons. Venice sent a fleet to the rescue, but the crew contracted plague from stowaway rats, and the ships limped home without having fired a shot.

Meanwhile, Venice was under threat by land from Holy Roman Emperor Frederick Barbarossa's plans to force Italy and the pope to recognise his authority. But after several strikes, Barbarossa found northern Italy a tough territory to control. When his army was struck by plague

John Julius Norwich's *History of Venice* (1981) is an engrossing, epic account of the city's maritime empire, if a bit long on naval battles and short on recent history.

828	957	1094	1172
According to legend, the corpse of St Mark the Evangelist is smuggled from Alexandria (Egypt) to Venice in a shipment of pork. St Mark is adopted as the patron saint of Venice.	Holy Roman Emperor Otto the Great recognises key trading rights for Venice, cutting the Eastern Byzantine Christian empire out of Venice's increasingly lucrative deals.	Basilica di San Marco is consecrated. The doge's spectacular Chiesa d'Oro (Church of Gold) stands for the glory of Venice, St Mark and a brain trust of Mediterranean artisans.	Venice establishes an elected Maggior Consiglio (Great Council). Though citizenry makes up 80% of the population, nobles are elected councillors.

THE STOLEN SAINT

Venice had all the makings of an independent trading centre – ports, a defensible position against Charlemagne and the Huns, leadership to settle inevitable trade disputes – but no glorious shrine to mark the city's place on the world map. So Venice did what any ambitious, God-fearing medieval city would do: it procured a patron saint. Under Byzantine rule, St Theodore (San Teodoro) had been the patron saint. But according to local legend, the evangelist St Mark (San Marco) had visited the lagoon islands and been told by an angel that his body would rest there – and some Venetian merchants decided to realise this prophecy.

In AD 828, Venetian smugglers stole St Mark's body from its resting place in Alexandria (Egypt), apparently hiding the holy corpse in a load of pork to deter inspection by Muslim customs officials. Venice summoned the best artisans from Byzantium and beyond to enshrine these relics in an official ducal church that would impress visitors with the power and glory of Venice. The usual medieval construction setbacks of riots and fires thrice destroyed exterior mosaics and weakened the underlying structure, and St Mark's bones were misplaced twice in the mayhem. With Basilica di San Marco under construction, the winged lion of St Mark was officially adopted as the emblem of the Venetian empire, symbolically setting Venice apart from Constantinople and Rome.

in 1167, Barbarossa was forced to withdraw to Pavia – only to discover that 15 Italian city-states, including Venice, had formed the Lombard League against him. Barbarossa met with spectacular defeat, and even worse, excommunication. Venice quickly recognised that it could only handle one holy war at a time, and through diplomatic manoeuvres, convinced Pope Alexander III and the repentant emperor to make peace in Venice in 1177.

The Dodgy Doge

For fast talking, even the shrewdest Venetian merchant couldn't top Doge Enrico Dandolo. The doddering nonagenarian might have seemed like an easy mark to Franks seeking Venice's support in the Fourth Crusade. But Doge Dandolo drove a hard bargain: Venice would provide a fleet to carry 30,000 crusaders, but not for less than 84,000 silver marks – approximately double the yearly income of the king of England at the time.

Only one-third of the proposed Frankish forces turned up in Venice the following year, and their leaders couldn't pay. But Venice had the ships ready, and figured it had kept its side of the bargain. To cover the

1203–04	1271	1297	1309
Doge Dandolo promises to transport Frankish crusaders to the Holy Land but heads to Constantinople; his forces massacre and pillage, then return to Venice with booty.	Traders Nicolò and Matteo Polo set sail for Xanadu, the court of Kublai Khan, with Nicolò's 20-year-old son, Marco. The Polos make a fortune in the jewellery business in Asia.	Venice ends constitutional monarchy, allowing only those from noble families to participate in the Assembly – until it runs low on funds, and allows merchants to buy noble titles.	For openly defying Rome's orders, Venice is excommunicated from the Church for the first time. Through its wealth and negotiation skills, Venice convinces Rome to relent.

balance due, Doge Dandolo suggested that the crusaders might help Venice out with a few tasks on the way to Palestine. This included invading Dalmatia and a detour to Constantinople in 1203 that would last a year, while Venetian and Frankish forces thoroughly pillaged the place.

Finally Doge Dandolo claimed that Constantinople had been suitably claimed for Christendom – never mind that it already was under Christian rule. At age 96, the doge declared himself 'Lord of a Quarter and a Half-Quarter of the Roman Empire' of Byzantium. This title conveniently granted Venice three-eighths of the spoils, including the monumental gilt-bronze horses in Basilica di San Marco. Venetian ships opted to head home loaded with booty instead of onward to Christian duty, leaving the Franks to straggle onwards to the Crusades.

Venice Versus Genoa

The puppet emperor Doge Dandolo put on the throne in Constantinople didn't last long: the Genoese conspired with the Byzantines to overthrow the pro-Venetian regime. Having taken Constantinople for all it was worth, Venice set its sights on distant shores. Through the overland trip of native son Marco Polo to China in 1271–91, Venetian trade routes extended all the way to China. Rival Genoa's routes to the New World were proving slower to yield returns, and the impatient empire cast an envious eye on Venice's spice and silk-trade routes.

In 1372 Genoa and Venice finally came to blows over an incident in Cyprus, initiating eight years of maritime warfare that took a toll on Venice. To make matters worse, plague decimated Venice in the 1370s. Genoa's allies Padua and Hungary took the opportunity to seize Venetian territories on the mainland, and in 1379 a Genoese fleet appeared off the Lido. Venetian commander Carlo Zeno's war fleet had been sent out to patrol the Mediterranean, leaving the city outflanked and outnumbered.

But the Genoese made a strategic mistake: instead of invading, Genoa attempted to starve out the city. With stores of grain saved for just such an occasion, Venice worked day and night to build new ships and defences around the islands. Mustering all of Venice's might, Venetian commander Vittore Pisani mounted a counter-attack on the Genoese fleet – but his forces were inadequate. All hope seemed lost, until ships flying the lion of St Mark banner appeared on the horizon: Carlo Zeno had returned. Venice ousted the Genoese, exerting control over the Adriatic and a backyard that stretched from Dalmatia (Croatia) to Bergamo (northern Italy).

Since Marco Polo's 1271–95 heyday, no Venetian palace has been complete without Chinese art – hence the chinoiserie drawing room at Ca' Rezzonico, and Ca' Pesaro's Museo d'Arte Orientale, featuring Prince Enrico di Borbone's Chinese porcelain hoard.

HISTORY FROM SWAMP TO EMPIRE

Top Five for Byzantine Splendour

Basilica di San Marco

Museo di Torcello

Chiesa di San Zaccaria

Chiesa dei SS Maria e Donato

Chiesa di San Giacomo dell'Orio

1310	1348–49	1386	1403
With rebellion afoot, a temporary security force called the Consiglio dei Dieci (Council of Ten) is convened; it lasts almost five centuries, effectively running Venice for two.	A horrific bout of the Black Death hits Venice, killing some 60% of the population. Venetian doctors observe that the worst-hit areas are by Dorsoduro's docks, where rats arrive.	A Jewish cemetery is established on the Lido, with land granted by the state. The cemetery remains in use until its abandonment with Mussolini's racial laws in 1938.	The world's first quarantine stations are established with proceeds from Venice's salt monopoly, saving lives by limiting contact with the bubonic plague.

Rats & Redemption

As a maritime empire, ships came and went through Venice's ports daily, carrying salt, silks, spices and an unintentional import: rats infested with fleas carrying bubonic plague. In 1348 the city was still recovering from an earthquake that had destroyed houses and drained the Grand Canal, when the plague struck. Soon as many as 600 people were dying every day, and undertakers' barges raised the rueful cry: *'Corpi morti! Corpi morti!'* (Bring out your dead!) Within a year, more than 50,000 Venetians died.

No one was sure how the disease had spread, but Venice took the unprecedented step of appointing three public health officials to manage the crisis. Observing that outbreaks seemed to coincide with incoming shipments, Venice decided in 1403 to intercept all incoming ships arriving from infected areas on Isola di Lazzaretto Nuovo. Before any ship was allowed to enter the city, it was required to undergo inspection, and its passengers had to wait for a *quarantena* (40-day period) while Venetian doctors monitored them for signs of plague. This was the world's first organised quarantine station, setting a precedent that has saved untold lives from plague and other infectious diseases since.

While the plague struck Italy's mainland as many as 50 more times before 1500, the outbreaks often seemed to miraculously bypass Venice. The city's faithful chalked up their salvation to divine intervention, and built the spectacular churches of Il Redentore and Basilica di Santa Maria della Salute as monumental thanks.

Those found guilty of crimes against the doge were bludgeoned or decapitated. Severed heads were placed atop columns outside the Palazzo Ducale and sundry parts displayed in *sestieri* (districts) for exactly three nights and four days, until they started to smell.

Traders & Traitors

Like its signature Basilica di San Marco, the Venetian empire was dazzlingly cosmopolitan. Venice turned arrivals from every nation and creed into trading partners with a common credo: as long as everyone was making money, cultural boundaries need not apply. Armenians, Turks, Greeks and Germans became neighbours along the Grand Canal, and Jewish and Muslim refugees and other groups widely persecuted in Europe settled into established communities in Venice.

Commerce provided a common bond. At the height of Venice's maritime prowess, 300 shipbuilding companies in the Arsenale had 16,000 employees. By the mid-15th century, Venice's maritime ventures had left the city swathed in golden mosaics, rustling silks and incense. In case of trade disputes or feuds among neighbours, La Serenissima instigated a complex political system of checks, balances and elections, with the doge as the executive presiding over council matters.

Yet inside the red-velvet cloak of its ruling elite, Venice was hiding an iron hand. Venice's shadowy secret service, the Consiglio dei Dieci

1444	1470	1492	1494
The second Rialto bridge collapses under spectators watching a wedding flotilla. After 148 years and huge cost overruns, a stone replacement is provided by Antonio da Ponte.	Cyprus is the latest of Venice's conquests, which stretch across the mainland to Bergamo, through the Aegean to Crete, and to Middle East trading outposts in Jaffa, Beirut and Alexandria.	Genoese Cristoforo Colombo's voyage kicks off the age of discovery and Venice's long slide into obsolescence, as the Portuguese and Spanish bypass its customs controls.	Aldo Manuzio founds Aldine Press, introducing mass-market paperbacks, including Dante's *Divine Comedy*. By 1500, one in six books published in Europe is printed in Venice.

(Council of Ten), thwarted conspiracies by deploying Venetian James Bonds throughout the city and major European capitals. Venice had no qualms about spying on its own citizens, and trials, torture and executions were carried out in secret. Still, compared with its neighbours at the time, Venice remained a haven of tolerance.

Friendly Foes

Never mind that Venice sacked Constantinople, or that Constantinople sided with Genoa against Venice: warfare wasn't enough to deter the two maritime powers from doing brisk business. When Constantinople fell to Ottoman rule in 1453, business carried on as usual. The rival powers understood one another very well; the Venetian language was widely spoken across the eastern Mediterranean.

After Suleiman the Magnificent captured Cyprus in 1571, Venice sensed its maritime power slipping, and allied with the papal states, Spain and even arch-rival Genoa to keep the Ottoman sultan at bay. The same year a huge allied fleet (much of it provided by Venice) routed the Turks off Lepanto (Greece) and Sebastiano Venier and his Venetian fleet sailed home with 100 Turkish women as war trophies.

Legend has it that when Turkish troops took over the island of Paros, the POWs included Cecilia Venier-Baffo, who was apparently the illegitimate daughter of Venice's noble Venier family, a niece of the doge, and possibly the cousin of Sebastiano (of Lepanto fame). Cecilia became the favourite wife of Sultan Salim II in Constantinople, and when he died in 1574 she took control as Sultana Nurbani (Princess of Light). Regent of Sultan Murad III, she was a faithful pen pal of Queen Elizabeth I of Britain and Catherine de Medici of France. According to historian Alberto Toso Fei, the Sultana's policies were so favourable to Venetian interests that the Venetian senate set aside special funds to fulfil her wishes for Venetian specialities, from lapdogs to golden cushions. Genoa wasn't pleased by her favouritism, and in 1582 she was poisoned to death by what appeared to have been Genoese assassins.

The Age of Decadence

While Italy's city-states continued to plot against one another, they were increasingly eclipsed by marriages cementing alliances among France, England and the Habsburg Empire. As it lost ground to these European nation-states and the seas to pirates and Ottomans, Venice took a different tack, and began conquering Europe by charm.

Top Five Landmarks of Multicultural Venice

Ghetto

Museo delle Icone

Scuola di San Giorgio degli Schiavoni

Fondaco dei Turchi

Palazzo Zenobio

HISTORY THE AGE OF DECADENCE

Venetian party planners outdid themselves with the 1574 reception for King Henry III of France. The king's barge was greeted with glass-blowers performing on rafts, bevvies of Venetian beauties dressed in white, a 1200-course meal, and decorations provided by an all-star committee of Palladio, Veronese and Tintoretto.

1498	1501	1508	1516
Portuguese explorer Vasco da Gama sails around the Cape of Good Hope, and the boom in trans-Atlantic trade shuts out many Venetian merchants.	The Magistrato alle Acque is created in order to maintain and regulate the delicate hydrological balance of the lagoon, on which Venice's security and fortune is built.	The Holy Roman Empire, papal states, Spain and France form the League of Cambrai against Venice – but with Venice cutting side deals, ensuring war doesn't change the map much.	A proclamation declares that Jewish residents of Venice are to live in a designated zone called the Ghetto, with access to the area closed at midnight by guards.

Sensations & Scandals

Venice's star attractions were its parties, music, women and art. Nunneries in Venice held soirées to rival those in its *ridotti* (casinos), and Carnevale lasted up to three months. Claudio Monteverdi was hired as choir director of San Marco in 1613, introducing multipart harmonies and historical operas with crowd-pleasing tragicomic scenes. Monteverdi's modern opera caught on: by the end of the 17th century, Venice's season included as many as 30 operas.

New orchestras required musicians, but Venice came up with a ready workforce: orphan girls. Circumstances had conspired to produce an unprecedented number of Venetian orphans: on the one hand were plague and snake-oil cures, and on the other were scandalous masquerade parties and flourishing prostitution. Funds poured in from anonymous donors to support *ospedaletti* (orphanages), and the great baroque composers Antonio Vivaldi and Domenico Cimarosa were hired to lead orphan orchestras. The Venetian state took on the care and musical training of the city's orphan girls, who earned their keep by performing at public functions and *ospedaletti* fund-raising galas. Visiting diplomats treated to orphan concerts were well advised to tip the orphan performers: you never knew whose illegitimate daughter you might be insulting otherwise.

VENICE'S 'HONEST COURTESANS'

High praise, high pay and even high honours: Venice's *cortigiane oneste* were no ordinary strumpets. An 'honest courtesan' earned the title not by offering a fair price, but by providing added value with style, education and wit that reflected well on her patrons. They were not always beautiful or young, but *cortigiane oneste* were well educated, dazzling their admirers with poetry, music, philosophical insights and apt social critiques. In the 16th century, some Venetian families of limited means spared no expense on their daughters' educations: beyond an advantageous marriage or career, educated women who become *cortigiane oneste* could command prices 60 times those of the average *cortigiana di lume* ('courtesan of the lamp' – streetwalker).

Far from hiding their trade, a catalogue of 210 of Venice's *piu honorate cortigiane* (most honoured courtesans) was published in 1565, listing contact information and going rates, payable directly to the courtesan's servant, her mother or, occasionally, her husband. A *cortigiana onesta* might circulate in Venetian society as the known mistress of one or more admirers, who compensated her for her company rather than services rendered, and with an allowance rather than pay per hour. Syphilis was an occupational hazard, and special hospices were founded for infirm courtesans.

1571	1575–6	1630	1669
Venice and the Holy League of Catholic states defeat Ottoman forces at the naval Battle of Lepanto, thanks in part to a technical advantage: cannons and guns versus archers.	Plague claims many lives, including Titian's. Quarantine aids Venice's recovery; a new painting cycle by Tintoretto is dedicated to San Rocco, patron saint of the plague-stricken.	The plague kills a third of Venice's population within 16 months. With few leaders surviving, Venice allows wealthy Venetians to buy their way into the Golden Book of nobles.	The Venetian colony of Crete is lost to the Ottoman Turks, yet the two powers continue to trade with one another – despite repeated objections from Rome.

Pulling Rank: The Pope & the Doge

Rome repeatedly censured Venice for depicting holy subjects in an earthy, Venetian light, and for playing toe-tapping tunes in churches – but such censorship was largely ignored. According to late-16th-century gossip, Cardinal Camillo Borghese had a beef with the Venetian ambassador to Rome, Leonardo Donà, ever since the two exchanged heated words in the Roman halls of power. The cardinal hissed that, were he pope, he'd excommunicate the entire Venetian populace. 'And I would thumb my nose at the excommunication', retorted Donà.

As fate would have it, by 1606 cardinal and ambassador were promoted to Pope Paul V and doge, respectively. Rome had never appreciated Venice's insistence on reserving a degree of control over Church matters, and when Venice claimed that zoning laws required its approval of Church expansion plans within the city, Pope Paul V issued a papal bull excommunicating Venice. As promised, Doge Donà defied the bull, ordering all churches to remain open on Venetian territory. Any church that obeyed the bull would have its doors permanently closed, property seized and clergy exiled from Venice.

Venetian-born monk and philosopher Paolo Sarpi convincingly argued Venice's case, claiming Venice's right to self-determination came directly from God, not through Rome. Before the excommunication could cause further loss of Church property in Venice, or other Catholic territories became convinced by Sarpi's argument, Pope Paul V rescinded his bull.

But the power struggle didn't stop there. Venice conducted an official 1767 audit of 11 million golden ducats in revenues rendered to Rome in the previous decade, and decided to cut its losses: 127 Veneto monasteries and convents were closed, cutting the local clerical population in half and redirecting millions of ducats to Venice's coffers.

Red Lights, White Widows & Grey Areas

While Roman clerics furiously scribbled their disapproval, Venetian trends stealthily took over drawing rooms across the continent. Venetian women's lavish finery, staggering platform shoes up to 50cm high and masculine quiff hairdos scandalised visiting European nobility, until Venice felt obliged to enact sumptuary laws preventing women from wearing manly hairstyles and blinding displays of jewels on dipping décolletages. Venetian noblewomen complained to the doge and the pope, and the restrictions were soon dropped.

With trade revenues and the value of the Venetian ducat slipping in the 16th century, Venice's fleshpots brought in far too much valuable foreign currency to be outlawed. Instead, Venice opted for regulation

Top Five Hallmarks of Venetian Decadence

Carnevale

Ca' Rezzonico

Ponte delle Tette

Palazzo Mocenigo

Palazzo Fortuny

HISTORY THE AGE OF DECADENCE

Venice's former leper colony of San Lazzaro degli Armeni became a monastery, founded by Armenian refugees in 1717, and frescoed Palazzo Zenobio remains an Armenian cultural centre and popular venue for concerts and Carnevale.

1678	1703–40	1718	1797
Venetian scholar Eleonora Lucrezia Cornaro Piscopia is the first woman to receive a university degree in Europe, earning her doctorate in philosophy at the University of Padua.	Antonio Vivaldi is musical director at La Pietà, composing many concertos for orchestras of orphan girls. He is fired in 1709 but swiftly recalled, to Venice's immense credit.	Venice and Austria sign the Treaty of Passarowitz with the Ottoman Empire, splitting prime coastal territory and leaving Venice with nominal control and some Ionian islands.	The segregation of Jewish Venetians comes to an end and the gates of the Ghetto are opened, just as Napoleon arrives in the city.

and taxation. Rather than baring all in the rough-and-ready streets around the Rialto, prostitutes could only display their wares from the waist up in windows, or sit bare-legged on window sills. Venice decreed that to distinguish themselves from noblewomen who increasingly dressed like them, ladies of the night should ride in gondolas with red lights. By the end of the 16th century, the town was flush with some 12,000 registered prostitutes, creating a literal red-light district.

Beyond red lights ringing the Rialto, 16th-to-18th-century visitors encountered broad grey areas in Venetian social mores. As free-spirited, financially independent Venetian women took lovers, there became a certain fluidity surrounding the definition of a *cortigiana* (courtesan). With their husbands at sea for months or years, Venice's 'white widows' took young, handsome *cicisbei* (manservants) to tend their needs. Not coincidentally, Venetian ladies occasionally fell into religious fervours entailing a trimester-long seclusion.

PRINCE OF PLEASURE

Never was a hedonist born at a better time and in a more appropriate place. Eighteenth-century Venice was well into its new career as the pleasure capital of Europe when Giacomo Casanova (1725–98) arrived on the scene. He was abandoned as a young boy, and became a gambler and rake while studying law in Padua. He graduated by age 17 to take up a position with the Church in Venice, but adventuring soon became Casanova's primary career. His charm won him warm welcomes into the homes of wealthy patrons – and the beds of their wives, lovers and daughters.

Venice was a licentious place, but some political limits still applied. Casanova's dalliances with Freemasonry and banned books were considered nothing less than a threat to the state. After an evening foursome with the French ambassador and a couple of nuns, Casanova was arrested on the nebulous charge of 'outrages against religion' and dragged to the Palazzo Ducale's dreaded attic prison. Sentenced to five years in a flea-infested cell, Casanova complained bitterly, and promptly escaped through the roof of his cell, entered the palace, and breezed past the guards in the morning.

Casanova fled Venice to make his fortune in Paris and serve briefly as a French spy. But his extracurricular habits caused him no end of trouble: he went broke in Germany, survived a duel in Poland, fathered and abandoned several children, and contracted venereal diseases in England. Late in life, he returned to Venice as a celebrity, and served the government as a spy – but he was exiled for publishing a satire of the nobility. He wound up as a librarian in an isolated castle in Bohemia, where boredom drove him to finally write his memoirs. In the end, he concludes, 'I can say I have lived'.

1807	1814	1836	1840
Napoleon suppresses religious orders to quell dissent. Upon Independence, some churches are reconsecrated – but many aren't, serving instead as archives or tourist attractions.	Austria takes Venice as a war trophy and imposes order with thousands of troops, a house-numbering system and heavy taxes that push Venice to the brink of starvation.	Fire guts Venice's legendary public opera house, but a new version soon rises from the ashes. When La Fenice (The Phoenix) burns again in 1996, an exacting replica is rebuilt.	At La Serenissima's height, Venice's fabled Golden Book of nobles included more than 1200 families – but by 1840, all but 200 were destitute and subsisting on charity.

From Colonisation to Revolution

When Napoleon arrived in 1797, Venice had been reduced by plague and circumstances from 175,000 to fewer than 100,000 people. Venetian warships managed to deter one French ship by the Lido, but when Napoleon made it clear he intended to destroy the city if it resisted, the Maggior Consiglio (Great Council) decreed the end of the Republic. The doge reportedly doffed the signature cap of his office with a sigh, saying, 'I won't be needing this anymore'. Rioting citizens were incensed by such cowardice, but French forces soon ended the insurrection, and began systematically plundering the city.

Though Napoleon only controlled Venice sporadically for a total of about 11 years, the impact of his reign is still visible. Napoleon grabbed any Venetian art masterpiece that wasn't nailed down, and displaced religious orders to make room for museums and trophy galleries in the Gallerie dell'Accademia and Museo Correr. Napoleon's city planners lifted remaining restrictions on the Jewish Ghetto, filled in canals and widened city streets to facilitate movement of troops and loot; his decorators established a style of gaudy gold cornices and whimsical grotesques. Napoleon lost control of Venice to the Austrians in 1814, and two years later one-quarter of Venice's population was destitute.

But Austria had grand plans for the city, and expected impoverished Venetians to foot the bill. They were obliged to house Austrian soldiers, who spent off-duty hours indulging in their new happy-hour invention, the *spritz* (a *prosecco*-and-bitters cocktail). Finding their way back home afterwards was a challenge in Venetian *calli* (alleyways), so the Austrians implemented a street-numbering system. To bring in reinforcements and supplies, they dredged and deepened entrances to the lagoon for ease of shipping access and began a train bridge in 1841 – all with Venetian labour and special Venetian taxes. To make way for the new train station in 1846, *scuole* (religious confraternities) and a palace were demolished.

With no say in the government, many Venetians voted with their feet: under the Austrians, the population fell from 138,000 to 99,000. When a young lawyer named Daniele Manin suggested reforms to Venice's puppet government in 1848, he was tossed into prison – sparking a popular uprising against the Austrians that would last 17 months. Austria responded by bombarding and blockading the city. In July, Austria began a 24-day artillery bombardment, raining some 23,000 shells down on the city and its increasingly famished and cholera-stricken populace, until Manin finally managed to negotiate a surrender to Austria with a guarantee of no reprisals. Yet the indignity of Austria's suppression continued to fester, and when presented with the option in 1866, the people

> Many Venetians dropped the mask of propriety altogether, openly cohabitating with lovers year-round and acknowledging illegitimate heirs in their wills. By the 18th century, less than 40% of Venetian nobles bothered with the formality of marriage.

1846	1848	1866	1895
The first train crosses to the mainland. The feat is bittersweet: churches were demolished for the station, trains brought occupying Austrian troops and Venetians footed the bill.	Daniele Manin leads an anti-Austrian rebellion and declares Venice a republic for 17 months. Austrians retake the city in 1849, and Venice remains under Austrian control for 17 years.	Venice and the Veneto join the new Kingdom of Italy. The unification of Italy is complete when Rome is made the capital in 1870.	The first Biennale reasserts the city's role as global taste maker. Other nations are eventually invited, though a provocative Picasso is removed from the Spanish pavilion in 1910.

of Venice and the Veneto voted to join the new independent kingdom of Italy under King Vittorio Emanuele II.

Life During Wartime

The Water Magistrate was the second-most important person of the Republic, and his word was law on anything to do with the lagoon. On his investiture, the doge presented him to the people with these words: 'Weigh him, pay him, and, if he makes a mistake, hang him'.

Glamorous Venice gradually took on a workaday aspect in the 19th century, with factories springing up on Giudecca and around Mestre and Padua, and textile industries setting up shop around Vicenza and Treviso. As an increasingly strategic industrial area, Venice began to seem like a port worth reclaiming. But when Austro-Hungarian forces advanced on Venice, they were confronted by Italy's naval marines. Two days after Italy declared war on Austria in 1915, air raids on the city began, and would continue intermittently throughout WWI until 1918. Venice was lucky: the bombardments caused little damage.

When Mussolini rose to power after WWI, he was determined to turn the Veneto into a modern industrial powerhouse and a model Fascist society – despite Venice's famously laissez-faire outlook. Mussolini constructed a roadway from the mainland to Venice, literally bringing the city into line with the rest of Italy. While Italy's largest Fascist rallies were held in Padua, with up to 300,000 participants, Italian Resistance leaders met in Padua's parks to plot uprisings throughout northern Italy. When Mussolini's grip on the region began to weaken during WWII, partisans joined Allied troops to wrest the Veneto from Fascist control.

Venice emerged relatively unscathed from Allied bombing campaigns that targeted mainland industrial sites, and was liberated by New Zealand troops in 1945 – but the mass deportation of Venice's historic Jewish population in 1943 shook Venice to its very moorings. When the Veneto began to rebound after the war, many Venetians left for the mainland, Milan and other postwar economic centres. The legendary lagoon city seemed mired in the mud, unable to reconcile its recent history with its past grandeur, and unsure of its future.

Keeping Venice Afloat

No one comes to Venice and fails to be struck by the uniqueness of the city. However, fewer people consider the utterly unique character of the lagoon in which it stands, despite the fact that it is the only lagoon in the world to have retained its equilibrium for over 1000 years.

Master of the Waters

By its very nature a lagoon is an unstable system, tending either towards erosion or, if the silt-bearing rivers prevail, towards swamps and then fields. In order to prevent either of these two fates, the Republic

1907	1918	1932	1933
Under the Italian government, the Magistrato alle Acque becomes part of the Ministry of Public Works and operational functions are devolved to the Consorzio Venezia Nuova.	Austro-Hungarian planes drop almost 300 bombs on Venice in WWI, but their aim is off, resulting in mercifully little loss of life or damage.	The world's first film festival is initially considered a dubious ploy for attention, but Greta Garbo, Clark Gable and 23,000 movie-goers prove the formula a success.	Mussolini opens the Ponte della Libertà (Freedom Bridge) from Mestre to Venice. The 3.85km-long, two-lane highway remains the only access to Venice by car.

of Venice brought to bear all its resources and technological know-how and enforced them autocratically under the aegis of the Magistrato alle Acque (Master of the Waters), which was established in 1501. This specially empowered office had absolute responsiblity for ensuring the hydraulic health of the lagoon.

Between the 14th and 16th centuries when the Brenta, Sila and Piave rivers threatened to overwhelm the lagoon with silt the magistrates ordered they be rerouted. Later, in the 18th century, they engineered the construction of Pellestrina's impressive *murazzi* (sea wall). To ensure the ebb and flow of the tides dealt effectively with the city's sewage, the three mouths to the sea were kept open just enough; and ships were required to unload cannons and cargo at Pola and the Lido to reduce weight in order to navigate the capillary canals (*ghebbi*) that ensured the city's security against both enemies and the force of the tidal influx. Anyone who sunk *briccole* (navigation poles) without permission was sent directly to prison, and in 1505 the Senate enacted a fine of 100 ducats (a colossal amount) for any unauthorised person who tampered with the lagoon in any way. Through this careful management the lagoon not only survived but thrived.

When the Republic fell in 1797 the unified management of the lagoon collapsed. Instead, Napoleonic, Austrian and Italian governments introduced new systems that validated the concept of private property. A third of the lagoon was reclaimed for agricultural use and aquaculture, and in 1917 the industrial zone of Marghera was constructed. To allow cargo ships to access Marghera, a deep water channel, the Vittorio Emanuele, was dug in 1925, with two additional channels – the Malamocco Canal and the Canale dei Petroli – dredged in the mid-1960s.

As the area into which high tides could expand and the area of absorbent capillary canals was reduced the level of the *acque alte* (high waters) increased. Then in 1966, a catastrophic flood hit. For hours the waters reached more than 200cm above sea level and the world feared that Venice would drown. Fifty organisations worldwide rallied to preserve the city, raising €50 million to cover 1500 restoration projects. Unesco took fright at the threatened loss and in 1987 awarded Venice and its lagoon World Heritage status.

Modern Lagoon Politics

More importantly for the city, in 1973, Italy passed the first 'special' law for Venice wherein the Italian state recognised the vital task of maintaining the lagoon in order to safeguard the city from environmental disaster. Debates were held, studies commissioned and it was agreed that any further reduction in the area of the lagoon should be forbidden.

Director Luchino Visconti takes on the novella by Nobel Prize–winner Thomas Mann with the story of a Mahleresque composer, an infatuation and a deadly outbreak in *Death in Venice* (1971).

One of Italy's most beloved graphic novels, *Corto Maltese in Fables of Venice* (originally published in 1967) follows Hugo Pratt's cosmopolitan sea captain as he cracks the mysteries of the *calli* (alleyways).

HISTORY KEEPING VENICE AFLOAT

1943	1948	1955	1966
From the Ghetto, 256 Jewish Venetians are rounded up and deported to concentration camps. A memorial in Campo del Ghetto commemorates those lost in the camps.	Peggy Guggenheim arrives with major modernists, renewing interest in Italian art, reclaiming Futurism from the Fascists and championing Venetian abstract expressionism.	Venice opens Italy's first museum of Jewish history, the Museo Ebraico, in the historic Ghetto. The museum opens the Ghetto's synagogues and Lido cemetery to visitors.	Record floods cause widespread damage and unleash debate on measures to protect Venice. Its admirers around the world rally to save the city, and rescue its treasures from lagoon muck.

As a cosmopolitan port city, Venice has always been a crowded place. Today, on its busiest summer days, the city accommodates around 143,450 residents and visitors combined, which falls short of the 170,000 residents the city accommodated c 1563.

A plan to build a third industrial zone was abandoned and ideas were discussed as to how best to regulate the increased force of the tides.

One idea, commissioned by the national Ministry of Public Works, was a proposed system of barriers – MoSE (Modulo Sperimentale Elettromeccanico) – at the three mouths of the lagoon, which could be raised to prevent flooding during high tides. Initial costs were estimated at €1.5 billion with a completion date set for 1995. Since then decades of controversy have ensued, ending in the exposure of a huge corruption scandal in 2014 that saw the arrest of the city mayor, undermined the scientific soundness of the idea and resulted in the dissolution of the 500-year-old Magistrato alle Acque, also implicated in the scandal. Many academics and hydrologists argue that relying on the mechanical fix of MoSE is an inadequate solution for a dynamic system like a lagoon, which needs constant regulation and effective, unitary environmental planning, as the Republic once provided.

But just as public opinion questions the efficacy of MoSE as a solution, Venice faces another rising tide – the boom in tourism. In 1999, cruise-ship passengers accounted for only 100,000 visitors a year to Venice. By 2012 the Port Authority published figures of 2.26 million arrivals. In protest, Venetians took to the Giudecca Canal in rowboats, symbolically blocking the entry of ships they argue endanger the very foundations of their city. The Port Authority countered that the city relies on the cruise industry to support 5000 jobs and the lagoon has never been a natural environment, but has always been adapted to serve the principal source of Venetian power – its port. In 2014, the protestors won a brief ban on outsized ships (over 96,000 gross tons) entering the lagoon, plus a limit on smaller ships to five per day. However, by January 2015 that ban had been overturned – that, too, was being contested.

Venice sorely misses the dedicated, centralised governance of the Republic – the lagoon now covers four provinces and is dependent on the policies and post-crisis finances of nine different city and town councils. Venice also has to negotiate over the direct stake of the national government in its museums, airport, railway station and port. As a result the city and its lagoon continue to degrade – the facts speak for themselves. A hundred years ago the average depth of the lagoon was 40cm, now it stands at 1.5m and in 50 years' time it's estimated it could increase to 2.5m. In other words, the floor of the lagoon on which Venice stands may gradually be washed out to sea, transforming the lagoon into a bay, with the city in danger of subsidence or actual collapse into the water as the foundations are undermined.

1973	1996	2003	2014
Italy's first 'special' law for Venice is enacted. It promises to protect urban settlements while maintaining the physical continuity of the lagoon.	La Fenice burns down for the second time; two electricians are found guilty of arson. A €90-million replica of the 19th-century opera house is completed in 2003.	After decades of debate, Berlusconi launches the construction of Modulo Sperimentale Elettromeccanico (MoSE) to prevent future flooding from rising water levels.	MoSE is mired in scandal. Venice mayor Giorgio Orsoni is arrested, the city council suspended and the venerable office of Magistrato alle Acque is dissolved.

Architecture

So what exactly is Venetian architecture? Everyone has a pet period in Venice's chequered architectural history, and hardly anyone agrees which is Venice's defining moment. Ruskin waxed rhapsodic about Venetian Gothic and detested Palladio; Palladians rebuffed baroque; fans of regal rococo were scandalised by the Lido's louche Liberty (Italian art nouveau); and pretty much everyone recoiled at the inclinations of industry to strip Venice of ornamentation. Now that the latest architectural trend is creative repurposing, it's all making a comeback.

Engineering Marvels

Over the centuries, Venetian architecture has evolved into such a dazzling composite of materials, styles and influences that you might overlook its singular defining feature: it floats. Thousands of wood pylons sunk into lagoon mud support stone foundations, built up with elegant brickwork and rustic ceiling beams, low *sotoportegi* (passageways) and lofty loggias, grand water gates and hidden *cortile* (courtyards). Instead of disguising or wallpapering over these essential Venetian structural elements, modern architects have begun highlighting them. With this approach, the Fondazione Giorgio Cini converted a naval academy into a gallery, Tadao Ando turned Punta della Dogana customs houses into a contemporary-art showplace, and Renzo Piano transformed historic Magazzini del Sale (salt warehouses) into a rotating gallery space for Fondazione Emilio Vedova. With original load-bearing supports and brickwork exposed to public admiration, Venice's new-old architecture seems more fresh and vital than ever.

More than 1000 years of architectural history are covered on the short trip down the Grand Canal, lined with 200 palaces that range from Venetian Gothic with Moorish flourishes (the Ca' d'Oro) to postmodern neoclassical (Palazzo Grassi).

Veneto-Byzantine

If Venice seems to have unfair aesthetic advantages, it did have an early start: cosmopolitan flair has made Venetian architecture a standout since the 7th century. While Venice proper was still a motley, muddy outpost of refugee settlements, the nearby island of Torcello was a booming Byzantine trade hub of 20,000 to 30,000 people. At its spiritual centre was the Basilica di Santa Maria Assunta (p149), which from afar looks like a Byzantine-style basilica on loan from Ravenna. But look closely: those 7th-to-9th-century apses have Romanesque arches, and the iconostasis separating the central nave from the presbytery is straight out of an Eastern Orthodox church. Back in Torcello's heyday, traders from France, Greece or Turkey could have stepped off their boats and into this church, and all felt at home.

But to signal to visitors that they had arrived in a powerful trading centre, Santa Maria Assunta glitters with 12th-to-13th-century golden mosaics. Excavations have revealed Torcello glassworks dating from the 7th century, and those furnaces would have been kept glowing through the night to produce the thousands of tiny glass *tesserae* (tiles) needed to create the mesmerising Madonna hovering over the altar – not to mention the rather alarmingly detailed *Last Judgment* mosaic, with hellfire licking at the dancing feet of the damned.

VENICE'S MOST CONTROVERSIAL BRIDGES

Ponte di Calatrava Officially known as Ponte della Costituzione (Constitution Bridge), Spanish architect Santiago Calatrava's contemporary bridge between Piazzale Roma and Ferrovia was commissioned for €4 million in 1999, and for a decade was variously denounced as unnecessary, inappropriate and wheelchair-inaccessible. Though the bridge cost more than triple the original estimate, it also received private backing, hence its local nickname 'Benetton Bridge'.

Ponte di Rialto The original 1255 wooden structure burned during a 1310 revolt, and its replacement collapsed under spectators watching a 1444 wedding parade. The state couldn't gather funds for a 1551 stone bridge project pitched for by Palladio, Sansovino and Michelangelo, and the task fell to Antonio da Ponte in 1588. Cost overruns were enormous: as the stonework settled, the bridge cracked, and legend has it that only a deal with the Devil allowed da Ponte to finish by 1592.

Ponte dei Pugni (Bridge of the Fists) Turf battles were regularly fought on this Dorsoduro bridge between residents of Venice's north end, the Nicolotti, and its south end, the Castellani. Deadly brawls evolved into full-contact boxing matches, with starting footholds marked in the corners of the bridge. Bouts ended with fighters bloodied, bruised and bobbing in the canal. King Henry III of France apparently enjoyed the spectacle, but escalation into deadly knife fights in 1705 ended the practice.

Ponte delle Tette 'Tits Bridge' got its name in the late 15th century, when neighbourhood prostitutes were encouraged to display their wares in the windows of buildings above the bridge instead of taking their marketing campaigns to the streets. According to local lore (and rather bizarre logic), this display was intended to curb a dramatic increase in sodomy.

Ponte dei Sospiri Built by Antonio Contino in 1600 and given its 'Bridge of Sighs' nickname by Lord Byron, the bridge connects the upper storeys of the Palazzo Ducale and Priggione Nove (New Prisons). According to Byron's conceit, doomed prisoners would sigh at their last glimpse of lovely Venice through the bridge's windows – but as you'll notice on Palazzo Ducale tours, the lagoon is scarcely visible through the stonework-screened windows.

Breakout Byzantine Style

When Venice made its definitive break with the Byzantine empire in the 9th century, it needed a landmark to set the city apart, and a platform to launch its golden age of maritime commerce. Basilica di San Marco (p50) captures Venice's grand designs in five vast gold mosaic domes, refracting stray sunbeams like an indoor fireworks display. Even today, the sight elicits audible gasps from crowds of international admirers. The basilica began with a triple nave in the 9th century but, after a fire two wings were added to form a Greek cross, in an idea borrowed from the Church of the Holy Apostles in Constantinople. The finest artisans from around the Mediterranean were brought in to raise the basilica's dazzle factor to jaw-dropping, from 11th-to-13th-century marble relief masterpieces over the Romanesque entry arches to the intricate Islamic geometry of 12th-to-13th-century inlaid semiprecious stone floors.

Since the basilica was the official chapel of the doge, every time Venice conquered new territory by commerce or force, the basilica displayed the doge's share of the loot – hence the walls of polychrome marble pilfered from Egypt and 2nd-century Roman bronze horses looted from Constantinople's hippodrome in 1204. The basilica's ornament shifted over the centuries from Gothic to Renaissance, but the message to visiting dignitaries remained the same: the glory above may be God's, but the power below rested with the doge.

Romanesque

Romanesque was all the rage across Western Europe in the 9th century, from the Lombard plains to Tuscany, southern France to northeast Spain, and later, Germany and England. While the materials ranged from basic brick to elaborate marble, Romanesque rounded archways, barrel-vaulted ceilings, triple naves and calming cloisters came to define medieval church architecture. This austere, classical style was a deliberate reference to the Roman empire and early martyrs who sacrificed all for the Church, reminding the faithful of their own duty through the Crusades. But in case the architecture failed to send the message, sculptural reliefs were added, heralding heroism on entry portals – and putting the fear of the devil into unbelievers, with angels and demons carved into stone capitals in creepy crypts.

As Venice became a maritime empire in the 13th century, many of the city's smaller Byzantine and early Romanesque buildings were swept away to make room for International Gothic grandeur. The finest examples of Romanesque in the Veneto – and possibly in northern Italy – are Verona's vast 12th-to-14th-century Basilica di San Zeno Maggiore (p179) and Padua's frescoed jewel of a Romanesque Baptistry. Within Venice, Romanesque simplicity awaits at Chiesa di San Giacomo dell'Orio (p91).

Venetian Gothic

Soaring spires and flying buttresses rose above Paris in the 12th century, making the rest of Europe suddenly seem small and squat by comparison. Soon every European capital was trying to top Paris with Gothic marvels of their own, featuring deceptively delicate ribbed cross-vaulting that distributed the weight of stone walls and allowed openings for vast stained-glass windows.

Europe's medieval superpowers used this grand international style to showcase their splendour and status. Venice one-upped its neighbours not with height but by inventing its own version of Gothic. Venice had been trading across the Mediterranean with partners from Lebanon to North Africa for centuries, and the constant exchange of building materials, engineering innovations and aesthetic ideals led to a creative cross-pollination in Western and Middle Eastern architecture. Instead of framing windows with the ordinary ogive (pointed) arch common to France and Germany, Venice added an elegantly tapered, Moorish flourish to its arches, with a trilobate (three-lobed) shape that became a signature of Venetian Gothic at Ca' d'Oro (p110).

Brick Gothic

While Tuscany, like France and Germany, used marble for Gothic cathedrals, Venice showcased a more austere, cerebral style with clever brickwork and a Latin cross plan at I Frari (p88), completed in 1443 after a century's work, and Zanipolo (p121), consecrated in 1430. The more fanciful brick Madonna dell'Orto was built on 10th-century foundations, but its facade was lightened up with lacy white porphyry ornament in 1460–64. This white stone framing red brick may have Middle Eastern origins: the style is pronounced in Yemen, where Venice's Marco Polo established trade relations in the 13th century.

Secular Gothic

Gothic architecture was so complicated and expensive that it was usually reserved for cathedrals in wealthy parishes – but Venice decided that if it was good enough for God, then it was good enough for the doge. A rare and extravagant secular Gothic construction, the Palazzo Ducale

Wagering which of Venice's brick *campanile* (bell towers) will next fall victim to shifting *barene* (mud banks) is a morbid Venetian pastime – but don't bet on the leaning tower of San Giorgio dei Greci, which has slouched ever since 1592. San Marco's *campanile* stood ramrod-straight until its 1902 collapse.

Top Five Divine Buildings

....

Basilica di San Marco

....

Chiesa di San Giorgio Maggiore

....

Scuola Grande dei Carmini

....

Chiesa di Santa Maria dei Miracoli

....

Schola Spagnola

(p53) was built in grand Venetian Gothic style beginning in 1340, with refinements and extensions continuing through the 15th century. The palace was just finished when a fire swept through the building in 1577, leaving Venice with a tricky choice: rebuild in the original *gotico fiorito* (flamboyant Gothic) style, or go with the trendy new Renaissance style proposed by Palladio and his peers. The choice was Gothic, but instead of brick, the facade was a puzzlework of white Istrian stone and pink Veronese marble with a delicate, lofty white loggia facing the Grand Canal. In 1853, critic and unabashed Gothic architecture partisan John Ruskin called the Palazzo Ducale the 'central building of the world'.

While the doge's palace is a show-stopper, many Venetian nobles weren't living too shabbily themselves by the 14th century. Even stripped of its original gilding, the Ca' d'Oro is a Grand Canal highlight. The typical Venetian noble family's *palazzo* (palace) had a water gate that gave access from boats to a courtyard or ground floor, with the grand reception hall usually on the *piano nobile* ('noble' or 1st floor). The *piano nobile* was built to impress, with light streaming through double-height loggia windows and balustraded balconies. The 2nd floor might also feature an elegant arcade topped with Venetian Gothic marble arches and trefoils, with crenellation crowning the roofline like a whimsical tiara.

Renaissance

For centuries Gothic cathedrals soared to the skies, pointing the eye and aspirations heavenward – but as the Renaissance ushered in an era of reason and humanism, architecture became more grounded and rational. Venice wasn't immediately sold on this radical new Tuscan world view, but the revival of classical ideals was soon popularised by Padua University and Venetian publishing houses.

With the study of classical philosophy came a fresh appreciation for strict classical order, harmonious geometry and human-scale proportions. A prime early example in Venice is the 1489 Chiesa di Santa Maria dei Miracoli (p109), a small church and great achievement by sculptor-architect Pietro Lombardo (1435–1515) with his sons Tullio and Antonio. The exterior is clad in veined multicolour marbles apparently 'borrowed' from Basilica di San Marco's slag-heap, kept in check by a steady rhythm of Corinthian pilasters. The stark marble interiors set off a joyous profusion of finely worked sculpture, and the coffered ceiling is filled in with portraits of saints in contemporary Venetian garb. This is ecclesiastical architecture come down to earth, intimate and approachable.

Sansovino's Humanist Architecture

Born in Florence and well versed in classical architecture in Rome, Jacopo Sansovino (1486–1570) was a champion of the Renaissance as Venice's *proto* (official city architect). His best works reveal not just a shift in aesthetics but a sea change in thinking. While the Gothic ideal was a staggeringly tall spire topped by a cross, his Libreria Nazionale Marciana is a role-model Renaissance landmark: a low, flat-roofed monument to learning, embellished with statues of great men. Great men are also the theme of Sansovino's Scala dei Giganti in the Palazzo Ducale, a staircase reserved for Venetian dignitaries and an unmistakable metaphorical reminder that in order to ascend to the heights of power, one must stand on the shoulders of giants.

Instead of striving for the skies, Renaissance architecture reached for the horizon. Sansovino changed the skyline of Venice with his work on 15 buildings, including the serenely splendid Chiesa di San Franc-

Venetians avoid walking between the San Marco quay pillars, where criminals were once executed. According to legend, anyone wandering between these pillars will meet an untimely demise – doomed Marin Falier was beheaded eight months after supposedly passing between them to accept the post of doge.

esco della Vigna (p128), completed with a colonnaded facade by Palladio and sculptural flourishes by Pietro and Tullio Lombardo. Thankfully, however, one of Sansovino's most ambitious projects never came to fruition: his plan to turn Piazza San Marco into a Roman forum.

Renaissance Palaces

As the Renaissance swept into Venice, the changes became noticeable along the Grand Canal: pointed Gothic arcades relaxed into rounded archways, repeated geometric forms and serene order replaced Gothic trefoils, and palaces became anchored by bevelled blocks of roughhewn, rusticated marble. One Renaissance trendsetter was Bergamo-born Mauro Codussi (c 1440–1504), whose pleasing classical vocabulary applied equally to churches, the 15th-century Torre dell'Orologio (p57) and several Grand Canal palaces, including Palazzo Vendramin-Calergi, better known today as Casinó di Venezia (p114).

Michele Sanmicheli (1484–1559) was from Verona but, like Sansovino, he worked in Rome, fleeing its sacking in 1527. The Venetian Republic kept him busy engineering defence works for the city, including Le Vignole's Forte Sant'Andrea, also known as the Castello da Mar (Sea Castle). Even Sanmicheli's private commissions have an imposing imperial Roman grandeur; the Grand Canal's Palazzo Grimani (built 1557–59) incorporates a triumphal arch on the ground floor, and feels more suited to its current use as the city's appeal court than a 16th-century pleasure palace. Sanmicheli is also occasionally credited with the other Renaissance Palazzo Grimani in Castello, along with Sansovino – but Venetian Renaissance man Giovanni Grimani seems to have mostly designed his own home as a suitably classical showcase for his collection of ancient Roman statuary, now in the Museo Correr.

Palladio

As the baroque began to graft flourishes and curlicues onto basic Renaissance shapes, Padua-born Andrea Palladio (1508–80) carefully stripped them away, and in doing so laid the basis for modern architecture. His facades are an open-book study of classical architecture, with rigorously elemental geometry – a triangular pediment supported by round columns atop a rectangle of stairs – that lends an irresistible logic to the stunning exteriors of San Giorgio Maggiore (p138) and Redentore.

Critic John Ruskin detested Renaissance architecture in general and Palladio in particular, and ranted about San Giorgio Maggiore in his three-volume book *The Stones of Venice* (1851–53): 'It is impossible to conceive a design more gross, more barbarous, more childish in conception, more servile in plagiarism, more insipid in result, more contemptible under every point of rational regard... The interior of the church is like a large assembly room, and would have been undeserving of a moment's attention, but that it contains some most precious pictures.' But don't take his word for it: Palladio's blinding white Istrian facades may seem stoic from afar, but up close they become relatable, with billowing ceilings and an easy grace that anticipated baroque and high modernism.

Baroque & Neoclassical

In other parts of Europe, baroque architecture seemed lightweight: an assemblage of frills and thrills, with no underlying Renaissance reason or gravitas. But baroque's buoyant spirits made perfect sense along the Grand Canal, where white-stone party palaces with tiers of ornament looked like floating wedding cakes. Baldassare Longhena (1598–1682) stepped into the role as the city's official architect at a moment when

ARCHITECTURE BAROQUE & NEOCLASSICAL

Top Five Palladio Landmarks

Chiesa di San Giorgio Maggiore (Isola di San Giorgio Maggiore)

La Malcontenta (Riviera Brenta)

La Rotunda (Vicenza)

Villa di Masèr (north of Vicenza)

Teatro Olimpico (Vicenza)

the city was breathing a sigh of relief at surviving the Black Death, and he provided the architectural antidote to Venice's dark days with the white bubble-dome of Basilica di Santa Maria della Salute (p76).

Architectural historians chalk up Longhena's unusual octagon-base dome to the influence of Roman shrines and cabbala diagrams, and the church's geometric stone floors are said to have mystical healing powers. Santa Maria della Salute's exterior decoration evokes pagan triumphal arches, with statues posing triumphantly on the facade and reclining over the main entrance. The building has inspired landscape artists from Turner to Monet, leading baroque-baiting Ruskin to concede that 'an architect trained in the worst schools, and utterly devoid of all meaning or purpose in his work may yet have such natural gift of massing and grouping as will render all his structures effective when seen from a distance'.

Although Ruskin deemed Longhena's fanciful facade of hulking sculptures at the Ospedaletto (p124) 'monstrous', baroque fans will think otherwise. Another Longhena-designed marvel is Ca' Rezzonico (p76), a wonder of sunny salons graced with spectacular Tiepolo ceilings. Soaring grandeur and mystical geometry in the Ghetto's Schola Spagnola's interior have led many to attribute it to Longhena, too.

Neoclassicism & Napoleon

Venice didn't lose track of Renaissance harmonies completely under all that ornament, and in the 18th century muscular neoclassicism came into vogue. Inspired by Palladio, Giorgio Massari (c 1686–1766) created the Chiesa dei Gesuati (p77) as high theatre, setting the stage for Tiepolo's trompe l'œil ceilings. He built the gracious Palazzo Grassi (p63) with salons around a balustraded central light well, and brought to completion Longhena's Ca' Rezzonico on the Grand Canal.

Napoleon roared into Venice like a bully in 1797, itching to rearrange its face. The emperor's first order of architectural business was demolishing Sansovino's Chiesa di Geminiano to construct a monument in his own glory: the Ala Napoleonica (now Museo Correr) by Giovanni Antonio Selva (1753–1819). Napoleon had an entire district with four churches bulldozed to make way for the Giardini Pubblici and Via Garibaldi in Castello. Though Napoleon ruled Venice for only 11 years, French boulevards appeared where there were once churches across the city. Among others, Sant'Angelo, San Basilio, Santa Croce, Santa Maria Nova, Santa Marina, San Mattio, San Paterniano, San Severo, San Stin, Santa Ternita and San Vito disappeared under the ambitious Gallic ruler.

Next to bridges, Venice's most common architectural features are its *poggi* (well-heads). Before Venice's aqueduct was constructed, more than 6000 wells collected and filtered rainwater for public use. Even today, overflow happy-hour crowds at neighbourhood *bacari* (bars) schmooze and toast around 600 surviving ancient watering holes.

The 20th Century

After Giudecca's baroque buildings were torn down for factories and the Ferrovia (train station) erected, the city took decades to recover from the shock. Venice reverted to 19th-century *venezianitá,* the tendency to tack on exaggerated Venetian elements from a range of periods – a Gothic trefoil arch here, a baroque cupola there. Rather than harmonising these disparate architectural elements, interiors were swagged in silk damask and moodlit with Murano chandeliers. The resulting hodgepodge seemed to signal the end of Venice's architectural glory days.

From Liberty Flounce to Fascist Sobriety

After nearly a century dominated by French and Austrian influence, Venice let loose on the Lido with the bohemian decadence of *stile liberty* (Liberty style, or Italian art nouveau). Ironwork vegetation wound around balconies of seaside villas and wild fantasy took root at grand hotels, including Giovanni Sardi's 1898–1908 Byzantine-Moorish Excelsior and Guido Sullam's Hungaria Palace Hotel. Eclectic references to Japanese art, organic patterns from nature and past Venetian styles give Lido buildings cosmopolitan flair with *stile liberty* tiles, stained glass, ironwork and murals.

By the 1930s, the Liberty party was well and truly over. The Fascists arrived to lay down the law on the Lido, applying a strict, functional neo-classicism even to entertainment venues such as the 1937–38 Palazzo della Mostra del Cinema (p145) and former Casinò. Fascist architecture makes occasional awkward appearances in central Venice too, notably the Hotel Bauer and the extension to the Hotel Danieli, which represent an architectural oxymoron: the strict Fascist luxury-deco hotel.

Scarpa's High Modernism

The Biennale introduced new international architecture to Venice, but high modernism remained mostly an imported style until it was championed by Venice's own Carlo Scarpa (1906–78). Instead of creating seamless modern surfaces, Scarpa frequently exposed underlying structural elements and added unexpectedly poetic twists. At Negozio Olivetti (p58), mosaic and water channels mimic *acqua alta* (high tide) across the floor, a floating staircase makes ascent seem effortless, and internal balconies jut out mid-air like diving boards into the infinite. Scarpa's concrete-slab Venezuelan Pavilion (p122) was ahead of its time by a full half-century, and inevitably steals the show at Biennales. High modernist architecture aficionados make pilgrimages outside Venice to see Scarpa's Brioni Tomb near Asolo, and Castelvecchio in Verona. Scarpa's smaller works can be spotted all over Venice: the cricket-shaped former ticket booth at the Biennale, the entry and gardens of Palazzo Querini Stampalia, spare restorations to the doorway of the Accademia, the elegant *boiserie* (panelling) inside the Aula Mario Baratto at Ca' Foscari, as well as the playful main gate at the Università Iuav di Venezia – Tolentini.

Contemporary Venice

Modernism was not without its critics, especially among Venice's preservationists. But when a disastrous flood hit Venice in 1966, architecture aficionados around the globe put aside their differences, and aided Venetians in bailing out *palazzi* and reinforcing foundations across the city. With the support of Unesco and funding from 24 affiliated organisations worldwide, Venice has completed over 1500 restoration projects in 40 years.

Today the city is open to a broader range of styles, though controversy is never far behind. Divisive projects that never left the drawing board include a 1953 design for student housing on the Grand Canal by Frank Lloyd Wright, Le Corbusier's 1964 plans for a hospital in Cannaregio, Louis Kahn's 1968 Palazzo dei Congressi project for the Giardini Pubblici, and the 2011 Palais Lumière, a three-finned skyscraper proposed by fashion designer Pierre Cardin and his architect nephew Rodrigo Basilicati. Planned for the industrial, mainland area of Porto Marghera, the 60-storey project ignited widespread opposition in Venice, with many Venetians arguing that its enormous scale and sci-fi design was highly inappropriate in the historic lagoon. Old also triumphed over new in the 2003 reconstruction of Teatro La Fenice, which opted for a €90-million replica of the 19th-century opera house instead of an edgier, modernised version proposed by the late architect Gae Aulenti.

Venice's first bridge to the mainland was built by the Austrians at Venetian taxpayers' expense in 1841–46, enabling troop and supplies transport by railway. Propped up by 222 arches, the bridge spans 2.7km. Explosives were originally planted under the piers, to be detonated in case of emergency.

ARCHITECTURE CONTEMPORARY VENICE

PHILIP LEE HARVEY / LONELY PLANET ®

1. Palazzo Ducale (p53) **2.** Chiesa di Santa Maria dei Miracoli (p109) **3.** Basilica di San Marco (p50) **4.** Basilica di Santa Maria della Salute (p76)

Architectural Marvels

➜ **Basilica di San Marco** (p50) Only if angels and pirates founded an architecture firm could there ever be another building like Venice's cathedral. Saints tip-toe across gold mosaics inside bubble domes, gilded horses pilfered from Constantinople gallop off the loggia, and priceless marbles lining the walls and floors are on exceedingly long-term loan from Syria and Egypt. Awed glee ensues.

➜ **Basilica di Santa Maria della Salute** (p76) The sublime white dome defies gravity, but thousands of wooden poles underfoot are doing the heavy lifting. Posts sunk deep into lagoon mud create an ingenious foundation for Baldassare Longhena's white Istrian stone masterpiece, influenced by mystical cabbala designs and rumoured to have curative powers.

➜ **Palazzo Ducale** (p53) Town halls don't get grander than this pink palace. Other medieval cities reserved Gothic graces for cathedrals, but Venice went all out to impress visiting dignitaries and potential business partners with pink Veronese marble and gilt staircases – you'd never guess there were spies and prisoners hidden upstairs.

➜ **Biennale Pavilions** (p122) International relations never looked better than in Venice's Giardini Pubblici, where Biennale pavilions are purpose-built to reflect national architectural identities from Hungary (futuristic folklore hut) to Korea (creative industrial complex). Venetian modernist Carlo Scarpa steals the show with his cricket-shaped ticket booth.

➜ **Chiesa di Santa Maria dei Miracoli** (p109) Small with outsized swagger, this corner church is a masterpiece of Renaissance repurposing. Pietro Lombardo and sons worked wonders from San Marco's marble slag-heap, creating a gleaming, aquarium-like space where carved mermaids and miracle-working Madonnas seem right at home.

Old is the New New

Despite the constraints of history, strict building codes, and the practical challenges of construction with materials transported by boat, lifted by crane and hauled by handcart, a surprising number of projects have turned Venice into a portfolio of contemporary architecture.

MIT-trained Italian architect Cino Zucchi kicked off the creative revival of Giudecca in 1995 with his conversion of 19th-century brick factories and waterfront warehouses into art spaces and studio lofts. A decade later, a triangular WWII bunker and bombs warehouse found new purpose as Teatro Junghans (p144), a hot spot for experimental theatre.

London-based firm David Chipperfield Architects has breathed new life into the cemetery island of San Michele with its sleek contemporary extensions. Among them is the House of the Dead, a bold, basalt-clad burial complex consisting of four open courtyards. The most striking of these is the Courtyard of the Four Evangelists. Featuring a black concrete colonnade, the courtyard's walls and pavement are inlaid with text from the gospels. Nearing completion, the next stage of the project will see a new island flanking the existing one. Separated by a canal, this supporting island is set to include gardens at water level and a series of elegant, sculpted tomb buildings. Meanwhile, rebirth of the artistic kind underscores Fondazione Giorgio Cini's Isola di San Giorgio Maggiore redevelopment, one that has transformed the island into a global cultural centre. Among its numerous features is a maze dedicated to Argentine writer Jorge Luis Borges behind the Palladian cloisters, as well as a dormitory-turned-humanities-library to complement Baldassare Longhena's original 17th-century science library. Across the Canale di San Marco, the continuing evolution of Venice's historic Arsenale (p119) shipyards has seen its medieval assembly-line sheds turned into fetching Biennale art galleries.

French billionaire art collector François Pinault hired Japanese minimalist architect Tadao Ando to repurpose two historic buildings into settings for his contemporary-art collection. Instead of undermining their originality, Ando's careful repurposing showcases the muscular strength of Giorgio Masari's 1749 neoclassical Palazzo Grassi (p63) in San Marco and Venice's late-17th-century Punta della Dogana (p78) customs houses in Dorsoduro. Around the corner from Punta della Dogana, Pritzker Prize–winning architect Renzo Piano reinvented the Magazzini del Sale (p77) as a showcase for the Fondazione Vedova, an art foundation dedicated to abstract Venetian painter Emilio Vedova. Similar to Ando's approach, Renzo's conversion embraces the building's original essence, its historic roof trusses and brick walls are integral elements of the modern makeover. Within this clear, uncluttered historical template, Piano added his respectful modern touches. The most unique of these is a conveyor system of 10 robotic arms, designed to rotate the gallery's art works like a team of cyborg curators. Renzo's transformation is only fitting: Venice's salt monopoly was once its dearest treasure, but now its ideas are its greatest asset.

From late 2015, culture and commerce will co-exist in Dutch architect Rem Koolhaas' redevelopment of the Fondaco dei Tedeschi, steps away from the Rialto Bridge in San Marco. Once a base for German merchants, the revamped 16th-century *palazzo* is set to house a department store, contemporary frescoes, a publicly accessible rooftop, as well as dedicated public and cultural spaces. Among these spaces is the *palazzo's* courtyard, to be used for events such as film screening, performances and meetings. The highly publicised incorporation of non-commercial spaces and events into the project is hoped to appease its opponents, who argue that the historical building's retail conversion undermines Venice's heritage.

The Arts

By the 13th century, Venice had already accomplished the impossible: building a glorious maritime empire on a shallow lagoon. But its dominance didn't last. Plague repeatedly decimated the city in the 14th century, new trade routes to the New World bypassed Venice and its tax collectors, and the Ottoman Empire dominated the Adriatic by the mid-15th century. Yet when Venice could no longer prevail by wealth or force, it triumphed on even loftier levels, with art, music, theatre and poetry.

Visual Arts

The sheer number of masterpieces packed into Venice might make you wonder if there's something in the water here, but the reason may be simpler: historically, Venice tended not to starve its artists. Multiyear commissions from wealthy private patrons, the city and the Church offered creatives a sense of security. Artists were granted extraordinary opportunities to produce new artwork without interference, with the city frequently declining to enforce the Inquisition's censorship edicts. Instead of dying young, destitute and out of favour, painters such as Titian and Giovanni Bellini survived into their 80s to produce late, great works. The side-by-side innovations of emerging and mature artists created schools of painting so distinct they still set Venice apart from the rest of Italy – and the world.

Early Venetian Painting

Once you've seen the mosaics at Basilica di San Marco and Santa Maria Assunta in Torcello, you'll recognise key aspects of early Venetian painting: larger-than-life religious figures with wide eyes and serene expressions floating on gold backgrounds and hovering inches above Gothic thrones. Byzantine influence is clearly present in *Madonna and Child with Two Votaries,* painted c 1325 by Paolo Veneziano (c 1300–62) and on display at the Gallerie dell'Accademia (p73): like stage hands parting theatre curtains, two angels pull back the edges of a starry red cloak to reveal a hulking Madonna, golden baby Jesus, and two tiny patrons.

By the early 15th century, Venetian painters were breaking with Byzantine convention. *Madonna with Child* (c 1455) by Jacopo Bellini (c 1396–1470) in the Accademia is an image any modern parent might relate to: bright-eyed baby Jesus reaches one sandalled foot over the edge of the balcony, while a seemingly sleep-deprived Mary patiently pulls him away from the ledge. Padua's Andrea Mantegna (1431–1506) took Renaissance perspective to extremes, showing bystanders in his biblical scenes reacting to unfolding miracles and martyrdoms with shock, awe, anger, and even inappropriate laughter.

Tuscan painter Gentile da Fabriano was in Venice as he was beginning his transition to Renaissance realism, and apparently influenced the young Murano-born painter Antonio Vivarini (c 1415–80), whose *Passion* polyptych in Ca' d'Oro shows tremendous pathos. Antonio's brother, Bartolomeo Vivarini (c 1432–99), created a delightful altarpiece in I Frari showing a baby Jesus wriggling out of the arms of the Madonna, squarely seated on her marble Renaissance throne.

Turbaned figures appear across Venice on the corners of Campo dei Mori, on diamond-encrusted jewels at Sigfrido Cipolato, and propping up I Frari funerary monuments. Misleadingly referred to as Mori (Moors), some represent Venetians from Greek Morea, others Turkish pirates, and others enslaved Africans who rowed merchant ships across the Mediterranean.

Detail of a mosaic in Basilica di San Marco (p50)

Venice's Red-Hot Renaissance

Jacopo Bellini's sons used a new medium that would revolutionise Venetian painting: oil paints. The 1500 *Miracle of the Cross at the Bridge of San Lorenzo* by Gentile Bellini (1429–1507) at the Accademia shows the religious figure not high on a throne or adrift in the heavens, but floating in the Grand Canal, with crowds of bystanders stopped in their tracks in astonishment. Giovanni Bellini (c 1430–1516) takes an entirely different approach to his Accademia *Annunciation,* using luminous reds and oranges to focus attention on the solitary figure of the kneeling Madonna awed by an angel arriving in a swish of rumpled drapery.

From Venice's guild of house painters emerged some of art history's greatest names, starting with Giovanni Bellini's apt pupils: Giorgione (1477–1510) and Titian (c 1488–1576). The two worked together on the frescoes that once covered the Fondaco dei Tedeschi (only a few fragments remain in the Ca' d'Oro), with teenage Titian following Giorgione's lead. Giorgione was a Renaissance man who wrote poetry and music, is credited with inventing the easel, and preferred to paint from inspiration without sketching out his subject first, as in his enigmatic, Leonardo da Vinci–style 1508 *La Tempesta* (The Storm) at Gallerie dell'Accademia.

When Giorgione died at 33, probably of the plague, Titian finished some of his works – but young Titian soon set himself apart with brushstrokes that brought his subjects to life, while taking on a life of their own. At Basilica di Santa Maria della Salute (p76), you'll notice Titian started out a measured, methodical painter in his 1510 *Saint Mark on the Throne.* After seeing Michelangelo's expressive *Last Judgment,* Titian let it rip: in his final 1576 *Pietà* he smeared paint onto canvas with his bare hands.

Winged lions carved onto Venetian facades symbolise St Mark, Venice's patron saint, but some served sinister functions. In the 1500s, the Consiglio dei Dieci (Council of Ten) established *bocca dei leoni* (lion's mouths) – stone lions' heads with slots for inserting anonymous denunciations of neighbours for crimes ranging from cursing to conspiracy.

But even for a man of many masterpieces, Titian's 1518 altarpiece *Assunta* (Ascension) at I Frari (p88) is nothing short of enigmatic, mysteriously lighting up the cavernous space with solar-like energy. Vittore Carpaccio (1460–1526) rivalled Titian's reds with his own sanguine hues – hence the dish of bloody beef cheekily named in his honour by Harry's Bar – but it was Titian's *Assunta* that cemented Venice's reputation for glowing, glorious hues.

Not Minding Their Manners: Venice's Mannerists

Although art history tends to insist on a division of labour between Venice and Florence – Venice had the colour, Florence the ideas – the Venetian School had plenty of ideas that repeatedly got it into trouble. Titian was a hard act to follow, but there's no denying the impact of Venice's Jacopo Robusti, aka Tintoretto (1518–94) and Paolo Cagliari from Verona, known as Veronese (1528–88).

A crash course in Tintoretto begins at Chiesa della Madonna dell'Orto (p109), his parish church and the serene brick backdrop for his action-packed 1546 *Last Judgment*. True-blue Venetian that he is, Tintoretto shows the final purge as a teal tidal wave, which lost souls are vainly trying to hold back, like human MoSE barriers. A dive-bombing angel swoops in to save one last person – a riveting image Tintoretto reprised on the upper floor of the Scuola Grande di San Rocco. The artist spent some 15 years creating works for San Rocco, and his biblical scenes read like a modern graphic novel. Tintoretto sometimes used special effects to get his point across, enhancing his colours with a widely available local material: finely crushed glass.

Veronese's colours have a luminosity entirely their own, earning him Palazzo Ducale commissions and room to run riot inside Chiesa di San Sebastiano – but his choice of subjects got him into trouble. When Veronese was commissioned to paint the *Last Supper* (in Gallerie dell'Accademia, p73) his masterpiece ended up looking suspiciously like a Venetian shindig, with apostles in Venetian dress mingling freely with Turkish merchants, Jewish guests, serving wenches, begging lapdogs and (most shocking of all) Protestant Germans. When the Inquisition demanded he change the painting, Veronese refused to remove the offending Germans and altered scarcely a stroke of paint, simply changing the title to *Feast in the House of Levi*. In an early victory for freedom of expression, Venice stood by the decision.

The next generation of Mannerists included Palma il Giovane (1544–1628), who finished Titian's *Pietá* after the master's death and fused Titian's early naturalism with Tintoretto's drama. Another Titian acolyte who adopted Tintoretto's dramatic lighting was Jacopo da Ponte from Bassano del Grappa, called Bassano (1517–92). Bassano's work is so high contrast and high drama, at first glance you might wonder how black-velvet paintings wound up in Gallerie dell'Accademia, Chiesa di San Giorgio Maggiore and Bassano del Grappa's Museo Civico.

VENETIAN PAINTINGS THAT CHANGED PAINTING

→ *Feast in the House of Levi* (Veronese, Gallerie dell'Accademia)

→ *Assunta* (Titian, I Frari)

→ *St Mark in Glory* (Tintoretto, Scuola Grande di San Rocco)

→ *La Tempesta* (Giorgione, Gallerie dell'Accademia)

→ *Madonna with Child Between Saints Caterina and Maddalena* (Giovanni Bellini, Gallerie dell'Accademia)

A Blast of Baroque

By the 18th century, Venice had endured plague and seen its ambitions for world domination dashed – but the city repeatedly made light of its dire situation in tragicomic art. Pietro Longhi (1701–85) dispensed with lofty subject matter and painted wickedly witty Venetian social satires, while Giambattista Tiepolo (1696–1770) turned religious themes into a premise for dizzying ceilings with rococo sunbursts. Ca' Rezzonico (p76) became a show place for both their talents, with an entire salon of Longhi's drawing-room scenarios and Tiepolo's trompe l'œil ceiling masterpieces.

Instead of popes on thrones, portraitist Rosalba Carriera (1675–1757) captured her socialite sitters on snuffboxes, and painted in a medium she pioneered: pastels. Her portraits at Ca' Rezzonico walk a fine line between Tiepolo's flattery and Longhi's satire, revealing her sitters' every twinkle and wrinkle.

As the 18th-century party wound down, the Mannerists' brooding theatricality merged with Tiepolo's pastel beauty in works by Tiepolo's son, Giandomenico Tiepolo (1727–1804). His 1747–49 *Stations of the Cross* in Chiesa di San Polo (p94) takes a dim view of humanity in light colours, illuminating the jeering faces of Jesus' tormentors. Giandomenico used a lighter touch working alongside his father on the frescoes at Villa Valmarana 'ai Nani' (p173) outside Vicenza, covering the walls with Chinese motifs, rural scenes and Carnivale characters.

Top Five Arts Workshops

Hands-on workshops (Venice Biennale)

Micro mosaic workshops (Orsoni Mosaici)

Printing & engraving workshops (Bottega del Tintoretto)

Screenprinting courses (Fallani Venezia)

Painting 'en plein air' (Painting in Venice)

The Vedutisti

Many Venetian artists turned their attention from the heavens to the local landscape in the 18th century, notably Antonio Canal, aka Canaletto (1697–1768). He became the leading figure of the *vedutisti* (landscape artists) with minutely detailed *vedute* (views) of Venice that leave admiring viewers with vicarious hand cramps. You might be struck how

TOP FIVE ARTISTS IN RESIDENCE

➡ **Albrecht Dürer** (1471–1528) left his native Nuremberg for Venice in 1494, hoping to see Venetian experiments in perspective and colour that were the talk of Europe. Giovanni Bellini took him under his wing, and once Dürer returned to Germany in 1495, he began his evolution from Gothic painter into Renaissance artist. When Dürer returned to Venice in 1505, he was feted as a visionary.

➡ **JMW Turner** (1775–1851) was drawn to Venice three times (in 1819, 1833 and 1840), fascinated by the former merchant empire that, like his native England, had once commanded the sea. Turner's hazy portraits of the city are studies in light at different times of day; as he explained to art critic John Ruskin, 'atmosphere is my style'. Ruskin applauded the effort, but in London many critics loathed Turner's work.

➡ **James Whistler** (1834–1903) arrived in Venice in 1879, bankrupt and exhausted after a failed libel case brought against John Ruskin. The American painter rediscovered his verve and brush in prolific paintings of the lagoon city, returning to London in 1880 with a formidable portfolio that re-established his reputation.

➡ **John Singer Sargent** (1856–1925) was a lifelong admirer of Venice; the American visited at a young age and became a part-time resident from 1880 to 1913. Sargent's intimate knowledge of the city shows in his paintings, which capture new angles on familiar panoramas and illuminate neglected monuments.

➡ **Claude Monet** (1840–1926) turned up in Venice in 1908, and immediately found Impressionist inspiration in architecture that seemed to dissolve into lagoon mists and shimmering waters. Despite claiming that the city was too beautiful to paint, the French artist set brush to 37 canvases during his short sojourn.

closely Canalettos resemble photographs – and, in fact, Canaletto created his works with the aid of a forerunner to the photographic camera, the *camera oscura* (camera obscura). Light entered this instrument and reflected the image onto a sheet of glass, which Canaletto then traced. After he had the outlines down, he filled in exact details, from lagoon algae to hats on passers-by.

Vedute sold well to Venice visitors; they were like rich man's postcards. Canaletto was backed by the English collector John Smith, who introduced the artist to such a vast English clientele that only a few of his paintings can be seen in the Veneto today, in Venice's Gallerie dell'Accademia (p73) and Ca' Rezzonico (p76), and further afield in Vicenza's Palazzo Leoni Montanari (p172). Canaletto's nephew Bernardo Bellotto (1721–80) also adopted the *camera oscura* in his painting process, though his expressionistic landscapes use strong *chiaroscuro* (shadow and light contrasts). His paintings hang in the Accademia alongside *San Marco Basin with San Giorgio and Giudecca* by Francesco Guardi (1712–93), whose Impressionistic approach shows Venice's glories reflected in the lagoon. Among the last great *vedutisti* was Venetian Impressionist Emma Ciardi (1879–1933), who captured Venetian mysteries unfolding amid shimmering early-morning mists in luminous landscapes at Ca' Rezzonico and Ca' Pesaro.

Lucky Stiffs: Venetian Funerary Sculpture

Bookending Venice's accomplishments in painting are its sculpted marvels. The city kept its sculptors busy, with 200 churches needing altars, fire-prone Palazzo Ducale requiring near-constant rebuilding for 300 years, not to mention the near-endless chiseling of tombs for nobles with political careers cut short by age, plague and intrigue. The tomb of Doge Marco Corner in Zanipolo (p121) by Pisa's Nino Pisano (c 1300–68) is a sprawling wall monument with a massive, snoozing doge that somewhat exaggerated his career: Corner was doge for less than three years.

Venice's Pietro Lombardo (1435–1515) and his sons Tullio (1460–1532) and Antonio (1458–1516) sculpted heroic, classical monuments to shortlived dogi: Nicolo Marcello, doge for a year (1473–74), Pietro Mocenigo (1474–76) and Andrea Vendramin (1476–78). This last gilded marble monument was probably completed under Tullio, who literally cut corners: he sculpted the figures in half relief, and chopped away part of Pisano's Corner tomb to make room for Vendramin. Tullio's strong suit was the ideal beauty of his faces, as you can see in his bust of a young male saint at Chiesa di Santo Stefano (p59).

The most prominent sculptor to emerge from the Veneto is Antonio Canova (1757–1822), whose pyramid tomb intended for Titian at I Frari (p88) would become his own funerary masterpiece. Mourners hang their heads and clutch one another, scarcely aware that their diaphanous garments are slipping off; even the great winged lion of St Mark is curled up in grief. Don't let his glistening Orpheus and Eurydice in Museo Correr fool you: Canova's seamless perfection in glistening marble was achieved through rough drafts modelled in gypsum, displayed at the Museo Canova near the hilltop town of Asolo.

Not Strictly Academic: Venetian Modernism

The arrival of Napoleon in 1797 was a disaster for Venice and its art. During his Kingdom of Italy (1806–14), Napoleon and his forces knocked down churches and systematically plundered Venice and the region of artistic treasures. Some works have been restored to Venice, including the bronze horses of Basilica di San Marco that arguably belong in Istanbul, given that Venice pilfered them from Constantinople. Yet even under 19th-century occupation, Venice remained a highlight

---

THE ARTS VISUAL ARTS

Top Five for Modern & Contemporary Art

Venice Biennale

Peggy Guggenheim Collection (Dorsoduro)

Ca' Pesaro (Santa Croce)

Punta della Dogana (Dorsoduro)

Palazzo Grassi (San Marco)

VENICE VIEWS INDOORS

→ *The Miracle of the Reliquary of the Cross at Rialto Bridge* (c 1494, Vittore Carpaccio; Gallerie dell'Accademia)

→ *Procession in San Marco* (c 1496, Gentile Bellini; Gallerie dell'Accademia)

→ *Rio dei Mendicanti* (1723–24, Canaletto; Ca' Rezzonico)

→ *Piazza San Marco, Mass after the Victory* (1918, Emma Ciardi; Museo Correr)

→ *San Marco Basin with San Giorgio and Giudecca* (1770–74, Francesco Guardi; Gallerie dell'Accademia)

Top Five for Modernism

Peggy Guggenheim Collection (Dorsoduro)

Ca' Pesaro (Santa Croce)

Fondazione Prada (Santa Croce)

Fondazione Giorgio Cini (Isola di San Giorgio Maggiore)

Museo Fortuny (San Marco)

of the Grand Tour, and painters who flocked to the city created memorable Venice cityscapes.

After joining the newly unified Italy in 1866, Venice's signature artistic contribution to the new nation was Francesco Hayez (1791–1882). The Venetian painter paid his dues with society portraits but is best remembered for Romanticism and frank sexuality, beginning with *Rinaldo and Armida* (1814), in the Gallerie dell'Accademia. Sexuality and Italian patriotism underline Hayez's brooding *Meditation* (1851) in Verona's Galleria d'Arte Moderna, a work driven by the artist's frustration at the failed pro-unification battles of 1848.

Never shy about self-promotion, Venice held its first Biennale in 1895 to reassert its role as global taste maker and provide an essential corrective to the brutality of the Industrial Revolution. A garden pavilion showcased a self-promoting, studiously inoffensive take on Italian art – principally lovely ladies, pretty flowers, and lovely ladies wearing pretty flowers. Other nations were granted pavilions in 1907, but the Biennale retained strict control, and had a Picasso removed from the Spanish pavilion in 1910 so as not to shock the public with modernity.

A backlash to Venetian conservatism arose from the ranks of Venetian painters experimenting in modern styles. Shows of young artists backed by the Duchess Felicita Bevilacqua La Masa found a permanent home in 1902, when the Duchess gifted Ca' Pesaro (p90) to the city as a modern-art museum. A leader of the Ca' Pesaro crowd was Gino Rossi (1884–1947), whose brilliant blues and potent symbolism bring to mind Gauguin, Matisse and the Fauvists, and whose later work shifted toward Cubism. Often called the Venetian van Gogh, Rossi spent many years in psychiatric institutions, where he died. Sculptor Arturo Martini (1889–1947) contributed works to Ca' Pesaro ranging from the rough-edged terracotta *Prostitute* (c 1913) to his radically streamlined 1919 gesso bust.

Future Perfect: From Futurism to Fluidity

In 1910, Filippo Tommaso Marinetti (1876–1944) threw packets of his manifesto from Torre dell'Orologio promoting a new vision for the arts: futurism. In the days of the doge, Marinetti would have been accused of heresy for his declaration that Venice (a 'magnificent sore of the past') should be wiped out and replaced with a new industrial city. The futurists embraced industry and technology with their machine-inspired, streamlined look – a style that Mussolini co-opted in the 1930s for his vision of a monolithic, modern Italy. Futurism was conflated with Mussolini's brutal imposition of artificial order until championed in Venice by a heroine of the avant-garde and refugee from the Nazis: American expat art collector Peggy Guggenheim, who recognised in futurism the fluidity and flux of modern life.

Artistic dissidents also opposed Mussolini's square-jawed, iron-willed aesthetics. Emilio Vedova (1919–2006) joined the *Corrente* movement of artists, which openly opposed Fascist trends in a magazine shut down by the Fascists in 1940. After WWII, Vedova veered towards abstraction, and his larger works are now in regular robot-assisted rotation at the Magazzini del Sale (p77). Giovanni Pontini (1915–70) was a worker who painted as a hobby until 1947, when he discovered Kokoschka, van Gogh and Rouault, who inspired his empathetic paintings of fishermen at the Peggy Guggenheim Collection (p75).

Venetian Giuseppe Santomaso (1907–90) painted his way out of constrictive Fascism with lyrical, unbounded abstract landscapes. Rigidity and liquidity became the twin fascinations of another avant-garde Italian artist – Unesco-acclaimed, Bologna-born and Venice-trained video artist Fabrizio Plessi (b 1940). His 1970s *Arte Povera* (Poor Art) experiments in humble materials, while his multimedia installations feature Venice's essential medium: water.

The fluidity that characterises Venice and its art continues into the 21st century, with new art galleries in San Marco and Giudecca showing a range of landscapes, abstraction, video and installation art.

Music

Over the centuries, Venetian musicians developed a reputation for playing music as though their lives depended on it, which at times wasn't far from the truth. In its trade-empire heyday, La Serenissima had official musicians, including the distinguished directorship of Flemish Adrian Willaert (1490–1562) for 35 years at Capella Ducale. But when the city fell on hard times in the 17th to 18th centuries, it discovered its musical calling.

With shrinking trade revenues, the state took the quixotic step of underwriting musical education for orphan girls, and the investment yielded unfathomable returns. Among the *maestri* hired to conduct orphan orchestras was Antonio Vivaldi (1678–1741), whose 30-year tenure yielded hundreds of concertos and popularised Venetian baroque music across Europe. Visitors spread word of extraordinary performances by orphan girls, and the city became a magnet for novelty-seeking moneyed socialites. Modern visitors to Venice can still experience music and opera performed in the same venues as in Vivaldi's day – *palazzi* (palaces), churches and *ospedaletti* (orphanages) such as La Pietà (p128), where Vivaldi worked – sometimes with 18th-century instruments.

Opera

Today's televised talent searches can't compare to Venice's knack for discovering talents like Claudio Monteverdi (1567–1643), who was named the musical director of the Basilica di San Marco and went on to launch modern opera. Today, opera reverberates inside La Fenice and across town in churches, concert halls and *palazzi* – but until 1637 you would have needed an invitation to hear it. Opera and most chamber music were the preserve of the nobility, performed in private salons.

Then Venice threw open the doors of the first public opera houses. Between 1637 and 1700, some 358 operas were staged in 16 theatres to meet the musical demands of a population of 140,000. Monteverdi wrote two stand-out operas, *Il ritorno di Ulisse al suo paese* (The Return of Ulysses) and *L'Incoronazione di Poppea* (The Coronation of Poppea), with an astonishing range of plot and subplot, strong characterisation and powerful music. Critical response couldn't have been better: he was buried with honours in I Frari.

A singer at the Basilica di San Marco under Monteverdi, Pier Francesco Cavalli (1602–76) became the outstanding 17th-century Italian opera composer, with 42 operas. With his frequent collaborator Carlo Goldoni and Baldassare Galuppi (1706–84), he added musical hooks to *opera buffa* (comic opera) favourites like *Il filosofo di campagna* (The Country Philosopher).

Besides *musica leggera* ('light' or pop music), jazz is another modern musical offering in Venice. The Venice Jazz Club features tribute nights year-round, and during July's Venice Jazz Festival, you may luck into a performance by Venetian saxophonist and composer Giannantonio De Vincenzo or Venetian trumpeter-musicologist Massimo Donà.

Classical

Get ready to baroque-and-roll: Venetian classical musicians are leading a revival of 'early music' from medieval through to Renaissance and baroque periods, with historically accurate arrangements played *con brio* (with verve) on period instruments. Venetian baroque was the rebel music of its day, openly defying edicts from Rome deciding which instruments could accompany sermons and what kinds of rhythms and melodies were suitable for moral uplift. Venetians kept right on playing stringed instruments in churches, singing along to bawdy *opera buffa* and writing compositions that were both soulful and sensual.

Modern misconceptions about baroque being a polite soundtrack to wedding ceremonies are smashed by baroque 'early music' ensembles. Among Vivaldi's repertoire of some 500 concertos is his ever-popular *The Four Seasons*, instantly recognisable from hotel lobbies and ringtones – but you haven't heard summer lightning strikes or icy winter rainfall until you've heard it played *con brio* by Interpreti Veneziani (p67).

The pleasure palace of Palazzetto Bru Zane (p100) is now restored to its original function: concerts to flirt and swoon over, with winking approval from Sebastiano Ricci's frolicking, frescoed angels. Venetian venues make all the difference: any classical performance in the grand salon of Palazzo Querini Stampalia (p126) will transport you to the 18th century in one movement, and catapult you into the 21st with the next. Seek out programs featuring Venetian baroque composer Tomaso Albinoni (1671–1750), especially the exquisite *Sinfonie e Concerti a 5*. For a more avant-garde take on classical music, look for works by Bruno Maderna (1920–73) or Luigi Nono (1924–90).

In trying to describe the *Inferno* to contemporary readers circa 1307, Dante compared it to Venice's Arsenale, with its stinking vats of tar, sparks flying from hammers and infernal clamour of 16,000 labourers working nonstop on its legendary ship-assembly lines.

Literature

In a surprising 15th-century plot twist, shipping magnate Venice became a publishing empire. Johannes Gutenberg cranked out his first Bible with a movable-type press in 1455, and Venice became an early adopter of this cutting-edge technology, turning out the earliest printed Quran. Venetian printing presses were in operation by the 1470s, with lawyers settling copyright claims soon thereafter. Venetian publishers printed not just religious texts but histories, poetry, textbooks, plays, musical scores and manifestos.

Early Renaissance author Pietro Bembo (1470–1547) was a librarian, historian, diplomat and poet who defined the concept of platonic love and solidified Italian grammar in his *Rime* (Rhymes). Bembo collaborated with Aldo Manuzio on an invention that revolutionised reading and democratised learning: the Aldine Press, which introduced italics and paperbacks, including Dante's *La Divina Commedia* (The Divine Comedy). By 1500, nearly one in six books published in Europe was printed in Venice.

Eighteenth-century Venetian grande dame Isabella Teotochi Albrizzi was practically wedded to her literary salon: when her husband received a post abroad, she got her marriage annulled to remain in Venice, and continue her discussions of poetry with the patronage of a new husband, her *cicisbeo* (manservant-lover) in devoted attendance.

Poetry

Shakespeare has competition for technical prowess from Veneto's Petrarch (aka Francesco Petrarca; 1304–74), who added wow to Italian woo with his eponymous sonnets. Writing in Italian and Latin, Petrarch applied a strict structure of rhythm (14 lines, with two quatrains to describe a desire and a sestet to attain it) and rhyme (no more than five rhymes per sonnet) to romance the idealised Laura. He might have tried chocolates instead: Laura never returned the sentiment.

Posthumously, Petrarch became idolised by Rilke, Byron, Mozart and Venice's *cortigiane oneste* (well-educated 'honest courtesans'). Tullia d'Aragona (1510–56) wrote sharp-witted Petrarchan sonnets that conquered men: noblemen divulged state secrets, kings risked their thrones to beg her hand in marriage, and much ink was spilled in panegyric praise of her hooked nose.

Written with wit and recited with passion, poetry might get you a free date with a high-end courtesan, killed, or elected in Venice. Leonardo Giustinian (1388–1446) was a member of the Consiglio dei Dieci (Council of Ten) who spent time off from spying on his neighbours writing poetry in elegant Venetian-inflected Italian, including *Canzonette* (Songs) and *Strambotti* (Ditties). Giorgio Baffo (1694–1768) was a friend of Casanova's whose risqué odes to the posterior might have affected his political career elsewhere – but in Venice, he became a state senator. To experience his bawdy poetry, head to Taverna da Baffo (p99), where his ribald rhymes may be chanted by night's end.

One of Italy's greatest poets, Ugo Foscolo (1778–1827) studied in Padua and arrived in Venice as a teenager amid political upheavals. Young Foscolo threw in his literary lot with Napoleon in a 1797 ode to the general, hoping he would revive the Venetian Republic, and even joined the French army. But Napoleon considered Foscolo a dangerous mind, and Foscolo ended his days in exile in London.

Memoirs & Travel Writing

Life on the lagoon has always been stranger than fiction, and Venetian memoirists were early bestsellers. Venice-born Marco Polo (1254–1324) captured his adventures across central Asia and China in memoirs entitled *Il Milione* (c 1299), as told to Rustichello da Pisa. The book achieved

VENICE'S BESTSELLING WOMEN WRITERS

At a time when women were scarcely in print elsewhere in Europe, Venetian women became prolific and bestselling authors in subjects ranging from mathematics to politics. Works from over 100 Venetian women authors from the 15th to 18th centuries remain in circulation today. Among the luminaries of their era:

➜ **Writer, Sara Copia Sullam** (1592–1641) A leading Jewish intellectual of Venice's Accademia degli Incogniti literary salon, Sullam was admired for her poetry and spirited correspondence with a monk from Modena. A critic accused her of denying the immortality of the soul, a heresy punishable by death under the Inquisition. Sullam responded with a treatise on immortality written in two days; her manifesto became a bestseller. Sullam's writings remain in publication as key works of early modern Italian literature.

➜ **Philosopher, Isotta Nogarola** (c 1418–66) The Verona-born teen prodigy corresponded with Renaissance philosophers and was widely published in Rome and Venice. An anonymous critic published attacks against her in 1439, claiming 'an eloquent woman is never chaste' and accusing her of incest. But she continued her correspondence with leading humanists and, with Venetian diplomat Ludovico Foscarini, published an influential early feminist tract: a 1453 dialogue asserting that since Eve and Adam were jointly responsible for expulsion from Paradise, women and men must be equals.

➜ **Musician and poet, Gaspara Stampa** (1523–54) A true Renaissance intellectual, Gaspara Stampa was a renowned lute player, literary-salon organiser, and author of published Petrarchan sonnets openly dedicated to her many lovers. Historians debate her livelihood before she became a successful author; some claim she was a courtesan.

➜ **Academic, Dr Eleonora Lucrezia Cornaro Piscopia** (1646–84) Another prodigy, she became the first female university doctoral graduate in Europe in 1678 at the University of Padua, where a statue of her now stands. Her prolific contributions to the intellectual life of Venice are commemorated with a plaque inside Venice's city hall.

bestseller status even before the invention of the printing press, each volume copied by hand. Some details were apparently embellished along the way, but his tales of Kublai Khan's court remain riveting. In a more recent traveller's account, *Venezia, la Città Ritrovata* (Venice Rediscovered; 1998), Paolo Barbaro (b 1922) captures his reverse culture shock upon returning to the lagoon city.

Memoirs with sex and scandal sold well in Venice. 'Honest courtesan' Veronica Franco (1546–91) kissed and told in her bestselling memoir, but for sheer *braggadocio* (boasting) it's hard to top the memoirs of Casanova (1725–98). Francesco Gritti (1740–1811) parodied the decadent Venetian aristocracy in vicious, delicious *Poesie in dialetto Veneziano* (Poetry in the Venetian Dialect) and satirised the Venetian fashion for memoirs with his exaggerated *My Story: The Memoirs of Signor Tommasino Written by Him, a Narcotic Work by Dr Pifpuf.* Modern scandal, corruption and a cast of eccentric Venetians drive *The City of Falling Angels* by John Berendt (b 1939), an engrossing account of the life in Venice following the devastating fire that gutted La Fenice in 1996.

Modern Fiction

Venetian authors have remained at the forefront of modern Italian fiction. The enduring quality of Camillo Boito's 1883 short story *Senso* (Sense), a twisted tale of love and betrayal in Austrian-occupied Venice, made it a prime subject for director Luchino Visconti in 1954. Mysterious Venice proved the ideal setting for Venice's resident expat American mystery novelist Donna Leon, whose inspector Guido Brunetti uncovers the shadowy subcultures of Venice, from island fishing communities *(A Sea of Troubles)* to environmental protesters *(Through a Glass Darkly)*. But the pride of Venice's literary scene is Tiziano Scarpa (b 1963), who earned the 2009 Strega Prize, Italy's top literary honour, for *Stabat Mater,* the story of an orphaned Venetian girl learning to play violin under Antonio Vivaldi.

Film

Back in the 1980s, a Venice film archive found that the city had appeared in one form or another in 380,000 films – feature films, shorts, documentaries, and other works archived and screened at the city's Casa del Cinema. But Venice's photogenic looks have proved a mixed blessing. This city is too distinctive to fade into the background, so the city tends to upstage even the most photogenic co-stars (which only partly excuses 2010's *The Tourist*).

Since Casanova's escapades and a couple of Shakespearean dramas unfolded in Venice, the lagoon city was a natural choice of location for movie versions of these tales. In the Casanova category, two excellent accounts are Alexandre Volkoff's 1927 *Casanova* and Federico Fellini's 1976 *Casanova,* starring Donald Sutherland. Oliver Parker directed a 1995 version of *Othello,* but the definitive version remains Orson Welles' 1952 *Othello,* shot partly in Venice, but mostly on location in Morocco. Later adaptations of silver-screen classics haven't lived up to the original, including Michael Radford's 1994 *The Merchant of Venice* starring Al Pacino as Shylock, and Swedish director Lasse Hallström's 2005 *Casanova,* with a nonsensical plot but a charmingly rakish Heath Ledger in the title role.

After WWII, Hollywood came to Venice in search of romance, and the city delivered as the backdrop for Katharine Hepburn's midlife Italian love affair in David Lean's 1955 *Summertime.* Of all his films, Lean claimed this was his favourite, above *Lawrence of Arabia* and *Doctor*

Venice's first movie role dates from the earliest days of cinema, as the subject of the 1897 short film *A Panoramic View of Venice.* But since Venice was complicated and expensive for location shooting, silver-screen classics set in Venice, such as the Astaire-Rogers vehicle *Top Hat,* were shot in Hollywood backlots.

A costumed Carnevale participant

Zhivago. Locals confirm that yes, Signora Hepburn did fall into that canal, and no, she wasn't happy about it. Gorgeous Venice set pieces compensated for some dubious singing in Woody Allen's musical romantic comedy *Everyone Says I Love You* (1996). But the most winsome Venetian romance is Silvio Soldini's *Pane e tulipani* (Bread & Tulips; 2000), a tale of an Italian housewife who restarts her life as a woman of mystery in Venice, trying to dodge the detective-novel-reading plumber hot on her trail.

More often than not, romance seems to go horribly wrong in films set in Venice. It turns to obsession in *Morte a Venezia* (Death in Venice), Luchino Visconti's 1971 adaptation of the Thomas Mann novel, and again in *The Comfort of Strangers* (1990), featuring Natasha Richardson and Rupert Everett inexplicably following Christopher Walken into shadowy Venetian alleyways. A better adaptation of a lesser novel, *The Wings of the Dove* (1997) was based on the Henry James novel and mostly shot in the UK, though you can scarcely notice behind Helena Bonham Carter's hair.

Venice has done its best to shock movie-goers over the years, as with Nicolas Roeg's riveting *Don't Look Now* (1973) starring Donald Sutherland, Julie Christie, and Venice at its most ominous and depraved. *Dangerous Beauty* (1998) is raunchier but sillier, a missed opportunity to show 16th-century Venice through the eyes of a courtesan.

Always ready for action, Venice made appearances in *Indiana Jones and the Last Crusade* (1989) and *Casino Royale* (2006), whose Grand Canal finale was shot in Venice with some help from CGI – don't worry, no Gothic architecture was harmed in the making of that blockbuster. To see the latest big film to make a splash in Venice, don't miss the Venice International Film Festival (p21).

Theatre & Performing Arts

Venice is an elaborate stage, and whenever you arrive, you're just in time for a show. Sit on any *campo* (square), and the *commedia dell'arte* (archetypal comedy) and *opera buffa* commence, with stock characters improvising variations on familiar themes: graduating university students lurching towards another round of toasts, kids crying over gelato fallen into canals, neighbours hanging out laundry gossiping indiscreetly across the *calle* (alleyway). Once you've visited Venice, you'll have a whole new appreciation for its theatrical innovations.

The Biennale Teatro (www.labiennale.org/en/theatre) is a showcase for experimental theatre, drawing on Venice's 400-year tradition of risk-taking performance. Avant-garde troupes and experimental theatres such as Teatro Junghans, Teatro Fondamenta Nuove and Laboratorio Occupato Morion also bring new plays, performance art and choreography to Venetian stages.

Commedia dell'Arte

During Carnevale, *commedia dell'arte* conventions take over, and all of Venice acts out with masks, extravagant costumes and exaggerated gestures. It may seem fantastical today, but for centuries, this was Italy's dominant form of theatre. Scholars attribute some of Molière's running gags and Shakespeare's romantic plots to the influence of *commedia dell'arte* – although Shakespeare would have been shocked to note that in Italy, women's parts were typically played by women. But after a couple of centuries of *commedia dell'arte,* 18th-century Venice began to tire of bawdy slapstick. Sophisticated improvisations had been reduced to farce, robbing the theatre of its subversive zing.

Comedy & Opera Buffa

Enter Carlo Goldoni (1707–93), a former doctor's apprentice, occasional lawyer, and whipsmart *librettist* (playwright) who wrote some serious tragic opera. But of his 160 plays and 80 or so *libretti,* he remains best loved for *opera buffa,* unmasked social satires that remain ripe and delicious: battles of the sexes, self-important socialites getting their comeuppance, and the impossibility of pleasing one's boss.

Goldoni was light-hearted but by no means a lightweight; his comic genius and deft wordplay would permanently change Italian theatre. His *Pamela* (1750) was the first play to dispense with masks altogether, and his characters didn't fall into good or evil archetypes: everyone was flawed, often hilariously so. Some of his most winsome roles were reserved for women and *castrati* (male soprano countertenors), from his early 1735 adaptation of Apostolo Zeno's *Griselda* (based on Boccaccio's *Decameron,* with a score by Vivaldi) to his celebrated 1763 *Le donne vendicate* (Revenge of the Women). Princess Cecilia Mahony Giustiniani commissioned this latter work, in which two women show a preening chauvinist the error of his ways with light swordplay and lethal wordplay.

But one Venetian dramatist was not amused. Carlo Gozzi (1720–1806) believed that Goldoni's comedies of middle-class manners were prosaic, and staged a searing 1761 parody of Goldoni – driving Goldoni to France in disgust, never to return to Venice. Gozzi went on to minor success with his fairy-tale scenarios, one of which would inspire the Puccini opera *Turandot.* But Gozzi's fantasias had little staying power, and eventually he turned to...comedy.

Meanwhile, Goldoni fell on hard times in France, after a pension granted to him by King Louis XVI was revoked by the Revolution. He died impoverished, though at his French colleagues' insistence, the French state granted his pension to his widow. But Goldoni got the last laugh: while Gozzi's works are rarely staged, Goldoni regularly gets top billing along with Shakespeare at the city's main theatre, Teatro Goldoni (p67).

The Fragile Lagoon

White ibis perch on rock outcroppings, piles of lagoon crab are hauled into the Pescaria, and waters change like mood rings from teal blue to oxidised silver: life on the lagoon is extraordinary, and extraordinarily fragile. When gazing across these waters to the distant Adriatic horizon, the lagoon appears to be an extension of the sea. But with its delicate balance of salty and fresh water, *barene* (mud banks) and grassy marshes, the lagoon supports a unique aquaculture.

Rivers & Tides

The lagoon is a great shallow dish, where ocean tides meet freshwater streams from alpine rivers. It's protected by a slender 50km arc of islands, which halt the Adriatic's advances. Between Punta Sabbioni and Chioggia, three *bocche di porto* (port entrances) allow the sea entry into the lagoon. When sirocco winds push ocean waves toward the Venetian gulf or *seiche* (long waves) gently unroll along the Adriatic coast, *acque alte* (high tides) ensue. These seasonal tides help wash the lagoon clean of extra silt and maintain the salty-sweet balance of its waters.

Rising Waters & Erosion

During the era of the Republic the *bocche di porto* were kept open just wide enough so the tide could enter the lagoon while also regulating its volume and flow. But this status quo proved incompatible with the development of the industrial zone at Marghera in the early 20th century. To facilitate the passage of modern tankers the port entrances were widened and three deep channels were dredged, the most controversial being the 12m-deep, 100m-wide Canale dei Petroli dredged in 1966.

These channels and the passage of boats through them have resulted in strong transversal currents across the lagoon. These currents flatten the *ghebbi* (capillary canals) and sandbanks that have historically acted to dissipate the force of the tidal influx. In a 2006 report highlighting their destruction, Lidia Fersuoch, president of Italia Nostra Venezia (www.italianostra-venezia.org), an NGO dedicated to the protection of Venice's natural and cultural heritage, argued that the lagoon's sandbanks are 'in need of protection as much as the churches and palaces of the city'.

Well-drilling by coastal industries in the 1960s and the lowering of the mainland water table has also caused the *caranto* (the layer of clay that forms the base of the lagoon) to subside, while the reduction in the lagoon's salt marshes from 255 sq km in the 17th century to 47 sq km by 2003 has allowed unobstructed wind to whip up large waves that further destabilise the lagoon bed. The effect of all this: a downward-eroding, sediment-exporting system that is slowly turning the lagoon into a marine bay and posing a critical danger to the city.

MoSE

The hot topic of the past three decades in Venice has been the mobile-flood-barrier project known as MoSE (Modulo Sperimentale Elettromeccanico – Experimental Electromechanical Module). These inflatable

Back in 1900, Piazza San Marco flooded about 10 times a year; now it's closer to 60. Engineers estimate that Venice may be able to withstand a rise of 26cm to 60cm in water levels in the 21st century – however, an intergovernmental panel on climate change has forecast increases as high as 88cm.

THE TIDE IS HIGH

The alarm from 16 sirens throughout the city is a warning that *acqua alta* (high tide) is expected to reach the city within two to four hours. Venetians aren't often surprised: most monitor Venice's Centro Maree 48-hour tidal forecast at www.comune.venezia. it for high-tide warnings between November and April. When alarms sound, it's not an emergency situation but a temporary tide that principally affects low-lying areas. Within five hours, the tide usually ebbs.

One even tone (up to 110cm above normal): barely warrants a pause in conversation.

Two rising tones (up to 120cm): you might need *stivali di gomma* (rubber boots).

Three rising tones (around 130cm): check Centro Maree to see where *passarelle* (gangplank walkways) are in use.

Four rising tones (140cm and up): shops close early, everyone slides flood barriers across their doorsteps.

Atlante della Laguna (www. atlantedella laguna.it), a website sharing key environmental data and maps of the lagoon, won the Smart Communities Award in Padua in 2015.

barriers 30m high and 20m wide are intended to seal the three *bocche di porto* whenever the sea approaches dangerous levels. However, since its proposal in 1988 both the science and the management of the project have been dogged by criticism and controversy, culminating, in 2014, in the exposure of a toxic corruption scandal in which the city mayor, the main contractor (Consorzio Venezia Nuova) and the government body responsible for the lagoon (Magistrato alle Acque) were implicated.

Despite an original completion date of 1995, MoSE remains a work in progress and a tentative completion date is now slated for 2017. The recent corruption scandal has only further undermined its credibility and even its supporters now concede that it offers only a partial solution, since it does nothing to address the issue of erosion in the lagoon, and if sea levels rise frequently enough above the 110cm barrier trigger, the gates may be closed so often as to compromise the entire lagoon as a tidal marsh.

Lagoon Conservation

High waters aren't the only concern. Venice's foundations are taking a pounding as never before, with new stresses from wakes of speeding motorboats and mega cruise ships as well as pollution. When pollution and silt fill in shallow areas, algae takes over, threatening building foundations and choking out other marine life. The increase in the salt content of the lagoon also corrodes stone foundations and endangers unique lagoon aquaculture. Since 1930 an estimated 20% of bird life has disappeared, 80% of lagoon flora has gone and lagoon water transparency has dropped 60%.

Although industrial waste from mainland Porto Marghera has been curbed since the 1980s, the spike in cruise ships entering the Bacino di San Marco (1096 in 2013) has created new environmental threats. In the wake of Tuscany's 2012 *Costa Concordia* shipwreck, Unesco expressed concern about the impact of cruise ships on the Unesco-protected lagoon. Critics like Venice's No Grandi Navi (No Big Ships) committee also oppose cruise-ship entry for introducing pollution to the lagoon, including sulphur that corrodes marble and canal banks.

In response, the Port Authority (controlled by the state rather than the city council) has proposed the dredging of a new deep-water canal, the Canale Contorta Sant'Angelo, which will allow cruise ships to reach the port without entering the Giudecca Canal. It will require the dredging of 7 million cubic metres of mud, the creation of 'marsh islands' to contain the vast wakes and will cost about €140 million. Such a solution, says Luigi d'Alpaos, one of the most experienced water engineers at the University of Padua, will simply replicate the devastation caused by the Canale dei Petroli and may well nudge the lagoon over the critical edge of survival.

Survival Guide

Transport

ARRIVING IN VENICE

Most people arrive in Venice by train, plane and more controversially, cruise ship. There is a long-distance bus service to the city and it is also possible to drive to Venice, though you have to park at the western end of the city and then walk or take a *vaporetto* (small passenger ferry).

Flights from New York to Venice take nine hours; from London, Paris or Madrid about two hours; and from most other destinations in Europe between one and two hours.

Trains from Paris to Venice take about 13 hours; from London 17 hours; from Berlin 16 hours; from Frankfurt 11 hours; from Milan three hours; and from Rome four hours.

Flights, tours and rail tickets can be booked online at lonelyplanet.com.

Marco Polo Airport

Most flights to Venice fly in to **Marco Polo Airport** (VCE; ☑ flight information 041 260 92 60; www.veniceairport. it), 12km outside Venice, east of Mestre.

There is a range of options to get from the airport to the heart of Venice, including buses, water taxis and reliable passenger ferry links.

A taxi ride to Venice's Piazzale Roma (the end of the road in the pedestrianised historic centre) costs €40 to €50, but from there you'll still need to either walk or get a water bus or taxi the remainder of the way. Alilaguna boats are likely to get you much closer to your final destination at least as fast.

The main reseller of public transport tickets, HelloVenezia, has a desk in the arrivals hall, where ACTV travel and Venice Card products preordered through the **VèneziaUnica** website (www. veneziaunica.it) can also be picked up.

The dock for water transfers to the historic centre is a 10-minute hike from the arrivals hall (exit left out of arrivals), largely beneath a covered walkway. Luggage trolleys (requiring a €1 deposit) can be taken to the dock.

Alilaguna Airport Shuttle

Alilaguna (☑ 041 240 17 01; www.alilaguna.it) operates four water-taxi lines that link the airport with various parts of Venice at a cost of €8 to Murano and €15 to all other landing stages. Discounted fares are available online and at www.veneziaunica.it. Passengers are permitted one suitcase and one piece of hand luggage. All further bags are charged at €3 per piece. It

takes approximately 1¼ hours to reach Piazza San Marco. Lines include the following:

➡ **Linea Blu** (Blue Line) Stops at Lido, San Marco, Stazione Marittima and points in between.

➡ **Linea Rossa** (Red Line) Stops at Murano and Lido.

➡ **Linea Arancia** (Orange Line) Stops at Stazione Santa Lucia, Rialto and San Marco via the Grand Canal.

➡ **Linea Gialla** (Yellow Line) Stops at Murano and Fondamente Nove.

Bus

Azienda del Consorzio Trasporti Veneziano (ACTV; ☑ 041 24 24; www.actv.it) runs bus 5 between Marco Polo Airport and Piazzale Roma (€6, 30 minutes, four per hour) with a limited number of stops en route. Alternatively, a bus+*vaporetto* ticket covering the bus journey and a one-way *vaporetto* trip within a total of 90 minutes costs €12.

Azienda Trasporti Veneto Orientale (ATVO; ☑ 0421 59 46 71; www.atvo.it) runs a direct bus service between the airport and Piazzale Roma (€6, 25 minutes, every 30 minutes from 8am to midnight). At Piazzale Roma you can pick up the ACTV *vaporetti* to reach locations around Venice.

Water Taxi

Private water taxis are available for hire at Marco Polo Airport. These can be booked at the **Consorzio Motoscafi Venezia** (☑041 522 23 03; www.motoscafivenezia.it) or **Veneziataxi** (☑041 72 31 12; www.veneziataxi.it) desks, or directly at the dock. Private taxis cost from €110 for up to four passengers and all their luggage. Extra passengers (up to a limit of 12 or 16) carry a small surcharge. Note: all taxis are metered and you should never be quoted a per-person fare.

If you don't have a large group, there is also the option of a shared Venice Shuttle. This is a shared water taxi and costs from €25 per person with a €6 surcharge for night-time arrivals. Seats should be booked online at www.venicelink.com. Boats seat a maximum of eight people and accommodate up to 10 bags. Those opting for a shared taxi should be aware that the service can wait for some time to fill up and has set drop-off points in Venice; only private transfers will take you directly to your hotel.

Venezia Santa Lucia Train Station

Trains run frequently to Venice's Stazione Santa Lucia (appearing on signs as Ferrovia within Venice). There are direct, intercity services to most major Italian cities (www.trenitalia.it), as well as major points in France, Germany, Austria, Switzerland, Slovenia and Croatia.

Local trains that link Venice to the Veneto are frequent, reliable and remarkably inexpensive, including Padua (€4.05, 25 to 50 minutes, three to four per hour), Verona (€8.60, 1¾ hours, three to four per hour) and points in between. Faster intercity trains also serve these Veneto destina-

tions, but the time saved may not be worth the 200% surcharge.

When getting train tickets, be sure to specify Venezia Santa Lucia (VSL), for the station in central Venice, as opposed to Venezia Mestre. The station has a rail-travel **information office** (☉7am-9pm) opposite the APT office and a **deposito bagagli** (Left Luggage Office; ☑041 78 55 31; Venezia Santa Lucia; per piece 1st 5hr €6, next 6hr €0.90, thereafter per hr €0.40; ☉6am-11pm) opposite platform 1.

Train tickets can be purchased at self-serve ticketing machines in the station, online at www.trenitalia.it, in the UK at **Rail Europe** (www.raileurope.co.uk) or through travel agents.

Validate your ticket in the orange machines on station platforms before boarding your train. Failure to do so can result in a hefty on-the-spot fine when the inspector checks tickets on the train.

Vaporetto & Water Taxi

Vaporetti connect Santa Lucia train station with all parts of Venice. There is also a handy water-taxi stand just out front if you are heavily laden.

Venezia Mestre Train Station

On the mainland (which is a 10-minute train ride from Santa Lucia), Venezia Mestre station offers rail

information, a hotel-booking office and a **deposito bagagli** (☑041 78 44 46; Venezia Mestre; per piece 1st 5hr €6, next 6hr €0.90, thereafter per hr €0.40; ☉7am-11pm). While many trains head all the way to Santa Lucia, some itineraries may require a change here.

Piazzale Roma

To get to Venice by car or motorcycle, take the often-congested Trieste–Turin A4, which passes through Mestre. From Mestre, take the 'Venezia' exit. Once over Ponte della Libertà from Mestre, cars must be left at a car park in Piazzale Roma or on the Isola del Tronchetto. Urban, regional and long-distance buses also arrive in Piazzale Roma, from where *vaporetti* connect with the rest of the city. Services include:

Eurolines (☑0861 199 19 00; www.eurolines.com) Operates a wide range of international routes.

Azienda del Consorzio Trasporti Veneziano (ACTV; ☑041 24 24; www.actv.it) Runs *vaporetti* and buses to Mestre and surrounding areas.

Azienda Trasporti Veneto Orientale (ATVO; ☑041 520 55 30) Operates buses from Piazzale Roma to destinations all over the eastern Veneto, including airport connections.

CHEAP THRILLS ON THE GRAND CANAL: TRAGHETTI

A *traghetto* is the gondola service locals use to cross the Grand Canal between its widely spaced bridges. *Traghetti* rides cost just €2 for non-residents and typically operate from 9am to 6pm, although some routes finish by noon. For major *traghetto* crossings, consult the main map section, though note that service can be spotty at times at all crossings.

Isola del Tronchetto

Isola del Tronchetto is an artificial island located at the westernmost tip of Santa Croce that now acts as the city's main car park. To reach Tronchetto from the causeway stay in the right-hand lane and follow the signs for 'Tronchetto' and car parks. Be warned: visitors who drive across the bridge into Venice pay a hefty price in parking fees, and traffic backs up at weekends.

Car Ferry

Car ferry 17 transports vehicles from Tronchetto to the Lido (vehicles up to 4m and motorcycles €13).

Monorail

To get from Tronchetto to Piazzale Roma, if you park on Tronchetto, the monorail known as the People Mover will whisk you from Tronchetto to Piazzale Roma via the cruise terminal.

Stazione Marittima

Cruise ships dock at Venice's main passenger terminal, the Stazione Marittima, which is located at the western end of Santa Croce between the Isola del Tronchetto, the Santa Lucia train station and Piazzale Roma.

The terminal is accessible by road but cars must be parked on the nearby Isola del Tronchetto. When in port, most big cruise ships provide their passengers with a complimentary shuttle bus or boat service into Venice.

Alilaguna Boat Shuttle

Alilaguna's blue line connects the cruise terminal with San Marco (one-way €8), the Lido and points in between. The service also continues on to the airport (one-way €15, two hours) for those departing Venice.

Bus

A frequent, free shuttle bus connects the cruise terminal to Piazzale Roma. It runs every 15 to 20 minutes from Monday to Saturday during cruise season and whenever a big ship is in port.

Monorail

The Monorail People Mover connects the terminal with Piazzale Roma. It takes less than two minutes and runs until 11pm at night.

Land & Water Taxi

Land taxis can ferry you and your luggage the brief 900m distance to Piazzale Roma (about €5) from where you can access the public *vaporetto* system. Be warned though, *vaporetto* stops at Piazzale Roma are usually very crowded at peak times.

Alternatively, a water taxi direct to your hotel will set you back about €40 to €65, but may be worth it if you have a significant amount of luggage.

A land taxi to the airport costs around €30 to €40.

Treviso Airport

Ryanair and some other budget airlines also use **Treviso Airport** (TSF; ☎0422 31 51 11; www.trevisoairport.it; Via Noalese 63), about 5km southwest of Treviso and a 30km, one-hour drive from Venice.

There are various public transport options between Treviso Airport and Venice. Taxis from Treviso Airport to Venice cost upwards of €75.

Bus

Barzi Bus Service (☎0422 68 60 83; www.barziservice. com) provides the most direct service to Tronchetto in Venice (€10, 40 minutes, one to two per hour from 8am to 10.30pm) from where you can jump on the Monorail to Piazzale Roma. Buy tickets on the bus or at the desk in the arrivals hall.

Azienda Trasporti Veneto Orientale (ATVO; ☎0422 31 53 81; www.atvo.it) also offers a service to Mestre and Piazzale Roma in Venice (€10, 40 minutes, one to two per hour from 5.30am to 11.30pm), but it takes a more circuitous route.

Train

Line 6 of **ACTT** (☎0422 23 40 23; www.mobilitadimarca. it) connects Treviso Airport with Treviso train station (€1.40, or €2.80 if purchased on the bus, 20 minutes, two to three an hour from 6am to 10.30pm), from where there are frequent services to Santa Lucia train station in Venice (€3.30, 30 to 40 minutes, half hourly).

San Basilio Terminal

Venezia Lines (☑385 524 228 96; www.venezialines.com) runs high-speed boats to and from Croatia and Slovenia in summer. Boats arrive and depart from the **San Basilio Terminal** (Old Stazione Marittime; Fondamenta Zattere Al Ponte) on the southern side of Dorsoduro.

Vaporetto

Vaporetto line 2 links the terminal with Tronchetto, Piazzale Roma and San Zaccaria.

Fusina Terminal

Anek Lines (www.anek.gr) runs four services a week between Venice and Greece with boats docking at Igoumenitsa and Patras. Boats arrive and depart from the **Fusina Terminal** (☑041 547 01 60; www.terminalfusina.it; Via dell'Elettronica, Fusina) on the mainland.

Vaporetto

To reach Fusina take the Circolare LineafusinA *vaporetto* from Zattere (€8, 25 minutes, hourly) or Alberoni (€7, 35 minutes, every two hours) at the southern end of the Lido.

GETTING AROUND VENICE

Vaporetto

The city's main mode of public transport is the *vaporetto*. **Azienda del Consorzio Trasporti Veneziano** (ACTV; ☑041 24 24; www.actv.it) runs public transport in the Comune di Venezia (the municipality), covering mainland buses

and all the waterborne public transport around Venice. Although the service is efficient and generally punctual, boats on main lines get full fast and can be overcrowded during Carnival and in peak season. One-way tickets cost €7.

Some lines make only limited stops, especially from 8am to 10am and 6pm to 8pm, so check boat signage. If in doubt, ask the person charged with letting people on and off the boat.

Inter-island ferry services to Murano, Torcello, the Lido and other lagoon islands are usually provided on larger *motonave* (big inter-island *vaporetti*).

Tickets

HelloVenezia (☑041 24 24) is the main reseller of public transport tickets, and you can purchase *vaporetti* tickets at their booths at most landing stations. Free timetables and route maps are also available at many of these ticket booths. Tickets and multiday passes can also be pre-purchased online through **VèneziaUnica** (www.veneziaunica.it).

If you're going to be using the *vaporetto* frequently (more than three trips per day), instead of spending €7 for every one-way ticket, it is advisable to consider a

Tourist Travel Card – a pass for unlimited travel within a set period beginning when you first validate your ticket in the yellow machine located at *vaporetto* stops. Swipe your card every time you board, even if you have already validated it upon your initial ride. If you're caught without a valid ticket, you'll be required to pay an on-the-spot fine of €59. No exceptions.

People aged 14 to 29 holding a Rolling Venice card (p247) can get a three-day ticket for €20 at Hello Venezia/VèneziaUnica ticket outlets.

Routes

From Piazzale Roma or the train station, *vaporetto* 1 zigzags up the Grand Canal to San Marco and onward to the Lido. If you're not in a rush, it's a great introduction to Venice. *Vaporetto* 17 carries vehicles from Tronchetto, near Piazzale Roma, to the Lido.

Frequency varies greatly according to line and time of day. *Vaporetto* 1 runs every 10 minutes throughout most of the day, while lines such as the 4.1 and 4.2 only run every 20 minutes. Night services can be as much as one hour apart. Some lines stop running by around 9pm, so check timetables.

USEFUL VAPORETTO ROUTES

The following *vaporetti* connect Santa Lucia train station and Piazzale Roma (the bus terminus and shuttle drop for cruise ships and car passengers) with all parts of Venice:

Line 1 Plies the Grand Canal to San Marco and Lido every 10 minutes.

Line 2 Follows the same route as Line 1, with fewer stops, returning via Giudecca.

Lines 4.1, 4.2 Circle the outside of Venice's perimeter in both directions.

Lines 5.1, 5.2 Follow the same routes as 4.1 and 4.2 but with fewer stops and adds in Lido.

Line N All-night local service for Giudecca, the Grand Canal, San Marco and Lido (11.30pm to 4am, every 40 minutes).

Keep in mind that routes, route numbers and schedules can change, and not all routes go both ways. Here are the key *vaporetto* lines and major stops, subject to seasonal changes:

No 1 Runs Piazzale Roma–Ferrovia–Grand Canal (all stops)–Lido and back (runs 5am to 11.30pm, every 10 minutes from 7am to 10pm).

No 2 Circular line: runs San Zaccaria–Redentore–Zattere–Trochetto–Ferrovia–Rialto–Accademia–San Marco.

No 3/DM 'Diretto Murano' connects Piazzale Roma and the railway station to all five stops on Murano.

No 4.1 Circular line: runs Murano–Fondamente Nove–Ferrovia–Piazzale Roma–Redentore–San Zaccaria–Fondamente Nove–San Michele–Murano (6am to 10pm, every 20 minutes).

No 4.2 Circular line in reverse direction to No 4.1 (6.30am to 8.30pm, every 20 minutes).

No 5.1 & 5.2 Runs the same route, Lido–Fondamente Nove–Riva de Biasio–Ferrovia–Piazzale Roma–Zattere–San Zaccaria–Giardini–Lido, in opposite directions.

No 6 Circular line, limited stops, weekdays only: runs Piazzale Roma–Santa Marta–San Basilio–Zattere–Giardini–Sant'Elena–Lido.

No 8 Runs Giudecca–Zattere–Redentore–Giardini–Lido. May to early September only.

No 9 Runs Torcello–Burano and back (7am to 8.45pm, every 30 minutes).

No 11 A coordinated, hourly bus+*vaporetto* service from Lido to Pellestrina and Chioggia.

No 12 Runs Fondamente Nove–Murano–Mazzorbo–Burano–Torcello and back.

No 13 Runs Fondamente Nove–Murano–Vignole–Sant'Erasmo–Treporti and back.

No 16 Connects Fusina Terminal with Zattere.

No 17 Car ferry: runs Tronchetto–Lido and back.

No 18 Runs Murano–Sant'Erasmo–Lido and back (infrequent and summer only).

No 20 Runs San Zaccaria–San Servolo–San Lazzaro degli Armeni and back. In summer it also connects with the Lido.

N All-stops night circuit, including Giudecca, Grand Canal, San Marco, Piazzale Roma, and the train station (11.30pm to 4am, every 40 minutes).

NMU (Notturno Murano) Night service from Fondamente Nove to Murano (all stops).

NLN (Notturno Laguna Nord) Infrequent night service between Fondamente Nove, Murano, Burano, Torcello and Treporti.

Gondola

A gondola ride offers a view of Venice that is anything but pedestrian. Official daytime rates are €80 for 30 minutes (it's €100 for 35 minutes from 7pm to 8am), not including songs or tips. Additional time is charged in 20-minute increments (day/night €40/50). You may negotiate a price break in overcast weather or around noon. Agree on a price, time limit and singing in advance to avoid unexpected surcharges.

Gondolas cluster at *stazi* (stops) along the Grand Canal, at the Ferrovia stop at the Venezia Santa Lucia station, the Rialto and near major monuments (such as I Frari, Ponte dei Sospiri and Accademia), but you can also book a pick-up by calling **Ente Gondola** (☑041 528 50 75; www.gondolavenezia.it).

You can book a cheaper, non-exclusive gondola ride at a designated time with **Tu.Ri.Ve** (www.turive.it), either online, through a number of travel agencies or at the tourist office. These rides all depart from the waterside in front of the Palazzina Selva Pavilion. In summer rides depart at 11am, 3pm and 5.15pm; in winter at 3pm only. Boats carry a maximum of six people.

Non-profit organisation **Gondolas 4 All** (☑328 243 13 82; www.gondolas4all.com), supported by the Gondoliers Association, is raising funds to create a new wheelchair-accessible dock at Piazzale Roma. Once up and running the service will be bookable online or by phone.

Water Taxi

Licensed **water taxis** (Consorzio Motoscafi Venezia; ☑24hr 041 522 23 03, Marco Polo airport desk 041 541 50 84; www.motoscafivenezia.it) are a costly way to get around Venice, though they may prove handy. Fares can be metered or negotiated in advance. Official rates start at €15 plus €2 per minute, €6 extra if they're called to your hotel. There's a €10 surcharge for night trips (10pm to 6am), a €5 surcharge for additional luggage (above five pieces) and a €10 surcharge for each extra passenger above the first five. Even if you're in a hurry, don't encourage your taxi driver to speed through Venice – this kicks up *motoschiaffi* (motorboat wakes) that expose Venice's ancient foundations to degradation

CAR PARKING

You'll find car parks in Piazzale Roma or on Isola del Tronchetto. Prices in Venice start at €3 per hour and rise to €21 for five to 24 hours. At peak times, many become completely full. However, you can book a parking place ahead of time at www.veneziaunica.it.

To avoid hassles (and to make the most of the cheaper car parks) consider parking in Mestre, and take the bus or train into Venice instead. Remember to take anything that looks even remotely valuable out of your car.

For a range of parking options in Venice and Mestre, including prices and directions, head to www.avmspa.it.

Garage Europa Mestre (☑041 95 92 02; www.garageeuropamestre.com; Corso del Popolo 55, Mestre; per day €15; ☉8am-10pm) Has 300 spaces; ACTV bus 4 to/from Venice stops outside the garage, or it's a 10-minute walk to the Mestre train station. It has the cheapest hourly rates.

ASM Autoremissa Comunale (☑041 272 73 07; www.asmvenezia.it; Piazzale Roma; compact car in low/peak period per day €24/26, car over 185cm €27/29; ☉24hr) Has 2182 spaces, the largest lot in Piazzale Roma. Discounts available with online reservations; free six-hour parking for people with disabilities.

Garage San Marco (☑041 523 22 13; www.garagesanmarco.it; Piazzale Roma 467F; per 12/24hr €26/30, overnight 5pm-4am €15; ☉24hr) Has 900 spaces; guests of certain hotels get discounts.

Parking Sant'Andrea (☑041 272 23 84; www.avmspa.it; Piazzale Roma; per 2hr or part thereof €7; ☉24hr) Has 100 spaces; best for short-term parking.

Interparking (Tronchetto Car Park; ☑041 520 75 55; www.veniceparking.it; Isola del Tronchetto; per 2/3-5/5-24hr €3/5/21; ☉24hr) Has 3957 spaces; the largest lot with the cheapest 24-hour rate; *vaporetti* connect directly with Piazza San Marco, while the People Mover provides connections to Piazzale Roma and the cruise terminal.

and rot. Make sure your water taxi has the yellow strip with the licence number displayed. Illegal water taxis can be an issue on the Isola del Tronchetto, where there is no taxi stand. If you're arriving here and want a taxi, prebook a pick-up.

Bicycle

Cycling is banned in central Venice. On the larger islands of Lido and Pellestrina, cycling is a pleasant way to get around and to reach distant beaches. **Lido on Bike** (☑041 526 80 19; www.lidoonbike.it; Gran Viale 21b; bikes per hr/day €5/9; ☉9am-7pm; ☑Lido) is near the *vaporetto* stop; ID is required for rental.

To sort out a set of wheels for a Veneto day trip contact **Veloce** (☑346 8471141; www.rentalbikeitaly.com; Via Gramsci 85, Mira; touring/mountain/racing bicycle per day €20/25/35; ☉8am-8pm), which offers a handy drop-off and pick-up service from train stations and hotels.

Boat

Aspiring sea captains can take on the lagoon (not the Grand Canal or canals in the historic centre) in a rented boat from **Brussa** (☑041 71 57 87; www.brussaisboat.it; Fondamenta Labia 331, Cannaregio; ☉7.30am-5.30pm Mon-Fri, to 12.30pm Sat & Sun). You can hire a 7m boat (including fuel) that can carry up to six people for an hour (€42.70) or a day (€195.20), or make arrangements for longer periods. You don't need a licence, but you will be taken on a test run to see if you can manoeuvre and park; be sure to ask them to point out the four boat-petrol stations around Venice on a map.

Car

Obviously you can't drive in Venice proper, but Lido and Pellestrina allow cars, and they can be the most efficient way of seeing far-flung sites across the Veneto. The

car-rental companies Avis, Europcar and Hertz all have offices both on Piazzale Roma and at Marco Polo Airport. Several companies operate in or near Mestre train station as well.

Avis (☑041 523 73 77; www.avis.co.uk; Piazzale Roma 496G)

Europcar (☑041 523 86 16; www.europcar.co.uk; Piazzale Roma 496H)

Hertz (☑041 528 40 91; www.hertz.co.uk; Piazzale Roma 496)

Monorail

Designed by the architect Francesco Cocco, Venice's wheelchair-accessible **People Mover monorail** (APM; www.apmvenezia.com; per ride €1.30; ☉7am-11pm Mon-Sat, 8.30am-9pm Sun) now connects the car parks on Tronchetto with the Stazione Maritima and Piazzale Roma. Purchase tickets from the vending machines near the station.

Directory A–Z

Customs Regulations

Goods are sold free of value-added tax (VAT) in European airports. Visitors coming into Italy from non-EU countries can import duty-free: 1L of spirits (or 4L of wine), 200 cigarettes and any other goods up to a total of €430 for air and sea travellers (€300 for all other travellers). Anything over this limit must be declared on arrival and the appropriate duty paid.

Courses

Venice Italian School

(☑347 963 51 13, 340 751 08 63; www.veniceitalianschool. com; Campo San Stin 2504; group course 1-/2-weeks €290/530, cultural lessons per person €60; ☑San Tomà) Founded by a Venetian brother and sister, Diego and Lucia Cattaneo, this language school offers excellent, immersive courses for adults and children between the ages of five and 13 years old. Teaching is based on the communicative Dogme technique and additional cultural lessons use associative physical activities (such as food and wine tasting, cooking lessons, glass and art workshops) to encourage students to practise what they've learnt.

Lessons for kids (€65 to €95 for 1½ hours) are entirely personalised to the child's and parents' needs, but include practical learning experiences using songs, books, games and social interactions.The school can also help arrange well-priced accommodation.

Discount Cards & Passes

VèneziaUnica

Although it is misleadingly referred to as a City Pass, **VèneziaUnica** (☑041 24 24; www.veneziaunica.it) is really a portal that brings together a range of discount passes and services and enables you to tailor them to your needs and pre-purchase online. Services and passes on offer include:

➡ Land and water transfers to the airport and cruise terminal

➡ ACTV Travel Cards

➡ Museum and church passes

➡ Select parking

➡ Citywide wi-fi

➡ Prepaid access to public toilets

If purchasing online you need to print out your voucher displaying your reservation number (PNR) and carry it with you, then simply present it at the various attractions for admission/access.

To use public transport, however, you will need to obtain a free card (you will need your PNR code to do this), which is then 'loaded' with the credit you have purchased. You can do this at the ACTV ticket machines at Marco Polo Airport (this is the only place where you'll find the self-service tickets), or at the ticket desks at *vaporetto* (small ferry) stops, HelloVenezia ticket booths and tourist offices.

The most useful discount tickets available are as follows:

TOURIST CITY PASS

The Tourist City Pass (adult/junior €39.90/29.90) replaces the Venice Card and is the most extensive (and expensive) discount card for the city, with an adult card for the over 30s, and a junior version for those aged between six and 29 years. Valid for seven days, it allows free entrance to 11 Civic Museums, 16 Chorus churches, the Querini Stampalia Foundation and the Jewish Museum. In addition, discounted rates are offered at a number of other museums such as the Palazzo Grassi, Punta della Dogana and the Peggy Guggenheim Collection. A reduced version, called the San Marco Pack (€25.90), is also available.

CHORUS PASS

The association of Venice churches offers a Chorus Pass (adult/student under 29 years €12/8) for single entry to 16 historic Venice churches any time within one year, including I Frari, Chiesa di Santa Maria dei Miracoli, Chiesa di San Sebastiano and the Gesuati. Otherwise, admission to these individual churches costs €3. Passes are also for sale at church ticket booths; proceeds from the pass support restoration and maintenance of churches throughout Venice.

CIVIC MUSEUM PASSES

The Civic Museum Pass (adult/reduced €24/18) is valid for six months and covers single entry to 11 Civic Museums, including Palazzo Ducale, Ca' Rezzonico, Ca' Pesaro, Palazzo Mocenigo, Museo Correr, the Museo del Vetro (Glass Museum) on Murano and the Museo del Merletto (Lace Museum) on Burano. Short-term visitors may prefer the San Marco Museums Pack (adult/reduced €17/10), which covers four museums around Piazza San Marco (Palazzo Ducale, Museo Correr, Museo Archeologico Nazionale and

Biblioteca Nazionale Marciana). Also available from the tourist office.

Other Combined Museum Tickets

For art aficionados planning to visit the Gallerie dell'Accademia and Palazzo Grimani, consider the combined ticket (adult/student/senior €11/9/free), which is good for three months.

A combined ticket to the Palazzo Grassi and Punta della Dogana costs adult/reduced €20/15.

Note that 'reduced' rate in our listings refers to the reduced rate for seniors and students (in Italy these are nearly almost the same).

Most attractions in Venice offer reduced admission for children. City-run museums (visitmuve.it) generally give a 60% to 70% discount to visitors aged six to 14, and free entry to those aged five and under. State-owned museums (www.polomuseale.

venezia.beniculturali.it) are free for those under 18.

Rolling Venice Card

Visitors aged 14 to 29 years should pick up the €4 Rolling Venice card (from tourist offices and most ACTV public transport ticket points), entitling purchase of a 72-hour public transit pass (€18) and discounts on museums, monuments and cultural event access, food, accommodation and entertainment.

Emergencies

For an ambulance, call ☑118. Call ☑112 or ☑113 for the police.

Police Headquarters
(☑041 271 55 11; Santa Croce 500) San Marco's head police station is off the beaten track in the ex-convent of Santa Chiara, just beyond Piazzale Roma.

PRACTICALITIES

Weights & Measures

The metric system is used for weights and measures.

Smoking

Since 2005 smoking in all closed public spaces (from bars to elevators, offices to trains and hotel rooms) has been banned.

Media

➡ The Veneto's major newspaper is *Il Gazzettino* (www.gazzettino.it). *La Nuova Venezia* (www.nuovavenezia.it) is Venice's own city paper and is a good source of information on local events. Of the nationals, *Corriere della Sera* (www.corriere.it) is the most widely read, followed closely by the centre-left *La Reppublica* (www.repubblica.it).

➡ State-owned RAI-1, RAI-2 and RAI-3 (www.rai.it) radio stations broadcast all over the country. Venice Classic Radio (www.veniceclassicradio.eu) mines the city's rich archive of classical, baroque and chamber music, while Teatro La Fenice has its own dedicated channel (www.lafenicechannel.it).

➡ Padua's Megamix FM (www.megamix.fm) offers a dance and pop repertoire (much of it in English), and Vicenza's Golden Radio Italia (www.goldenradio.it) offers two internet channels, one featuring the Top 40 and the other dedicated to the best of the '80s.

➡ Turn on the box to watch the state-run RAI-1, RAI-2 and RAI-3 (www.rai.it) and the main commercial channels (mostly run by Silvio Berlusconi's Mediaset company): Canale 5 (www.canale5.mediaset.it), Italia 1 (www.italia1.mediaset.it), Rete 4 (www.rete4.mediaset.it) and LA 7 (www.la7.it).

Electricity

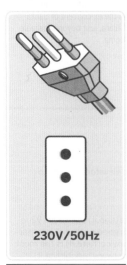

230V/50Hz

230V/50Hz

Gay & Lesbian Travellers

Homosexuality is legal in Italy and generally accepted in Venice and the Veneto. **ArciGay** (www.arcigay.it), the national gay, lesbian, bisexual and transgender organisation, has information on the GLBT scene in Italy. The useful website www.

gay.it (in Italian) lists gay and lesbian events across the country, but options in Venice are slim. Head to Padua for a wider range of gay-friendly nightlife and the nearest GLBT organisation, **ArciGay Tralaltro** (☑049 876 24 58; www.tralaltro.it; Corso Garibaldi 41).

Internet Access

If you plan to carry your notebook or computer, consider bringing a grounded power strip – it will allow you to plug in more appliances and protect your computer from the power fluctuations that can occur in Venice's older buildings.

Wi-Fi

Wi-fi access is widely available in hotels, B&Bs and rental apartments, and increasingly in cafes, though less than in other parts of Europe. Another option is to buy a PCMCIA card pack with one of the Italian mobile-phone operators, which gives wireless access through the mobile telephone network. These are usually prepaid services that you can top up as you go.

If you don't have access to wi-fi in your accommodation you can purchase a connection through VèneziaUnica. The cost of connection is €5/15 for 24/72 hours, and €20 for a week.

Medical Services

All foreigners have the same right as Italians to free emergency medical treatment in a public hospital in Venice. However, other medical care is not necessarily covered.

EU, Switzerland, Norway & Iceland Citizens are entitled to the full range of health-care services in public hospitals free of charge upon presentation of a European Health Insurance Card (EHIC).

Australia Thanks to a recipro-

cal arrangement with Italy, Australian citizens are entitled to free public health care – carry your Medicare card.

New Zealand, USA & Canada Citizens of these and other countries have to pay for anything other than emergency treatment. Most travel-insurance policies include medical coverage.

Emergency Clinics

Opening hours of medical services vary, though most are open 8am to 12.30pm Monday to Friday, and some open for a couple of hours on weekday afternoons and Saturday mornings.

Guardia Medica (☑041 238 5648) This service of night-time call-out doctors in Venice operates from 8pm to 8am on weekdays and from 10am the day before a holiday (including Sunday) until 8am the day after.

Ospedale Civile (☑041 529 41 11; Campo SS Giovanni e Paolo 6777; ⬛Ospedale) Venice's main hospital; for emergency care and dental treatment.

Ospedale dell'Angelo (☑041 965 71 11; Via Paccagnella 11, Mestre) Vast modern hospital on the mainland.

Pharmacies

Most pharmacies in Venice are open from 9am to 12.30pm and 3.30pm to 7.30pm, and are closed on Saturday afternoons and Sundays. Information on rotating late-night pharmacies is posted in pharmacy windows and listed in the free magazine *Un Ospite di Venezia* as well as on its website (www.unospitedi venezia.it).

Money

As in the 19 other EU nations, the currency in Italy is the euro.

Euro notes come in denominations of €500, €200, €100, €50, €20, €10 and €5, in different colours and sizes. Euro coins are in denominations of €2, €1, 50c, 20c, 10c, 5c, 2c and 1c.

ATMs

There are ATMs (*bancomats*) that accept international ATM cards throughout the city, with many near Piazza San Marco, Ponte di Rialto and the train station. ATMs are the most convenient and cost-effective way to access cash in Venice and most have multilingual menus. On many machines there's a daily limit on withdrawals of €250.

Changing Money

You can exchange money in banks, at post offices or in bureaux de change. See www.xe.com for the most current exchange rates. The post office and banks are reliable, but always ask about commissions. Also, keep a sharp eye on commissions at bureaux de change, which sometimes exceed 10% on travellers cheques. Travelex has three branches:

Travelex (☑041 541 68 33; Marco Polo Airport; ☺7.30am-9.30pm)

Travelex (☑041 528 73 58; Piazza San Marco 142; ☺9am-7pm Mon-Fri, 9am-6pm Sat, 9.20am-6pm Sun)

Travelex (☑041 528 73 58; Riva del Ferro 5126, San Marco; ☺9.30am-6.45pm Mon-Sat, to 5pm Sun)

Credit Cards

Major cards such as Visa and MasterCard are accepted throughout Italy. Check charges with your bank beforehand to avoid any nasty surprises later. American Express and Diners Club are also accepted, though not as widely.

Most banks now build a fee of around 2.75% into every foreign transaction.

In addition, ATM withdrawals attract a fee, which can range from a flat fee to 1.5% of the withdrawal, or both.

Tipping

A 10% tip is customary at restaurants where a service charge is not included, and you can leave small change at cafes and bars. Tipping water-taxi drivers is not common practice; hotel porters are tipped €1 per bag.

Opening Hours

The hours listed here are a general guide; individual establishments can vary, sometimes widely. Also note that hours at shops, bars and restaurants can be somewhat flexible in Venice, as they are in the rest of Italy.

Banks 8.30am to 1.30pm and 3.30pm to 5.30pm Monday to Friday, though hours vary; some open Saturday mornings.

Restaurants Noon to 2.30pm and 7pm to 10pm.

Shops 10am to 1pm and 3.30pm to 7pm (or 4pm to 7.30pm) Monday to Saturday.

Supermarkets 9am to 7.30pm Monday to Saturday.

Post

There are a couple of post offices in every Venetian *sestiere* (district), with addresses and hours online at www.poste.it.

Post Office (Calle Larga de l'Ascension 1241; ☺8.20am-1.35pm Mon-Fri, to 12.35pm Sat) A convenient regional branch located behind Piazza San Marco.

Public Holidays

For Venetians, as for most Italians, the main holiday periods are summer (July and especially August), the Christmas–New Year period and Easter. Restaurants, shops and most other activity also grind to a halt around Ferragosto (Feast of the Assumption; 15 August).

Capodanno/Anno Nuovo (New Year's Day) 1 January

Epifania/Befana (Epiphany) 6 January

Lunedì dell'Angelo (Good Friday) March/April

Pasquetta/Lunedì dell'Angelo (Easter Monday) March/April

Giorno della Liberazione (Liberation Day) 25 April

Festa del Lavoro (Labour Day) 1 May

Festa della Repubblica (Republic Day) 2 June

Ferragosto (Feast of the Assumption) 15 August

Ognissanti (All Saints' Day) 1 November

Immaculata Concezione (Feast of the Immaculate Conception) 8 December

Natale (Christmas Day) 25 December

Festa di Santo Stefano (Boxing Day) 26 December

Taxes & Refunds

VAT (value-added tax) of around 20%, known as Imposta di Valore Aggiunto (IVA), is slapped onto just about everything in Italy. If you are a non-EU resident and spend more than €155 in a single transaction on selected purchases, you can claim a refund when you leave – or sometimes at the time of purchase. The refund only applies to purchases from affiliated retail outlets that display a 'tax free for tourists' (or similar) sign. For more information, visit www.taxrefund.it.

Telephone

National and international numbers can be requested at ☑1254 or online at 1254.virgilio.it.

Domestic Calls

Italian telephone area codes all begin with 0 and consist of up to four digits. The area code is an integral part of the telephone number and must always be dialled. When calling Venice land lines, even from within the city, you must dial the ☎041 city code.

Mobile-phone numbers begin with a three-digit prefix such as 330. Toll-free (free-phone) numbers are known as *numeri verdi* and usually start with ☎840, 841, 848, 892, 899, 163, 166 or 199.

International Calls

The cheapest options for calling internationally are free or low-cost computer programs such as Skype, FaceTime and Viber, cut-rate call centres or international dialling cards, which are sold at newsstands and tobacconists. All of these offer cheaper calls than the Telecom payphones.

If you're calling an international number from an Italian phone, you must dial ☎00 to get an international line, then the relevant country and city codes, followed by the telephone number.

To call Venice from abroad, call the international access number for Italy (☎011 in the United States, 00 from most other countries), Italy's country code 39, then the Venice area code 041, followed by the telephone number.

Mobile Phones

Italy uses GSM 900/1800, so GSM and tri-band mobile phones can be used in Venice with the purchase of a local SIM card. Buy these at Vodafone and Telecom Italia Mobile (TIM) outlets across the city. However, be sure to check with your provider before you leave home, as some phones may be code blocked. Prepaid plans are fairly reasonable, and most offer the option to have inter-net access for an additional fee.

US mobile phones generally work on a frequency of 1900MHz, so your US hand-set will have to be tri-band to be usable in Italy.

Pay-as-you-go SIM cards are readily available at telephone and electronics stores. Once you're set up with an Italian SIM card, you can easily purchase recharge cards at many tobacconists and newsstands. Of the main mobile-phone companies, TIM and Vodafone have the best coverage in Venice.

You'll need your passport to open any kind of mobile-phone account, prepaid or otherwise.

Phonecards

You can buy phonecards (€3, €5 or €10) at post offices, tobacconists and news-stands, and from vending machines in Telecom offices. Snap off the perforated corner before using it.

PUBLIC PHONES

Most orange Telecom payphones only accept *carte/schede telefoniche* (phonecards), though there are payphones that accept coins around the Santa Lucia train station, Piazzale Roma, Campo Santa Margherita and Piazza San Marco.

Time

Italy (and hence Venice) is one hour ahead of GMT/UTC during winter and two hours ahead during the daylight-saving period, which runs from the last Sunday in March to the last Sunday in October. Note that times are often listed using a 24-hour clock (ie 2pm is written as 14 hours).

Toilets

Most bars and cafes reserve the restroom for paying customers only. Look before you sit: even in women's bath-rooms, some toilets don't have seats, and sometimes there is no toilet at all – just a hole with footrests. Public toilets (€1.50) are scattered around Venice near tourist attractions (look for the 'WC Toilette' signs), and are usually open from 7am to 7pm (sometimes closing earlier in winter).

Tourist Information

The useful monthly booklet *Un Ospite di Venezia* (www.unospitedivenezia.it), published by a group of Venetian hoteliers, is distributed in many hotels and can also be viewed online. In tourist offices, ask for *La Rivista di Venezia*, a bimonthly free magazine with articles in Italian and English, with a handy *Shows & Events* listings insert. Another useful listings freebie in Italian and English is *Venezia da Vivere* (www.veneziadavivere.com). You may find it in printed form in bars and shops. The Veneto section of *Corriere della Sera* (www.corriere.it) is also useful for current and upcoming events.

Tourist Offices

Azienda di Promozione Turistica (☎041 529 87 11; www.turismovenezia.it; Arrivals Hall, Marco Polo Airport; ◷8.30am-7.30pm) has several branches that can provide information on sights, suggested itineraries, day trips from Venice, transport, special events, shows and temporary exhibitions. There are a number of official APT outlets providing tourist information – all open daily:

Airport Tourist Office (☎041 529 87 11; www.turismovenezia.it; Arrivals Hall, Marco Polo Airport; ◷8.30am-7.30pm)

Piazzale Roma Tourist Office (☎041 529 87 11;

www.turismovenezia.it; ground fl, multistorey car park, Piazzale Roma; ☺8.30am-2.30pm; 🚤Santa Chiara)

San Marco Tourist Office (☎041 529 87 11; www.turismovenezia.it; Piazza San Marco 71F; ☺8.30am-7pm; 🚤San Marco)

Santa Lucia Station Tourist Office (☎041 529 87 11; www.turismovenezia.it; Stazione di Santa Lucia; ☺8.30am-7pm; 🚤Ferrovia Santa Lucia)

Travellers with Disabilities

With all the foot bridges and stairs, Venice is not the easiest place to visit for travellers with disabilities. But the city has made an effort to provide access to key monuments.

In its favour, Venice is a compact city and the public *vaporetti* are relatively easy to access when not crowded. Water ferries are also the most effective way to access sites and avoid bridges. Planning ahead is the key. The most accessible tourist office is the one off Piazza San Marco.

Of the other islands, Murano, Burano, the Lido and Torcello are all fairly easy to access, although there are no stair-lifts on Murano and Burano.

Also note: the wheelchair lift across the Ponte di Calatrava takes an estimated 16 minutes roundtrip plus waiting time, so travellers with disabilities may want to opt for the *vaporetto* between the Piazzale Roma bus station and the train station.

Maps

A printable 'Accessible Venice' map is available on the Comune di Venezia website (www.comune.venezia.it) in the 'Tourism' section. The map delimits the area around each water-bus stop that can be accessed without cross-

ing a bridge. In addition, the website provides information on accessible attractions, including 12 'barrier-free' itineraries, which can also be downloaded. The maps are also available from the APT tourist offices.

Public Transport

Vaporetti have access for wheelchairs, offering an easy way to get around town. Passengers in wheelchairs travel for just €1.30, while their companion travels free.

Virtually all local buses connecting Venice with mainland destinations are also wheelchair accessible.

Tours

Gondolas 4 All (☎328 243 13 82; www.gondolas4all.com) At the time of research, this non-profit organisation, backed by the Gondoliers Association, was building a new dock where wheelchair users will be able to access gondola tours. Once up and running the service will be bookable online or by phone.

L'Altra Venezia (www.laltravenezia.it; tours for 4 €180) Guided tours of the northern lagoon, the gardens of Sant'Erasmo and the monastery of San Lazzaro degli Armeni are now possible in wheelchair-adapted boats that can accommodate up to four wheelchair users and three other passengers.

Organisations

Accessible Italy (www.accessibleitaly.com) A San Marino–based company that specialises in holiday services for people with disabilities. This is the best first port of call.

Città Per Tutti (☎041 965 54 40, 041 274 81 44; www.comune.venezia.it/informa handicap) This city program is devoted to improving disabled access in Venice and can provide the latest information about access issues around the city.

Visas

Citizens of EU countries, Iceland, Norway and Switzerland do not need a visa to visit Italy. Nationals of some other countries, including Australia, Brazil, Canada, Israel, Japan, New Zealand and the USA, do not require visas for tourist visits of up to 90 days. For more information and a list of countries whose citizens require a visa, check the website of the Italian foreign ministry (www.esteri.it).

The standard tourist visa issued by Italian consulates is the Schengen visa, valid for up to 90 days. This visa is valid for travel in Italy and in several other European countries with which Italy has a reciprocal visa agreement (see www.eurovisa.info for the full list). These visas are not renewable inside Italy.

Permits

EU citizens do not need permits to live, work or start a business in Italy, but they are advised to register with a police station (*questura*) if they take up residence. If you are a non-EU citizen coming to Venice for work or long-term study, you'll require study and work visas, which you must apply for in your country of residence.

Women Travellers

Of the major travel destinations in Italy, Venice is among the safest for women, given the low rate of violent crime of any kind in Venice proper. Chief annoyances would be getting chatted up by other travellers in Piazza San Marco or on the more popular Lido beaches, usually easily quashed with a '*Non mi interessa*' (I'm not interested), or that universally crushing response, the exasperated eye roll.

Language

Standard Italian is spoken throughout Italy, but regional dialects are an important part of identity in many areas, and this also goes for Venice. You'll no doubt hear some Venetian (also known as Venet) spoken or pick up on the local lilt that standard Italian is often spoken with. This said, you'll have no trouble being understood – and your efforts will be much appreciated – if you stick to standard Italian, which we've also used in this chapter.

Italian pronunciation is straightforward as most sounds are also found in English.

Note that ai is pronounced as in 'aisle', ay as in 'say', ow as in 'how', dz as the 'ds' in 'lids', and that r is a strong, rolled sound. Keep in mind that Italian consonants can have a stronger, emphatic pronunciation – if the consonant is written as a double letter, it should be pronounced a little stronger, eg *sonno* son·no (sleep) and *sono* so·no (I am). If you read our coloured pronunciation guides as if they were English (with the stressed syllables in italics), you'll be understood.

BASICS

Italian has two words for 'you' – use the polite form *Lei* lay if you're talking to strangers, officials or people older than you. With people familiar to you or younger than you, you can use the informal form *tu* too.

In Italian, all nouns and adjectives are either masculine or feminine, and so are the articles *il/la* eel/la (the) and *un/una* oon/oo·na (a) that go with the nouns.

WANT MORE?

For in-depth language information and handy phrases, check out Lonely Planet's *Italian Phrasebook*. You'll find it at **shop. lonelyplanet.com**, or you can buy Lonely Planet's iPhone phrasebooks at the Apple App Store.

In this chapter the polite/informal and masculine/feminine options are included where necessary, separated with a slash and indicated with 'pol/inf' and 'm/f'.

Hello.	*Buongiorno.*	bwon·*jor*·no
Goodbye.	*Arrivederci.*	a·ree·ve·*der*·chee
Yes./No.	*Sì./No.*	see/no
Excuse me.	*Mi scusi.* (pol)	mee skoo·zee
	Scusami. (inf)	skoo·za·mee
Sorry.	*Mi dispiace.*	mee dees·*pya*·che
Please.	*Per favore.*	per fa·*vo*·re
Thank you.	*Grazie.*	*gra*·tsye
You're welcome.	*Prego.*	*pre*·go

How are you?
Come sta/stai? (pol/inf)   *ko*·me sta/stai

Fine. And you?
Bene. E Lei/tu? (pol/inf)   *be*·ne e lay/too

What's your name?
Come si chiama? pol   *ko*·me see *kya*·ma
Come ti chiami? inf   *ko*·me tee *kya*·mee

My name is ...
Mi chiamo ...   mee *kya*·mo ...

Do you speak English?
Parla/Parli   *par*·la/*par*·lee
inglese? (pol/inf)   een·*gle*·ze

I don't understand.
Non capisco.   non ka·*pee*·sko

ACCOMMODATION
I'd like to book a room, please.
Vorrei prenotare una   vo·*ray* pre·no·*ta*·re oo·na
camera, per favore.   *ka*·me·ra per fa·*vo*·re

Is breakfast included?
La colazione è   la ko·la·*tsyo*·ne e
compresa?   kom·*pre*·sa

How much is it per ...?	*Quanto costa per ...?*	*kwan*·to *kos*·ta per ...
night	*una notte*	oo·na *no*·te
person	*persona*	per·*so*·na

air-con	*aria condizionata*	a·rya kon·dee·tsyo·na·ta
bathroom	*bagno*	ba·nyo
campsite	*campeggio*	kam·pe·jo
double room	*camera doppia con letto matrimoniale*	ka·me·ra do·pya kon le·to ma·tree·mo·nya·le
guesthouse	*pensione*	pen·syo·ne
hotel	*albergo*	al·ber·go
single room	*camera singola*	ka·me·ra seen·go·la
youth hostel	*ostello della gioventù*	os·te·lo de·la jo·ven·too
window	*finestra*	fee·nes·tra

DIRECTIONS

Where's ...?
Dov'è ...? · do·ve ...

What's the address?
Qual è l'indirizzo? · kwa·le leen·dee·ree·tso

Could you please write it down?
Può scriverlo, per favore? · pwo skree·ver·lo per fa·vo·re

Can you show me (on the map)?
Può mostrarmi (sulla pianta)? · pwo mos·trar·mee (soo·la pyan·ta)

at the corner	*all'angolo*	a·lan·go·lo
behind	*dietro*	dye·tro
far	*lontano*	lon·ta·no
in front of	*davanti a*	da·van·tee a
left	*a sinistra*	a see·nee·stra
near	*vicino*	vee·chee·no
next to	*accanto a*	a·kan·to a
opposite	*di fronte a*	dee fron·te a
right	*a destra*	a de·stra
straight ahead	*sempre diritto*	sem·pre dee·ree·to

EATING & DRINKING

I'd like to reserve a table.
Vorrei prenotare un tavolo. · vo·ray pre·no·ta·re oon ta·vo·lo

What would you recommend?
Cosa mi consiglia? · ko·za mee kon·see·lya

What's in that dish?
Quali ingredienti ci sono in questo piatto? · kwa·li een·gre·dyen·tee chee so·no een kwe·sto pya·to

What's the local speciality?
Qual è la specialità di questa regione? · kwa·le la spe·cha·lee·ta dee kwe·sta re·jo·ne

That was delicious!
Era squisito! · e·ra skwee·zee·to

KEY PATTERNS

To get by in Italian, mix and match these simple patterns with words of your choice:

When's (the next flight)?
A che ora è (il prossimo volo)? · a ke o·ra e (eel pro·see·mo vo·lo)

Where's (the station)?
Dov'è (la stazione)? · do·ve (la sta·tsyo·ne)

I'm looking for (a hotel).
Sto cercando (un albergo). · sto cher·kan·do (oon al·ber·go)

Do you have (a map)?
Ha (una pianta)? · a (oo·na pyan·ta)

Is there (a toilet)?
C'è (un gabinetto)? · che (oon ga·bee·ne·to)

I'd like (a coffee).
Vorrei (un caffè). · vo·ray (oon ka·fe)

I'd like to (hire a car).
Vorrei (noleggiare una macchina). · vo·ray (no·le·ja·re oo·na ma·kee·na)

Can I (enter)?
Posso (entrare)? · po·so (en·tra·re)

Could you please (help me)?
Può (aiutarmi), per favore? · pwo (a·yoo·tar·mee) per fa·vo·re

Do I have to (book a seat)?
Devo (prenotare un posto)? · de·vo (pre·no·ta·re oon po·sto)

Cheers!
Salute! · sa·loo·te

Please bring the bill.
Mi porta il conto, per favore? · mee por·ta eel kon·to per fa·vo·re

I don't eat ...	*Non mangio ...*	non man·jo ...
eggs	*uova*	wo·va
fish	*pesce*	pe·she
nuts	*noci*	no·chee
(red) meat	*carne (rossa)*	kar·ne (ro·sa)

Key Words

bar	*locale*	lo·ka·le
bottle	*bottiglia*	bo·tee·lya
breakfast	*prima colazione*	pree·ma ko·la·tsyo·ne
cafe	*bar*	bar
cold	*freddo*	fre·do
dinner	*cena*	che·na

drink list	lista delle bevande	lee·sta de·le be·van·de
fork	forchetta	for·ke·ta
glass	bicchiere	bee·kye·re
grocery store	alimentari	a·lee·men·ta·ree
hot	caldo	kal·do
knife	coltello	kol·te·lo
lunch	pranzo	pran·dzo
market	mercato	mer·ka·to
menu	menù	me·noo
plate	piatto	pya·to
restaurant	ristorante	ree·sto·ran·te
spicy	piccante	pee·kan·te
spoon	cucchiaio	koo·kya·yo
vegetarian (food)	vegetariano	ve·je·ta·rya·no
with	con	kon
without	senza	sen·tsa

Meat & Fish

beef	manzo	man·dzo
chicken	pollo	po·lo
duck	anatra	a·na·tra
fish	pesce	pe·she
herring	aringa	a·reen·ga
lamb	agnello	a·nye·lo
lobster	aragosta	a·ra·gos·ta
meat	carne	kar·ne
mussels	cozze	ko·tse
oysters	ostriche	o·stree·ke
pork	maiale	ma·ya·le
prawn	gambero	gam·be·ro
salmon	salmone	sal·mo·ne
scallops	capasante	ka·pa·san·te
seafood	frutti di mare	froo·tee dee ma·re
shrimp	gambero	gam·be·ro
squid	calamari	ka·la·ma·ree
trout	trota	tro·ta
tuna	tonno	to·no
turkey	tacchino	ta·kee·no
veal	vitello	vee·te·lo

Fruit & Vegetables

apple	mela	me·la
beans	fagioli	fa·jo·lee
cabbage	cavolo	ka·vo·lo
capsicum	peperone	pe·pe·ro·ne
carrot	carota	ka·ro·ta
cauliflower	cavolfiore	ka·vol·fyo·re
cucumber	cetriolo	che·tree·o·lo
fruit	frutta	froo·ta
grapes	uva	oo·va
lemon	limone	lee·mo·ne
lentils	lenticchie	len·tee·kye
mushroom	funghi	foon·gee
nuts	noci	no·chee
onions	cipolle	chee·po·le
orange	arancia	a·ran·cha
peach	pesca	pe·ska
peas	piselli	pee·ze·lee
pineapple	ananas	a·na·nas
plum	prugna	proo·nya
potatoes	patate	pa·ta·te
spinach	spinaci	spee·na·chee
tomatoes	pomodori	po·mo·do·ree
vegetables	verdura	ver·doo·ra

Other

bread	pane	pa·ne
butter	burro	boo·ro
cheese	formaggio	for·ma·jo
eggs	uova	wo·va
honey	miele	mye·le
ice	ghiaccio	gya·cho
jam	marmellata	mar·me·la·ta
noodles	pasta	pas·ta
oil	olio	o·lyo
pepper	pepe	pe·pe
rice	riso	ree·zo
salt	sale	sa·le
soup	minestra	mee·nes·tra
soy sauce	salsa di soia	sal·sa dee so·ya
sugar	zucchero	tsoo·ke·ro
vinegar	aceto	a·che·to

Drinks

beer	birra	bee·ra
coffee	caffè	ka·fe
(orange) juice	succo (d'arancia)	soo·ko (da·ran·cha)
milk	latte	la·te
red wine	vino rosso	vee·no ro·so

soft drink	bibita	bee·bee·ta
tea	tè	te
(mineral) water	acqua (minerale)	a·kwa (mee·ne·ra·le)
white wine	vino bianco	vee·no byan·ko

EMERGENCIES

Help!
Aiuto! — a·yoo·to

Leave me alone!
Lasciami in pace! — la·sha·mee een pa·che

I'm lost.
Mi sono perso/a. (m/f) — mee so·no per·so/a

Call the police!
Chiami la polizia! — kya·mee la po·lee·tsee·a

Call a doctor!
Chiami un medico! — kya·mee oon me·dee·ko

Where are the toilets?
Dove sono i gabinetti? — do·ve so·no ee ga·bee·ne·tee

I'm sick.
Mi sento male. — mee sen·to ma·le

SHOPPING & SERVICES

I'd like to buy ...
Vorrei comprare ... — vo·ray kom·pra·re ...

I'm just looking.
Sto solo guardando. — sto so·lo gwar·dan·do

Numbers

1	uno	oo·no
2	due	doo·e
3	tre	tre
4	quattro	kwa·tro
5	cinque	cheen·kwe
6	sei	say
7	sette	se·te
8	otto	o·to
9	nove	no·ve
10	dieci	dye·chee
20	venti	ven·tee
30	trenta	tren·ta
40	quaranta	kwa·ran·ta
50	cinquanta	cheen·kwan·ta
60	sessanta	se·san·ta
70	settanta	se·tan·ta
80	ottanta	o·tan·ta
90	novanta	no·van·ta
100	cento	chen·to
1000	mille	mee·le

Signs

Entrata/Ingresso	Entrance
Uscità	Exit
Aperto	Open
Chiuso	Closed
Informazioni	Information
Proibito/Vietato	Prohibited
Gabinetti/Servizi	Toilets
Uomini	Men
Donne	Women

Can I look at it?
Posso dare un'occhiata? — po·so da·re oo·no·kya·ta

How much is this?
Quanto costa questo? — kwan·to kos·ta kwe·sto

It's too expensive.
È troppo caro/a. (m/f) — e tro·po ka·ro/a

Can you lower the price?
Può farmi lo sconto? — pwo far·mee lo skon·to

There's a mistake in the bill.
C'è un errore nel conto. — che oo·ne·ro·re nel kon·to

ATM	bancomat	ban·ko·mat
post office	ufficio postale	oo·fee·cho pos·ta·le
tourist office	ufficio del turismo	oo·fee·cho del too·reez·mo

TIME & DATES

What time is it?	Che ora è?	ke o·ra e
It's one o'clock.	È l'una.	e loo·na
It's (two) o'clock.	Sono le (due).	so·no le (doo·e)
Half past (one).	(L'una) e mezza.	(loo·na) e me·dza

in the morning	di mattina	dee ma·tee·na
in the afternoon	di pomeriggio	dee po·me·ree·jo
in the evening	di sera	dee se·ra

yesterday	ieri	ye·ree
today	oggi	o·jee
tomorrow	domani	do·ma·nee

Monday	lunedì	loo·ne·dee
Tuesday	martedì	mar·te·dee
Wednesday	mercoledì	mer·ko·le·dee
Thursday	giovedì	jo·ve·dee
Friday	venerdì	ve·ner·dee
Saturday	sabato	sa·ba·to
Sunday	domenica	do·me·nee·ka

January	gennaio	je·*na*·yo
February	febbraio	fe·*bra*·yo
March	marzo	*mar*·tso
April	aprile	a·*pree*·le
May	maggio	*ma*·jo
June	giugno	*joo*·nyo
July	luglio	*loo*·lyo
August	agosto	a·*gos*·to
September	settembre	se·*tem*·bre
October	ottobre	o·*to*·bre
November	novembre	no·*vem*·bre
December	dicembre	dee·*chem*·bre

TRANSPORT

At what time does the ... leave/arrive?	A che ora parte/ arriva ...?	a ke o·ra par·te/ a·ree·va ...
boat	la nave	la *na*·ve
bus	l'autobus	*low*·to·boos
city ferry	il vaporetto	eel va·po·*re*·to
ferry	il traghetto	eel tra·*ge*·to
plane	l'aereo	la·e·re·o
train	il treno	eel *tre*·no
bus stop	fermata dell'autobus	fer·*ma*·ta del ow·to·boos
one-way	di sola andata	dee *so*·la an·*da*·ta
platform	binario	bee·*na*·ryo
return	di andata e ritorno	dee an·*da*·ta e ree·*tor*·no
ticket	biglietto	bee·*lye*·to
ticket office	biglietteria	bee·lye·te·*ree*·a
timetable	orario	o·*ra*·ryo
train station	stazione ferroviaria	sta·*tsyo*·ne fe·ro·*vyar*·ya

Does it stop at ...?
Si ferma a ...?　　　　see fer·ma a ...

Please tell me when we get to ...
Mi dica per favore　　mee dee·ka per fa·vo·re
quando arriviamo a ...　kwan·do a·ree·vya·mo a ...

I want to get off here.
Voglio scendere qui.　vo·lyo shen·de·re kwee

I'd like to hire a/an ...	Vorrei noleggiare un/una ... (m/f)	vo·ray no·le·ja·re oon/oo·na ...
bicycle	bicicletta (f)	bee·chee·*kle*·ta
car	macchina (f)	*ma*·kee·na
motorbike	moto (f)	*mo*·to

bicycle pump	pompa della bicicletta	*pom*·pa de·la bee·chee·*kle*·ta
helmet	casco	*kas*·ko
mechanic	meccanico	me·*ka*·nee·ko
petrol/gas	benzina	ben·*dzee*·na
service station	stazione di servizio	sta·*tsyo*·ne dee ser·*vee*·tsyo

Is this the road to ...?
Questa strada porta a ...?　kwe·sta stra·da por·ta a ...

(How long) Can I park here?
(Per quanto tempo)　　(per kwan·to tem·po)
Posso parcheggiare qui?　po·so par·ke·ja·re kwee

I have a flat tyre.
Ho una gomma bucata.　o oo·na go·ma boo·ka·ta

I've run out of petrol.
Ho esaurito la　　　o e·zow·ree·to la
benzina.　　　　　ben·dzee·na

VENETIAN BASICS

A few choice words in Venetian (or Venet, as it is also known) will endear you to your hosts, especially at happy hour. To keep up with the *bacaro* banter, try mixing them with your Italian:

Yes, sir!	Siorsi!
Oh, no!	Simènteve!
You bet!	Figuràrse!
How lucky!	Bénpo!
Perfect.	In bròca.
Welcome!	Benvegnù!
Cheers!	Sanacapàna!
Watch out!	Òcio!

cheap wine	brunbrùn
glass of wine	ombra (lit: a shade)
happy hour	giro di ombra (lit: round of shade)
to become Venetian	Venexianàrse
Venetian	venexiano/a (m/f)
you guys	voàltri

FOOD GLOSSARY

alla busara Venetian prawn sauce

anatra wild lagoon duck

baccala mantecato creamed cod

bigoli Venetian whole-wheat pasta

branzino sea bass

bruscandoli wild hop buds

canoce mantis prawn

capasanta/canastrelo large/small scallops

carpaccio finely sliced raw beef

castraure baby artichokes from St Erasmo Island

cicheti Venetian tapas

contorni vegetable dishes

crostini open-faced sandwiches

crudi Venetian sushi

curasan croissant

dolci sweets

dolci tipici venexiani typical Venetian sweets

fatto in casa house-made

fegato alla veneziana liver lightly pan-roasted in strips with browned onion and a splash of red wine

filetto di San Pietro fish with artichokes or *radicchio trevisano*

fritole sweet fritters

fritto misto e pattatine lightly fried lagoon seafood and potatoes

frittura seafood fry

gnochetti mini-gnocchi

granseola spider crab

krapfen doughnuts

latte di soia soy milk

lingue di suocere biscuit; 'mother-in-law' tongues'

macchiatone espresso liberally 'stained' with milk

margherite ripiene all'astice com sugo di pesce ravioli stuffed with lobster in fish sauce

moeche soft-shell crabs

moscardini baby octopus

mozzarella di bufala fresh buffalo-milk mozzarella

orechiette 'little ear' pasta

pan dei dogi 'doges' bread'; hazelnut-studded biscuits

panino sandwich

pastine pastry

peoci mussels

pizza margherita pizza with basil, mozzarella and tomato

pizzette mini-pizzas

polpette meatballs

radicchio trevisano feathery red radicchio

risotto di pesce fish risotto

saor Venice's tangy marinade

sarde sardines

sarde in saor sardines fried in tangy onion marinade with pine nuts and sultanas

senza limone without lemon

seppie squid

seppie in nero squid in its own ink

sfogio sole

sopressa Venetian soft salami

sopressa crostini soft salami on toast

sorbetto sorbet

spaghetti alla búsera spaghetti with shrimp sauce

surgelati frozen

tramezzini sandwiches on soft bread often with mayo-based condiments

verdure vegetables

zaletti cornmeal biscuits with sultanas

zuppa di pesce thick seafood soup

Behind the Scenes

SEND US YOUR FEEDBACK

We love to hear from travellers – your comments keep us on our toes and help make our books better. Our well-travelled team reads every word on what you loved or loathed about this book. Although we cannot reply individually to your submissions, we always guarantee that your feedback goes straight to the appropriate authors, in time for the next edition. Each person who sends us information is thanked in the next edition – the most useful submissions are rewarded with a selection of digital PDF chapters.

Visit **lonelyplanet.com/contact** to submit your updates and suggestions or to ask for help. Our award-winning website also features inspirational travel stories, news and discussions.

Note: We may edit, reproduce and incorporate your comments in Lonely Planet products such as guidebooks, websites and digital products, so let us know if you don't want your comments reproduced or your name acknowledged. For a copy of our privacy policy visit lonelyplanet.com/privacy.

AUTHOR THANKS

Cristian Bonetto

First and foremost, *grazie di cuore* to Stefano Baldan for his incredible generosity. A heartfelt thanks also to Giovanna and Silvia Vendramin, Marco Guerra, Alessandro Durante, Sara Costenaro, Laura Durante Poloni, Gian Luigi Sartor, Francesca Zerbo, Lucia Sartor, Pietro Manno, Diana Pedone, Lisa Crawshaw, and Diego Vianello. At Lonely Planet, *grazie mille* to Anna Tyler for the commission and to my talented co-author and friend Paula Hardy.

Paula Hardy

Thank you to the wonderfully warm Venetians for sharing the best of their island home: Michela Guggia, Diego and Lucia Cattaneo, Monica Cesarato, Francesca Giubilei, Luca Berta, Marco Secchi, Veronica Green, Nan McElroy, Jane Caporal, Eliana Argine, Niccoló at Bragora and Julia Curtis. *Brava*, too, to co-author Cristian Bonetto for being such a supportive partner in crime; to Lonely Planet destination editor, Anna Tyler, for steering a steady course; and, to Rob for all the laughs along the way.

ACKNOWLEDGMENTS

Illustration pp60-61 by Javier Martinez Zarracina.

Cover photograph: A gondola on a canal. Danita Delimont Stock Photography/AWL ©

THIS BOOK

This 9th edition of Lonely Planet's *Venice & the Veneto* guidebook was researched and written by Cristian Bonetto and Paula Hardy. The previous two editions were written by Alison Bing, Paula Hardy and Robert Landon. This guidebook was produced by the following:

Destination Editor Anna Tyler

Product Editors Briohny Hooper, Luna Soo

Senior Cartographer Anthony Phelan

Book Designer Jessica Rose

Assisting Editors Nigel Chin, Melanie Dankel, Carly Hall, Jodie Martire

Assisting Cartographer James Leversha

Assisting Book Designer Katherine Marsh

Cover Researcher Naomi Parker

Thanks to Sasha Baskett, Harriet Copelyn, Bruce Evans, Mark Griffiths, Andi Jones, Anne Mason, George Moss, Claire Murphy, Karyn Noble, Martine Power, Samantha Russell-Tulip, Dianne Schallmeiner, Rosemary Slater, Gabrielle Stefanos, Lauren Wellicome, Amanda Williamson, Alexander & Caroline Wrigley

See also separate subindexes for:

✗ **EATING P263**

🍷 **DRINKING & NIGHTLIFE P264**

☆ **ENTERTAINMENT P264**

🔒 **SHOPPING P264**

🏃 **SPORTS & ACTIVITIES P265**

🛏 **SLEEPING P265**

Index

🍴 EATING

🍷 DRINKING & NIGHTLIFE

⭐ ENTERTAINMENT

🛍️ SHOPPING

he
aps

Routes

	Tollway
	Freeway
	Primary
	Secondary
	Tertiary
	Lane
	Unsealed road
	Road under construction
	Plaza/Mall
	Steps
	Tunnel
	Pedestrian overpass
	Walking Tour
	Walking Tour detour
	Path/Walking Trail

Boundaries

	International
	State/Province
	Disputed
	Regional/Suburb
	Marine Park
	Cliff
	Wall

Hydrography

	River, Creek
	Intermittent River
	Canal
	Water
	Dry/Salt/Intermittent Lake
	Reef

Areas

	Airport/Runway
	Beach/Desert
	Cemetery (Christian)
	Cemetery (Other)
	Glacier
	Mudflat
	Park/Forest
	Sight (Building)
	Sportsground
	Swamp/Mangrove

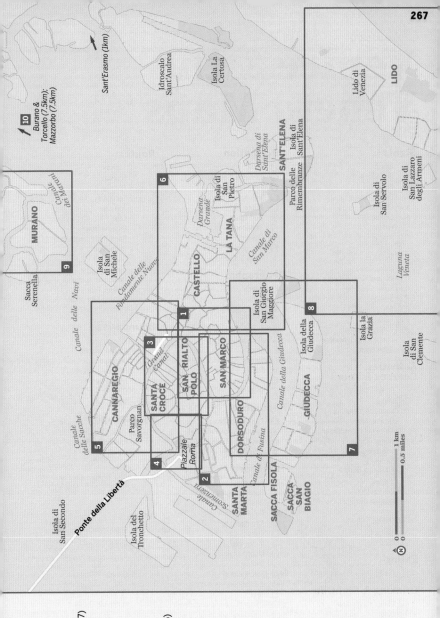

MAP INDEX

SAN MARCO

Key on p270

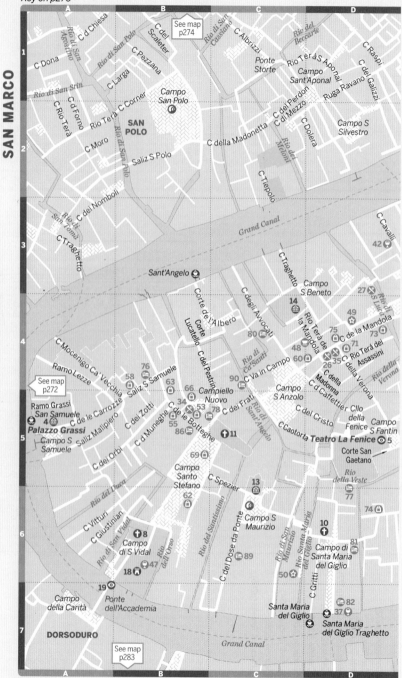

SAN MARCO

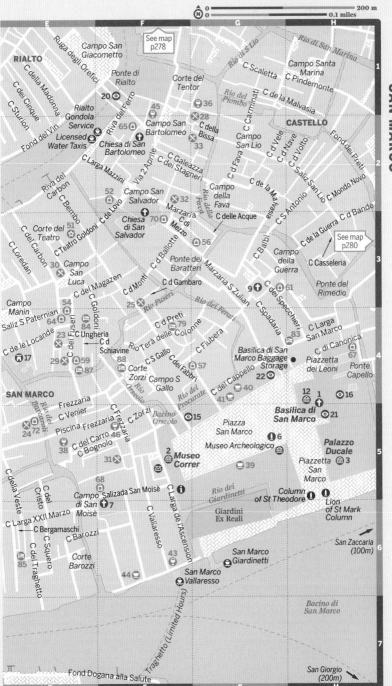

RIALTO

Ruga degli Orefici
Campo San Giacometto

C della Madonna
C dei Cinque
C Sturion
Fond del Vin

Ponte di Rialto

20

Rialto Gondola Service
65
Licensed Water Taxis
Chiesa di San Bartolomeo

Riva del Ferro
45
Campo San Bartolomeo
33

Corte del Tentor
36
28
C della Bissa

Rio di S Lio
C Scaletta

Rio di San Marina
Campo Santa Marina
C Pindemonte
C de la Malvasia

CASTELLO

C Larga Mazzini
Via 2 Aprile
C dei Stagneri
C Galeazza

Campo San Lio
C de Vele
C d Nave
C d Volto
Saliz San Lio
C Mondo Novo
Fond dei Preti

Riva del Carbon
C Bembo
52
Campo San Salvador
C de Lovo
Chiesa di San Salvador
70
32
Marzaria
C di Mezo
Campo della Fava
C delle Acque
C S Antonio
C Bande

Corte del Teatro
51
C Teatro Goldoni
30
Campo San Luca
C del Magazen
C d Monti
C d Ballote
Ponte dei Baratteri
56
C Balbi
Campo della Guerra
C de la Guerra
C Casseleria
Ponte del Rimedio

See map p280

Campo Manin
54
64
Saliz S Paternian
23
C de le Locande
17
29
59
87
C dei Fuseri
84
C Ungheria
C d Schiavine
25
Rio Pusteri
C d Gambaro
Rio del Ferali
Marzaria S Zulian
C d Preti
79
Rio Terà delle Colonne
C S Gallo
C Fiubera
C Larga San Marco
83
9
C d Specchieri
61
C Spadaria

Corte Zorzi
88
C dei Fabbri
57
Campo S Gallo
Rio del Procurate
C del Cappello
40
Basilica di San Marco Baggage Storage
22
C di Canonica
67
Piazzetta dei Leoni
Ponte Capello

SAN MARCO

Frezzaria
C Venier
Piscina Frezzaria
C del Carro
C Bognolo
31
38
24
72
46
C Zorzi
Rio Orseolo
Bacino Orseolo
15
41
Piazza San Marco
Museo Archeologico
6
12
1
16
Basilica di San Marco
21

C della Veste
C del Cristo
68
Campo di San Moisè
7
Salizada San Moisè
2
Museo Correr
39
Palazzo Ducale
3
Piazzetta San Marco

C Larga XXII Marzo
C Bergamaschi
C Barozzi
C Squero
C del Traghetto
85
Corte Barozzi
44
43
C Larga de l'Ascension
C Vallaresso
Rio dei Giardinetti
Giardini Ex Reali
Column of St Theodore
Lion of St Mark Column
San Zaccaria (100m)

San Marco Giardinetti
San Marco Vallaresso
Bacino di San Marco

Fond Dogana alla Salute
Traghetto (Limited Hours)
San Giorgio (200m)

0   200 m
0   0.1 miles

See map p278

SAN MARCO *Map on p268*

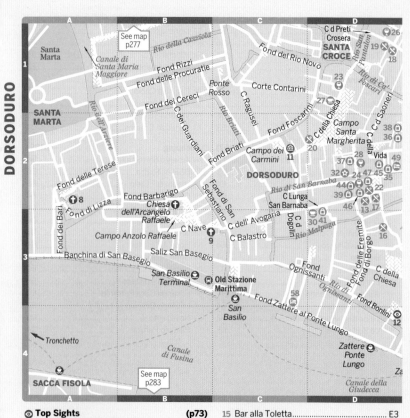

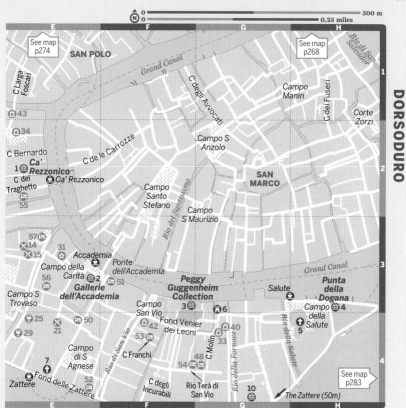

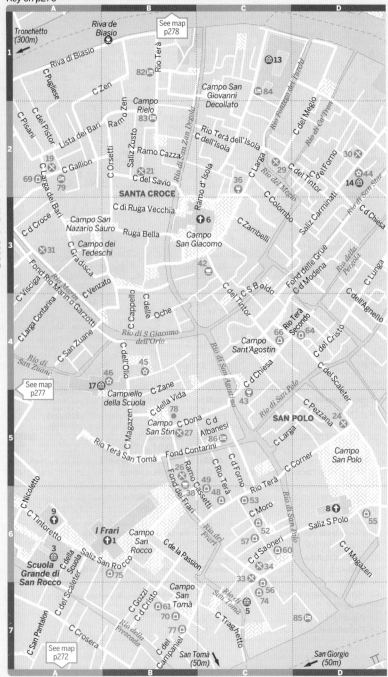

Key on p276

See map p278

See map p277

See map p272

Tronchetto (300m)

Riva de Biasio

Riva di Biasio

C Pugliese

C Zen

Rio Terà

Campo San Giovanni Decollato

Campo Rielo

C del Megio

Rio di Ca' Tron

C del Pistor

C Pisani

Lista dei Bari

Ramo Zen

Saliz Zusto

Ramo Cazza

Rio Terà dell'Isola

C dell'Isola

C Orsetti

C Gallion

C Larga dei Bari

C del Savio

Ramo d'Isola

C Larga

C del Tintor

C del Forno

Saliz Carminati

SANTA CROCE

C di Ruga Vecchia

C Colombo

C d Croce

Campo San Nazario Sauro

Ruga Bella

Campo San Giacomo

C Zambelli

Rio di San Stae

C d Chiesa

C della Pergola

Campo dei Tedeschi

C Gradisca

Fond delle Grue

C d Modena

C Lunga

C dell'Agnello

Fond Rio Marin o Garzotti

Rio Marin

C Venzato

C del Tintor

C S B oldo

Rio Terà Secondo

C del Cristo

C Visciga

C Larga Contarina

C San Zuane

C Cappello

C delle Oche

Campo Sant'Agostin

C del Scaleter

Rio di S Giacomo dell'Orto

Rio di San Zuane

C dell'Olio

Rio di San Agostin

C d Chiesa

SAN POLO

C Pezzana

Campiello della Scuola

C Zane

C della Vida

Campo San Stin

C Doña

C Albanesi

C Larga

Rio di San Polo

C Corner

Campo San Polo

C Magazen

Rio Terà San Tomà

Fond Contarini

Ramo Cassetti

C Rio Terà

C d Forno

Rio Terà

C Moro

Fond dei Frari

Saliz S Polo

C Nicoletto

C Tintoretto

I Frari

Campo San Rocco

C de la Passion

Rio dei Frari

C d Saoneri

C d Magazen

C della Scuola

Saliz San Rocco

C Gozzi

C d Cristo

Campo San Tomà

Rio di San Tomà

Scuola Grande di San Rocco

C del Scaleter

C San Pantalon

C Crosera

Rio della Frescada

C del Campaniel

C Traghetto

San Tomà (50m)

San Giorgio (50m)

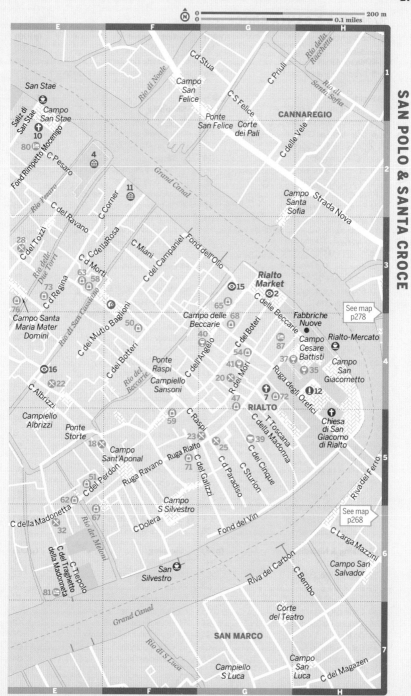

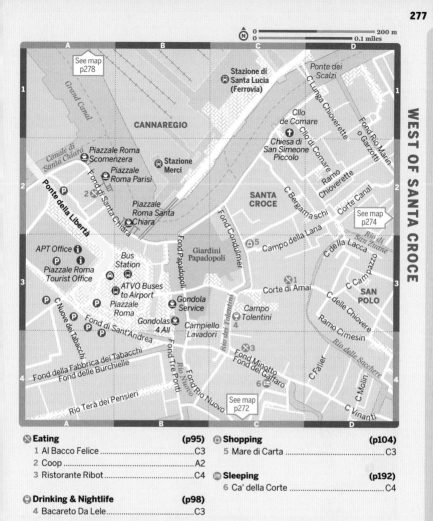

See map p277

See map p274

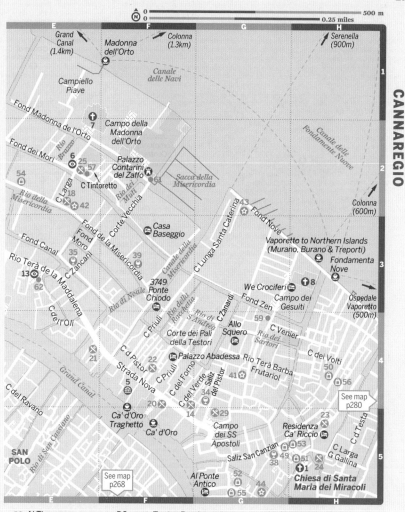

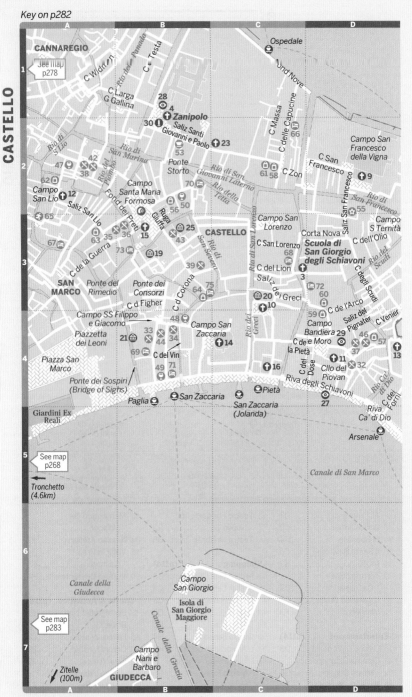

CASTELLO

CANNAREGIO

See map
p278

Ospedale

Fond Nove

C Widman

Rio tera Pompea

C Testa

C Larga
G Gallina

28

4

Zanipolo

30

Saliz Santi
Giovanni e Paolo

23

53

C Massa

C delle Capucine

66

Campo San
Francesco
della Vigna

C San
Francesco

9

Rio di Sta Marina

Rio del Piombo

47

42

38

62

Campo
San Lio

12

Campo
Santa Maria
Formosa

Ponte
Storto

Rio di San
Giovanni Laterno

Rio della
Tetta

61 58

C Zon

Saliz San Francesco

Rio di San Francesco

55

Campo
S Ternità

Saliz San Lio

65

Fond dei Preti

70

56

50

Campo San
Lorenzo

Corta Nova

C dell'Olio

Rio dei
Scudi

67

63 35

36

Ruga
Giuffa

15

25

43

CASTELLO

68

C San Lorenzo

Scuola di
San Giorgio
degli Schiavoni

C degli Scudi

73

19

Rio di San Severo

39

C del Lion

3

72

60

C de l'Arco

SAN
MARCO

C de la Guerra

Ponte del
Rimedio

Ponte dei
Consorzi

C d Cotona

64

75

Saliz dei Greci

20

10

59

Campo
Bandiera
e Moro

29

Saliz del
Pignater

C Venier

46

37

57

C d Figher

Campo SS Filippo
e Giacomo

48

Campo San
Zaccaria

13

Piazzetta
dei Leoni

21

33

34

44

14

11

32

69

C del Vin

Rio di Greci

16

C de la Pietà

Cllo del
Piovan

Rio Cat
di Dio

27

Riva degli Schiavoni

C del Forni

Piazza
San
Marco

49

71

Ponte dei Sospiri
(Bridge of Sighs)

Paglia

San Zaccaria

Pietà

San Zaccaria
(Jolanda)

Riva
Ca' di Dio

Giardini Ex
Reali

Arsenale

See map
p268

Canale di San Marco

Tronchetto
(4.6km)

Canale della
Giudecca

Campo
San Giorgio

Isola di
San Giorgio
Maggiore

See map
p283

Canale della Grazia

Campo
Nani e
Barbaro

Zitelle
(100m)

GIUDECCA

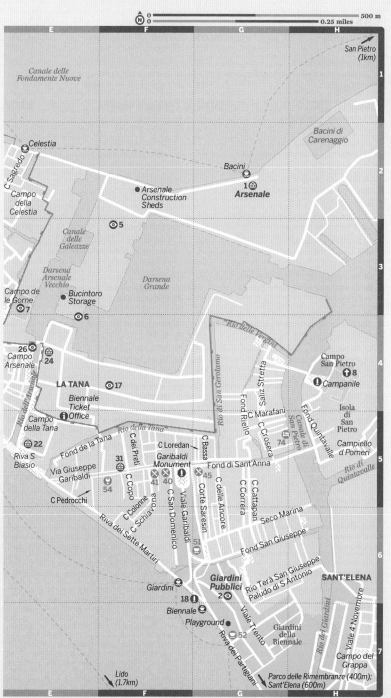

0 ———————— 500 m
0 ———————— 0.25 miles

San Pietro
(1km)

Canale delle
Fondamente Nuove

Celestia

Bacini di
Carenaggio

C Sagredo

Bacini

Campo
della
Celestia

Arsenale
Construction
Sheds

1 Arsenale

Canale delle
Galeazze

5

Darsena
Grande

Darsena
Arsenale
Vecchio

Bucintoro
Storage

Campo de
le Gorne

Rio delle Vergini

7

6

Campo
San Pietro

8

26

Campanile

24

Campo
Arsenale

Rio di San Gerolamo

Salizz Stretta

LA TANA

17

C Marafani

Isola
di
San
Pietro

Fond Riello

C Crosera

Biennale
Ticket
Office

74

Campiello
d Pomeri

Campo
della Tana

Rio della Tana

C Loredan

Fond Quintavalle

Rio di
Quintavalle

22

C Bassa

Fond de la Tana

Garibaldi
Monument

Fond di Sant'Anna

Riva S
Biasio

C dei Preti

45

31

C Copo

41

40

C delle Ancore

C Cattapan

Via Giuseppe
Garibaldi

54

C San Domenico

C Correra

Seco Marina

C Pedrocchi

C Colonne

C S Schiavona

Viale Garibaldi

Corte Saresin

Riva dei Sette Martiri

Fond San Giuseppe

SANT'ELENA

51

Giardini
Pubblici

2

Rio dei Giardini

Giardini

18

Rio Terà San Giuseppe
Paludo di S Antonio

Biennale

Viale Trento

Giardini
della
Biennale

Playground

52

Viale 4 Novembre

Lido
(1.7km)

Riva dei Partigiani

Parco delle Rimembranze (400m);
Sant'Elena (600m)

Campo del
Grappa

282

CASTELLO *Map on p280*

GIUDECCA

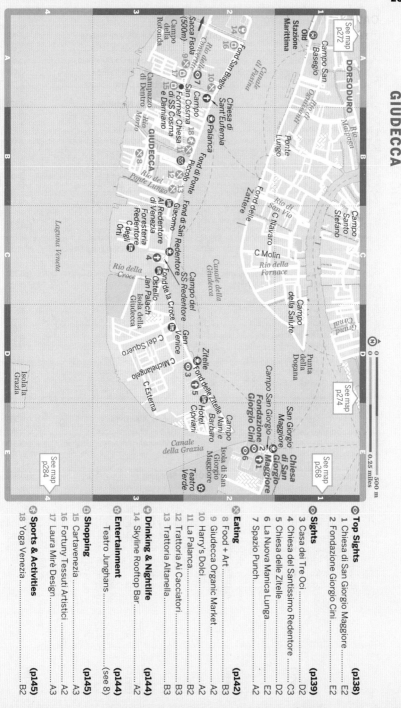

LIDO DI VENEZIA

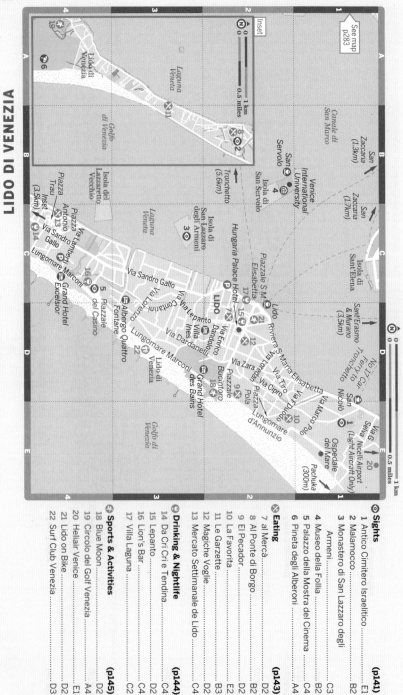

MURANO

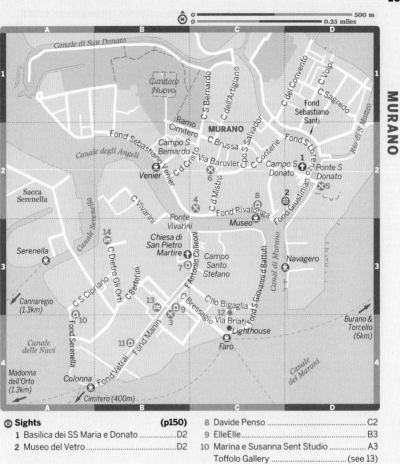

BURANO & TORCELLO

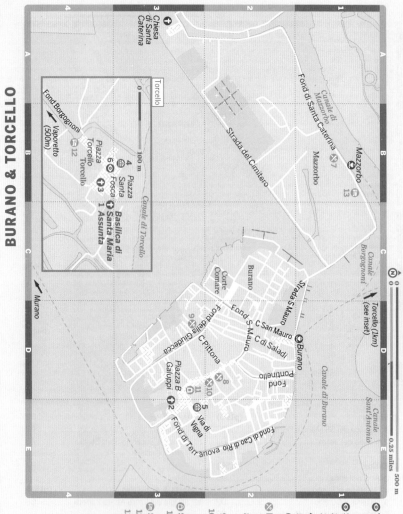

Our Story

A beat-up old car, a few dollars in the pocket and a sense of adventure. In 1972 that's all Tony and Maureen Wheeler needed for the trip of a lifetime – across Europe and Asia overland to Australia. It took several months, and at the end – broke but inspired – they sat at their kitchen table writing and stapling together their first travel guide, *Across Asia on the Cheap*. Within a week they'd sold 1500 copies. Lonely Planet was born.

Today, Lonely Planet has offices in Franklin, London, Melbourne, Oakland, Beijing and Delhi, with more than 600 staff and writers. We share Tony's belief that 'a great guidebook should do three things: inform, educate and amuse'.